HANDBOOK OF LEARNING AND COGNITIVE PROCESSES

Volume 6

I0113388

LINGUISTIC FUNCTIONS IN COGNITIVE THEORY

HANDBOOK OF LEARNING AND COGNITIVE PROCESSES

Volume 6

Linguistic Functions in Cognitive Theory

Edited by
W. K. ESTES

Routledge
Taylor & Francis Group

LONDON AND NEW YORK

First published 1978 by Lawrence Erlbaum Associates, Inc

2 Park Square, Milton Park, Abingdon, Oxon OX14 4RN
711 Third Avenue, New York, NY 10017, USA

Routledge is an imprint of the Taylor & Francis Group, an informa business

First issued in paperback 2016

British Library Cataloguing in Publication Data
A catalogue record for this book is available from the British Library

ISBN: 978-1-84872-347-4 (Set)
ISBN: 978-1-84872-398-6 (Volume 6) (hbk)
ISBN: 978-1-848-72399-3 (Volume 6) (pbk)

Publisher's Note
The publisher has gone to great lengths to ensure the quality of this book but
points out that some imperfections from the original may be apparent.

Disclaimer
The publisher has made every effort to trace copyright holders and would
welcome correspondence from those they have been unable to trace.

Handbook
of Learning and
Cognitive Processes

Volume 6
Linguistic Functions in
Cognitive Theory

EDITED BY

W. K. ESTES

Rockefeller University

LAWRENCE ERLBAUM ASSOCIATES, PUBLISHERS
1978   Hillsdale, New Jersey

DISTRIBUTED BY THE HALSTED PRESS DIVISION OF
JOHN WILEY & SONS
New York   Toronto   London   Sydney

Lawrence Erlbaum Associates, Inc., Publishers
62 Maria Drive
Hillsdale, New Jersey 07642

Distributed solely by Halsted Press Division
John Wiley & Sons, Inc., New York

Library of Congress Cataloging in Publication Data

Main entry under title:

Linguistic functions in cognitive theory.

  (Handbook of learning and cognitive processes; v. 6)
  Includes bibliographies and indexes.
  1. Cognition. 2. Psycholinguistics. 3. Memory.
I. Estes, William Kaye.
BF311.H334 vol. 6   153s [153]   78-13661
ISBN 0-470-26311-3

Printed in the United States of America

Contents

Foreword

This volume concludes the survey of research and theory on learning and cognitive processes that was envisaged when the plan for this *Handbook* was sketched out some 10 years ago. I say "conclude," not "complete," for there may well have been as much new research output during this decade as in the two preceding. Still, except for lacunae left by a few defecting authors, the plan has been fairly well realized. The best laid plans often run behind the course of events, however, and even though a great deal of material has been covered, some readers will nonetheless find conspicuous gaps.

The primary orientation in planning the *Handbook* was to concentrate on research and models aimed toward the development of general cognitive theory. Thus, very large bodies of literature restricted as to the phylogenetic level or age of the subjects or the specific action system studied have not been systematically surveyed—among them literature on cognitive development, acquisition of language, ethology, operant behavior, and aspects of psycholinguistics having to do with syntax, grammars, and the subjective lexicon. In each case, extensive treatises or handbooks are already available. In the present volumes we have attempted only to provide "pointers" to these bodies of literature and to examine their relationships to research in the core areas of the *Handbook*.

The first five chapters of this volume are organized in relation to one of the research areas that has expanded most vigorously during the period of planning and writing of the *Handbook*. These chapters treat aspects of psycholinguistics most closely related to research and theory covered in the other volumes. Perhaps the most fertile source of new concepts and models closely related to other branches of cognitive theory has been research on semantic memory. This work is given a critical review and interpretation by Smith in the first chapter of this volume, following which some lines of theoretical developmental leading "upward" into problems of comprehension of meaningful material are reviewed by Kintsch, then connections "downward" into more elementary problems of coding in memory by Johnson. Also, Johnson's chapter shades into the very active current body of work on perceptual and memorial processes in reading, carried further by Baron's examination of perceptual learning in relation to letter and word recognition. Finally, we consider inputs to the psycholinguistic system via speech and speech perception. The strong emphasis of Pisoni's chapter on speech perception rather than production simply reflects both the predominance of research on perceptual aspects of speech in the current cognitive literature and the close relationships of this research to other lines of investigation of perception and short-term memory.

Detailed examination of research findings and theory in the many areas that have been covered in these volumes yields at least some small comfort to the beleaguered reader. First, although the vast acceleration in research output yields a commensurate increase in the sampling of varieties of cognitive performance, there is reason to doubt that this broadened sampling often uncovers new theoretical insights of a fundamental character or even points up new theoretical issues. Second, a great deal of the harvest of superficially new theory is achieved by various forms of translation and the playing of variations on long familiar themes. Some knowledge of the history of the subject and some understanding of the way some of the more pervasive concepts and principles have evolved may serve present-day investigators better than boosting their reading rates. The final chapter of the present volume provides some documentation for this last suggestion.

W. K. ESTES

1

Theories of Semantic Memory

Edward E. Smith

Stanford University

I. INTRODUCTION

A. The Domain of Semantic Memory

The phrase *semantic memory* has been used to denote three views about meaning and memory that vary in how inclusive they are. At the broadest level, semantic memory is assumed to be our store for meaningful material, be it our permanent knowledge of the meanings of words or our transient memory of a particular sentence that was presented to us in a laboratory experiment. Under this definition, theories of semantic memory include, among others, the large-scale memory models developed by Anderson and Bower (1973), Kintsch (1974), and Norman and Rumelhart (1975). A second definition restricts the domain of semantic memory to a subset of the above. This is Tulving's (1972) distinction between semantic and episodic memory, where the former refers to our permanent knowledge about the language and basic facts of the world, while the latter essentially includes everything else. Under Tulving's definition, semantic memory would contain the meaning of *cat* as well as the fact that Columbus is commonly credited with the discovery of America, but not a particular sentence that was just presented to us in a psychological experiment. The third definition, that semantic memory contains only knowledge about the language, specifically, the meanings of words and rules for operating them, is the most restrictive of all.

It would be advantageous in several respects to adopt the most restrictive definition. This would permit us to focus our review on a well-defined domain. Also, it might allow us to relate psychological studies of semantic memory to some well-known linguistic and philosophical approaches to semantics, like that of Katz (1972), though perhaps at the cost of less contact with rival formulations in linguistic semantics. There are, however, two problems with adopting the

1

most restrictive definition. One is that even if we limit our attention to the psychological literature that is explicitly referred to as semantic-memory research, we find studies dealing with knowledge other than that contained in word meanings. The second problem is that accepting the most restricted definition seems to entail taking sides on an unresolved empirical issue, namely, whether a separable knowledge system exists that deals only with linguistic (as opposed to real-world) information. In view of these considerations, we will have to remain somewhat open on the question of a definition. In the following discussion, we will take semantic memory to be a system that certainly contains word meanings and rules for operating on them, and possibly includes some general world knowledge as well. Though this is an awfully fuzzy stance to take on a definitional matter, it will allow us to be restrictive in our coverage of meaning and memory, and at the same time treat the distinction of linguistic versus real-world knowledge as an open question.

Given our quasi-definition, where exactly does semantic memory fit into the broader scheme of cognitive psychology? While it is possible to view this topic in the general context of concept attainment and utilization (Rosch, 1974; Smith, Rips, & Shoben, 1974a), in this chapter semantic memory will be treated as a component of language comprehension. Consider, then, the process involved when an attentive listener comprehends a single sentence. At a minimum, three types of procedures must come into play: pattern-recognition devices that encode the words of the sentence, syntactic procedures that parse the sentence and make apparent the grammatical role of each word, and semantic procedures that interpret the meaning of the sentence. There is good reason to believe that these three types of procedures are mutually interactive rather than sequentially ordered and independent. Thus, pattern-recognition devices can use the information available from syntactic and semantic analyses to facilitate the perception of words (for example, Morton, 1969), while parsing procedures may consider semantic and pragmatic facts as well as syntactic information (for example, Winograd, 1972). But despite the complexities resulting from these interactions, researchers have considered it a legitimate endeavor to focus on one of these procedures for intensive study, while keeping in mind how the procedure of interest could be interfaced with the other processes. Our particular concern is with the set of processes that are involved in semantic interpretation. These include: (a) retrieving the semantic representations of individual words, (b) combining these individual meanings into an overall meaning of the entire sentence (where such combinatorial processes may be partly directed by context), (c) possibly relating this overall meaning to a real-world situation so that the truth or falsity of the sentence can be established, e.g., determining whether a sentence is a true description of a particular scene, and (d) using the meaning of the entire sentence to draw some permissible inferences (where again context may play a decisive role). These four aspects of semantic interpretation are precisely what the study of semantic memory is about. Under this view, then, semantic memory is a critical ingredient in the study of language comprehension.

B. Goals of a Theory of Semantic Memory

Each of the above-mentioned processes—retrieving word meanings, combining meanings, interfacing meanings with real-world situations, and drawing inferences—relates to a particular goal that any theory of semantic memory should aspire to.[1]

The first goal is to stipulate the psychological representations of word meanings. In principle, this will be accomplished when we have a theory that: (a) offers a general description of meaning components and their structure and (b) tells us how we can proceed to determine detailed aspects of meaning for individual cases. Given both (a) and (b), we could then account for why people judge some word pairs to be synonyms (for example, *lad* and *boy*), others contradictories (for example, *dead* and *alive*), others coordinates (for example, *apple* and *peach*), and so on. These are some of the standard phenomena that linguists have traditionally been concerned with (for example, Katz, 1972; Lyons, 1968). To see how far we are from being able to do this, one need only consider that even if we included linguistic and philosophical research in conjunction with psychological work, we could not offer such lexical specifications for more than a handful of words, and even these might prove problematic. (See, for example, Katz's 1972 treatment of *buy* and *sell* for an indication of the detailed analysis needed to stipulate word meanings and the problems inherent in doing so.) It seems that, for now, we must settle for a more limited goal and accept as a contribution any research that specifies some general structural properties of semantic representations. Such properties might, for example, be that the semantic representation of a word contains only those meaning components needed to define it literally or that the components of such a representation must be hierarchically organized. Most semantic memory research has been primarily concerned with establishing such general properties.

The second goal involves a description of the combinatorial processes that operate on individual semantic representations to yield larger meaning units. These processes must have the cast of productive rules, since they operate on a finite set of lexical entries, yet produce an indefinite number of larger meaning units, like sentence meanings. A list of such processes and their exact input and output conditions would, in principle, constitute a means of fulfilling our second goal. Obviously, progress on this line of reserach will be critically dependent on progress on our first goal, though it is possible to work on this combinatorial problem without firm foundational knowledge about the nature of semantic representations (see, for example, Rips, Shoben, & Smith, 1975; Rips, Smith & Shoben, 1978).

The third goal is to determine how to relate semantic representations, whether for individual words or for larger units, to real-world situations. That is, we want to provide an interface between semantic representations and perceptual pro-

---

[1]I am indebted to Lance Rips for much of the following discussion of goals.

cesses so we can account for how one recognizes objects from descriptions, or answers questions about visual objects, or calls another's attention to aspects of the physical environment. At this point in time, it is not even clear what form a solution to these problems would take. It might consist of showing that semantic representations include the type of information needed to identify their perceptual referents. This implies that both linguistic descriptions and perceptual representations of events can be reduced to the same semantic representation, a position argued by Clark and Chase (1972) and Pylyshyn (1973). Alternatively, a solution to this goal might consist of a set of rules that interrelate separate semantic and perceptual representations, a proposal similar to one noted by Kosslyn and Pomerantz (1977). In any event, we can see that again progress on this endeavor will be intimately related to progress on the prior goals, though once more it is possible to make progress on the current problem without firm solutions to the prior ones (see, for example, Clark & Chase, 1972).

The final goal is to be able to specify the kinds of inferences that one makes on the basis of sentence meaning, particularly those based on the meanings of the constituent words, for example, *Dan is a bachelor* implies *Dan is male*. A conceivable solution to this problem would involve some sort of formal system that generates only acceptable inferences, and possibly a set of psychological principles that accounts for our preferences for drawing some semantic inferences over others. The kinds of formal systems I have in mind are of two types. In one (for example, Katz, 1972), words are specified in terms of primitive meaning components (for example, one sense of *bachelor* includes the components of being male and unmarried), and permissible inferences are based on these components (for example, *Dan is male* can be inferred from *Dan is a bachelor*). In the other kind of system, permissible inferences are determined by a set of general inference rules or meaning postulates (for example, Fodor, Bever, & Garrett, 1974; Stillings, 1975). Under either type of system, there is again a dependence of the present goal on the previous ones since, for example, questions about inferences are inextricably bound to questions about semantic representations.

While I have repeatedly emphasized how success on a particular goal depends on progress on previously mentioned goals, the situation is not nearly as sequential as my discussion might suggest, for all of these goals are thoroughly interdependent, and how we approach any one of them will have implications for the others. As one example of this, Fodor *et al.*, (1974) noted that there is a tradeoff between issues about semantic representation and issues about inferences, such that many aspects of semantic knowledge may either be incorporated directly into semantic representations or handled indirectly via semantic inference rules. As another illustration of this interdependence, consider how our conceptualization of semantic representations can be affected by our notions about combinatorial rules, semantic/perception interfaces, and inferences. In the preceding discussion of my first goal involving semantic representations, it was mentioned that such representations may be explicated in terms of meaning components, but no constraints on potential components were suggested. Having discussed the other goals, it is now apparent how partially to constrain potential meaning components. Specifically, these components should be capable of: (a) being readily employed by compositional rules, (b) making contact with perceptual representations (though this is too strong a constraint for all meaning components to meet), and (c) fostering the semantic inferences that people in fact draw. That is, the general constraint on meaning components is that they be compatible with solutions to the other goals.

These goals provide a natural way of structuring the field of semantic memory and all its offshoots. However, in this chapter I will concentrate primarily on research related to the first goal—specifying the general properties of semantic representations. The reason for doing so is simple: the bulk of semantic-memory research has been primarily concerned with this issue of lexical representations and with the related questions of how these representations are accessed and utilized in comprehending sentences, particularly those whose meanings can be determined without extensive use of combinatorial processes. In the next, or second, section some critical distinctions that will serve to elucidate and organize semantic-memory theories in general will be considered. One of these distinctions is drawn from linguistics and philosophy, while others derive from psychology proper. Armed with these, I will, in Section III, present the major models of semantic memory, all of which are fundamentally concerned with the nature of semantic representations. (For reasons that are not entirely clear, these models deal primarily with nouns and generally neglect the semantics of other syntactic categories.) In addition to describing these models, I will offer critiques of their ability to account for the most important empirical findings. Finally, in Section IV, I will evaluate semantic-memory research against three rather abstract criteria: generally, extendability, and sufficiency. I believe that this kind of appraisal will indicate the major virtues and failings of semantic-memory research as it has thus far been conducted.

Before proceeding to the next section, however, there is one more introductory issue to be dealt with—the problem of how to interrelate our psychological approach to semantics with the more formal approaches of linguistics and philosophy.

C. The Relation of Psychological Semantics to Formal Semantics

Our statement of primary goals makes it clear that a psychological approach to semantics has much in common with linguistic and philosophical studies of semantics, for the latter two disciplines would presumably concur that the study of semantics should be directed toward an understanding of (a) semantic representations of lexical items, (b) combinatorial meaning rules, and (c) inference procedures. The only goal of psychology that may not be a legitimate concern of the other two disciplines is an analysis of the semantics/perception interface, though this itself is a matter of debate among linguists (see Katz, 1972 versus Fillmore, 1974). Given this communality of goals, it behooves the psychologist interested in semantics to take a long and hard look at the work done in these other two fields.

In doing so, though, it is important to appreciate some of the differences between psychological approaches to semantics and those of linguistics and philosophy. A major difference is that the latter disciplines have tended to approach semantic analysis in a purely structural way, that is, in the same way one would approach the study of any formal system (like an arithmetic one). Thus, linguists and philosophers from Frege (1892) to Chomsky (1957) have argued that: To explicate language use, we must first understand the object of such use—the language—and to do this, we must analyze language as a system unto itself, uncontaminated by the idiosyncrasies of actual language users. According to this view, one should treat words as abstract objects interconnected by some sort of semantic structure and ignore the functions of these entities to language users, at least for the time being. The major argument for this approach is its precedent in the history of science. Thus, one would not attempt to study how children acquire simple arithmetic concepts without first having some understanding of the nature of these concepts in a mathematical sense; that is, you have to know something about how arithmetic "works" before you can study its acquisition.

Let us refer to this position as a "competence" approach to semantics. For it, like Chomsky's (1957) approach to syntax, is concerned with a kind of idealized knowledge available only to ideal comprehenders (where, under some views, an ideal comprehender is simply a normal adult speaker freed from performance constraints like limited attention and memory capacity). This is in contrast to the "performance" approach of many psychologists who argue that semantic interpretation can best be understood by studying linguistic performances that involve semantic knowledge. There are two major arguments in favor of this view. First, as psychologists, we will only be satisfied with an account of semantic knowledge that details how it is actually used and the idiosyncracies or individual differences therein. This is not incompatible with the formal approaches, but rather ancillary or auxiliary to it, as a competence model may be a component of a performance model. Second, it may be helpful to study semantic knowledge with respect to the language user, because the functions of such knowledge (for example, the retrieval and combination of semantic representations) may affect the very nature of the representations themselves or at least affect our theoretical descriptions of such representations.[2] What all this comes

[2]It should be noted that some linguists and philosophers (for example, Chafe, 1973; Grice, 1968) would accept this functionalist argument.

down to, then, is that a psychological approach to semantics shares with its linguistic and philosophical counterparts a common set of goals but differs in metatheory. And this difference in metatheory is responsible for differences in the type of methodology and theory that characterize performance versus competence approaches to semantics.

II. DISTINCTIONS AMONG SEMANTIC-MEMORY MODELS

A. A Competence-Based Distinction

In view of the above, what psychologists need to do is survey the literature on competence approaches to semantics, keeping in mind the differences that have been mentioned, and look for constructs and distinctions that may prove useful in performance models of semantics. One such distinction was alluded to in our earlier consideration of definitional problems. This is the contrast that some linguists and philosophers draw between the kind of semantic information that is linguistic knowledge versus that which is knowledge of the world. Or to phrase it in another way, it is the distinction between the knowledge contained in an idealized dictionary versus that included in an idealized encyclopedia (for example, Frege, 1892; Katz & Fodor, 1963; Lyons, 1968).

Each dictionary entry would presumably contain only the most essential aspects about the meaning of a word, roughly those that are invariant over context and are the basis of the strongest semantic inferences we can draw. In contrast, each encyclopedia entry would contain all of a language user's knowledge of the world that is relevant to the word in question. To illustrate, consider the meanings of *bachelor* and *spinster*. A dictionary might represent the meaning of *bachelor* in terms of three component properties: maleness, adulthood, and the property of never having been married. Similarly, the dictionary entry for *spinster* would include the attributes of femaleness, adulthood, and the property of never having been married. Hence, according to this analysis, the two terms differ only with respect to the dimension of sex (male versus female). But to most people *bachelor* and *spinster* also differ in ways this dictionary-based analysis does not capture. For one thing, *bachelor* has at least a neutral connotation, but *spinster*, a decidedly negative one; for another, *bachelor* suggests a young man of marriageable age, or is at least neutral with respect to the age dimension, while *spinster* suggests an older woman, one past society's conception of the standard age of marriage. These latter two differences—of evaluation and age—would presumably be part of our encyclopedic knowledge of the two terms.

Let me extend this example a bit to insure the distinction is clear. Suppose a friend tells you that his acquaintance, Annie, is a spinster. If he should then add that Annie is married, intuition strongly suggests that you will accuse your friend of not knowing the meaning of *spinster*. Your friend simply has a gap in his linguistic knowledge, a deficit in his internal dictionary. But now suppose instead that your friend, after noting Annie's spinsterhood, adds that Annie is a vivacious, youthful, eligible, woman who is constantly sought after by men, but prefers not to marry. In this case, intuition suggests that you may merely note that you and your friend have different world-views about what spinsters are typically like. Here, the discrepancy between you and your friend concerns world knowledge rather than linguistic knowledge, that is, encyclopedia information not dictionary entries.

One implication of this dictionary/encyclopedia distinction can be seen when the distinction is viewed in relation to the task usually used by psychologists to study semantic memory. In this verification task, a subject is presented with simple statements of the form *An S is a P*—where S designates a subject noun and P a predicate noun—and has to decide whether the statement is true or false. The data of primary interest are the times needed to reach these decisions. Sample true statements would include *A robin is a bird* and *An apple is a fruit,* while sample false statements would be *A chair is a fruit* and *A dog is a cat.* In these examples one can determine truth or falsity solely by the meanings of the constituent words, without any recourse to particularized world knowledge, and this is the case for many of the statements used in studies of semantic memory. The relation of this to the dictionary/encyclopedia distinction is as follows. If this distinction has psychological reality, and there is a separable psychological entity akin to a dictionary, then many of the true and false statements used in the experimental research should be verifiable solely on the basis of the dictionary. That is, the verification task provides us with a "road into" the mental dictionary. This is only a claim. It can be evaluated empirically by determining whether world knowledge of the supposed encyclopedia variety plays a substantial role in the verification of statements like the above. If it does, then either there is no psychological entity akin to a dictionary or such an entity exists but may not be functionally separable from an internal encyclopedia.

There are, however, two problems with this dictionary/encyclopedia distinction that should be noted. First, it will often prove difficult to determine whether or not the distinction is incorporated into a theory of semantic memory. Semantic-memory models may obscure this distinction even though they implicitly take a stance on it, either because the models were not formulated with this issue in mind or because the statement of the processing model in some way blurs the distinction of interest. The second and more serious problem is that the distinction itself has lately come under attack in linguistic and philosophical circles (see, for example, Bolinger, 1965; Fillmore, 1974). Consider, for example, an argument noted by Fillmore (originally due to Macnamara, 1971). Fillmore argued that we have no reason to believe that when we learn a word we store linguistic information about it (a dictionary entry) separately from our experiences associated with the word (an encyclopedia entry). This, in essence, challenges the dictionary/encyclopedia distinction on psychological grounds. So the question of whether this dichotomy has value for psychological models remains an open one, and in our subsequent analysis of models we will inquire of each theory whether it incorporates such a distinction, and, if so, how it is utilized in the processing part of the model. This kind of approach should shed further light on the psychological utility of the distinction at issue.

B. Performance-Based Distinctions

There appears to be only one major performance distinction among semantic-memory models, and it has run into problems. I am referring to the contrast between network and set-theoretic models (Rips, Shoben, & Smith, 1973), where network theories depict the meaning of a word in terms of a network of labeled relations, while set-theoretic models represent word meanings by sets of unrelated meaning components. The basic problem with this distinction was pointed out by Hollan (1975). He noted that the network versus set contrast was essentially a difference in the type of language used to describe a model and might be relatively devoid of empirical content.

Though the content of the network versus set distinction has been challenged, there still seems to be something very useful about it. This distinction partitions the existent models into two classes that appear to have substantive differences between them, though these differences may have little to do with the network versus set-representational format. The question is, What are these supposed substantive differences? The following attempts to answer this.

1. The Computation versus Prestorage Distinction

Consider how a subject might go about confirming the statement *A robin is a bird*. At a general level, he has either stored this exact knowledge prior to being presented the test statement, or he has not and must somehow compute it from whatever knowledge he has stored. This contrast, between prestorage and computation of the relevant information, can help us to distinguish among semantic-memory models. Each model can be characterized by (*a*) the types of information it prestores versus the type it computes and (*b*) the kinds of computations it performs. Let me first deal with (*a*), the computation versus prestorage distinction.

To explicate the distinction, let us start by contrasting two simple models. The first is similar to the attribute model discussed by Meyer (1970), and it is presented on the left-hand side of Figure 1. Here each word (for example, *bird*) is represented by a set of prestored semantic attributes (for example, animate and feathered). The precise nature of these attributes need not concern us now, except to note that they are assumed to correspond to components of the meaning of a word that are singly necessary and jointly sufficient to define the word. According to the model, a statement such as *A robin is a bird* is verified by comparing

ATTRIBUTE MODEL   HIERARCHICAL NETWORK MODEL

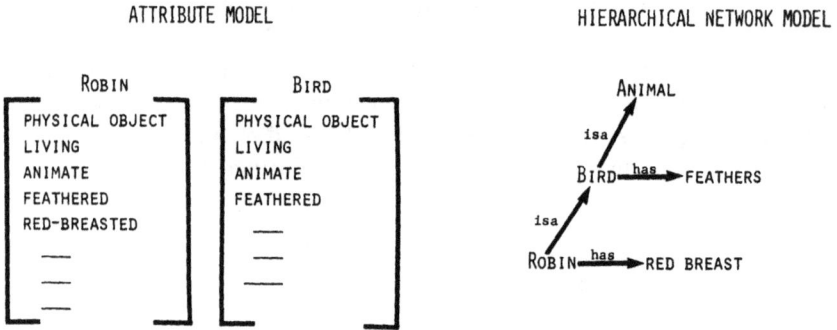

FIGURE 1.   Two illustrative models of semantic categorization.

the stored attribute set of the predicate (*bird*) to that of the subject (*robin*), with the sentence being true if and only if the former set is a subset of the latter. Thus, the categorical relation between the subject and predicate is computed at the time of verification.

Now contrast this with our second model, presented on the right-hand side of Figure 1. This formulation depicts a segment of the hierarchical-network model of Collins and Quillian (1969), which will be discussed later in detail. For now, all that we need concern ourselves with is the following. First, words are represented as nodes in a network, interconnected by prestored labeled links, where attribute relations are labeled *has* and category relations are labeled *isa*. Second, in addition to the prestored attribute and category relations, other relations may be computed by a simple inference procedure. For example, given a prestored *isa* relation between *robin* and *bird* and another between *bird* and *animal,* one can infer an *isa* relation between *robin* and *animal*. This model, then, would confirm a statement like *A robin is a bird* by entering the network at the nodes for the subject and predicate terms and searching for either a prestored relation (link) between the two or for a set of prestored relations that would inferentially connect the two.

The above contrast demonstrates how two models may differ with respect to what information they prestore and what information they compute. The attribute model prestores certain attributes and computes all categorical relations of the kind we have been discussing; the hierarchical-network model prestores attribute and category relations that are directly related to a particular node and computes (infers) all other relations. This gives us a means for distinguishing between models at an abstract level, which is exactly what we need in order to organize the various models of semantic memory. In fact, given existent semantic-memory models, we may simplify the distinction. As the models are primarily concerned with an analysis of categorical relations, we may simply note whether such relations are always computed (as in the attribute model), or sometimes prestored (as in the hierarchical-network model). Let us refer to the former as computation models and to the latter as prestorage models, keeping in mind that the distinction holds only with regard to the categorical relations and that even prestorage models posit some computations (inferences).

Having drawn this distinction, it can now be related to the earlier one between set-theoretic and network models. Note that the attribute model, which is of the computation type, lends itself to a set-theoretic representation, while the hierarchical-network model, which is of the prestorage type, is more conducive to a network representation. That is, there is a correlation between the possibly superficial distinction of network versus set representations and our newer distinction about how information is represented. This correlation seems to hold across most semantic-memory models, and thus the computation/prestorage contrast gives us a viable way of distinguishing between the models originally partitioned into classes of network and set theories.

There is, however, one obvious problem with the above reasoning. It seems that our distinction between computation and prestorage models itself rests on the distinction between attributes and categories. For example, in discussing the attribute model, I noted that certain attributes, like animate, are prestored while all categorical relations are computed. But, logically, any attribute can define a category, as, for example, the attribute of being animate defines the category of all animate things. The problem then becomes one of supplying some criteria that will distinguish between the entities we have characterized as attributes and those we have labeled categories. Syntactic criteria may be of some help. For example, the relation between *robin* and *bird* is usually expressed by an *is a* construction, while that between *robin* and *animate* is most often expressed by an *is* construction. Another possible criterion concerns the notion of primitiveness. Some of the entities we have called attributes may well have the potential to serve as primitive semantic components in a general theory of semantics, for a component like being animate would be part of the meaning of many terms. In contrast, the entities we have called categories (for example, *birds*) are unlikely candidates for primitive components. I am not at all confident that these criteria will work, but there is little more I can say here about this problem. In what follows, I will pursue the computation versus prestorage distinction and not fret over its potentially shaky foundation.

One good reason for pursuing this distinction is that it seems to have wide applicability in psychology. The distinction is similar to that between procedural (computational) and declarative (prestored) knowledge, which is widely used in artificial intelligence (for example, Winograd, 1975), and in recent psychological models that have come out of this approach (for example, Anderson, 1976). Our distinction also seems relevant to some well-known dichotomies in the psychology of memory. As an example, consider the kinds of theories that have been developed to account for recognition-memory tasks, where a subject must decide whether or not a test item was on a previously memorized list. In a recent review of this work, Wescourt and Atkinson (1976) argued that some theories assume that recognition is based on a comparison of the strength or familiarity of an item with a criterion value (a computation process), while other models hold that recognition occurs when one retrieves a fact indicating the item had occurred previously (a prestorage notion). Indeed, it is hard to think of an area in cognitive psychology where this distinction could not play a role. Along these lines, it is of some interest to note that Neisser, in the last chapter of his classic book *Cognitive Psychology* (1967), argued for the centrality of this computation/prestorage distinction (though he called it the utilization/reappearance issue).

2. Correlated Distinctions

The computation/prestorage contrast explicitly deals with how information is represented but carries with it some implications about how information is processed or computed (previously discussed by Rips, Smith, & Shoben, 1975b). To appreciate these processing distinctions, consider again how the attribute model would verify the statement *A robin is a bird.* Since the answer cannot be computed directly from the words *robin* and *bird,* one must first expand these terms into semantic attributes that can be operated on. That is, some semantic decomposition is a prerequisite for verification. Then the two sets of attributes must be compared, and the statement is confirmed if all of the attributes of the predicate can be matched to those of the subject term. Thus, a comparison process is required that is both exhaustive (confirmation is based on all of the attributes of the predicate) and conjunctive (confirmation is based on the conjunction of the outcomes for specific attributes). This type of comparison process is crucial in the attribute model, as it is assumed to be the primary source of variations in verification times (Meyer, 1970). These two aspects of the attribute model— decomposition and an emphasis on comparison processes—follow from its computational nature, and so should be true of all computation models.

Now let us turn to the hierarchical-network model. For both prestored and inferred categorical relations, there is no need for any decomposition. The major process involved is a search of the network. One must search through the prestored and inferred paths looking for a path that connects the subject and predicate terms. (Of course such a search can be construed as a comparison process, where the comparisons are self-terminating and disjunctive; but to keep things simple, I will continue to refer to this process as a *search* and reserve the term *comparison* for the kind of process that goes on in the attribute model.) Once the search has found a path linking the subject and predicate, the relations manifested in this path must be compared to those in the test sentence. Here again is a comparison process, but it is assumed that this process plays a negligible role in accounting for variations in verification times; that is, in the hierarchical-network model, empirical findings are attributed to the search process and not to a subsequent comparison operation. This emphasis on search processes appears to be true of all existent prestorage models.

What we end up with, then, is that computation models require some decomposition and emphasize comparison processes, while prestorage models require no decomposition and emphasize search processes. These distinctions will soon prove useful.

III. MODELS OF SEMANTIC REPRESENTATIONS AND RETRIEVAL PROCESSES

We are finally ready to consider the models themselves. In all, four theories will be discussed in detail.[3] Each of them is an attempt to say something substantial about the representation and utilization of word meanings. Some justification should be given for why only four models are considered here when there are clearly more than that around. In order to determine which models were worth extended treatment, I adopted as one criterion that the theoretical statement be relatively precise and detailed, not just a discussion at one end of an experimental report. A second criterion was more complex and gets at the heart of what my review is intended to be about. While I think it worthwhile to present various models in detail so one can get an idea of their comparative strengths and weaknesses, an equally important goal is to convey the kinds of assumptions theorists have made about semantic memory. That is, I am concerned with what one may learn about representational and processing assumptions by looking across rather than just within models. So I have selected models that seem to contrast in the kinds of assumptions they make, rather than theories that may be viewed as hybrids of other models. As a final criterion for inclusion, I considered only those models that deal primarily with semantic memory as I have roughly defined it. This excluded large-scale theories of meaning and memory—such as those of Anderson (1976), Anderson and Bower (1973), Kintsch (1974), and Norman and Rumelhart (1975). The interested reader should consult Anderson (1976) for a systematic review of these models.

The models to be discussed here will be grouped into two pairs. The first contains early models that were introduced between 1969 and 1970 and dominated the scene for about five years. The second pair contains more recent models that seem to offer more adequate statements about semantic representations. The rationale for this organization is that both of the early models share certain failings that the recent theories have explicitly tried to circumvent. But while the consideration of models will be chronological, I will make extensive use of the previously described distinctions in structuring the discussion of each theory and interrelating them in summary statements. For each model, I will consider its basic assumptions and how they line up with our distinctions, then discuss its important predictions, and finally offer an overall evaluation.

[3]Here and elsewhere, the terms *theory* and *model* are used interchangeably.

One last matter before going on to the theories. All of the models are mainly concerned with accounting for performance in a verification task, and it seems useful to remind the reader of the nature of this task. Recall that in this paradigm, subjects are presented with statements of the form *An S is a P* (for example, *An apple is a fruit*) and have to decide as rapidly as possible whether the statement is true or false. The data of primary interest are the times needed to confirm true statements and to disconfirm false ones. There are several reasons for this emphasis on times. For one, the statements presented for verification are so simple that error rates are often too low to serve as sensitive dependent measures. Another is that decision times can be assumed to reflect directly mental operations; that is, we can assume that the retrieval and utilization of semantic representations goes on in real time and so latencies directly reflect the times needed to execute these operations in vivo. Also, analytic techniques have been worked out for latency measures that allow one to draw strong inferences about the nature of mental operations (for example, Sternberg, 1969).

A. Early Models

1. The Hierarchical-Network Model

a. Description. Perhaps the best known theory of semantic memory is the hierarchical-network model proposed by Collins and Quillian (1969, 1972a), which was used earlier to explicate some of our distinctions. To gain a deeper understanding of the model, it is helpful to separate its general assumptions about semantic representations from its more specific ones about hierarchical organization. With regard to the former assumptions, Collins and Quillian postulated that the conceptual counterparts of words are represented as independent units connected in a network of labeled relations. Figure 2 illustrates this idea.

While the assumption of a network representation may not be a critical one (Hollan, 1975), there are four important assumptions embedded in Figure 2. First, there are two different kinds of relations represented in the model: subset relations, labeled *isa*, and attribute relations, designated by the labels *is, has,* and *can*. (The *isa* label was only implicit in the Collins and Quillian (1969) formulation; for purposes of exposition I have made it explicit.) Second, as noted in our earlier discussion, the model is a prestorage one, as some subset relations are represented directly (and, consequently, there is a minimum of decomposition and an emphasis on search rather than comparison processes). Third, the meaning of a word, such as *robin,* is the entire complex of labeled relations leading to and from this word (node) in the network. This suggests that the present formulation does not include a dictionary/encyclopedia distinction since there is no attempt to restrict semantic knowledge to only its essential aspects. But things are a bit fuzzy here, for the present model is based on Quillian's work in artificial intelligence, and there the properties of a word have sometimes been charac-

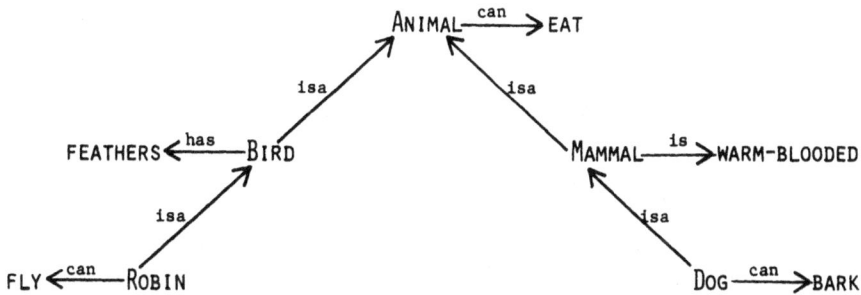

FIGURE 2. An illustration of the hierarchical-network model.

terized by how essential they are in defining the word (see Bell & Quillian's 1971 notion of criteriality). The fourth critical assumption relates to a distinction I have not explicitly considered, namely, whether or not one can depict the meanings of all words in terms of a fixed set of semantic primitives (see, for example, Katz, 1972, and Norman & Rumelhart, 1975). In the present model, the meaning of a word concept is expressed only in terms of other concepts, and so the idea of semantic primitives is explicitly denied.

The other general assumptions of this model concern how these representations are processed. These assumptions have already been considered in the earlier discussion of the model, but it will not hurt to reiterate them here. When presented with a sentence to verify, for example, *A robin is a bird,* a subject enters semantic memory at the nodes for the subject and predicate nouns (*robin* and *bird,* respectively), looks for a path that relates them (a search process), and checks that the path found is labeled in a way consistent with the relations asserted in the sentence (a comparison process). Variations in the times needed to confirm statements are assumed to be due to variations in the search process. In the example given above, verification would be relatively quick because the subject has to search only the one link between *robin* and *bird.* There is only one link between the two concepts because the subset relation between *robin* and *bird* is presumably stored directly in semantic memory. However, if a subject was presented with the sentence *A robin is an animal,* verification would take longer because the relevant concepts are now two links apart. In this case, the subject has to infer *A robin is an animal* from the stored propositions *A robin is a bird* and *A bird is an animal.*

We are now ready to deal with the specific assumptions about hierarchical organization. First, the model holds that noun concepts are arranged hierarchically in semantic memory. That is, a noun concept is in some sense closer to an immediate superordinate than to a distant superordinate; and in relating a noun concept to one of its distant superordinates, one must consider or go through some direct superordinate along the way. For example, in Figure 2, *robin* is closer to *bird* than to *animal,* and one must go through *bird* in relating *robin* and *animal.* A second assumption deals with properties rather than nouns and has been referred to as the cognitive-economy assumption (Conrad, 1972). It holds that properties are stored at the highest, or most general, node to which the property applies. As examples, in Figure 2 the property *can eat* is attached only to *animal* and not to the lower node like *bird,* while *can fly* is attached to *robin* and not to *bird* since not all birds can fly.

Collins and Quillian (1969, 1972a) used the above assumptions to generate two critical predictions for the verification task. One concerned subset statements, such as (1) *A robin is a bird* and (2) *A robin is an animal,* that is, statements in which a subject term is paired with either an immediate superordinate or a distant one. It follows from the general assumptions and the specific one about hierarchical organization that (1) should be verified faster than (2), because the former has been prestored while the latter must be inferred. This prediction was confirmed. The other prediction dealt with property statements, such as (3) *A bird has feathers* and (4) *A bird can eat,* that is, statements in which a subject term is either paired with a property stored directly with it (as in 3) or a property stored at a higher node (as in 4). It follows from the general assumptions plus the specific one about cognitive economy that (3) should be verified faster than (4), because the former requires less of a search (or because the former is prestored while the latter must be inferred). Again, the critical prediction was confirmed.

b. Evaluation.   This model offered the first detailed description of how one represents and retrieves semantic information. It proved sufficiently attractive that it was soon adopted by other semantic-memory researchers (Freedman & Loftus, 1971; Loftus, 1973) or incorporated wholesale into a more general theory of language comprehension (Rumelhart, Lindsay, & Norman, 1972).

But despite initial popularity, the model was soon to fall on hard times, with problems stemming from its specific assumptions about hierarchical organization in the storage of nouns and about cognitive economy in the storage of properties. With regard to the cognitive-economy issue, Conrad (1972) was the first to provide some damaging evidence. She argued that Collins and Quillian (1969) had confounded an important factor with their variation in the number of hierarchical links separating a noun concept and its property. This factor was the extent to which the noun and property were associatively related, independent of their supposed separation in a semantic hierarchy. To illustrate, *A bird has feathers* may have been confirmed faster than *A bird can eat* because *bird* is more associated to *feathers* than to *eat,* rather than because of the positioning of these terms in a semantic network. To separate these two factors, Conrad first obtained norms on the strength of associative relations for various noun-property pairs. She then manipulated both this variable and the number of hierarchical links separating noun-property pairs in a verification task. She found that verification time decreased as the associative relation between the noun and property became stronger, but did not vary consistently with the number of links supposedly separating the two terms in a semantic network. This seems like direct evidence against the assumption of cognitive economy. More recent studies have also failed to find any hint of cognitive economy (see, for example, Kosslyn, 1976, who actually found the reverse of a cognitive-economy effect).

There is now also evidence against the assumption that noun concepts are organized hierarchically. Both Collins and Quillian (1971) and Rips *et al.* (1973) showed that, in some cases, subset statements involving immediate superordinates actually took longer to verify than those with distant ones. As an example, *A dog is a mammal* took longer to confirm than *A dog is an animal,* even though there should be fewer links separating the two concepts in the former case. More recent work has generalized this result and shown that the critical determinant of verification times is again the strength of the relation between the two terms (Smith, Shoben, & Rips, 1974). That is, verification time decreases as the associative relation between the two nouns of a category statement increases, while the supposed number of hierarchical links has no effect at all. This evidence, then, suggests that prestored relations are not verified faster than inferred ones, if we take the logic of class relation to determine which ones are prestored.

There are other problems with the hierarchical-network model. One is that it does not readily explain why some instances of a category can be verified faster than others, for example, *A robin is a bird* can be confirmed faster than *A chicken is a bird* (for example, Rosch, 1973). Another problem is that the model has difficulty in accounting for how statements are disconfirmed (see, for example, Schaeffer & Wallace, 1970). This issue turns out to be a sticky one though. While Collins and Quillian (1969) initially failed to offer a viable mechanism for disconfirmations, they did address this problem in a later paper (1972a). Their proposed account of disconfirmations was quite complex and some of it lacks experimental support, but it did introduce the important notion that a false statement is difficult to disconfirm when its component terms contain extraneous links between them, that is, relations other than the one specified in the test statement. Suffice it to say that, while one should not fault the model too much for its treatment of disconfirmations, the results presented in the preceding two paragraphs do offer counterevidence to the specific assumptions of the model. However, its more general assumptions (for example, those aspects having to do with its prestorage format) are not challenged by these findings.

One final point about this model. While my discussion of the model seems faithful to how many other workers in this field have interpreted it, Collins and Loftus (1975) argued that this standard interpretation is not the one intended by Collins and Quillian (1969). They hold, in particular, that the specific assumptions of hierarchical organization and cognitive economy were not intended to be completely general. This protest is supported by a caveat in the original (1969) report of Collins and Quillian (see p. 242, of that paper). However, if this caveat is accepted, and the assumptions in question are not essential parts of the model, then it is not clear that the theory makes any empirical predictions. And a psychological theory without empirical claims is really not much of a theory at all. For these reasons, I have presented the standard interpretation of the hierarchical-network model.

2.   The Predicate-Intersections Model

a.   Description. The next theory to be considered is the predicate-intersections model of Meyer (1970). It is depicted in Figure 3. The model has two stages, and both are required to confirm statements like *All robins are animals.* In the first stage, the subjects initially retrieve the names of all categories that intersect the predicate, that is, all categories that have some member in common with the predicate category (animal). The subjects then search these names for that of the subject category (*robin*). If they fail to find it, they can disconfirm the sentence at that point. But if their search is successful, they must go on to a second stage.

Let us begin by focusing on the mechanics of the first stage. The order of search in this stage is determined by the number of exemplars that are not shared by the predicate category and each of the intersecting categories, that is, by the category difference. This notion is a bit complicated, but an example should make things clear. The predicative category of animals intersects the categories for both birds and robins; since there are fewer nonshared exemplars between animals and birds than between animals and robins, *bird* will be searched before *robin* during the first stage. Or, to put it slightly differently, the category difference between animals and robins is the number of animals that are not robins, that between animals and birds is the number of animals that are not birds, and

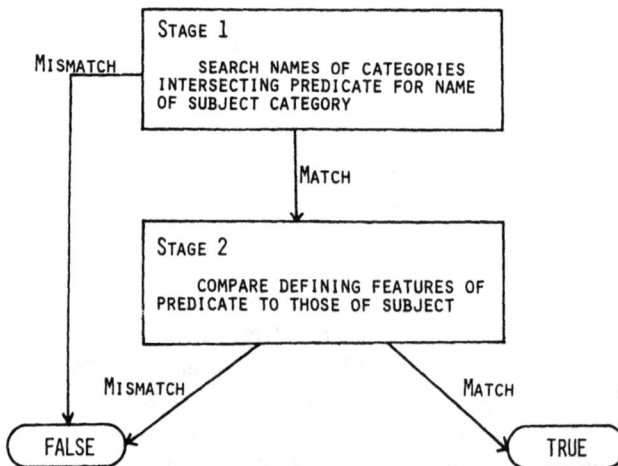

FIGURE 3.   The predicate-intersections model. The figure illustrates only the processing of statements quantified by *all;* see text for remarks on the processing of statements quantified by *some.*

since the latter category difference is the smaller one, *bird* will be searched first.

In the second stage of the model, the subject consider a different kind of semantic information. Here they access the defining attributes of the subject and predicate categories, where such attributes are presumably the most essential aspects of the meaning of a word. The subjects compare the two sets of attributes and confirm the statement if each attribute of the predicate category matches one in the subject category; otherwise, they disconfirms the statement.

It is instructive to take a further look at what kinds of statements require only first-stage processing and what kinds necessitate both stages. The statements that Meyer (1970) worked with may be divided into four types on the basis of the set-theoretic relation of the subject to the predicate term. There are: (a) subset statements, where the subject is a subset of the predicate concept (for example, *robins are animals*); (b) superset statements, where the subject concept is a superset of the predicate (for example, *stones are rubies*); (c) overlap statements, where the subject and predicate only partially overlap (for example, *mothers are writers*); and (d) disjoint statements, where the subject and predicate concepts denote mutually exclusive sets (for example, *houses are vacuums*). When such statements are quantified by *all*, only the disjoint ones can be rejected by the first state since this stage checks for intersections. The other three types must be passed on to the second stage, which will determine that subset statements are true while the remaining two types are false. However, the situation changes when the four statement types are quantified by *some*. Now all types can be evaluated solely by the first stage, since any intersection or shared exemplar between subject and predicate concepts is sufficient grounds for confirming the statements. Thus, the number of stages needed to verify a statement depends both on its set-theoretic type and on the quantifier, where *all* demands that a subset relation be present, while *some* will settle for any intersection.[4]

Now let us turn to our usual distinctions. With regard to statements quantified by *all*, this model is a computational one. For subset relations (which must be established if one is to confirm an *all* statement) are never prestored; rather, they must be computed during the second stage in exactly the same manner as in the simple attribute model. However, for statements quantified by *some*, the model is of the prestorage type. This is because the first stage prestores intersection relations between categories. Hence, the model is something of a hybrid with respect to our computation/prestorage distinction.

With regard to our competence-based distinction, things are a bit sticky. The information used in the second stage appears to approximate an internal dictionary, as it contains only the most essential attributes of the meaning of a word (though it is not clear that Meyer (1970) intended these attributes to reflect

---

[4]Many verification studies have not used explicit quantifiers such as *all* and *some* but rather have employed the form *An S is a P*. In such cases, it seems plausible that subjects interpret the first indefinite article to mean *all*, though this may depend on the nature of the statements used.

linguistic knowledge). The type of information used in the first stage is even harder to classify. Since it tells us whether categories intersect, it seems like part of an essential, dictionary entry; but because it may be based on real-life exemplars of categories, it seems somewhat encyclopedic in nature. In any event, the model does include something like the dictionary entries for words that are studied by numerous linguists (for example, Bierwisch, 1971; Katz, 1972).

From this model Meyer (1970) derived and tested a number of critical predictions. First, as has already been noted, the theory implies that subset statements (for example, *Robins are animals*) can be confirmed by the first stage when quantified by *some*, but require both stages when quantified by *all*. Therefore, subset statements should be confirmed faster when quantified by *some* than *all*. Meyer confirmed this prediction. The next prediction deals only with disjoint statements, such as (1) *All (some) robins are chairs*, and (2) *All (some) robins are furniture*. These statements share a subject term, but vary in the size of the predicate category, with *furniture* denoting a larger category than *chair*. According to the model, (1) and (2) will both be disconfirmed in the first stage, when a search of those categories intersecting the predicate fails to turn up *robin*. But this search will take longer for (2) than (1), because there are more intersecting categories to be searched with larger predicate categories than with smaller ones. This category-size effect was obtained by Meyer. A third prediction deals only with subset statements quantified by *some*, like (3) *Some robins are animals* and (4) *Some birds are animals*. This sample pair shares a predicate term, but differs with respect to the size of the subject category. Both statements should be confirmed by the first stage. So the only way for predicting verification differences between the two would be on the basis of search order. Since the category difference between robins and animals is greater than that between birds and animals, *birds* (in Statement 4) should be searched earlier than *robins* (in Statement 3). Hence, (4) should be confirmed faster than (3). Again, Meyer's data supported this category-size prediction.[5]

b.   Evaluation.   In contrast to the first theory considered, the predicate-intersections model has a straightforward way of accounting for disconfirmations as well as confirmations. Also, it makes some interesting distinctions about processing requirements for statements and quantifiers of various types. In addition, the model was successfully extended by Meyer (1973, 1975) to account for the verification of statements containing negatives, as in *Some animals are not reptiles*. The present model was also investigated by Landauer and Meyer

---

[5]There is one other prediction of the model that deserves some mention. In confirming subset statements quantified by *all*, the duration of the second stage should be briefer for larger than smaller predicate categories. This is because larger categories contain fewer attributes than do smaller ones, and so the time needed to compare all attributes should be less for larger categories. Meyer (1970) found support for this prediction, but it required a relatively derived test.

(1972), who referred to it as the category-search model, and was shown to be consistent with other findings in the semantic-memory literature, including those of Collins and Quillian (1969).

More recent research, however, has challenged the model by questioning the support for its critical predictions. Consider first the finding that subset statements are confirmed faster when quantified by *some* than *all*. In Meyer's (1970) study demonstrating this effect, *some* and *all* statements were presented in separate blocks of trials. In the blocks of *some* statements, the true sentences (subset, superset, and overlap statements) tended to contain related noun pairs (for example, *some birds are animals*), while the false sentences (disjoint statements) contained mainly unrelated noun-pairs (as in *Some houses are vacuums*). Thus, the true–false difference was correlated with a difference in relatedness. This correlation was greatly diminished in the blocks of *all* statements. Here the true sentences (subset statements) again contained related noun pairs, but now the false sentences included superset and overlap statements as well as disjoint ones, and the former two statement types often contained related noun pairs (as in *All stones are rubies*). If subjects were able to use differences in relatedness as a clue to their true–false decisions, this clue would have been available in the *some* blocks but not in the *all* blocks. This in itself could account for why subset statements were verified faster when quantified by *some* than by *all*. Rips (1975a) tested this line of reasoning in two experiments, and found support for it in both. In one study, which used Meyer's blocked-trial procedure, the latency advantage of *some* over *all* statements was substantially reduced when the false *some* statements contained related noun pairs (just as the false *all* statements did). In a second study, Rips randomly intermixed *some* and *all* statements. This procedure effectively reduced the possibility of using relatedness differences as a clue to true–false decisions. Here he found a complete absence of differences in verification times associated with the two quantifiers. This same null finding has also been reported by Glass and Holyoak (1974), Glass, Holyoak, and O'Dell (1974) and Holyoak and Glass (1975). Thus, a major prediction of the predicate-intersections model has been robustly discredited.

Rips (1975a) also assessed the major category-size predictions of the predicate-intersections model—verification times should (*a*) increase with the size of the predicate category for disjoint statements and (*b*) decrease with the size of the subject category for subset statements quantified by *some*. In Rips' data, neither of these predicted effects were significant, although some of the results were in the expected direction. However, in other studies by Meyer (1973, 1975), there was some support for these predictions. These conflicting findings question the robustness of predictions derived from the predicate-intersections model. The model has other difficulties. In its present form, it cannot explain Rips' (1975) finding that the time needed to disconfirm disjoint statements increased with the associative relatedness of the nouns in the statements (see also Smith *et al.*, 1974b). Similarly, the model has no natural way of explaining why some instances of a concept are verified faster than others (for example, Rosch, 1973).

3. Summary of the Early Models

The two models considered differ dramatically in their general assumptions about semantic representations, and in how such representations are thought to be utilized in verifying simple statements. Consider first the issue of representational differences. In the hierarchical-network model, word concepts are defined by the total set of their interrelations to other concepts, including subordinates and superordinates as well as properties or attributes. Furthermore, these interrelations are highly structured, as all relations are explicitly labeled. In contrast, the predicate-intersections model contains a second stage where word concepts seem to be depicted only in terms of their essential attributes, with no specific structure interrelating them. (These remarks must be qualified by the fact that this model also contains a first stage where word concepts are represented by their intersections with subordinates and superordinates.)

With regard to assumptions about processing, the theories again provide some striking differences. Here the differences are captured by our distinction between computation and prestorage theories. The hierarchical-network model is clearly of the prestorage type. It assumes that some subset relations are stored directly while others are inferred, that there is little in the way of semantic decomposition during verification, and that the effects obtained in verification tasks are primarily due to variations in search processes. On the other hand, the predicate-intersections model is a computational one when it comes to verifying *all* statements. The computations involve comparisons of decomposed semantic entries, and the durations of these comparisons can affect verification times (see Footnote 5 for an example). (Again these remarks must be qualified, for the first stage of this model functions like a prestorage theory, and many verification-time effects are attributed to variations in the duration of this stage).

Although these general aspects are of great importance, it is really the specific assumptions of the models that are responsible for their critical predictions. And with regard to these specific assumptions, there is surprising agreement among the models. The critical predictions of the hierarchical-network model rest on the assumption of a hierarchical organization of noun concepts, where this hierarchy was presumed to follow the logic of class relations. It was this assumption that led to the notion that a word concept was closer to an immediate superordinate than to a distant one. This same notion is incorporated into the predicate-intersections model via the assumption that the order of search in the first stage was determined by category differences, again defined with respect to the logic of class relations. Hence, both models were argued to be consistent with the original Collins and Quillian (1969) finding that category statements were confirmed faster when they involved immediate rather than distant superordinates.

This specific notion now appears to be precisely what is wrong with these early models. For since these models have been formulated, evidence has accumulated indicating that one cannot use the logic of class relations to determine how close two concepts are in semantic memory. Perhaps the most critical results come from the studies of Rips *et al.* (1973) and Rosch (1973, 1974). Rips *et al.*, it will be recalled, found that the time to confirm a category statement depended on how related the two-word concepts were and not on their proximity in the logic of class relations. This is direct counterevidence to the central notion of the early models. Both Rips *et al.* and Rosch also found that, for any given category, some instances of it could be verified faster than others. Moreover, these within-category differences could be predicted by ratings of how typical each instance was judged to be of its category. For example, in the category of birds, *robin* is judged to be a typical member and *chicken* an atypical one, and *A robin is a bird* can be confirmed faster than *A chicken is a bird*. This typicality effect does not sit well with the notion that the organization of semantic memory somehow follows the logic of class relations, as the latter makes no differentiation among members of a category.

What it all comes down to is this. To account for verification, we not only have to represent logical relations between concepts but must also include in our models representational and processing aspects that focus on the strength of relations between word concepts and their superordinates and subordinates. The next two models try to accomplish these goals.

B. Recent Models

1. *The Feature-Comparison Model*

a. Description.   The first recent theory to be considered is the feature-comparison model, proposed by Smith, Shoben, and Rips (1974b). Its assumptions about representations are as follows. Each word is represented by a set of attributes, called semantic features. These vary continuously in the degree to which they confer or define category membership, that is, they are weighted by their degree of "definingness." Thus, features at one extreme are essential for defining the word concept, whereas features at the other extreme are only characteristic of the concept. For example, the term *bird* would include as defining features the facts that it is animate and feathered and as characteristic features the notions that it is of a particular size and has certain predatory relations to other animals. The characteristic features thus serve to fill in or concretize terms like *bird,* thereby creating a prototype for each word category.

The processing assumptions of this model are portrayed in Figure 4. It is assumed that verification of a statement such as *A robin is a bird* involves a two-stage process. The first compares all of the features of the subject and predicate nouns and assesses the degree of featural similarity between the two

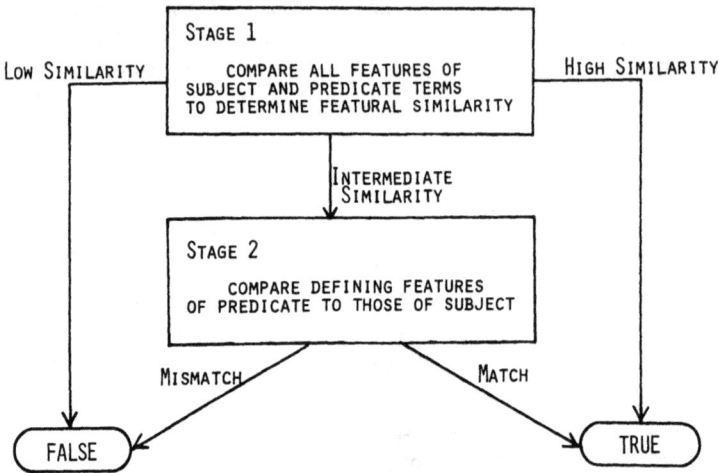

FIGURE 4. The feature-comparison model.

terms. No consideration is given here as to whether the similar features are defining or only characteristic. It is further assumed that if the featural similarity is either very high or very low, one can decide immediately whether or not the subject term designates a subset of the predicate, and respond *true* or *false* accordingly. More precisely, if the overall featural similarity between the two nouns is greater than a high criterion (as might be the case for *robin* and *bird*), one decides that the statement is true; if the featural similarity between the two nouns is less than a low criterion (as in *robin* and *pencil*), one decides that the statement is false; and, finally, if the featural similarity falls between the two criteria (as in *chicken* and *bird* or *bat* and *bird*), one goes on to the second stage. This assumption is critical, because the model holds that measures of both typicality and associative relatedness primarily reflect featural similarity. Therefore, highly typical or highly associated noun pairs can be confirmed by just a single processing stage. When the second stage is executed, it isolates the more defining features of the two terms and compares those of the predicate with those of the subject term. If all of these features match, the statement is true; otherwise, it is false.

The feature-comparison model is entirely a computational one. In fact, the essential proposal of the model is that people have two ways of computing subset relations, where these correspond to the two stages. Decisions based on only the first stage involve a heuristic computation, for such computations, though rapid, are sometimes in error (that is, when many of the similar features are characteristic rather than defining ones, as in *A bat is a bird*). Decisions based on the second stage, however, involve an algorithmic computation, since such computations, although slow, consider only logically sufficient conditions. Using this terminology, it becomes apparent that the main way the present model differs from the predicate-intersections model is that its first stage involves a heuristic computation procedure that allows it to account for those typicality and association effects that plagued its predecessor. Both heuristic and algorithmic computations are alike, however, in requiring decomposition of the semantic representations and using variations in comparison processes to explain verification effects.

Consider now our competence-based distinction. The feature-comparison model is perhaps the first to maintain explicitly a partition akin to the dictionary/ encyclopedia split. The defining features of the second stage are like those in dictionary entries, while the characteristic features of the first stage depict information found only in an encyclopedia (such as the fact that birds tend to be of a particular size value). However, three qualifications or additions to this must be noted. For one, the features of the second stage of the model would correspond to a dictionary entry only when the former are restricted to necessary conditions for category membership, that is, to those with maximal definingness weights. But all the model actually postulates is that the second stage considers the more defining features, that is, those with definingness weights above some threshold. A second qualification is that the characteristic features presumably do not exhaust one's encyclopedia knowledge of a word concept, and thus such features are at best only an approximation of encyclopedia knowledge. The third point is perhaps the most telling. Although the model contains something akin to a dictionary/encyclopedia division, it explicitly denies the claim mentioned earlier that only dictionary knowledge is used in verifying simple sentences. This denial is a major assumption of the model. The best evidence for this assumption is the typicality effect, and the finding that typicality variations among bird and mammal instances can be accounted for partly by the variation of these instances on two dimensions—size values and predatory relations (Rips *et al.*, 1973). These two dimensions seem to depict characteristic or encyclopedia information about birds and mammals, and such information clearly seems to play a role in verifying simple statements. If the assumption in question is indeed correct, we have hit upon an important limit to what competence approaches to dictionary meaning can tell us about the real-time usage of semantic knowledge.

Smith *et al.* (1974b) generated a number of predictions from their model. All are based on the idea that latencies are faster for statements verifiable by the first stage alone than for those requiring both stages. Let us first look at the predictions for true statements. For the case where various instances of the same category are presented (*A robin is a bird, A chicken is a bird,* etc.), Smith *et al.* assumed that typicality ratings reflect similarity relations between instances and category. So if *robin* is judged to be more typical of *bird* than *chicken* is, the features of *robin* presumably provide a better match to the characteristic features of *bird* than do those of *chicken*. Therefore, statements involving more typical instances should be more likely to exceed the high criterion for similarity, more likely to be confirmed by first-stage processing only, and more likely to be verified faster. As mentioned earlier, this has been shown by Rips *et al.* (1973) and Rosch (1973). For cases where subset statements from various categories are presented (*A robin is a bird, A tomatoe is a plant,* etc.), and where the associative strength of the noun pairs has been measured by some norms, Smith *et al.* assumed that this measure also reflects the featural similarity between the nouns. Hence, statements with higher associative strength are more likely to be confirmed by first-stage processing and be verified quickly. This prediction is perhaps the best-documented finding in the literature (for example, Loftus, 1973; Glass, Holyoak, & O'Dell, 1974; Holyoak & Glass, 1975; Smith, 1967; Smith *et al.*, 1974b). Notice that according to these arguments, the effects of both typicality and associative strength result from the same mechanism—overall featural similarity.

A similar logic is used for false statements. The more similar the terms in such a statement (as established by any of a number of ratings), the less likely the statement will fall below the low criterion of similarity. Consequently, such similar statements (for example, *A bat is a bird*) should be more likely to require second-stage processing, and so take longer to disconfirm, than those containing dissimilar noun pairs (for example, *A pencil is a bird*). This finding has also been confirmed numerous times (for example, Herrmann, Shoben, Klun, & Smith, 1975; Rips, 1975; Shoben, 1974; Smith *et al.*, 1974b; Wilkins, 1971).

b. Evaluation.   One of the strengths of the model is its ability to account for most semantic-memory findings with a single principle—featural similarity speeds confirmations and slows disconfirmations. This parsimony in explanatory principles is achieved through the assumptions about characteristic features. Such assumptions mark a significant departure from previous models of semantic memory in that they lead to a different view of natural-language concepts. The notion of characteristic features essentially makes each full semantic representation a prototype or stereotype of the concept (Rosch, 1974), and thereby allows for degrees of category membership (for example, a *robin* is more of a *bird* than a *chicken* is). These views differ markedly from the earlier notion that the organization of semantic memory follows the logic of class relations.

Though the feature-comparison model is relatively recent, it has already run into some problematic findings. One is concerned with the confirmation of true statements. For such statements, if the degree of featural similarity is held constant while the size of the predicate category is varied, the model predicts a decrease in confirmation times with increasing category size. The reasoning is as follows. For nouns, category size is confounded with abstractness, with predicates of larger size being more abstract. But the more abstract a term, the fewer its defining features. As an illustration, *animal* contains fewer defining features than *bird* since every defining feature of the former is also one of the latter. Consequently, as the predicate term becomes more abstract, there is a decrease in the number of features that must be compared in the second stage, and the expected duration of this stage decreases. The two most relevant sets of data to this prediction can both be found in Smith *et al.* (1974b), and, unfortunately, they are not in agreement. In the first experiment in that report, both featural similarity and the size of the predicate category were varied, and statistical procedures were used to determine the effect of category size when featural similarity was held constant. No effect of category size was found, in contrast to the predicated facilitation (as pointed out by Glass & Holyoak, 1975). In the second experiment of this same report, however, there was evidence for the critical prediction. Here a mathematical model was fit to the results of a verification task, and the estimated duration of the second stage was less for larger than for smaller predicate categories.

A more serious problem for the model is presented by some recent findings of Holyoak and Glass (1975) on disconfirmation times. They found two cases where false statements containing similar nouns were actually verified faster than those containing less similar ones. (Similarity was determined by asking raters to assess directly the similarity of meaning between a pair of nouns.) This is evidence against one of the major predictions of the model. In one case, similar statements, but not dissimilar ones, expressed contradictions that were assumed to be represented directly in semantic memory, for example, *All dogs are cats*. (This notion of a direct contradiction will be explicated when the next model is considered.) In the other case studied by Holyoak and Glass, similar statements, but not dissimilar ones, could be disconfirmed by a salient counterexample, for example, *All animals are birds* can be disconfirmed by the salient counterexample *reptiles*. While these findings on contradictories and counterexamples appear to offer strong evidence against the model, Shoben *et al.* (1978) argued for a reinterpretation of the results in question. They showed that when the similarity of the Holyoak and Glass statements were re-rated by asking the raters "How easily can one concept be transformed into another?" the statements reflecting direct contradictions were now considered less similar than those that did not. This, in essence, removed the conflict between the feature-comparison model and the Holyoak and Glass findings, since the results now showed disconfirmations were faster for the less similar statements.

At best, the preceding argument suggests that it may be difficult to capture a theoretical notion like sematic similarity by a single average number from a single rating procedure. And since the predictions of the feature-comparison model rest on such numbers, they are somewhat shaky. There is also another reason to be troubled about the reliance of the model on ratings. Most of the support for the model rests on correlations between decision times and ratings, yet there is no way of knowing whether the ratings really reflect what they purport to. This is a problem of validity, one that arises with most ratings. It would thus be preferable to have some independent way of establishing, for example, typicality variations among the members of a given category. Smith *et al.* (1974b) suggested that this may be accomplished by noting that typical instances-category relations can be modified by *a true*, as in *A robin is a true bird*, while atypical relations are modified by *technically speaking*, as in *Technically speaking, a chicken is a bird*. While this linguistic criterion for typicality (which is derived from Lakoff, 1972) is certainly useful, some might argue that it is just another rating (for example, a rating of the acceptability of *A robin is a true bird*), and so the model still lacks a firm foundation for many of its predictions. (For a more detailed critique of this model, see Glass & Holyoak, 1975.)

2. *The Marker-Search Model*

a. Description.   The findings on disconfirmations just considered led Glass and Holyoak (1975) to propose a new theory, called the marker-search model. Its assumptions about representations are rather complex. Each word concept is represented by markers, a notion borrowed from Katz (1972). It is assumed that most common words are directly associated with only a single defining marker. Thus, the terms *bird* and *robin* would be represented by the markers "avian" and "robin," where, for example, the marker "robin" can be glossed as "possessing the essential properties of a robin." A second assumption is that markers are interrelated, so that one marker dominates or implies a set of other markers. As an illustration, "robin" implies "avian" which in turn implies "animate," where the latter is the defining marker for *animal*.

This implicational structure, which is intended to capture Katz's (1972) idea of redundancy rules, is illustrated in Figure 5. There it can be seen that these assumptions result in a semantic network, like that of the hierarchical-network model. However, further assumptions serve to distinguish the present theory from the earlier network model. The third assumption of the present model is that hierarchical connections can sometimes be shortcut by direct pathways between nonadjacent markers. This is exemplified in Figure 5 by the shortcut path between "chicken" and "animate." The final representational assumption is that information about contradictions can be represented directly in the network. Specifically, a contradiction arises whenever two paths with the same label (the letters on the arrows in Figure 5) meet at the same marker; for example, in Figure 5, "robin" and "chicken" contradict at "avian," since both have the label *a*. Note that two conditions—intersection at a common node and identical labeling—must be met for a pair of paths to be contradictory. If intersection at a common node was the only criterion for a contradiction, then, for example, "avian" and "pet," which intersect at "animate" in Figure 5, would form a contradiction, which would erroneously imply that something cannot be both a bird and a pet.

As for processing assumptions, the basic idea is that verification rests on a search of the network. When a statement of the form *All birds are animals* is presented, the subject accesses the defining markers of the two nouns and all other markers they imply or are implied by, for example, "avian," "animate," "living," "robin," and "mammalian." This specifies a target section of the

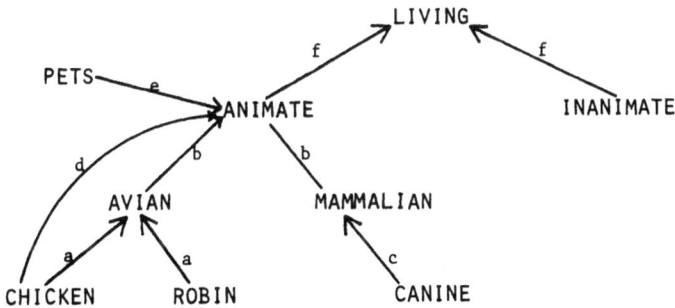

FIGURE 5.   An illustration of the marker-search model. Lowercase letters designate the labels on relations.

semantic network that is then searched. For true statements, the search terminates when one finds an acceptable path linking the markers of the two terms, that is, when one establishes that the marker for the subject term implies that for the predicate term. In the above example, this would occur when one finds the directly stored implicational relation between "avian" and "animate." This is as it was in the hierarchical-network model, but to see where the two theories diverge, consider again Figure 5. There is only one path from "robin," and that goes to "avian," so *All robins are birds* should be confirmed rapidly; however, to get from "robin" to "animate," one must trace two paths, and so *All robins are animals* will take longer to confirm. But the situation reverses when one considers the paths from "chicken." There are two paths from this marker, one to "avian" and the other a shortcut to "animate"; if the shortcut tends to be searched first, *All chickens are birds* will be confirmed relatively slowly while *All chickens are animals* will be responded to quickly. Thus, the concept of shortcut paths, along with the notion that some paths from a marker are searched sooner than others, provides a means of accounting for the effects of associative strength and typicality. All that must be assumed is that measures of associative strength and typicality directly reflect search order.

We are now ready to deal with the processing of false statements. The crucial assumption is that disconfirmation rests on a search eventuating in a contradiction. The search process is identical to that described for true statements, and all that needs to be added is a description of the kinds of contradictions that can terminate the search. There are two such kinds: (*a*) a contradiction between the markers of the subject and predicate terms, as would occur in disjoint statements (such as *All robins are chickens*—see Figure 5); or (*b*) a contradiction between the marker of the predicate and a marker that implies the marker of the subject, as would occur in overlap and superset statements (such as *All birds are chickens*, where "robin" implies "avian" and contradicts "chicken"—see Figure 5).

The model, then, is of the prestorage type. Many subset relations are represented directly (for example, the implicational relation between "robin" and "avian"), while others are inferred (for example, the relation between "robin" and "animate"). Furthermore, no expansion of these terms is required for verification. Rather, verification is a matter of searching for these direct connections, or of drawing inferences from these connections, or of searching for two connections that contradict one another. In all these cases, the critical determinant of verification times is the order in which the paths are searched. Consequently, most verification results, for both confirmations and disconfirmations, are accounted for by means of variations in search order. This is as it should be in a prestorage model.

The present theory, when contrasted with the feature-comparison model, also raises another potential distinction between prestorage and computation models. To see this, note that in the present theory both typicality and association effects are handled by shortcut paths and variations in search order. It is further assumed here that cooccurrence frequency is the major factor that determines which shortcuts are formed and which paths are searched first; presumably, the more frequently subject and predicate terms are used together (in a single proposition, perhaps), the more likely one will establish a path between them that is searched early. In contrast, recall that in the feature-comparison model, featural similarity was assumed to be the major determinant of typicality and association effects. In explaining the same set of effects, then, a computational model emphasizes a structural aspect—featural similarity—while a prestorage model emphasizes a functional aspect—cooccurrance frequency. This may be a fairly general distinction between the two classes of models, since all prestorage models seem to attribute typicality and association effects to cooccurrence frequency (Anderson & Bower, 1973; Rumelhart et al., 1972). However, the present dichotomy is unlike the processing distinctions that we considered earlier, because it does not arise from the basic computation versus prestorage contrast.

The marker-search model is also interesting when viewed in the light of our dictionary/encyclopedia division. Because the representational assumptions are heavily based on Katz's (1972) formal theory of semantics, the representations seem to have the cast of dictionary entries. However, it has already been suggested that any model of semantic memory must include some encyclopedia information if it is to explain certain verification effects. The current theory accomplishes this via its assumptions about shortcut paths and search order that, being based on cooccurrence frequencies, bring a certain kind of encyclopedia information into the model. Encyclopedia knowledge can also enter into the model via the labeling of paths. To see this, consider the markers for *women* and *writers*. Suppose they both imply the marker for *person*. Then to insure that the first two markers are not represented as contradictories, they must be given different labels. But knowing that women can be writers is encyclopedia-type knowledge and not something that follows from the essential meanings of the words. It seems, then, that a dictionary/encyclopedia distinction is maintained in the model.

It is time to turn to the major predictions of the model as derived by Glass and Holyoak (1975). For a true statement, confirmation time should depend on when a path between the markers of the subject and predicate terms is searched relative to other operative paths. To get a handle on this, it is necessary to have an independent measure of search order. The measure used by Glass and Holyoak is production frequency. To illustrate, the production frequency for *All robins are birds* would be the number of times a normative group of raters completed the frame *All robins are?* with *birds,* when instructed to complete the frame so as to form a true statement. The essential prediction, therefore, is that confirmation time should decrease with production frequency. Since such production-frequency measures have often been used to measure associative strength, this prediction has been confirmed many times (for example, Glass *et al.,* 1974; Holyoak & Glass, 1975; Loftus, 1973; Smith, 1967; Smith *et al.,* 1974b).

The predictions are more complex for false statements, though the basic idea is always the same: disconfirmation time increases with the time needed to find a contradiction. For statements qualified by *all,* Glass and Holyoak's (1975) analysis essentially divides false statements into two types: (1) disjoint statements, such as *Birds are mammals,* and (2) superset and overlap statements, such as *Birds are robins* and *Birds are pets.* Consider first the disjoint statements. These can be further divided into three subtypes: (1a) high contradictories— statements containing relatively similar nouns that express a contradiction directly represented in semantic memory (for example, *All robins are chickens,* see Figure 5); (1b) low contradictories—statements containing relatively similar nouns that contradict only indirectly (for example, *All robins are dogs,* where the marker for *dog,* "canine," leads to the marker "mammalian," which in turn contradicts the marker "avian," see Figure 5); and (1c) anomalies—statements containing unrelated nouns, where a contradiction can only be achieved at a marker high in the hierarchy (for example, *All pencils are birds,* where a contradiction occurs when markers like "nonliving" and "living" intersect).

This tripart division is based on production frequencies (where subjects complete frames so as to form false statements) and, in some cases, on intuitions. In any event, the model clearly predicts disconfirmations should be faster for high than for low contradictories because less search is needed for the former. As noted earlier, Holyoak and Glass (1975) have obtained this result (see also Anderson & Reder, 1974). With regard to anomalies, however, the model is simply mute, as no predictions for such statements are given in Glass and Holyoak (1975). In another paper, however, Holyoak and Glass (1975) suggested that anomalies can be disconfirmed as quickly as high contradictories. The rationale here is that there are presumably numerous shortcuts to markers high in the hierarchy, and some of these should be searched early, leading to the rapid detection of a contradiction. The data of Holyoak and Glass supported this suggestion.

Finally, consider the other type of false statements, superset and overlap statements. Here, two subtypes are distinguished: (a) statements with salient counterexamples (for example, *All prisoners are women*), where one can back up from the marker of the subject term and readily find a marker (for example, "male") that contradicts the one for the predicate (for example, "female"), and (b) statements without salient counterexamples (for example, *All prisoners are thieves*), where a back-up search from the subject may have trouble finding a marker that contradicts the predicate one. The prediction is that the latter subtype should require a longer search to find a contradiction and, hence, take longer to disconfirm. Again the Holyoak and Glass data supported the prediction of interest.

b. Evaluation.   Like the previous model, the marker-search model is consistent with most of the relevant data. Furthermore, the present model takes pains to explicate the notion of a contradiction, an idea handled implicitly or casually in numerous other theories. This explication leads to a taxonomy of false statements that is far richer than that offered by any rival theory, and this is one of the major contributions of the present model.

But like all other theories considered, there are some difficulties. Two of these involve the predictions of the model for disconfirmations. First, the prediction that disconfirmations are faster for high than low contradictories depends on how similarity is rated, as mentioned in our evaluation of the previous model. While this does not invalidate the finding, it challenges the grounds for the distinction between high and low contradictories. Second, the model has difficulty dealing with some findings on anomalous statements. The Holyoak and Glass (1975) data supported their suggestion that anomalous statements are disconfirmed as quickly as high contradictories, but there are two other studies that failed to show this. Glass *et al.* (1974) themselves found that anomalous statements were disconfirmed faster than high contradictories, and so did Shoben *et al.* (1978). It thus appears there is little support for the suggested treatment of anomalies.

Finally, a few of the assumptions of the model are somewhat problematic. For one, there is the question of how to decide whether two intersecting paths have the same label and, hence, will form a contradiction. One cannot simply assume that two intersecting paths are labeled identically whenever they come from disjoint concepts, because this will produce inconsistencies in the theory (see Shoben *et al.*, 1978). Thus, the only basis for giving two paths the same label appears to be the theorist's intuitions. Similarly, one of the divisions of false statements—that between low contradictories and anomalies—is based mainly on intuitions rather than production frequencies. Finally, like the previously considered theory, the marker-search model assumes its fundamental theoretical variable can be assessed by a single average number from a single rating procedure. We have already had occasion to question the wisdom of this kind of assumption. For a further critique of the model, see Shoben *et al.* (1978).

3. Summary of the Recent Models

The most notable thing about the feature-comparison and marker-search models is that they do a comparable job of accounting for verification results, but by means of very different assumptions. Take, for example, some of the assumptions about representations. In the feature-comparison model, word concepts are represented by sets of features that are unstructured but weighted by their degree of definingness. These weights form the basis for the distinction between characteristic and defining features. The characteristic features provide the model with a way of accounting for typicality and association effects, while the defining features insure that strictly logical relations between concepts are preserved in semantic memory. In contrast, the marker-search model assumes word concepts are defined in terms of a set of markers that are structured, but unweighted. The structure is in terms of the implicational relations between pairs of markers, as well as in the labeling of these relations. The specific structural assumption that shortcut relations (paths) exist is critical in accounting for typicality and association effects, while logical relations are preserved by the very nature of the implication relation. In short, one model uses variations in structural relations to accomplish what the other does by variations in weights, and we get some feel for the kinds of tradeoffs permissible in representational assumptions.

A representational aspect that the models share, though, is that both have something of a dictionary/encyclopedia division. By maintaining this distinction, the models provide a means of making contact with competence-based approaches to semantics. The marker-search model may be viewed as an explicit attempt to incorporate some of Katz's (1972) linguistic proposals into a performance model. And by taking this tack, the model is able to bring to psychology a number of linguistic notions—such as semantic-redundancy rules and the distinction between contradictory and anomalous statements. The feature-comparison model also makes contact with certain linguistic proposals, in particular Lakoff's (1972) partition of meaning components on their basis of definingness (though Lakoff, 1973, himself has eschewed the distinction between dictionary and encyclopedia meaning, or even that between competence and performance).

The two models also differ with respect to the computation/prestorage dichotomy and all of its correlated distinctions. There is no need to repeat these differences here. Rather, we can concern ourselves with the question of whether there is any evidence that favors one set of processing assumptions over the other. For the basic question of whether all subset relations are computed or not, I know of no relevant experimental evidence, though Collins and Loftus (1975) have argued that in many cases intuition decidedly favors the prestorage position. Similarly, there seems to be little published evidence on the issue of whether comparison or search processes underlie verification effects.

Relevant data do exist, though, on the issue of whether semantic decomposition is necessary for verification. The data, however, are mixed, and so are their implications. In his work on the semantic processing of adjectives, prepositions, and verbs, Clark (1974) finds considerable evidence for these terms being decomposed during comprehension. For example, Clark's studies indicate that when a subject is told *John is absent,* he decomposes *absent* into semantic components corresponding to *not* and *present,* and then uses these components to answer questions about the implications of the original sentence. In contrast to this work, Kintsch's (1974) studies show no evidence at all for decomposition during verification. To illustrate one of Kintsch's experiments, subjects were given fragments, such as *The boy's unusual ability,* and asked to complete them so as to form a sentence; the fragments varied with respect to the lexical complexity of their terms (for example, *ability* is derived from *able* and therefore more complex than a comparable but nonderived noun), but the results failed to show any effect of this variation. Kintsch argued that such an effect should have obtained if the words in the fragment had to be decomposed in order for the subject to complete the fragment.

How, then, can we reconcile Kintsch's (1974) and Clark's (1974) results on decomposition? One obvious solution is to assume that subjects can decompose words in order to understand a sentence, but sentences can often be understood without such decomposition. That is, there may be different levels of sentence comprehension, with "deep" levels requiring decomposition of the constituent words, "shallow" levels requiring no decomposition, and the level of comprehension being under the subject's control. (Norman and Rumelhart, 1975, have in fact suggested this kind of view.) Alternatively, one may postulate that people do not decompose words, but rather use inference rules to determine the semantic interrelationship of words in a sentence, with subjects applying these rules for deep but not shallow comprehension. Either of these solutions seems plausible at this point in time. And both suggest that there is not a true dichotomy between the decomposition of computation models and the lack of such decomposition in prestorage models.

We need to note one more point about this issue. In the above, the evidence for decomposition came from Clark's (1974) studies that involved adjectives, prepositions, and verbs. None of these experiments used nouns such as those employed in semantic-memory studies. The latter designate entities like animals and plants, which are referred to as natural-kind terms in linguistic and philosophical writings. In that literature, it has sometimes been argued that natural-kind terms, referring as they do to taxonomies of things that are somehow directly given by the world, cannot be analyzed by a system of primitive semantic features (see, for example, Fillmore, 1974). According to this view, *robin,* for example, has no lexical structure that can be elucidated by an analysis of semantic features. (Clark and Clark, 1977, also consider this position.) Under this view, then, the notion of a featural decomposition during verification is misguided from the outset. But there are opposing views in formal semantics. Katz (1972), for one, has argued that natural-kind terms can be decomposed into more primitive entities. The point of all this is simply that we have little direct evidence for decomposition of natural-kind terms, and some reason to be skeptical about obtaining such evidence. But the issue is still open.

There are also data relevant to the question of whether featural similarity or cooccurrence frequency determines association and typicality effects. Smith *et al.* (1974a) cited a number of arguments that favor their featural-similarity view. Let me mention just one of them. Rips *et al.* (1973) applied a multidimensional-scaling analysis to typicality ratings of bird and mammal instances. They found these ratings could be represented in a two-dimensional space, where the dimensions were interpreted as reflecting variations in size and predatory relations among the instances. Now, if these ratings reflected variations in how frequently the terms were used together, rather than in featural similarity, it is a complete mystery why the ratings should be reducible to variations in size and predacity. One could argue in return, though, that this evidence for the featural-similarity viewpoint may hinge on the scaling method used and that some other method may not present the same picture.

Perhaps the most relevant research on this question is contained in a recent paper by Rosch, Simpson, and Miller (1976). These authors used artificial materials to study the issue of featural similarity versus cooccurrence frequency. In one of their experiments, Rosch *et al.* used two experimentally defined categories of stick figures, where each figure varied on four dimensions. They defined the typicality of each figure in a category by its featural similarity to that of a prototype figure, where the latter possessed the mean value of the four dimensions for that category. This measure of featural similarity is consistent with how Rips *et al.* (1973) determined typicality in their scaling solutions. Rosch *et al.* found that, after the categories has been learned, this measure predicted subjects' ratings of typicality as well as the frequency with which figures could be produced (the latter is the usual way of indexing the association effects). An explicit variation in featural similarity thus accounted for variations in judged typicality and production frequency, thereby suggesting that featural similarity is a key factor in the semantic-memory studies as well.

In looking over this last issue, one is again struck by the possibility that both positions are correct to some degree. That is, both featural similarity and cooccurrence frequency may underly typicality and association effects in studies of semantic memory, for the issue is not really one of a dichotomy. As I have already noted, the same may be true of the decomposition question. Similarly, the issue concerning comparison versus search processes may not be a true dichotomy either. For example, we know that the marker-search model must contain some comparison processes, for one has to be able to compare each relation found in the search with that given in the test sentence, as well as to compare the labels of relations to determine whether they are contradictory or not. From here, it seems just a short step to envision situations where variations in these processes could contribute substantially to variations in verification times. The point of all this is simply that while the distinctions I have raised are worth worrying about, some of them may not form true dichotomies. This is the way of most distinctions in psychology, including the useful ones.

C. Newer Directions

There are also some newer directions in semantic-memory theorizing that are worth commenting on. One is that the process of verification may sometimes involve an examination of exemplars of the relevant concepts, rather than the concepts themselves. To see how this works, consider a modification of a proposal by Walker (1975). According to this view, when presented with a statement of the form *An S is a P,* the verifier retrieves an exemplar of the subject concept, determines whether it is a member of the predicate category, and then continues to sample and interrogate exemplars of the subject category until sufficient information has accumulated to indicate whether the statement is probably true or probably false. On this argument, verification is an inductive process, not a deductive one as was assumed in the models we discussed in detail. A critical problem with this proposal, however, is that it offers no account of how people can be so supremely confident in confirming statements like *All robins are birds.* For if this verification is based on an induction from robin exemplars, one's conclusion about the sentence can only be probabilistic. Yet I know of few people (aside from Kripke, 1972, and Putnam, 1962) who would assign any non-zero probability to the event that there is really a robin out there that is not a bird. But, in response to this criticism, one could argue that some semantic verifications that lack this feeling of certainty are indeed based on an induction from exemplars (Holyoak & Glass, 1975).

Another new direction is the development of hybrid models (for example, Collins & Loftus, 1975; Collins & Quillian 1972b). These theories posit both computational and prestorage mechanisms that are separately capable of establishing subset relations. (This is unlike the predicate-intersections model, which, though a hybrid, did not allow for the prestorage of subset relations.) The most important of the hybrid models is Collins and Loftus' (1975) revision of the Hierarchical-network model. This revised model comes close to being a summation of the feature-comparison and marker-search models. Like the former, the revised model posits that features (or properties) are weighted by how essential they are for category memberships and that all such properties may enter into comparison processes in the determination of subset relations. Like the marker-search model, the revised theory assumes that subset statements can also be confirmed via either prestored relations or inferences from such relations, while false statements can be disconfirmed by means of direct contradictions. With so many postulated mechanisms it is not surprising that the revised model does a good job of accounting for empirical findings. Its weaknesses lie in its disregard of parsimony and failure to lead to many clear-cut empirical predictions.

The revised model also brings another novel idea into semantic-memory theorizing. With regard to its prestorage mechanisms, the notion of a discrete search of network links is replaced by a spreading activation process. When relevant concepts are accessed, activation from them spreads out along the paths of a network, decreasing as it moves further from its sources. To see how this process accounts for the verification of a statement such as *A robin is a bird,* some further assumptions are needed. Presumably, activation from the two sources (*robin* and *bird*) can summate, and when the two streams of activation intersect at the node for *bird,* the total activation exceeds a threshold value. The path producing the intersection is then evaluated by a decision process, which continuously evaluates intersections until a clearcut true or false decision is indicated. While these ideas have some intuitive appeal, it is not yet clear what substantive issues hinge on this change from a discrete search to a spreading activation process. But suffice it to say that the latter notion has proven useful in studies of lexical access (for example, Meyer & Schvaneveldt, 1971), and sentence memory (Anderson, 1976), and may do so in semantic-memory studies as well.

IV. GENERALITY, EXTENDABILITY, AND SUFFICIENCY OF SEMANTIC-MEMORY RESEARCH

Having sated ourselves with specific theoretical proposals, it is time to take a broader look at matters. In this last section, we will see how the semantic-memory research reviewed in this chapter stacks up against three rather general criteria. They include: (*a*) generality, with regard to both specific findings and the representations and processes assumed to account for these findings; (*b*) extendability, or the degree to which current formulations are, in principle, capable of being extended to more complex psycholinguistic situations; and (*c*) sufficiency, or the extent to which the theories we reviewed have offered accounts of verification that can reproduce all relevant aspects of the performances involved.

A. Generality of Findings and Assumptions

So far I have dealt almost exclusively with the verification of category statements. In reviewing this work, I have hit upon some major findings, as well as some theoretical mechanisms that have been proposed to account for them. Now the generality of both these findings and mechanisms will be considered. The main findings whose generality we seek to establish include the effects of associative relatedness and typicality on classifications. To establish generality here, I will first consider some paradigms that are similar to our standard verification task but do not invovle category relations and then mention some studies that are far removed from verification, yet touch on the issue of semantic classifications. With regard to establishing the generality of theoretical mechanisms, things are a bit stickier. Ideally, we would like to have a taxonomy of the theoretical mechanisms involved in various situations, so the generality of the mechanisms postulated in semantic-memory research could be directly determined. In the absence of such a taxonomy, we will have to settle for less. What I will do is point out that the mechanisms involved in our computation models also seem to be operative in many perceptual-based decisions, while the mechanisms of our prestorage models appear to be operative in many memory-based decisions. Admittedly, this is not much of a case to make for generality of processes, but it is at least a start.

1. Generality of Findings

The question of interest is whether the findings obtained in the category-verification task are reproducible in other semantic-memory paradigms. The answer is overwhelmingly yes. Some illustrative findings should suffice. As mentioned in our discussion of the hierarchical-network model, a number of investigators have studied the verification of property statements (for example, *A bird can eat*). The best of these studies produce the same kinds of results as those found in the verification of category statements. As one example, Glass *et al.* (1974) found that confirmation times decreased as the associative relation between the noun and property increased, while disconfirmation times were fastest for anomalous statements, next fastest for high contradictories, and slowest for low contradictories.

As another illustration of the generality of findings, consider the same–different paradigm developed by Schaeffer and Wallace (1970). In this task a subject must decide whether a pair of test nouns are from the same or different categories, the categories being specified before a trial. Shoben (1976) performed what is perhaps the most extensive study in this paradigm. He found that the latencies of *same* decisions decreased with the typicality of each test noun to the appropriate category, whereas the times for *different* decisions increased with the similarity of the second test word to the category of the first, presumably because the subject initially categorized the first word and then compared this category to the second test word. Again, the results are identical to those obtained in our standard verification task.

For our third illustration we will take the studies of Loftus (for example, 1974). In her semantic-production task, a subject is given a category term plus a property (for example, *fruit–red*) and is asked to produce a response consistent with these restrictions (for example, *apple*). In a host of studies, Loftus has consistently found that the time to produce a correct response decreases with the degree to which it is associatively related to the prespecified category.

Of course a skeptic could claim that this commonality of findings is due to all of the paradigms requiring rapid semantic categorizations. What about typicality or association effects in situations without these task demands? A number of recent studies that bear on the issue of semantic classifications have attempted to answer this challenge. Again, I will note just a few illustrative studies.

In one study, Rosch (1974) had subjects generate sentences about category terms. For example, a subject given the term *fruit* might generate *The bowl contained a lot of fruit*. The constructed predications were then shown to be more applicable to typical instances of the category than to atypical ones (see what happens when you replace *fruit* in the above example with either the typical instance *apple,* or the atypical one *watermelon*). Apparently, when we think of a category term, we think of something akin to its typical instances, which is in agreement with the work on semantic categorization reviewed earlier in this chapter.

In another experiment by Rosch (1975), subjects placed pairs of number terms (for example, *ten* and *eleven*) into sentence frames like *? is essentially ?.* They were more likely to assign the typical term (*ten*) to the second or reference position and the atypical term (*eleven*) to the first or comparison position, then vice versa. This result suggests that typical terms are closer to cognitive reference points, which is in line with typical instances resembling category prototypes.

Lastly, Rips (1975b) studied inductive reasoning and showed that typical instances had greater inductive power than atypical ones. In this task, for a particular category (for example, *mammals*), subjects were told one of the species (for example, *horses*) had a specific property and had to estimate the proportion of instances in the other species that also possessed this property. These estimates were greater when the species known to have the property formed a typical subset of the category.

Note, then, that all three of the preceding experiments share only one essential aspect with the semantic-categorization experiments—the requirement to use semantic representations to accomplish the task—and this is sufficient to bring out typicality effects.

2. Generality of Theoretical Mechanisms

Consider now whether the kinds of representations and processes posited to account for the above findings are operative in situations far removed from semantic memory. Let us start with the mechanisms in computation models.

One line of relevant evidence derives from studies of pattern recognition (for example, Posner & Keele, 1968; Reed, 1972). These experiments require a subject to classify patterns (for example, dot patterns, schematic faces) into categories, where the patterns involve variations along relatively continuous dimensions and the categorization rules are ill-defined. The results suggest that a subject forms a prototype for each category (defined by the average values of all exemplars on the relevant dimensions) and then classifies patterns on the basis of their similarity to the prototype. (Interestingly, this same kind of process has also been proposed for some nonperceptual situations, namely, situations where one must produce nominal or numerical categorizations of uncertain events [Kahneman & Tversky, 1973].) This prototype-comparison process is clearly reminiscent of the feature-comparison model.

The kinds of representations and processes characterizing our computations models also seem relevant to work on perceptual judgments. In these studies, a subject decides whether two multidimensional forms are the same or different, and again latencies are the data of interest (see Nickerson, 1972, for a review). One finding that occurs consistently is that *different* latencies increase with the similarity of the two test forms (for example, Egeth, 1966; Hawkins, 1969). This finding is comparable to the semantic-memory result that disconfirmation latency increases with the similarity of the two test words in a verification task. And the explanation of the perceptual finding is close in form to that of the semantic result. It is assumed in these perceptual tasks that a subject encodes the visual features of the two forms and then compares the forms feature-by-feature; hence, the more features a *different* pair share, the more comparisons it will take to find a criterial difference. This account sounds like the feature-comparison model, where extra comparisons are also required for disconfirming similar items. Another point of commonality is that in these perceptual tasks, *same* decisions can be made faster when irrelevant dimensions of the test forms are also identical. This is analogous to a claim of the feature-comparison model about its first stage. Here features not strictly relevant to establishing subset relations (characteristic features) are considered in the decision, and similarity on these extra features can speed confirmation times. In view of these commonalities, it should come as no surprise that some explanations of perceptual judgments assume a two-stage comparison process (Hawkins & Shipley, 1972; Snyder, 1972), similar in form to the computation models reviewed earlier.

The mechanisms of prestorage models seem just as widespread, but to see this we need to consider experiments concerned with memory-based decisions. The best-known paradigm of this genre is the Sternberg task. A subject first memorizes a short list of arbitrary symbols and then has to decide whether or not a test item was on the list. One way to model these results is to assume that a subject searches through short-term memory for the critical test symbol, with search time being proportional to list length (Stenberg, 1969). This is a prestorage theory, and it obviously shares many assumptions with prestorage theories of semantic categorization. More recently, studies of retrieving stored information have focused on structured materials like sentences. Thus, Anderson (1974) and Anderson and Bower (1973) have reported numerous experiments where a subject first memorizes a list of unrelated sentences and then decides whether test sentences are old (on the memorized list) or new. Again, latency is the principal measure, but now the variation of interest is the number of memorized propositions that each word concept in the test sentence enters into. The major result is that the more memorized propositions the test words are involved in, the longer it takes to respond either old or new. The preferred explanation of these results is as follows. Given a test sentence, the subject enters memory at nodes corresponding to the words in the sentence, sequentially searches stored propositions from these nodes, and responds old if he finds the test statement among these propositions and new otherwise (Anderson & Bower, 1973). This is a prestorage model once more. And it has many assumptions in common with the hierarchical-network and marker-search models of semantic categorizations, including that some of the information needed for response is directly represented in memory and that the duration of the search needed to find the critical information is the major determinant of variations in response times.

B. Extendability of Semantic-Memory Research

Let us return now to our focus on semantic memory as a component of language comprehension and consider whether the approach taken is extendable to more complex cases of semantic interpretation. I have primarily dealt with the semantic interpretation of sentences that can be assigned a truth value on the basis of their constituent words. But what about sentences where something must be added to word meanings for interpretation to occur, or sentences whose interpretation depends on preceding and subsequent context? At this point of progress, there is no way one can offer a detailed analysis of these sentence-types in terms of existent semantic-memory models; however, a crucial pretheoretical question can be addressed, namely, are the semantic-memory models capable, in principle, of being extended to this new domain?

Recent research has led some to be skeptical about the extendability of our models. I have in mind, in particular, the work of Bransford and his colleagues (notably, Barclay, Bransford, Franks, McCarrell, & Nitsch, 1974; Bransford & Johnson, 1973; Bransford & McCarrell, 1974), as well as the recent report of Anderson and Ortony (1975). These investigators suggest two general and interrelated arguments against the extendability of semantic-memory models. The first stems from the notion that the meaning of a word is not a fixed entity but, rather, depends on its context, both the context of the sentence it is embedded in and that given by surrounding sentences. The challenge to semantic-memory models concerns whether or not this contextual dependence is consistent with models of the type I have reviewed. The second argument against extendability holds that an approach to semantic interpretation based on simple sentences may be doomed from the start, because the proper unit of semantic interpretation is something larger than a sentence. In what follows, I will first present each of these arguments in detail and then try to argue that, contrary to initial impressions, this work does not seriously challenge the extendability of semantic-memory models.

1. Word Meanings as Fixed Entities

a. The case against extendability.   Bransford and McCarrell (1974) suggested that semantic representations for individual words contain only a few constraints on their usage and that the meaning of a word in a sentence is in some sense developed through other items in that sentence and preceding context. Let me first illustrate the part of the argument concerned with preceding context. Consider the sentence *Gordon startled when the cloth ripped.* How we interpret terms like *startled* and *cloth* depends on the context preceding this sentence. If we know it is about parachute jumping, then we may assume that the startle may have been one of fear rather than of just surprise and that the cloth referred to is the fabric of a parachute. The context thus allows us to fill in the meanings of the individual words, to concretize them in some fashion. And this context effect shows up in comprehension and recall measures, as Bransford and his coworkers (for example, Bransford & Johnson, 1973) have shown that sentences like the above are better understood and better recalled when the relevant context is given prior to the sentence than when it is given after the sentence or is lacking entirely.

This filling in or concretizing of word meanings also occurs within a single sentence. Take an illustration from Anderson and Ortony (1975). Compare the interpretation of *container* in *The container held the apples* versus that in *The container held the cola.* In the first sentence, most people would interpret *container* to mean something like a basket; but in the sentence about *cola,* the preferred interpretation of *container* would be a bottle. So, the argument goes, the meaning of a word depends on the precise sentence it is a constituent of, thus endowing word meanings with something akin to emergent properties and suggesting that a study of word meanings ala semantic-memory research is unworkable.

More evidence along these lines comes from the experiment of Barclay *et al.* (1974). Sample statements from this study include: *The man lifted the piano* and *The man tuned the piano.* These sentences emphasize different aspects of the meaning of *piano,* where the one containing *lifted* presumably emphasizes that pianos are usually heavy, while the *tuned* sentence directs our attention to the musical quality of pianos. An empirical support for this, Barclay *et al.* presented statements such as the above and probed subjects' memories by probes such as *heavy* or *musical.* They showed, for example, that *heavy* was a better probe than *musical* for the *lifted* sentence, while this ordering or probe effectiveness reversed for the *tuned* sentence. Anderson and Ortony (1975) have obtained similar results.

b. The case for extendability.   Now let me try to make the case that these findings are not at all inconsistent with current semantic-memory models. To make my arguments clear, I will adopt a computational approach and assume that the meaning of a word can be specified in terms of features. Within this approach, there are three general ways in which the meaning of a word can be changed: (*a*) some features can be added, (*b*) some features can be deleted, or (*c*) some features can be added while others are deleted. It seems to me that the findings and arguments I just reviewed indicate that primarily the first way of changing meaning is involved. Thus, in the sentence *The container held the cola*, the occurrence of *cola* allows you to concretize the meaning of *container* by adding extra features to it. The question for semantic-memory models is, where do these extra features come from? In what follows, I will explore two possible answers to this question. The first holds that the extra features arise as a consequence of the procedures needed to combine word meanings into larger units (our second, and relatively unexplored, goal of semantic-memory research). The second answer assumes that context allows us to replace general concepts with specific ones and that the extra features are really features of the specific concepts. That is, word meanings are not changed by context, but, rather, are replaced by other, more specific, word meanings.

According to our first proposal, word meanings are fixed (as assumed in the semantic-memory models), and apparent changes in word meanings are really due to the creation of larger meaning units. That is, once we start to fill out the details of semantic-combination rules, some of the so-called "extra features" will be shown to be necessary consequences of these rules. To appreciate this, consider some possible ways these rules might work on just two words. In some cases where one must combine the meaning of a noun and an adjectival modifier, such as *silver* and *knife*, one may simply add the features of the modifier to those of the noun (Katz & Fodor, 1963). Other cases of adjectival modification, however, will require more complicated rules. For example, to determine the composite meaning of *good knife*, the rule must pick out the function of *knife* (cutting) and then have *good* operate on this function (for example, Katz, 1972). In still other cases, the meanings of the two words may contain some common features, as in *lifted weights*. Here we might suppose that regardless of the specifics of the combinatorial process, shared features are given greater emphasis than nonshared ones in the composite meaning. (This idea was suggested to me by Lance Rips.) Note that in all three cases, the features of the composite differ from those of each of its constituents. But one would not want to call these changes "emergent properties of word meaning"; for one thing, the apparent changes are really properties of meaning composites rather than of single words, and for another, there is nothing "emergent" about such properties, since they can be determined by well-defined combinatorial procedures.

Now let us try to use the above to account for how a sentence itself can affect the meanings of its constituent terms. We can start with the Barclay *et al.* (1974) findings. As Barclay *et al.* themselves note, when contrasting *The man lifted the piano* with *The man tuned the piano*, there may be no alteration in the basic meaning of *piano*, that is, no features are added. But there is certainly a change in which aspects of its meaning are salient (weight in the first example, musical quality in the second). If the meaning of *piano* is represented by features, the facts that a piano is heavy (for an instrument) and capable of producing music would likely be among them. In the sentence containing *lifted,* the feature of weight would also be noted in the representation of the verb and, consequently, this feature occurs in two representations in the sentence. As mentioned before, when two representations are combined, it is possible that repeated features are given extra weight or salience in the final composite, and this would explain the phenomenon of interest. A similar explanation holds for the sentence containing *tuned,* where the feature of music-producing now occurs twice.

Let us move on to the Anderson and Ortony (1975) examples, *The container held the apples* and *The container held the cola,* where *container* seems to be concretized to something like *basket* in the first case and to *bottle* in the second. With regard to the second sentence, it seems reasonable to assume that one of the characteristic features of *cola* is that it is often contained in bottles. Hence, when *cola* is combined with the rest of the sentence to form a composite, this characteristic feature of *cola* may be added to (or replace) the features of *container.* This would be an example of the simple addition-of-features rule I mentioned earlier. The sentence about *apples,* however, is more problematic. It seems implausible that any of the characteristic features of *apple* deal with containers, so the addition-of-features rule cannot be used here. However, it may turn out that this sentence can be handled by a combinatorial rule such as that used earlier to deal with *good knife.* That is, when combining *apples* with *container,* one may first pick out the function of *container* (to hold things), and then use the features of *apple* (solid, having nonnegligible weight) to modify or add new features to *container.* Admittedly, this is very vague, but it is the best we can do until more theoretical work is done on combinatorial rules.

Thus far our argument has run as follows. The findings on intra-sentence context offer no clear-cut reasons against extending semantic-memory models to more complex domains, though these findings do highlight the need to consider combinatorial processes. However, in attempting to analyze the *apples* sentence in terms of combinatorial rules, we hit a snag, and it is quite likely we would run into similar problems with other sentences (say, some of the other examples in the Anderson & Ortony, 1975, report). In view of this, it seems judicious to move on to our second possible answer to the question of where the extra features come from. This answer, unlike that based on combinatorial rules, will require more than just a straightforward extension of semantic-memory models, but the extensions we propose will at least be interfaceable with such models.

The basic idea is that context allows you to replace general concepts with specific ones. To get a handle on this proposal, let us return to where we started, to the effects of intersentence or prior context on interpretation, as in our example *Gordon startled when the cloth ripped.* Here again context seems to add features; knowing that the sentence is about parachute jumping allows you to add features to the meanings of *startle* and *cloth,* where, for example, these extra features contain some of the information you know about the fabric of parachutes. To account for this, we may assume that semantic memory contains not only general concepts, such as those corresponding to startle and cloth, but also more specific ones such as startle-of-fear and parachute-cloth, and that preceding context plays its role by allowing the substitution of the specific concepts for the general ones. (This proposal, which was suggested to me by Charles Clifton, has much in common with the work of Caramazza and Grober, 1976.)

There is, however, an obvious problem with the above analysis. Preceding context may sometimes lead to the substitution of a specific concept for a general one, where the specific concept seems too detailed to be stored in semantic memory. For example, consider the sentence *The torn canvas forced Herb to quit early*. If the preceding context were an athletic one, and further specified that Herb wears canvas tennis shoes, then presumably one would substitute the concept of canvas tennis shoes for the more general concept of canvas. But it seems unrealistic to posit that many people have canvas tennis shoes stored as a concept in semantic memory. Rather, it appears more reasonable to posit that this specific concept is computed on the spot. That is, in understanding the above sentence in context, one might retrieve a concept of tennis shoes and then add to it some information about canvas materials. In this case, the computation involves information that is not in semantic memory, and, thus, we have a context effect whose explanation requires us to go beyond the limits of existent semantic-memory models. This limitation, however, seems to be a principled one. For we would not want theories of semantic memory to give up their concern with general semantic representations that are useful in a wide variety of situations. Also, while the explanation at issue invokes procedures other than semantic-memory ones, these procedures are such that they can easily be interfaced with some existent semantic-memory models.

One final issue deserves mention. Most of my analyses of the context problems rest on the notion that, given the chance, people will concretize concepts, yet I have offered no indication of what functions are served by such concretization. Let me then mention two ways in which concretization may foster comprehension and memory. First, concretization may allow one to determine that different words refer to the same concept, which will permit a reduction in the amount of conceptual information that needs to be stored in episodic memory. To illustrate, suppose you experienced the following pair of sentences (adapted from Bransford & Johnson, 1973): *Put things in piles, making sure you have the necessary equipment. Colored objects must be treated separately.* If these sentences occurred in a context concerned with washing clothes, then you would presumably realize that both *things* and *objects* denote the concept of clothes, and, consequently, you would need to store only one concept in episodic memory. The other way in which concretization may foster comprehension is by allowing you to relate sentences to general causal principles that interconnect either various clauses of a sentence or various sentences. As an example, let us return to our standby, *Gordon startled when the cloth ripped*. Here, substituting startle-of-fear and parachute-cloth for the more abstract concepts in the sentence might permit you to relate the sentence to a causal principle like "Imminent danger leads to emotional reactions." Again, I should note that the proposed procedure—invoking causal principles—presumably exceeds the limits of existent semantic-memory models, but is capable of being interfaced with such models.

2. Units of Interpretation

a. The case against extendability.   We are now ready to deal with the second argument against extendability, that the proper unit of analysis for studying interpretation is larger than a sentence. Bransford and Johnson (1973) provide many ingenious demonstrations of how the interpretation of a sentence may critically depend on the topic of conversation, as in the *cloth* sentence. In some studies, subjects can read entire stories without being fully able to comprehend any of its sentences, unless they are told something about the situation being described. On the basis of these results, Bransford and his colleagues have suggested that people are not really trying to interpret sentences but rather are trying to develop a representation of the situation described by the sentences. That is, sentences and their constituent words merely function as clues for constructing cognitive representations of situations. From this point, it takes but a single leap to suggest that people have stored away some rather abstract representations of such situations, and it is these situation representations that are the appropriate unit for studying interpretation (an idea currently in favor in the artificial intelligence community—see Minsky's [1975] discussion of frames). This argument, though a bit sketchy, has already had great influence in moving psycholinguists away from a narrow syntactic-semantic orientation and toward a broader pragmatic one.

b. The case for extendability.   I for one believe there is a good deal right about the above argument. But I contend that even if such higher order units of interpretation are operative, this in no way mitigates the need to study simultaneously interpretation at the level of word representations. Relegating the role of word meanings to clues does not get rid of the problem of how we get such clues in the first place and then employ then in subsequent interpretation processes. For no one has seriously maintained that we can use sentences to construct cognitive representations without interpreting some of the words in the sentences. Or to put it another way, while higher order units (representations for situations) may exist, they must take as their input lower order units (representations for words and sentences), and, hence, one cannot possibly form a full theory of interpretation in terms of just higher order units.

Such multiunit approaches are common in all disciplines. For example, the linguistic reality of syntactic rules does not mitigate the need to study purely phonological rules; rather, the two endeavors go on simultaneously and interactively. Or take an example from within psychology. In the study of reading, the existence of higher order perceptual units for whole words does not rule out the study of perceptual units for single letters, for most theories about the former rest on theories of the latter (for example, Rumelhart & Siple, 1974). In sum, the evidence at best speaks to the need for a multiunit approach to interpretation, one that carefully considers interactions between the various units, and not to a downgrading of semantic-memory research.

C.   Sufficiency of Semantic-Memory Models

As a final topic, let us address the question of sufficiency. In most discussions on this topic, the concern is with whether models are specified in enough detail to reproduce all the phenomena of interest or, whether they beg critical questions instead. This will be the first aspect of sufficiency considered. A second aspect that will be of concern to us deals with a previously neglected problem. Specifically, it is possible for modelers to be so concerned with matters of sufficiency that they cram their theoretical descriptions with massive detail and neglect to emphasize their stances on major issues.

1.   Question Begging

The hierarchical-network model was among the first psycholinguistic theories to offer a relatively sufficient description of representations and processes. It was sufficient in several respects. Because it identified the organization of semantic memory with the logic of class relations, there were no begged questions in its assumptions about the representation of subset relations (at least for certain domains). Thus, one knew a priori what subset relations emanated from *robin* and that *bird* was only one hierarchical link away while *animal* was two. Similarly, the model specified an exact search procedure, and when this was coupled with the representational assumptions, there was no ambiguity about what the predictions of the theory were. Least there be any doubt about the ability of the model to reproduce all the relevant details of verification performance, the model was coupled with a computer program that supposedly could simulate verification (Quillian, 1969). So the model was sufficient in that it offered a detailed description of everything anyone ever wanted to know about the verification of a restricted group of simple sentences. (Whether this description was accurate or not is another matter.)

But things have gone downhill since. A major problem is that computation theories assume word concepts are decomposed into attributes or features but do not specify the exact nature of these more primitive entities. Thus, the predicate intersections model posits sets of defining attributes for each word concept but does not specify the nature of these attributes. This omission is particularly troublesome in light of longstanding arguments about the futility of looking for necessary and sufficient attributes of word meanings (see, for example, Bolinger, 1965; Kripke, 1972; Wittgenstein, 1953). The feature-comparison model also glides over the question of what the defining features are and contributes some new begged questions as well. In its assumptions about characteristic features, this model offers no way of distinguishing what kinds of encyclopedia information are contained in the semantic representation and what kinds are excluded.

Things are better with regard to the sufficiency of processing assumptions in semantic-memory models, though there are problems here as well. In the feature-comparison model, there is a lack of detail about the mechanics of the critical first stage. And in the marker-search model, there is no a priori way of establishing what distant markers have shortcut paths between them nor of determining the order in which various pathways are searched. Yet these two factors underlie all the critical predictions of the model.

Given this indictment of semantic-memory models, what can be said in their behalf? One defense is simply to reaffirm what we mentioned in the statement of goals in the Introduction: the problem of specifying detailed semantic representations for word concepts is so difficult that, for now, we must settle for determining general properties of semantic representations. Unfortunately, belief in this argument seems to require as much faith as logic. Perhaps a more persuasive way to defend semantic-memory models is to point out that many aspects of verification can, in theory, be ascertained without recourse to the exact contents of representations. Let me illustrate with our two most recent theories. According to the feature-comparison model, the major determinant of verification times is the featural similarity between word concepts. Even if we do not know the exact features of two concepts, we can empirically determine their featural similarity by ratings such as typicality measures. So, while the question of features is begged, the issue of featural similarity is confronted, and though this confrontation is indirect, it leads to testable empirical consequences. The marker-search model adopts a comparable approach. In this theory, the major determinants of verification latencies is the order of search from particular markers. Although search order cannot be known a priori, it can be estimated empirically by norms of productions frequencies. Again an essential question is begged, but some constraint is placed on this issue, and the constraint leads to empirical claims.

Our defense of the semantic-memory theories amounts to the claim that one can make progress while begging some questions. This is hardly new. It is done all the time in science. For example, in mathematics there was a good deal learned about number systems long before foundational work was done in this area. And to bring things closer to home, psychologists interested in perception were espousing featural theories of pattern recognition (for example, Selfridge, 1959) before they had firm foundational evidence for such features (for example, Hubel & Wiesel, 1962).

2. The Sufficiency/Transparency Tradeoff[6]

Suppose that someone developed a theory of semantic memory with no begged questions, so sufficient, in fact, that it was embodied in a computer program that perfectly simulated all relevant aspects of verification performance. Would all things then be right in the world? I doubt it. For anyone who has tried to read a theory embedded in a program knows how difficult it is to arrive at the general principles of the theory. More likely than not, whatever general principles there are, are buried in the mass of details needed to make the theory sufficient, i.e., to make the program run. More generally, as theories become increasingly suffi- cient they must by nature contain more details, and consequently their major claims become less transparent. There is, if you will, a tradeoff between suffi- ciency and transparency.

Some would argue that semantic-memory models have already traded too much transparency for sufficiency, notwithstanding the previously mentioned begged questions. Thus, if you read Smith *et al.*'s (1974b) mathematical version of the feature-comparison model or Glass and Holyoak's (1975) description of the marker-search model, you will be confronted with a substantial number of detailed assumptions that are there for purposes of sufficiency, but which can make it difficult to determine the major claims of the model or even whether the critical empirical predictions result from these major claims or from the less important details. For example, the mathematical version of the feature- comparison model contains assumptions about underlying distributions of featural similarity, as well as estimates of where high and low criteria for similar- ity fall in reference to these distributions. These details merely make explicit what is already in the qualitative statement of the model, but they do so at the cost of transparency. And this is only a mathematical model. Computer- simulation models are even worse offenders of transparency, for being more sufficient than mathematical models (simulations can mimic extremely complex real-time processes), they contain even more details.

While the transparency problem is not yet too severe in semantic-memory research, it promises to get worse. As researchers tackle some of the outstanding begged questions and as they continue to move in the simulation direction out- lined by some of the more general models of meaning and memory, the major claims of semantic-memory models are almost certain to become more opaque. To appreciate the extent of this potential problem, let us temporarily move outside the domain of semantic memory and consider some of the more general theories of meaning and memory. The Anderson and Bower (1973) model, which in many respects follows the simulation line, is one of the most sufficient

---

[6]The ideas discussed here grew out of conversations with Steven Kosslyn and Amos Tversky. In particular, the notion of a sufficiency/transparency tradeoff is due to Tversky.

theories of memory around. But some of its major assertions seem so entangled with sufficiency details that researchers are already experiencing difficulty in knowing what findings count as evidence against the model. Norman and Rumelhart's (1975) theory is another case in point. This formulation is primarily concerned with the sufficiency of representational assumptions. A reader of it might be hard pressed to list its central assumptions at other than a vague and abstract level. Or, as an extreme example, take Winograd's (1972) simulation of language comprehension in a limited domain. In many respects, this model is the most sufficient one in cognitive psychology. It is also one of the most opaque. For example, it is immensely difficult to go through this model and isolate the major principles it espouses about the parsing of sentences. Indeed when one gets to the level of computer modeling, so much transparency has been lost that it is sometimes doubtful if even the theorist himself knows all the major claims of the model.

This trend toward sufficient but opaque computer theories may be endemic to information-processing models, because such models rely on the computer program both as a guiding metaphor of cognitive processes and as the ultimate means of testing sufficiency and accuracy of a model. It is perhaps partly because of the transparency problem in such models that there currently seems to be a general reaction against information-processing models. Witness, for example, Craik and Lockhart's (1972) assault on the processing model that has dominated human memory for the past decade. Particularly noteworthy is their claim that this approach has distracted researchers from important problems (presumably because they were attending to details of sufficiency) and the fact that they proposed an alternative theory that is quite vague (insufficient) in comparison to processing models. As another example, take the work of Bransford and his colleagues discussed earlier. This work essentially refutes an approach to comprehension that had employed transformational grammar in phrasing a relatively sufficient theory of sentence representations. But again the model offered in place of the older one is vague or insufficient by comparison. These two examples seem to highlight the growing frustration with the opaqueness of sufficiency-minded processing models.[7]

[7]Note that the critics of the process-model approach are bothered by sufficiency, not by complexity. The alternative theories mentioned in the above examples are not so much simpler as they are vaguer. These recent theorists do not believe things are simpler than the process modelers claim, but rather suggest that cognitive psychology is not yet ready to seek totally sufficient theoretical explanations. Another reason for not equating the tradeoff between sufficiency and transparency with that between complexity and transparency is Craik and Lockhart's (1972) claim that the processing approach has distracted investigators from important problems; if this claim is valid, complexity could not be the cause of the difficulty because the added complexities would constitute as important problems as the better understood issues. This is not to say there is no tradeoff between complexity and transparency (of course there is), but rather to argue that above and beyond this, there is a sufficiency/transparency tradeoff. And the latter is in some sense the more problematic of the two tradeoffs, for highly complex theories are clearly undesirable because they violate a standard goal of

It is time to come back to models of semantic memory. Granted there is a sufficiency/transparency tradeoff that can undo these theories and future ones, what can be done about it? One solution is to forego our concern with sufficiency and adopt a vague level of theorizing like that which characterized gestalt psychology. This strikes me as far too extreme. Selling out sufficiency may seriously undermine the goals of semantic-memory research. For to aim for a theory that can specify detailed semantic representations for lexical items (our first goal) is to aim for a sufficient theory.

Another possible solution is to dismiss the sufficiency/transparency tradeoff as a pseudoproblem and argue that one should always completely sacrifice transparency for sufficiency, and not concern oneself an iota with the difficulties some people may have in figuring out the basic claims of a model. According to this argument, the business of science is to construct theories that are accurate, general, parsimonious, and sufficient, and not to worry about how difficult or transparent its theoretical descriptions are. This position seems far too extreme for two reasons. First, one can argue that one of the most important aims of science is to construct theories capable of being disproved, and the less transparent a theory, the less likely other researchers are to determine what counts as evidence against it. Thus the transparency of a theory is essential to the conduct of research and not just a nicety of style. Second, one can argue (and many have done so) that the primary business of science is to construct theories that enhance one's understanding, and the less transparent a theory, the less we understand about the domain of study. That is, what we have called transparency is just an aspect of understanding and to compromise on transparency is to compromise on our major goal. Note that under this view, simulation programs are not very satisfactory theories if they offer accurate, sufficient, and general predictions at the cost of understanding.

A moderate solution to the sufficiency/transparency tradeoff is to encourage processing theories of semantic memory in their present pursuit of sufficiency but to ask something of them in addition. Each theorist should assume the responsibility of stating the major aspects and claims of his model (for example, the assumptions that account for the principal findings of concern), so that all can tell what counts as evidence against the model. There are, however, problems with this solution as well. For one thing, it is not at all clear how to determine the major claims of a model (the model cannot tell us that). For another, this solution seems to assume that the transparency problem is due to the theorist's exposition of his model rather than to the nature of the model itself, and this assumption may be mistaken.

If part of the problem is indeed due to the nature of the models, then even a moderate solution to the transparency problem may call for a different kind of

---

theory construction, namely, parsimony. But highly sufficient theories are in this sense desirable because they satisfy a standard goal of theory construction, namely, sufficiency itself.

modeling. We may have to settle for models that sacrifice sufficiency in certain domains but provide a totally explicit account of others. Perhaps the best example of this is contained in the elegant work of Sternberg (for example, 1969). Sternberg developed a methodology (the additive-factors method) that allowed him to isolate a particular conceptual component (the so-called scanning operation) and then provided a relatively sufficient treatment of this component. But if this work is to be taken as a model of how to do future work in psycholinguistics, it may well be necessary to develop a new methodology, for it is becoming apparent that Sternberg's method leans too heavily on assumptions of strict serial processing.

I have concluded this chapter on something of a metatheoretical note. I think this is unavoidable. For the concern with transparency is currently threatening process model in general, and if semantic-memory models have contributed anything, it is the utility of the processing approach for studying problems in meaning. Any challenge to this general approach is, consequently, a matter of concern to those who choose to theorize about semantic memory.

ACKNOWLEDGMENTS

This chapter has benefited greatly from the extensive comments of Charles Clifton, William K. Estes, Keith Holyoak, Ellen Markman, and Lance Rips. Preparation of the chapter was supported in part by U.S. Public Health Service Grant MH-19705.

REFERENCES

Anderson, J. R. Retrieval of propositional information from long-term memory. *Cognitive Psychology*, 1974, **6**, 451–474.

Anderson, J. R. *Language, memory, and thought*. Hillsdale, New Jersey: Lawrence Erlbaum Associates, 1976.

Anderson, J. R., & Bower, G. H. *Human associative memory*. Washington, D.C.: Winston, 1973.

Anderson, J. R., & Reder, L. M. Negative judgments in and about semantic memory. *Journal of Verbal Learning and Verbal Behavior*, 1974, **13**, 664–681.

Anderson, R. C., & Ortony, A. On putting apples into bottles—A problem of polysemy. *Cognitive Psychology*, 1975, **7**, 167–180

Barclay, J. R., Bransford, J. D., Franks, J. J., McCarrell, N. S., & Nitsch, K. Comprehension and semantic flexibility. *Journal of Verbal Learning and Verbal Behavior*, 1974, **13**, 471–481.

Bell, A., & Quillian, M. R. Capturing concepts in a semantic net. In E. L. Jacks (Ed.), *Associative information techniques*. New York: Elsevier, 1971. Pp. 3–25.

Bierwisch, M. On classifying semantic features. In D. D. Steinberg & L. A. Jakobovits (Eds.), *Semantics: An introductory reader in philosophy, linguistics and psychology*. Cambridge: University Press, 1971, Pp. 410–435.

Bolinger, D. The atomization of meaning. *Language*, 1965, **41**, 555–573.

Bransford, J. D., & Johnson, M. K. Considerations of some problems of comprehension. In W. G. Chase (Ed.), *Visual information processing*. New York: Academic Press, 1973. Pp. 383–438.

Bransford, J. D., & McCarrell, N. S. A sketch of a cognitive approach to comprehension: Some thoughts about what it means to comprehend. In W. B. Weimer & D. S. Palermo (Eds.), *Cognition and symbolic processes.* New York: Winston & Sons, 1974. Pp. 189–229.

Caramazza, A., & Grober, E. H. *Polysemy & the Structure of the Subjective lexicon.* In C. Rameh (Ed.), Georgetown University round table on languages and linguistics 1976. Washington, D.C.: Georgetown University Press, 1976. Pp. 181–206.

Chafe, W. L. Language and memory. *Language,* 1973, **49**, 261–281.

Chomsky, N. *Syntactic structures.* The Hague: Mouton, 1957.

Clark, H. H. Semantics and comprehension. In T. A. Sebeok (Ed.), *Current trends in linguistics, Vol. 12: Linguistics and adjacent arts and sciences.* The Hague: Mouton, 1974. Pp. 1291–1498.

Clark, H. H., & Chase, W. G. On the process of comparing sentences against pictures. *Cognitive Psychology,* 1972, **3**, 472–517.

Clark, H. H., & Clark, E. V. *Psychology and language: An introduction to psycholinguistics.* New York: Harcourt, Brace, Jovanovich, 1977.

Collins, A. M., & Loftus, E. F. A spreading activation theory of semantic processing. *Psychological Review,* 1975, **82**, 407–428.

Collins, A. M., & Quillian, M. R. Retrieval time from semantic memory. *Journal of Verbal Learning and Verbal Behavior,* 1969, **8**, 240–248.

Collins, A. M., & Quillian, M. R. *Categories and subcategories in semantic memory.* Paper presented at the meeting of the Psychonomic Society, St. Louis, 1971.

Collins, A. M., & Quillian, M. R. Experiments on semantic memory and language comprehension. In L. W. Gregg (Ed.), *Cognition in learning and memory.* New York: John Wiley & Sons, 1972. Pp. 117–147.(a)

Collins, A. M., & Quillian, M. R. How to make a language user. In E. Tulving & W. Donaldson (Eds.), *Organization of memory.* New York: Academic Press, 1972. Pp. 309–351.(b)

Conrad, C. E. H. Cognitive economy in semantic memory. *Journal of Experimental Psychology,* 1972, **92**, 149–154.

Craik, F. I. M., & Lockhart, R. S. Levels of processing: A framework for memory research. *Journal of Verbal Learning and Verbal Behavior,* 1972, **11**, 671–684.

Egeth, H. E. Parallel versus serial processes in multidimensional stimulus discrimination. *Perception & Psychophysics,* 1966, **1**, 245–252.

Fillmore, C. J. The future of semantics. In C. Fillmore, G. Lakoff, & R. Lakoff (Eds.), *Berkeley studies in syntax and semantics.* Vol. 1. Berkeley: Institute of Human Learning, 1974. IV, 1–38.

Fodor, J. A., Bever, T. G., & Garrett, M. F. *The psychology of language: An introduction to psycholinguistics and generative grammar.* New York: McGraw-Hill, 1974.

Freedman, J. L., & Loftus, E. F. Retrieval of words from long-term memory. *Journal of Verbal Learning and Verbal Behavior,* 1971, **10**, 107–115.

Frege, G. On sense and reference. *Zeitschrift für philosophie und philosophische kritik,* 1892, **100**, 25–50.

Glass, A. L., & Holyoak, K. J. The effect of *some* and *all* on reaction time for semantic decisions. *Memory & Cognition,* 1974, **2**, 436–440.

Glass, A. L., & Holyoak, K. J. Alternative conceptions of semantic memory. *Cognition,* 1975, 3(4), 313–339.

Glass, A. L., Holyoak, K. J., & O'Dell, C. Production frequency and the verification of quantified statements. *Journal of Verbal Learning and Verbal Behavior,* 1974, **13**, 237–254.

Grice, H. P. Utterer's meaning, sentence-meaning, and word-meaning. *Foundations of Language,* 1968, **4**, 1–18.

Hawkins, H. L. Parallel processing in complex visual discrimination. *Perception & Psychophysics,* 1969, **5**, 56–64.

Hawkins, H. L., & Shipley, R. H. Irrelevant information and processing mode in speeded discrimination. *Journal of Experimental Psychology,* 1972, **96**, 389–395.

Herrmann, D. J., Shoben, E. J., Klun, J. R., & Smith, E. E. Cross-category structure in semantic memory. *Memory & Cognition,* 1975, **3**, 591–594.

Hollan, J. D. Features and semantic memory: Set-theoretic or network model? *Psychological Review,* 1975, **82**, 154–155.

Holyoak, K. J., & Glass, A. L. The role of contradictions and counterexamples in the rejection of false sentences. *Journal of Verbal Learning and Verbal Behavior,* 1975, **14**, 215–239.

Hubel, D. H., & Wiesel, T. N. Receptive fields, binocular interaction and functional architecture in the cat's visual cortex. *Journal of Physiology,* 1962, **160**, 106–154.

Kahneman, D., & Tversky, A. On the psychology of prediction. *Psychological Review,* 1973, **80**, 237–251.

Katz, J. J. *Semantic theory.* New York: Harper & Row, 1972.

Katz, J. J., & Fodor, J. A. The structure of a semantic theory. *Language,* 1963, **39**, 170–210.

Kintsch, W. *The representation of meaning in memory.* Hillsdale, New Jersey: Lawrence Erlbaum Associates, 1974.

Kosslyn, S. M. Can imagery be distinguished from other forms of internal representation? Evidence from studies of information retrieval times. *Memory & Cognition,* 1976, **4**, 291–297.

Kosslyn, S. M., & Pomerantz, J. R. Imagery, propositions, and the form of internal representation. *Cognitive Psychology,* 1977, **9**, 52–76.

Kripke, S. Naming and necessity. In D. Davidson & G. Harman (Eds.), *Semantics of natural language.* Dordrecht, Netherlands: Reidel, 1972. Pp. 253–355.

Lakoff, G. Hedges: A study in meaning criteria and the logic of fuzzy concepts. *Papers from the Eighth Regional Meeting, Chicago Linguistics Society.* Chicago: University of Chicago Linguistics Department, 1972, Pp. 183–228.

Lakoff, G. Fuzzy grammar and the performance/competence terminology game. *Papers from the Ninth Regional Meeting, Chicago Linguistics Society.* Chicago: University of Chicago Linguistics Department, 1973. Pp. 271–291.

Landauer, T. K., & Meyer, D. E. Category size and semantic memory retrieval. *Journal of Verbal Learning and Verbal Behavior,* 1972, **11**, 539–549.

Loftus, E. F. Category dominance, instance dominance and categorization time. *Journal of Experimental Psychology,* 1973, **97**, 70–74.

Loftus, E. F. Activation of semantic memory. *American Journal of Psychology,* 1974, **86**, 331–337.

Lyons, J. *Introduction to theoretical linguistics.* London: Cambridge University Press, 1968.

Macnamara, J. Parsimony and the lexicon. *Language,* 1971, **47**, 359–374.

Meyer, D. E. On the representation and retrieval of stored semantic information. *Cognitive Psychology,* 1970, **1**, 242–299.

Meyer, D. E. Verifying affirmative and negative propositions: Effects of negation on memory retrieval. In S. Kornblum (Ed.), *Attention and performance IV.* New York: Academic Press, 1973. Pp. 379–394.

Meyer, D. E. Long-term memory retrieval during the comprehension of affirmative and negative sentences. In R. A. Kennedy & A. L. Wilkes (Eds.), *Studies in long-term memory.* London: John Wiley & Sons, 1975. Pp. 289–312.

Meyer, D. E., & Schvaneveldt, R. W. Facilitation in recognizing pairs of words. *Journal of Experimental Psychology,* 1971, **90**, 227–234.

Minsky, M. A framework for representing knowledge. In P. H. Winston (Ed.), *The psychology of computer vision.* New York: McGraw-Hill, 1975. Pp. 211–277.

Morton, J. Interaction of information in word recognition. *Psychological Review,* 1969, **76**, 165–178.

Neisser, U. *Cognitive psychology.* New York: Appleton-Century-Crofts, 1967.

Nickerson, R. S. Binary-classification reaction time: A review of some studies of human information-processing capabilities. *Psychological Monograph Supplements,* 1972, **4**(Whole No. 65), 275–318.

Norman, D. A., & Rumelhart, D. E. *Explorations in cognition.* San Francisco: Freeman, 1975.

Posner, M. I., & Keele, S. W. On the genesis of abstract ideas. *Journal of Experimental Psychology,* 1968, **77,** 353–363.

Putnam, H. It ain't necessarily so. *Journal of Philosophy,* 1962, **59,** 658–671.

Pylyshyn, Z. W. What the mind's eye tells the mind's brain: A critique of mental imagery. *Psychological Bulletin,* 1973, **80,** 1–24.

Quillian, M. R. The teachable language comprehender. *Communications of the Association for Computing Machinery,* 1969, **12,** 459–476.

Reed, S. K. Pattern recognition and categorization. *Cognitive Psychology,* 1972, **3,** 382–407.

Rips, L. J. Inductive judgments about natural categories. *Journal of Verbal Learning and Verbal Behavior,* 1975, **14,** 665–681. (b)

Rips, L. J. Quantification and semantic memory. *Cognitive Psychology,* 1975, **7,** 307–340. (a)

Rips, L. J., Shoben, E. J., & Smith, E. E. Semantic distance and the verification of semantic relations. *Journal of Verbal Learning and Verbal Behavior,* 1973, **12,** 1–20.

Rips, L. J., Shoben, E. J., & Smith, E. E. Performance models of semantic composition. In R. Grossman, J. San, & T. Vance (Eds.), *Papers from the parasession on functionalism.* Chicago: Chicago Linguistics Society, 1975. Pp. 450–467. (a)

Rips, L. J., Smith, E. E., & Shoben, E. J. Set-theoretic and network models, reconsidered: A comment on Hollan's "Features and semantic memory." *Psychological Review,* 1975, **82,** 156–157. (b)

Rips, L. J., Smith, E. E., & Shoben, E. J. Semantic composition in sentence verification. *Journal of Verbal Learning and Verbal Behavior,* 1978, in press.

Rosch, E. H. On the internal structure of perceptual and semantic categories. In T. E. Moore (Ed.), *Cognitive development and acquisition of language.* New York: Academic Press, 1973. Pp. 111–144.

Rosch, E. H. Universals and cultural specifics in human categorization. In R. Brislin, W. Lonner, & S. Bochner (Eds.), *Cross-cultural perspectives on learning.* London: Sage Press, 1974. Pp. 177–206.

Rosch, E. H. Cognitive reference points. *Cognitive Psychology,* 1975, **1,** 532–547.

Rosch, E. H., Simpson, C., & Miller, R. S. Structural bases of typicality effects. *Journal of Experimental Psychology: Human Perception and Performance,* 1976, **2,** 491–502.

Rumelhart, D. E., Lindsay, P. H., & Norman, D. A. A process model for long-term memory. In E. Tulving & W. Donaldson (Eds.), *Organization and memory.* New York: Academic Press, 1972. Pp. 197–246.

Rumelhart, D. E., & Siple, P. Process of recognizing tachistoscopically presented words. *Psychological Review,* 1974, **81,** 99–118.

Schaeffer, B., & Wallace, R. The comparison of word meanings. *Journal of Experimental Psychology,* 1970, **86,** 144–152.

Selfridge, O. G. Pandemonium: A paradigm for learning. In *Mechanization of thought processes.* Vol. 1. London: Her Majesty's Stationery Office, 1959. Pp. 511–526.

Shoben, E. J. Semantic features in semantic memory. Unpublished doctoral dissertation, Stanford University, 1974.

Shoben, E. J. The verification of semantic relations in a same–different paradigm: An asymmetry in semantic memory. *Journal of Verbal Learning and Verbal Behavior,* 1976, **15,** 365–379.

Shoben, E. J., Rips, L. J., & Smith, E. E. *Issues in semantic memory: A response to Glass and Holyoak.* Center for Study of Reading Technical Report. 1978, in press.

Smith, E. E. Effects of familiarity on stimulus recognition and categorization. *Journal of Experimental Psychology,* 1967, **74,** 324–332.

Smith, E. E., Rips, L. J., & Shoben, E. J. Semantic memory and psychological semantics. In G. H. Bower (Ed.), *The psychology of learning and motivation.* Vol. 8. New York: Academic Press, 1974. Pp. 1–45. (a)

Smith, E. E., Shoben, E. J., & Rips, L. J. Structure and process in semantic memory: A featural model for semantic decisions. *Psychological Review,* 1974, **81,** 214–241. (b)

Snyder, C. R. R. Selection, inspection, and naming in visual search. *Journal of Experimental Psychology,* 1972, **92,** 428–436.

Sternberg, S. Memory scanning: Mental processes revealed by reaction time experiments. *American Scientist,* 1969, **57,** 421–457.

Stillings, N. A. Meaning rules and systems of inference for verbs of transfer and possession. *Journal of Verbal Learning and Verbal Behavior,* 1975, **14,** 453–470.

Tulving, E. Episodic and semantic memory. In E. Tulving & W. Donaldson (Eds.), *Organization and memory.* New York: Academic Press, 1972. Pp. 381–403.

Walker, J. H. Real-world variability, reasonableness judgments, and memory representations for concepts. *Journal of Verbal Learning and Verbal Behavior,* 1975, **14,** 241–252.

Wescourt, K. T., & Atkinson, R. C. Fact retrieval processes in human memory. In W. K. Estes (Ed.), *Handbook of learning and cognitive processes.* Vol. 4. Hillsdale, New Jersey: Lawrence Erlbaum Associates, 1976. Pp. 363–413.

Wilkins, A. T. Conjoint frequency, category size, and categorization time. *Journal of Verbal Learning and Verbal Behavior,* 1971, **10,** 382–385.

Winograd, T. Understanding natural language. *Cognitive Psychology,* 1972, **3,** 1–191.

Winograd, T. Frame representations and the declarative/procedural controversy. In D. Bobrow & A. M. Collins (Eds.), *Representation and understanding.* New York: Academic Press, 1975. Pp. 185–210.

Wittgenstein, L. *Philosophical investigations.* (Translated by G. E. M. Anscombe.) Oxford: Blackwell, 1953.

2
Comprehension and Memory of Text

Walter Kintsch

University of Colorado

Investigators of verbal learning have for the most part been interested in list-learning studies. Traditionally, lists of nonsense syllables or words have been the principal learning materials employed, to which lists of unrelated sentences were added more recently. Simultaneously, however, there has been a trickle of studies concerned with text materials. Throughout the history of verbal-learning research, the number of investigations of texts never represented more than a small fraction of the total research output and remained relatively insignificant. Worst of all, it never successfully merged with the main stream of verbal-learning research and theory. Even such well-known work as that of Bartlett, which was published in 1932, was for a long time regarded by academic psychologists as a slightly exotic curiosity—certainly interesting and probably important, but not of direct relevance for learning theory or models of memory. Much of the work on prose learning during this period was performed by educational psychologists. Only in the last few years has this situation begun to change. It seems possible today that the study of comprehension and memory of texts may finally overcome its status of benign neglect and even assume a central role in the research on cognitive processes.

Many of the problems arising in the study of memory for word lists reappear in research with textual materials. There is, however, a new set of problems specific to these materials, which could be called the comprehension problem. A person who reads or listens to a text and comprehends it can then perform a whole set of appropriate behaviors: He can recall it, paraphrase it, summarize it, answer questions about it, or translate it into another language. How can we characterize the competence he has acquired that permits him to perform these tasks? In order to answer this question we must find a way to deal with the meaning of the text.

Early psychological work on text comprehension and memory was hampered by the lack of a theory for the representation of the meaning of texts. Therefore, little progress was made in explicating the dependence of comprehension and memory upon the characteristics of the learning material. Indeed, it has sometimes been concluded that the structure of a text is unimportant in learning vis-a-vis the readers' activities during learning (for example, Frase, 1976). These studies of comprehension parallel earlier verbal-learning work concerned with "task variables"; up-to-date reviews of this work are available (Frase, 1976; Rothkopf, 1972). In the present chapter a different set of studies will be emphasized, those concerned with "materials variables," that is, the complexity of the content of the text itself and such notions as theme or gist. A prerequisite for such work is a theory for the representation of meaning. Such a theory is needed for the design of experiments to specify both the independent and dependent variables; that is, the particular aspects of the text content that are to be studied on the one hand and the relevant characteristics of the response protocols on the other. A number of investigators have proposed models for the representation of meaning suitable for work in experimental psychology and artificial intelligence (for example, Anderson & Bower, 1973; Crothers, 1975; Frederiksen, 1975a; Kintsch, 1974; Norman & Rumelhart, 1975; Schank, 1972. These proposals, for the most part based directly upon original work in linguistics and logic, differ in elaborateness and in the purposes for which they were constructed, as well as in some substantive issues. However, these differences need not concern us here since we are interested at present in the use to which these models are put, rather than in the models themselves. Our discussion will be based upon the model of Kintsch (1974) alone, with the understanding that rather similar arguments could be developed within some of the other theories mentioned.

I. TEXT BASES[1]

The meaning of a *text* is represented by its *text base,* which consists of a connected, partially ordered list of *propositions.* Propositions contain one or more *arguments* plus one *relational term.* The arguments and relations are *concepts* expressed in English by a word, or they may be other propositions. Relational terms are expressed in English as verbs, modifiers, or sentence connectors. If the relational term (or predicator) is a verb, case grammar provides a helpful notational system (Fillmore, 1968). Each verb is characterized, in part, by its corresponding verb frame. Thus, the frame for *buy* indicates that its use involves a human agent, a human source, an object that humans may possess, and money, though not all of these semantic cases are obligatory. Furthermore, *buy* implies a

---

[1]The terms text, prose, and discourse are used here interchangeably. According to the Oxford English Dictionary, discourse is derived from the Latin verb *discurrere,* running to and fro; hence "discontinuous discourse" is a contradiction in terms and "continuous discourse," a tautology.

2. COMPREHENSION AND MEMORY 59

transfer of possession of the object from the source to the agent and a reverse transfer of money. Additional information about this concept is also available in semantic memory, for example, that the agent wants the object he buys. Thus, semantic memory defines (BUY,agent:JOHN,object:RING,instrument:$1,000) as an acceptable proposition, while (BUY,agent:JOHN,object:SNOWFLAKE) or (BUY,agent:FROG,object:RING) would be rejected, though these propositions would be acceptable if they occurred in a fairy tale or as metaphors.

Modifiers of various kinds, expressed in English by words such as *tall, swift,* or *very,* may also serve as relational terms of propositions, as in (VALUABLE, RING), (VERY,(VALUABLE, RING)), or (HASTY,(BUY,agent:JOHN, object:RING))—*The ring is valuable, The ring is very valuable,* and *Hastily, John bought a ring.* In the last two examples, whole propositions are used as arguments of other propositions. This capability to embed one proposition as an argument of another provides much of the descriptive power of the system.

An example of a predicator that is normally expressed in English by means of a sentence connector would be (CAUSALITY,(BUY,agent:JOHN,object:RING), (NICE,RING)), which underlies such English sentences as *John bought a ring because it was nice* or *The ring was nice; therefore, John bought it.* It is impossible to comment here on such aspects of these sentences as the use of definite articles, or verb tenses; for this, the reader must be referred to the original source.

Connections among propositions are established through the repetition of arguments: each proposition in a text base must share an argument with at least one other proposition. Connection via argument repetition is not a sufficient condition for the coherence of a text base, but it is a necessary condition. Propositions forming a text base are partially ordered in a hierarchy. One or more propositions are the superordinate propositions of the text base; all propositions that share an argument with propositions at this superordinate level form the next highest level of the hierarchy: all propositions sharing an argument with any of the second level propositions, but not with propositions at the first level, form the third level in the text base hierarchy; lower levels are similarly defined.

While it is impossible to even sketch the theory here in any detail, a simple example will show how one operates with these concepts. In Table 1, a sentence from a story from Boccaccio's *Decameron* is reprinted together with the corresponding text base. For convenience, each proposition is written on a separate line and given a reference number. The first proposition is (BUY,agent:LANDOLFO,object:SHIP). The second proposition introduces the modifier *large;* the third one is a further modifier. Here we have an instance where a proposition appears as the argument of another proposition: *very* modifies *large ship*—not just *large,* which alone is undefinable. Proposition (4) contains the sentence connective *after* as its relational term and again has other propositions as arguments. The remaining propositions can be similarly interpreted.

The hierarchical structure of this portion of the text base is shown in Figure 1. The superordinate proposition (RUINED,LANDOLFO) is not actually repre-

TABLE 1
Fragment of an Episode from a Short Story and the Corresponding Text Base[a]

Text	Text base
This Landolfo, then, having made the sort of preliminary calculations merchants normally make, purchased a very large ship, loaded it with a mixed cargo of goods paid for out of his own pocket, and sailed with them to Cyprus. (The episode continues with a description of how this endeavor finally resulted in Landolfo's ruin.)	1(PURCHASE,agent:L,object:SHIP) 2(LARGE,SHIP) 3(VERY,2) 4(AFTER,1,5) 5(CALCULATE,agent:L) 6(PRELIMINARY,5) 7(LIKE,5,8) 8(CALCULATE,agent:MERCHANT) 9(NORMAL,8) 10(LOAD,agent:L,goal:SHIP,object:CARGO) 11(MIXED,CARGO) 12(CONSIST OF,object:CARGO,source:GOODS) 13(PAY,agent:L,object:GOODS,instrument:MONEY) 14(OWN,agent:L,object:MONEY) 15(SAIL,agent:L,object:GOODS,goal:CYPRUS)

[a]Modified from Kintsch (1976).

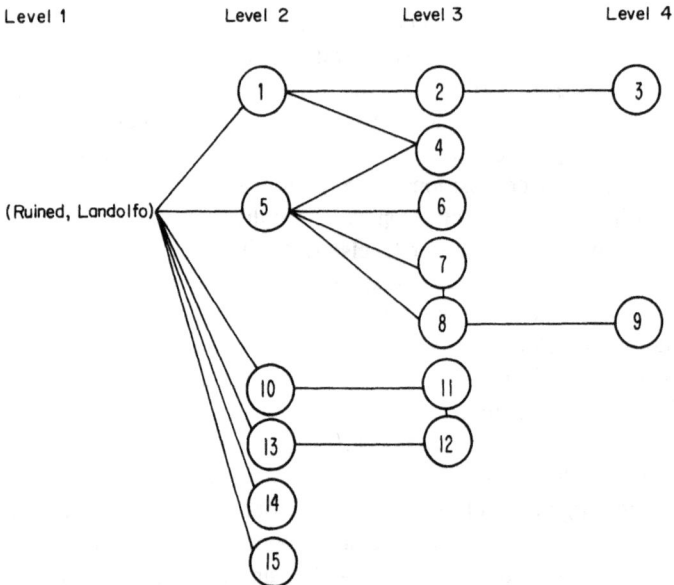

FIGURE 1.   The text base hierarchy for the fragment of a text base shown in Table 1. Propositions are indicated only by their number; shared arguments among them are shown as connecting lines.

sented in this part of the text; however, it is the topic of the episode to which the sentences analyzed here belongs. Since it contains only one argument, *Landolfo*, all propositions containing this argument are assigned to Level 2 of the text base. Proposition (2) is a Level 3 proposition because it repeats the argument *ship* that appears in a Level 1 proposition. Proposition (3) is connected to (2) that appears as its argument and hence is a Level 2 proposition. All other propositions are assigned to levels of the hierarchy in the same way. Thus, the levels are objectively defined for a given proposition list and a topical superordinate proposition. The text base shown in Table 1 is only the microstructure of a part of the text; we also need to be concerned with the overall organization of the text, that is, its *macrostructure*. The topic proposition (RUINED,LANDOLFO) is, in fact, part of that macrostructure, but we shall delay a further discussion of macrostructures until the last section of this chapter.

The text in Table 1 is only one possible paraphrase derivable from this text base. The rules for generating texts from a text base, or for constructing a text base from a given text will not be elaborated here. Given a particular text base, good agreement among raters can be achieved about the corresponding text. For present purposes such a procedure is sufficient, since we are only interested in exploring some psychologically relevant aspects of text bases. The rules for constructing text bases, and for generating text from them are, of course, of primary importance in artificial intelligence.

Once a text is analyzed into propositions, several rather straightforward experimental predictions can be obtained. For instance, such analyses suggest when a word should be a good recall cue: if the word concept corresponding to the word appears as an argument in many propositions of a text, it should be a more successful recall cue than when the corresponding word concept is used as an argument in only a few text propositions. Wanner (1974) obtained some data confirming this prediction. Consider the following sentence pair:

The governor asked the detective to $\left\{ \begin{array}{c} \text{cease} \\ \text{prevent} \end{array} \right\}$ drinking.

The corresponding text bases are, respectively,

(ASK,GOVERNOR,DETECTIVE,(CEASE,DETECTIVE,(DRINK,DETECTIVE)))
(ASK,GOVERNOR,DETECTIVE,(PREVENT,DETECTIVE,(DRINK,SOMEONE)))

In the *cease* sentence, *detective* is involved in all three propositions; but in the *prevent* sentence, *detective* is involved in only two propositions. Hence, *detective* should be a better recall cue for the *cease* sentence than for the *prevent* sentence. Wanner reported that the recall likelihood for the two sentence types were .39 and .30, respectively. For comparison, *governor*, which appears only once in each sentence, produced essentially the same recall proportions for the two sentences, .27 and .25. Thus, the differential effectiveness of *detective* as a recall cue can be attributed to its greater importance in one sentence than in the other.

A very similar cued sentence-recall experiment with corroborating results has been reported by Anderson and Bower (1973, p. 256), and the same phenomenon has also been observed in free recall of prose paragraphs. The likelihood that a particular word will be recalled increases as a function of the number of times the corresponding word concept appears in the text base (Kintsch, Kozminsky, Streby, McKoon, & Keenan, 1975).

When subjects recall a short text, propositions appear to be the units of recall. Kintsch and Keenan (1973) have shown that the time subjects take to read texts bears a regular relationship to the amount they can recall. Subjects were given sentences and paragraphs to read that were controlled for length (that is, number of words) but were derived from text bases with different numbers of propositions. For instance, *Romulus, the legendary founder of Rome, took the women of the Sabine by force* and *Cleopatra's downfall lay in her foolish trust of the fickle political figures of the Roman world* contain almost the same number of words, but the first sentence is based upon four propositions, while the second one is based upon eight propositions. Subjects read sentences such as these, pressed a response button when they were finished, and immediately attempted

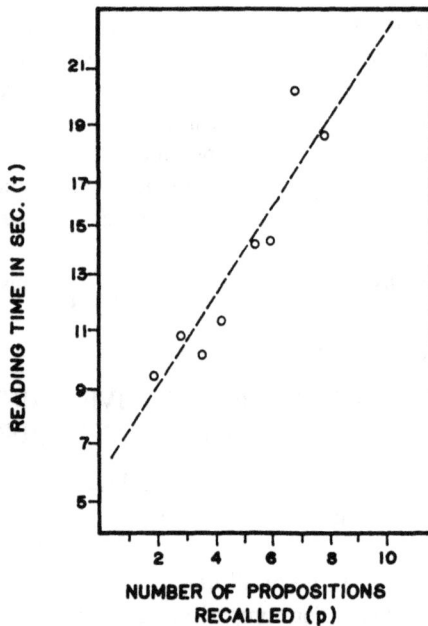

FIGURE 2. Reading time as a function of the number of propositions recalled for 16 to 17 word sentences, with different number of propositions in their base. The least square line is $t = 5.53 + 1.48p$. (after Kintsch & Keenan, 1973).

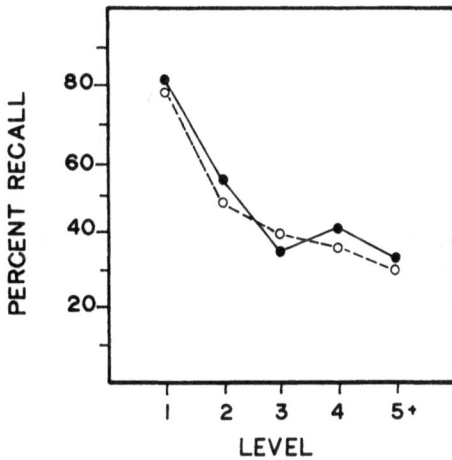

FIGURE 3.   Recall probability as function of the level of a proposition in the text base hierarchy. The data are for 70-word paragraphs about history (filled circles) and science (open circles) (after Kintsch *et al.*, 1975).

to recall each sentence in writing, not necessarily verbatim. A plot of the average reading time versus the number of propositions recalled is shown in Figure 2. For each additional proposition recalled, an additional 1.5 seconds of reading time was required. Therefore, the number of propositions, not the number of words, determined reading time in this study. The value of 1.5 seconds per additional proposition encoded is not a constant but varies with the nature of the text.

Propositional analyses also permit one to predict which particular propositions of a given text base will be recalled. In a number of studies it has been observed that propositions high in the text-base hierarchy (as defined in Figure 1) are recalled much better than subordinate propositions (Kintsch & Keenan, 1973; Kintsch *et al.*, 1975). A typical result is shown in Figure 3. While subjects recalled about 80% of the Level 1 propositions of 70-word paragraphs, they recalled only 30% of the most subordinate propositions. A similar observation was reported by Meyer (1975), who inserted a paragraph into a longer text in such a way that it was either high or low in the text hierarchy. Recall was substantially better when the paragraph was in the high position than when it was in the low position. After 1 week, this effect was even more pronounced: recall of the subordinate paragraph was only 27% of the recall of the same paragraph in the superordinate position. Kintsch *et al.* also suggested that superordinate propositions are not only encoded better but may also be remembered better.

Why are the superordinate propositions in a text recalled so well? Consider how levels are defined: the superordinate propositions are those that introduce new arguments into the text; subordinate propositions repeat the arguments of the higher level propositions. Furthermore, repeated arguments always have the same referent. Thus, if one assumes that whenever the subject processes a subordinate proposition he must identify the repeated argument with one already introduced, it follows that processing a subordinate proposition entails an implicit reprocessing of its superordinate proposition. During the reading of a text, superordinate propositions receive more implicit repetitions and are therefore recalled better.

This interpretation of the levels effect in terms of implicit repetition is plausible, because it can be shown that explicit repetition of arguments improves recall. Kintsch *et al.* (1975) gave subjects texts to read that were controlled both for the number of words (approximately 70) and number of propositions (approximately 24). The texts differed in how many different word concepts were used as the arguments of the propositions. In one case, a few concepts (7 or 8) were frequently repeated, in the other twice as many concepts were used, with correspondingly fewer repetitions. The paragraphs with few arguments and many repetitions were read faster than the paragraphs with many arguments when reading time was subject controlled and recall was equal for the two types of texts. When reading times were restricted by the experimenter, the many argument paragraphs were recalled more poorly, indicating that subjects did not have enough time to encode these texts as well as the paragraphs with fewer different concepts.

Corroborating evidence for the importance of repetition in memory was obtained by Manelis and Yekovich (1976). These authors had subjects recall connected sentences (for example, *Arnold lunged at Norman. Norman called the doctor. The doctor arrived.*) and shorter, but unconnected control sentences (for example, *Arnold lunged. Norman called. The doctor arrived.*). The longer sentences were recalled 51% of the time, while the shorter but textually deviant sentences were recalled only 43% of the time.

Each sentence builds upon the previous sentences in the text or upon the extralinguistic context. Referring to an object or event that is perceptually present in a situation serves the same function as repeating a concept from one sentence to the next. Thus, imagine a situation where a party arrives at a picnic spot, and someone lifts some beer out of the trunk of the car and says, "the beer is warm." Comprehension of this sentence is assured, because *the beer* is identified by the situational context. Lacking such a context in a laboratory situation, one can establish a linguistic context, as Haviland and Clark (1974) did:

(1)   *We got some beer out of the trunk. The beer was warm.*

Subjects who were asked to press a response button as soon as they had comprehended each sentence needed 835 msec for *The beer was warm* in context (1). On the other hand, if the context was only a general one as in (2) comprehension times were 181 msec longer on the average:

(2)   *We checked the picnic supplies. The beer was warm.*

Concept repetition facilities comprehension times. Haviland and Clark (1974) also showed that identity of reference of the concepts is crucial for this facilitation effect and that mere identity of words is not enough. Thus, the word *beer* is repeated in (3):

(3) *Andrew was especially fond of beer. The beer was warm.*

However, the referent of beer in the two sentences of context (3) are not the same (in one case it is beer in general, in the other some particular six-pack), and comprehension times increased by 137 msec. In both (2) and (3) the reader must somehow infer a specific connection between the two sentences. In (1), on the other hand, this connection is given in the text. Haviland and Clark (1974) hypothesized that in each sentence of a text, the reader identifies the old repeated concepts, uses them as an address to the relevant parts of his memory, and then connects the new information that the sentence provides with what he already knows. This is the given-new strategy of text comprehension. The more a text facilitates this comprehension strategy, the easier it is to comprehend the text.

There are many linguistic devices that are used to mark which parts of a sentence are new information and which are already known. In English, sentences are usually constructed so that the old, familiar information comes first, and new information is put at the end of the sentence. Thus, if someone says *The girl is petting the cat,* he usually assumes that the listener already knows about the girl and tells him what she is doing. On the other hand, if *cat* is the topic of conversation and the speaker wants to tell the listener what is happening to it, he might use the passive voice: *The cat is being petted by the girl* (Hornby, 1972). In both cases, the old information appears at the beginning of the sentence, allowing the listener to prepare himself for the new information to come, which must be integrated with the already existing knowledge.

If a speaker wants to emphasize the new information in a sentence more heavily than normal, he may violate normal word order, or use intonation, as in *The girl is petting the cat,* or a cleft sentence as in *It is the girl who is petting the cat.* With both of these sentences, the speaker signals to the listener that the girl is the newsworthy part of the sentence and that he assumes that the listener already knows about the cat being petted by someone. That listeners respond to sentences in this intended manner was shown in an experiment by Hornby (1974). Hornby's subjects listened to sentences such as *It is the girl that petted the cat* and *The one that is petting the cat is the girl.* After hearing each sentence, subjects were shown a picture for 50 msec only and had to determine whether sentence and picture were consistent or not. Two types of inconsistencies occurred: either a boy was shown petting the cat, or a girl was shown petting a dog. In the first case, the old information was misrepresented; in the second case, the new, focused information was misrepresented. The interesting result of the study was that many more errors occurred when the old information was misrepresented (2.16 errors) than when the focused information was misrepresented (1.17

errors). Cleft and pseudocleft sentences thus are quite successful in focusing attention upon a particular part of the sentence: in verifying pictures against sentences, subjects rarely make errors about the focused part, but they are almost twice as likely to make errors about that part of the sentence that was marked as old information.

The given-new strategy is therefore quite basic to sentence and text comprehension. It helps the comprehender to identify old knowledge—repeated concepts as well as repeated propositions—and thereby to integrate the new information contained in the sentences with his already existing knowledge structure. The text hierarchy shown in Figure 1 is the direct result of this information-processing strategy of linking repetitions. Hence, the superior recall of high-level propositions in a text base can ultimately be attributed to an interaction between the material and the subjects' processing activities. The material provides the propositions to work with, and the processing activities order them in a levels hierarchy.

The studies reported above have been concerned with comprehension and memory of texts as a function of characteristics of their propositional text base. To avoid misunderstandings, a brief discussion of the epistomological status of the concept "text base" is necessary. For the psychologist, text bases, and hence meaning, are not real-world objects but simply the outcome of certain psychological processes. When we read a text, the only things outside the reader's mind are some letter shapes on a page: the words that are communicated by these visual objects, the phrases and sentences in which these words are organized, and their meaning, are the results of complex hierarchical psychological processes taking place in the reader's mind. In particular, the meaning of the text that the reader constructs from the actual physical stimulus, the situational context, and his world knowledge, is not something that resides in the text, but a response on the part of the reader to the text. The properties of the graphemic stimulus, plus the reader's world knowledge, usually determine quite precisely what that response will be. That is, normally a text, at least a simple, unambiguous one such as those used in the experiments above, means one thing (or, in the technical language used here, corresponds to a particular text base). However, this is only what normally happens in comprehension with cooperative, unbiased subjects. There is always room for originality in comprehension, and, given the right set and motives, a reader can construct almost anything from any kind of text. Comprehension is an active process; we have concentrated here upon the case where the activity was mainly one of reproduction. Below we shall turn to inferential activity during comprehension. However, it must be remembered that constructing the propositions (LOVE,PETER,MARY) from the graphic stimulus "Peter loves Mary" is just as active a process as inferring on the basis of that stimulus that "Peter is an old fool" (Peter's friend), or "I'll get a divorce" (Peter's wife).

II. INFERENCES

A speaker or writer has some message to communicate. We have represented the meaning of that message by a text base, that is, a hierarchically organized set of propositions. This text base is expressed as a natural language text. The listener or reader must decode this text and derive from it the meaning of the message, in other words, attempt to reproduce the original text base. Therefore, meaning is something the reader creates in response to a text, not something directly given by the text. In this sense propositions are always inferred from a text. However, some propositions are cued directly by a text while others are not. Consider, for example, the following two-sentence text:

(4)   *A heater exploded. The house burned down.*

This text contains two explicit propositions. (EXPLODE,HEATER) and (BURN,HOUSE). According to the model of Kintsch (1974), these two propositions do not form a text base, because they are not connected by repeated arguments. Hence, a connecting proposition must be inferred. People know what can happen when a heater explodes, and therefore might construct the following text base for (4):

(5)   (CONSEQUENCE,(EXPLODE,HEATER),(BURN HOUSE)).

We shall say that the (CONSEQUENCE,X,Y) proposition is implicit in (4). Several of the experiments reviewed above show that texts in which all propositions are explicit are easier to comprehend and remember than texts in which some implicit propositions must be inferred. We shall now investigate (*a*) whether readers actually infer implicit propositions during reading and (*b*) in which way the memory representations for explicit and implicit propositions differ. There are obviously many more kinds of implicit propositions other than those that have to be inferred in order to make a text base coherent, as in (5). However, we shall consider this particularly simple type first.

In a series of studies, Keenan and Kintsch (1974) and McKoon and Keenan (1974) compared memory for explicit and implicit propositions. Texts, varying in length from 17 to 160 words, were constructed in such a way that in one version a particular proposition was expressed explicitly but was left implicit in another. An example of one of the short paragraphs is given in Table 2. A subject read either the explicit or the implicit version of a paragraph and was then given the task of verifying a test sentence. The test sentence always corresponded to the proposition that was left implicit in one version of the paragraph. (For methodological reasons there were, of course, other kinds of test sentences, too, but these need not concern us here). The test sentences were presented either immediately upon reading the paragraph or after a 20-minute delay, filled with reading other, unrelated material. Figure 4 shows some representative results. First, note

TABLE 2
Explicit and Implicit Paragraphs and Their Corresponding
Test Sentences in the Experiment of Keenan and Kintsch (1974)

Input:

EXPLICIT:
A gas leak developed in the heating system
of a house on 5th Street. The gas caused
an explosion which destroyed the house and
started a fire that threatened several
neighboring structures.

IMPLICIT:
A gas leak developed in the heating system
of a house on 5th Street. An explosion
destroyed the house and started a fire
that threatened several neighboring
structures.

Delay:
∅ or 20 minutes

Verification test:
The gas caused an explosion.

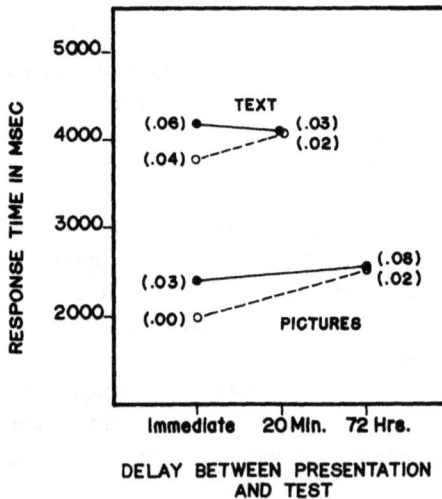

Figure 4.   Verification times for explicit (open circles) and implicit (filled circles) test sentences and pictures. Error rates are shown besides each point. Story data after Keenan and Kintsch (1974), Experiments I and II, short paragraphs; picture data after Baggett (1975).

that most of the responses were correct: subjects correctly maintained that the test sentences were true with respect to the story, whether or not they had actually seen them before. However, subjects made their response more rapidly when they had seen the test sentence than when the test sentence was implicit. At least, this was the case when the test sentence was presented right after reading the paragraph. If it was delayed by 20 min filled with an interfering task, verification times for explicit and implicit sentences were the same (note that one cannot argue that after a delay the response times for implicit sentences would have been longer, except for a speed-accuracy trade off; there were, in fact, fewer errors after a delay for implicit sentences than there were on the immediate test).

The data have some important theoretical implications. First, subjects in general correctly made the invited inferences, though that is hardly a surprising result. More interesting is the evidence that the implicit propositions were indeed inferred at the time of reading and not merely when the subjects were asked a question about them. The fact that after a delay, response times for explicit and implicit propositions were equal indicates that by that time the memory representations for explicit and implicit propositions were the same and argues against the notion that subjects inferred the implicit propositions at the time of test, which would have resulted in a lengthening of response times.

This leaves us to explain the shorter response times for explicit propositions on immediate tests. This is the only response time that is significantly lower than the others. We know that sentences are represented in memory not only in terms of their meaning (that is, at the propositional level) but also in terms of their actual physical stimulus properties (for example, Kolers & Ostry, 1974), as well as their linguistic characteristics (that is, the actual words, phrases, and sentences used). That sentences can be remembered verbatim hardly requires experimental proof. If we assume that 20 minutes of reading was enough to interfere with this verbatim memory representation of the sentences, the data in Figure 4 are readily explained. Subjects always infer the crucial proposition, whether it is implicit or explicit in the text, because without it no coherent text base is possible, that is, the text cannot be comprehended. However, while the implicit sentence is represented in memory only propositionally, the explicit sentence is represented both propositionally and at visual/linguistic levels. Hence, on an immediate test the explicit test sentence can be matched against both propositional and verbatim memory traces, resulting in shorter response times. After a 20-minute delay, explicit sentences lose this advantage, because the verbatim memory traces are weakened from the interference produced by reading other texts. Memory for meaning, on the other hand, is less susceptible to interference from unrelated texts.

Figure 4 also shows the results from an experiment by Baggett (1975), using pictures rather than verbal materials. Simple stories, consisting of a sequence of four pictures were constructed, each in an explicit version where all the important steps in the story were pictured and in an implicit version where one step was left implicit. Care was taken that the implicit picture should be easily inferrable in the context of the other pictures. For instance, one of her picture series showed a little boy sitting on the bank of a lake fishing. In the explicit version, he was actually shown pulling a fish out of the water with his rod. In the implicit version this picture was replaced by one showing the boy taking a fish—still dripping water—from his rod. Finally, the boy puts the fish into a bucket. In both cases the picture showing the actual catch was the test picture, and the subject had to respond whether or not this picture sensibly fitted into the picture story. Again, a high percentage of correct answers was obtained, and, as with the verbal materials, response times were approximately equal for explicit and implicit pictures after a delay, as well as for immediately tested implicit pictures. However, when a picture that subjects had actually seen was tested immediately, they responded about half a second faster than in the other three conditions (Figure 4). We again take this to be evidence that immediately after looking at the pictures, subjects had complex multilevel memory representations available, while after a sufficiently long delay, they were able to use only the memory for the meaning of the story.

People do not ordinarily confuse their inferences with what they have actually experienced, however. If, instead of being asked whether the implicit test picture is true with respect to the other pictures, subjects are asked whether they recognize this particular picture as one they have seen before, they can tell very well that they have never seen it before: 100% of the subjects reject the picture when the test is immediate; after 3 days, 98% still reject the implicit test picture, and even after 4 weeks, 76% do the same. However, the subjects' ability to recognize correctly that they have not seen the implicit picture before does not help them on the true–false judgment. Baggett (1975) found that after 72 hours the response time to reject as new implicit test pictures is greater than the response time to accept the same pictures as true (3133 msec and 2542 msec, respectively).

Frederiksen (1975b) has also reported a study showing that inferences are performed as part of the comprehension activity during reading, rather than at the time of recall. Frederiksen considered three different types of constructions: overgeneralizations, pseudodiscriminations, and inferences. An overgeneralization occurs when a subject recalls a more general term than the one used in the text, for example, dropping a modifier (*best administrator* is recalled as *administrator*). A pseudodiscrimination occurs when the subject makes a finer distinction than the text (for example, *administrator* is recalled as *successful administrator*). An example of an inference would be the recall of *rich ranchers* when the text only mentions *rich senators* and the fact that all *senators are ranchers*. Frederiksen hypothesized that these three types of constructive processes occur

2. COMPREHENSION AND MEMORY   71

during reading and that the reader does not regard them as errors. Hence, when multiple study and recall trials are given, overgeneralizations, pseudodiscriminations, and inferences should not drop out over trials, as errors would, but instead should remain constant or increase and, therefore, be positively correlated with the amount of veridical recall. Indeed, this tended to be the case, though the correlations were small. Another type of construction Frederiksen called *elaborations*. Elaborations introduce new material into the recall protocol, as when a subject recalls that *senators were elected by the majority of the people,* although the text said nothing at all about elections. Elaborations are a kind of inference, though less direct ones: in the example above, the elaboration obviously reflects the person's knowledge about how one usually gets to be a senator, but it is not something that is closely integrated with the rest of the text. Indeed, elaborations decrease over trials and are negatively correlated with the amount of veridical recall. Unlike true constructions, elaborations may be the product of the recall activity itself, rather than the comprehension process. Lacking much else to say, the subject elaborates a concept such as *senator* at the time of recall, but as he learns more about the text on successive trials, such elaborations become unnecessary and are discarded. Frederiksen's recall protocols, therefore, provide evidence both for constructive processes at the time of comprehension and reconstructive processes at the time of recall.

Another type of inference that plays an important role in comprehension has to do with the presuppositions of sentences. Sentences have two functions: they assert new information and also provide cues about the old information that is relevant to the new assertions. The importance of reference to already established concepts has already been discussed. Presuppositions are references to already established facts. In uttering a sentence, the speaker assumes that certain facts are already known to the listener; these are the presuppositions of the sentence. Semantic presuppositions are defined technically as implications of the sentence that remain true when the sentence is negated. Thus, both *The girl opened the door* and *The girl did not open the door* imply that the door was closed; both *John ignored the fly in his soup* and *John did not ignore the fly in his soup* imply there was a fly in John's soup. However, the term *presupposition* is used more broadly today in the sense of pragmatic presupposition. For example, *Mr. Smith, can I get your coat?* indicates to the listener that Mr. Smith is either a social superior or a distant acquaintance of the speaker. Similarly, *I simply love your tie* presupposes that the speaker is female. If these expectations are violated, the result would be humorous or ironical (Bates, 1976).

It can be shown that information contained in the presupposition of sentences is used during the comprehension processes and is encoded in memory. Just as repeating a concept from one sentence to the next facilitates comprehension, spelling out the presupposition of a sentence in a previous sentence also facilitates comprehension. In an experiment already mentioned, Haviland and Clark (1974) asked subjects to read two sentences in succession and press a key when they had comprehended the second sentence. Comprehension time for the second sentence was the dependent variable of interest. In some sentence pairs, the second sentence contained the word *again (still, either,* and *too* were also used). The presupposition of *again* is that whatever is being talked about has happened before. If the first sentence spells out this presupposition as in (6), comprehension was facilitated over control sentences such as (7):

(6) *Last Christmas Eugene became absolutely smashed.*
     This Christmas he got very drunk again.
(7) *Last Christmas Eugene went to a lot of parties.*
     This Christmas he got very drunk again.

Comprehension times for sentences like (6) averaged 984 msec versus 1040 msec for sentences like (7).

The inferred presuppositions of a sentence are stored in memory, along with the actual assertions. Offir (1973) demonstrated this experimentally. She constructed her sentences from two propositions:

(8) *I know a man.*
(9) *A man (the same one) embezzled $1,000,000.*

If one wants to communicate these two propositions in English to someone who is ignorant of both, either one of the following sentences would be appropriate:

(10) *I know a man who embezzled $1,000,000.*
(11) *A man I know embezzled $1,000,000.*

These sentences are equivalent, and Offir showed that on a recognition test, subjects frequently confused them.

On the other hand, suppose the speaker assumes that the listener already knows that there is someone who embezzled $1,000,000 and wants to assert that he knows that man. In this case he would say:

(12) *I know the man who embezzled $1,000,000.*

Sentence (12) asserts (8) but presupposes (9). In the opposite case, when the speaker wants to assert that a certain man, whom the listener already knows about, embezzled $1,000,000, he asserts (9) but presupposes (8):

(13) *The man I know embezzled $1,000,000.*

Sentences (12) and (13) are not equivalent in the same way as (10) and (11) are; they differ in their pragmatic structure. Apparently, information about this pragmatic structure is encoded as part of the memory code for these sentences, because in Offir's recognition experiment, subjects were much less likely to confuse (12) and (13) than the earlier, pragmatically equivalent sentence pair (10) and (11).

It is quite easy to bias what people remember by inviting them to infer certain presuppositions; often these will then be stored in memory as actual facts. For instance, Loftus and Palmer (1974) showed subjects a film about a car accident and then asked them, *How fast were the cars going when they smashed/collided/ bumped?* A week later subjects were asked some more questions about the film, among them whether they had seen broken glass (they had not). More subjects reported seeing broken glass when the experimenter had talked about the accident using the word *smashed,* than when *collided* or *bumped* were used.

Witnesses in a court of law are liable for perjury when they make false assertions, but not for false presuppositions. Hence, it is an accepted courtroom tactic to ask leading questions and to bias the jury in this way. A witness asked *Mr. Eugene, are you still getting drunk every Christmas?* is in a poor position, no matter whether his answer is yes or no. Even people who know about these possibilities of unfair bias find it very difficult to distinguish, in their own mind, fact and presupposition. Harris, Teske, and Gins (1975) gave subjects a mock trial testimony containing 18 critical sentences, each of which occurred either as a direct assertion or as a pragmatic implication. Thus, one subject might hear:

(14) *I walked away without taking any money,*

while the other would hear:

(15) *I was able to walk away without taking any money.*

Half of the subjects received detailed instructions about distinguishing facts from inferences, while the other subjects only received general instructions such as those given to actual juries. Either right afterwards or after 2 days subjects were given a true-false test. The results were rather disturbing: subjects remembered 80% of the direct assertions—but also 71% of the implications! Instructions about the pitfalls of treating implications as assertions were of some help when an immediate test was given, but no help at all after 2 days. Thus, it appears that the confusion between pragmatic implication and asserted fact may be widespread. Even if subjects are specifically instructed to avoid such confusion they may be unable to do so.

People frequently do not say what they mean, but they are still understood on the basis of general conventions about communication. A mother who asks her child:

(16) *Can you empty the trash can?*

is not asking a question at all; when she says:

(17)   *Your bed is not made.*

she is by no means merely asserting a fact; nor is she when she says:

(18)   *I can't remember whether today is Wednesday or Thursday.*

Conversational rules have been described by Grice (1967), Searle (1969), and Gordon and Lakoff (1971) that govern the interpretation of these sentences. One just does not ask someone whether he can do something that one knows very well he can; (16) violates this rule, and hence the listener knows that it was not intended as a question and reinterprets it as a request. Similarly, one does not tell people things they know already; hence, (17) cannot be an assertion but is intended as a request. Sentence (18) violates a conversational rule that communications must be relevant; again, it does not function as an assertion but as a question. Clark and Lucy (1975) have studied how people comprehend sentences such as these. They hypothesized that people first comprehend the literal meaning of a sentence, reject that meaning on the basis of general conversational conventions, and then infer the pragmatically intended meaning. If this is the case, it should take longer to comprehend conveyed requests than direct requests. Clark and Lucy had subjects read a sentence that was either a conveyed or direct request of the form *Color the circle blue,* or *Can you color the circle blue?* and then judge whether a given circle was colored in accordance with the request. Subjects responded correctly to both kinds of requests, but responses to conveyed requests were slower than responses to direct requests. Furthermore, Clark and Lucy found some evidence indicating that the extra time in comprehending conveyed requests is taken up by processing the literal meaning of the sentence. This evidence rests on the well-established fact that negations require extra processing time in sentence-verification experiments. Consider the sentence pair:

(19)   *I'll be very happy if you make the circle blue.*
(20)   *I'll be very sad unless you make the circle blue.*

Both sentences have the same conveyed meaning, and subjects correctly responded yes when the circle was actually blue. However, (19) contains no negations, while (20) contains two negations in its surface structure—*sad* and *unless.* Therefore, if subjects process the literal meaning of these sentences, the two negations in (20) should slow them down. Indeed, verification times for (20) were 500 msec longer than for (19). Thus, Clark and Lucy concluded that conversationally conveyed requests are understood by first computing the literal meaning of the sentence, rejecting it, and recomputing the conveyed meaning. The last two steps of this process are governed by general conversational rules as in Grice (1967) or Searle (1969), or by more specific conversational postulates, as in Gordon and Lakoff (1971).

We have now described three types of inferences that occur in text comprehension: inferring a missing link between propositions in order to make a text base coherent, inferring presuppositions, and inferring conversationally implied meaning. It has been shown that these inferences are an integral part of the comprehension process as well as the memory trace of sentences, rather than mere reconstructions at the time of recall. This does not mean, of course, that such reconstructions never occur or that they would be insignificant. Bartlett (1932) has described many instances of true reconstructions occurring in the recall of stories. His subjects often did not remember much about the rather complicated, unfamiliar story they read, but then proceeded to reconstruct a story around some remembered detail or attitude. Wulff (1922) made similar observations about the recall of pictures and observed that reconstructions tend to make the recalled objects more normal and regular. Frederiksen (1975b) also concluded that the errors occurring during the recall of stories may in part represent elaborations occurring at the time of recall, though for the most part they were constructions occurring during comprehension. James, Thomson, and Baldwin (1973) investigated the mechanisms underlying reconstructions that may, at least in part, explain the trend towards regularization in recall observed by some authors. They first analyzed normal speech production and established norms, for example, about people's preference for the use of the active voice. Then they collected recall protocols and found the same bias in these protocols. Thus, recall protocols tend to approach the usual speech pattern, with the result that the syntax of the recall protocols does not reproduce unusual syntactic patterns in the original story. Similar processes at the semantic level have not yet been demonstrated but appear plausible.

Therefore, we have clear evidence for both constructive and reconstructive processes in recall; in addition, we know that recall can be simply reproductive. Thus, arguments about whether recall of prose is reproductive, constructive, or reconstructive appear to be misguided. Bartlett (1932) stressed the reconstructive aspects of recall. His subjects were English college students, and he gave them a rather curious Indian story to recall. Much of what they recalled could be classified as elaborations occurring at the time of recall. Later investigators, using more conventional materials, found much less evidence for constructions and reconstructions than Bartlett did; the recall protocols in those studies consisted for the most part of reproductions, and the main error subjects made was that they omitted much of the material (for example, Cofer, 1973; Gomulicki, 1956; Kintsch et al. 1975; Zangwill, 1972). This led some investigators to question Bartlett's findings and to insist that recall was reproductive (or abstractive) rather than constructive (for example, Gomulicki, 1956; Zangwill, 1972). However, recall is reproductive, constructive, and reconstructive at the same time, and an important problem is to determine under what conditions one or the other of these aspects predominates.

The length of a text obviously has much to do with how reproductive recall is. One can only reconstruct a long novel, with very little reproduction. Indeed, even for moderately long texts (1000 words), free-recall protocols contain relatively few reproductions of text propositions. However, such protocols do not reflect accurately what is stored about the text in memory. If, instead of recalling the whole text, the subject is asked only to recall one particular episode from the long text, one finds an astonishing amount of accurate, reproductive recall for that episode. Kintsch and Turner (in preparation) gave subjects 1000-word passages of various kinds to read. One of them was a biography of Abraham Lincoln. After reading subjects were told to recall, as well as they could, but not necessarily verbatim, a single 70-word paragraph from the long text. For instance, they might be told to "recall the episode about Lincoln's participation in the Indian war." Of course, the subjects did not know beforehand which passage they would be asked to recall. Under these conditions, recall for the cued paragraph was almost as good as when they read only the 70-word paragraph and recalled it immediately after reading. For the Lincoln paragraph, subjects reproduced 44% of the propositions when they read it in isolation and 34%, on the average, when it was embedded in the longer text, either at the beginning, middle, or end. Since the complete text consisted of 14 paragraphs like the test paragraph, we can estimate that subjects retained in memory 34% of all propositions after reading this text once, that is, about 140 propositions! Furthermore, cued recall showed the same levels effect as the recall of the isolated paragraph (see Figure 2) and resulted in relatively few constructions and elaborations. At the same time, however, if subjects had been asked to recall the whole text or summarize it, they would have responded mostly with constructions rather than with direct reproductions from the text.

The familiarity of the material is another important variable that determines the amount of constructive and reconstructive activity, and it interacts in an interesting way with time of testing. Kintsch et al. (1975) used two types of learning materials: short, unfamiliar paragraphs taken from *Scientific American,* or paragraphs about relatively familiar topics from classical history. As already mentioned, immediate recall was mostly reproductive. When recall was delayed for a day, however, this pattern changed drastically for the familiar history texts, in that the subjects liberally supplemented their memory for the paragraph from their general knowledge about the topic. For instance, subjects who read a short paragraph about the Biblical story of Joseph and his brothers faithfully reproduced this text when recall was immediate (with many omissions, of course). After one day the number of omissions rose, but the recall protocols became longer because the subjects mentioned many things they knew about this story that were not part of the original text. Sulin and Dooling (1974) reported some similar observations about the loss of differentiation between the subjects' episodic memory for a text and their general knowledge about it.

Other variables that can greatly influence the amount of constructive activity a subject engages in are the instructions given to the subjects (Cofer, 1973; Frederiksen, 1975b), and the subject's interest in the material he reads (Paul, 1959). From all this information, we may safely conclude that inference processes form an important component of comprehension and recall. We also know something of the conditions under which these processes occur. The next question is how they occur.

III. SCHEMATA

Where do inferences come from? Certainly, these are not logical inferences. Logicians require inferences to be based upon formal, syntactic criteria, and to be decidably true or false. In most cases mentioned above, neither requirement is met. The inferences are not formal at all, but usually based upon knowledge about word use or about causal chains in the real world. Furthermore, these inferences are fuzzy: they are not precise, nor can one be sure about their truth. Given the mini-text:

A heater exploded. The house burned down.

a reader readily infers that the first event caused the second. This inference is based upon the reader's knowledge about explosions and fires. He is justified in assuming the normal sequence of events here because the rules governing conversations require the speaker to provide all relevant information; that is, if the normal sequence were violated, the speaker would have to indicate this somehow.

Knowledge about concepts is an important source of inferences. For instance, people know what normally belongs in a living room, so that they can continue:

John walked into the livingroom

with:

The window was open

on the basis of the inference that ''the'' window is part of the room. Verb frames are another rich source of inferences. Given:

The secretary types

subjects readily infer that she uses a typewriter and paper, types some kind of a text, and is skilled. Given:

Seymour carved the turkey

the inference is made that he uses a knife and that the turkey is cooked. From:

Cecil continued eating

subjects conclude that he eats food, has been eating before, and is hungry (data from Kintsch, 1972).

The examples above illustrate inferences on the basis of knowledge frames. Information about a complex concept is stored in memory and becomes available when the concept is activated. Furthermore, an element that is part of a knowledge frame is able to activate the whole frame. This process is one of pattern completion: a partial-stimulus pattern is matched with its representation in memory and activates the total knowledge unit, as when a visual stimulus activates the corresponding word concept in semantic memory. The tendency of parts to complete themselves has long been known to psychologists. Hamilton's "law of redintegration" was an early formulation of this pattern-completion process (Hamilton, 1859). Selz (1922) and Bartlett (1932) generalized this notion by introducing the concept of a *schema*. A schema is a representation of a situation or of an event; it is a prototype or norm and specifies the usual sequence of events that is to be expected. Just like other concepts, schemata are fuzzy and imprecise. A part of the schema can reintegrate the whole schema, and once a schema is activated, its components are available and need not be specified separately. Just as the verb *type* presupposes the use of a *typewriter,* the *children's birthday party* schema implies that there were *guests* and *presents.* Minsky (1975) called these "default assignments": unless otherwise specified, one assumes that these default assignments can be filled in in the usual way as specified by the schema. The notion of schema or frame has, under various names, become extremely popular in recent years in artificial intelligence and cognitive psychology (for example, Minsky, 1975; Winograd, 1975), and we need to take a look at the possible role that schemata might play in comprehending and remembering texts.

An excellent example of the use of schemata in text processing is Schank's (1975) computer program called SAM. SAM understands stories, is able to paraphrase them, summarize them, and even translate them into Chinese—if it has the required schemata stored in its memory. An example of such a schema is the restaurant script. Part of the script is reproduced here (without Schank's technical language):

script: restaurant
roles: customer, waitress, chef, cashier
reason: to get food as to go up in pleasure and down in hunger
scene 1: entering
         go into restaurant
         look for empty tables
         decide where to sit
         go there
         sit down

The next scene is called "ordering," and this is followed by "eating" and "exiting."

With this script Schank provided the computer with a detailed instruction sequence for how to behave in a restaurant. Actually, there are many different paths in a restaurant script; how one behaves in a cafeteria and in an expensive French restaurant is not at all the same; only the acts of eating and paying are essential to the restaurant script, but all this information can be incorporated in the computer's memory.

When reading a text, information in the text is identified in terms of its place in the restaurant script. The script is a long and explicit causal chain, and if a text mentions some members of that chain, the rest of the chain can be inferred. Thus, the input:

(21)   *John went to a restaurant. He ate a hamburger and left.*

could easily be paraphrased by filling in all the normal default assignments from the restaurant frame. All of these operations occur at a conceptual level, resulting in a string of propositions. As a final step, these propositions must be translated into verbal form. Schank (1975) reported that it makes little difference whether one uses English or Chinese at this point: once the conceptual structure is there, the problem of generating a text from it appears to be a relatively minor one.

Not only can SAM produce shorter or longer paraphrases of texts about restaurant visits, it can also answer questions about them. Given (21), SAM obviously can determine whether John ordered a hamburger, whether he left a tip, and so on.

All of this is done by the suitable use of preknowledge about restaurants. One can say that SAM can only understand a story when it already knows everything about it. Therefore, the use of schemata in comprehension must be supplemented with other more local inference rules. Real-world events usually deviate from the norm, and certainly stories are always about something more or less interesting and unexpected; to tell people the obvious is considered boring and a violation of conversational conventions. Thus, the story comprehender must be able to deal with deviations from the norm. Consider, for instance, the following input:

(22)   *John went to a restaurant. He got a cold hamburger, became angry and left.*

There are two pieces of information in this story that deviate from the script: the hamburger was cold, and John became angry. Becoming angry implies that there was some event that caused it; the only thing not accounted for by SAM's script is the cold hamburger. By the conversational principle that only relevant information should be mentioned, the comprehender can infer that the cold hamburger caused John to become angry. Further knowledge about cold food reinforces this conclusion.

The examples given above illustrate a problem but do not provide solutions. We know that numerous inferences are required in understanding text. Schema theory suggests how preknowledge can function in many of these inferences. Schank's SAM puts all the emphasis on preknowledge. Alternatively, one can imagine a system that relies mostly upon general inference rules of a more local character. Probably both are needed in comprehension, but how they are to be combined is far from clear today. Nevertheless, the idea that schemata or frames play a central role in comprehension appears to be equally attractive to computer scientists and psychologists, and even though the manner in which this might happen is still quite vague, it is worthwhile to ask whether there are any psychological data suggesting that text comprehension is, in fact, schema based.

The first line of evidence that suggests the operation of schemata derives from studies by Bartlett (1932) and Wulff (1922). These studies have already been noted above as examples of reconstructions that occur in the recall of stories and pictures.[2] What is relevant here is that these reconstructions tend to be more normal than the original story. Subjects might remember a particular poorly understood detail from a story, but in recalling it they try to provide some kind of a rationale for this detail, and they embed it into a more or less reasonable context. According to Bartlett, they have a schematic knowledge of what normally happens when Indians fight or when a man is wounded. The default assignments from that schema provide the reconstructions observed in recall. Thus, recall—especially repeated recall as more and more forgetting of the original material occurs—becomes ever more like the schema, and a story (or a picture) loses its individuality and idiosyncrasies.

While Bartlett's data are relevant mostly with respect to the role of schemata in recall, a study by Kintsch and van Dijk (1975) shows that schemata are also important in comprehension. Their argument is quite simple: if subjects read a story that has a familiar structure they should find it easier to comprehend than a story from a different culture for which they do not have the right schema. Consider first a typical story (about 1800 words) from Boccaccio's *Decameron*. It is about a single hero and tells several episodes about him. In each episode something interesting happens, and each is built in the same way: a setting (often the previous episode) and introduction is followed by some complication and its eventual resolution. All events are causally and temporally related. This is the prototype of a story in the European cultural tradition. Most literary products deviate from this norm in one way or another, so that it is not unfair to say that the norm exists only as an idealization that actual stories reflect more or less clearly. The *Decameron* stories used here are simple and come rather close to the norm. Therefore, if schema use is important, they should be easy to understand.

---

[2]Wulff's original interpretation was in terms of an autonomous change in the memory trace itself towards a better Gestalt, but later research is more in line with the view expressed here (for example, Riley, 1962).

Apache Indian stories of about the same length, on the other hand, are constructed according to a rather different schema: there is no consistent causal sequence, and the hero and topic of each episode change in ways that cannot be predicted from the story schema described above. Hence such stories should be more difficult to process for someone unfamiliar with the Apache story schema.

As a comprehension test, Kintsch and van Dijk (1975) selected a summarizing task. Subjects were simply asked to read each story and then to write a 60- to 80-word summary of it. The restriction in the length was necessary to insure some comparability among the summaries different subjects write. The summaries were scored by counting the number of propositions about which subjects agreed, determined by whether they included them in their summaries. Among American college students, there was much better agreement about what belongs in the summary of a *Decameron* story than in the summary of an Apache Indian story. Presumably, the availability of a schema for the first kind of story accounts for this difference. This relative lack of agreement about how to summarize the Indian story was obtained in spite of the fact that sentence-by-sentence the Indian story was by no means hard to understand. When subjects were given a random sample of sentences from all the stories to rate for comprehensibility and imagery value, they rated the sentences from the Indian story as slightly easier to comprehend and higher in imagery value than the sentences from the *Decameron* stories! Thus, out of context the sentences of the Indian story provided no difficulty; but lacking the proper schema, it was hard to put them together to form a story.

At the same time, subjects did understand something about the Indian story. Comprehension without the right schema was certainly possible, but when a story conformed to a familiar schema comprehension was facilitated. Indeed, Kintsch and van Dijk (1975) observed that the comprehender can reorder distorted stories with surprising ease if the story structure conforms to his schema. They asked subjects to read *Decameron* stories in which the order of paragraphs was randomized. Subjects had very little trouble with these scrambled texts. They took more time to read the scrambled texts than the stories in natural order (the means were 9.85 and 7.45 min, respectively), but the summaries they wrote after reading the scrambled stories (either immediately afterwards or after a 45-min delay) were as good as those written after reading the stories in their right order. Indeed, raters were unable to sort the summaries into those based upon natural and scrambled stories with better than chance results.[3]

These results suggest that the availability of schemata is psychologically important, both in the comprehension and in the recall of stories. As yet, these

---

[3]Note that scrambling the paragraphs of a story does not disrupt the coherence of the text in the same manner as scrambling the sentences of a paragraph: it was noted above that the latter operation makes the text unintelligible, for example, because the referents of pronouns and definite articles can no longer be determined. This is much less of a problem when paragraphs are displaced.

conclusions are only tentative, and other types of texts need to be investigated. However, assuming that schemata are used in comprehension, we can go on to ask how they are used.

Kintsch and van Dijk (1975) have suggested that a schema functions like an outline with empty slots. When one reads a story, this outline is filled in and becomes the macrostructure of that story. The schema is essentially the set of expectations the reader has about the story: that it will consist of a series of episodes, each based upon the setting–complication–resolution structure; that there will be a temporal–causal sequence of events; that a hero is required; that the events told must be unusual and interesting, etc. As the subject reads the story, he generates macrostructure propositions, that is, labels derived from the text for the various structural units of the story. Thus, in reading the story from which the sentence in Table 1 is taken, he ends up with several episodes. The label for the first one is *Landolfo is ruined* (hence the superordinate proposition in Figure 1); another episode is *Landolfo is shipwrecked*. The internal structure of this shipwrecking episode consists of an exposition *Landolfo is successful as a pirate,* the complication *Landolfo is captured and shipwrecked,* and the resolution *Landolfo survives by clinging to a spar in the water.* The claim is not that every reader will organize the story in precisely this way. The schema merely tells him to look for this kind of a structure, and the macrostructure he actually arrives at will depend upon how carefully he processes the text, as well as his personal interests and background. Kintsch and van Dijk have assumed that these macrostructure propositions are used to generate summaries of the story and, hence, have used the amount of intersubject agreement in summaries as an indication of the generality of the macrostructure: when the right kind of schema is available, this agreement is considerably higher than for stories from foreign cultures for which no schemata exist. The macrostructure is also used in recall to organize the story. Indeed, Kintsch and van Dijk could describe recall as based upon the macrostructure plus whatever microstructure propositions were encoded by the subject and were still retrievable. Empirically, recall protocols turn out to be like summaries plus idiosyncratic detail.

How are macrostructure propositions derived from the text? For the most part, they must be inferred. Often, there are no sentences in the text from which they could be directly constructed. Kintsch and van Dijk (1975) have described three kinds of macrostructure operations: deletion of nonessential detail as in:

(23)   *Mary played with a blue ball → Mary was playing,*

generalization, as in:

(24)   *We heard a coyote in the bushes → We heard an animal in the bushes,*

and construction, as in:

(25)   *Peter poured a foundation, erected walls, made a roof, put in the plumbing → Peter built a house.*

The conditions governing the use of these macrostructure operations are not yet well understood. Obviously, deletion and generalization are operations that cannot be applied indefinitely. Rumelhart (1975) has written a story grammar that addresses many of the same problems. He has classified the semantic relationships that occur in a story (AND, CAUSE, ALLOW, MOTIVE, THEN, and INITIATE) and provided a set of summarization rules for these structures. These summarization rules play the same role as the macrostructure operations above. For instance, take the relationship ALLOW, which is a weak form of causation. Rumelhart analyzed the relationship between the snake turning and killing in (26) as an instance of the ALLOW relationship:

(26) *The snake turned toward the boy and killed him.*

Three summarization rules for ALLOW are described, which, when applied successively to (26), generate the summary sentence:

(27) *The snake killed the boy.*

Rumelhart's grammar contains a total of 13 summarization rules. He has shown that actual summaries written by subjects can be rather well accounted for by judicious application of these rules.

In summary, we arrive at the following picture of text comprehension and memory. Through an analysis of the stimulus input at various levels from the physical to the linguistic to the conceptual, the reader (or listener) constructs from the text a propositional text base. Most of the propositions are directly cued by the text, but some must be inferred. These propositions are hierarchically ordered, and it is much more likely that the subject will process the more superordinate propositions than the subordinate ones. We have called this list of propositions the microstructure of the text. In addition, long texts need to be organized into higher units. A schema—that is, a set of expectations that the reader has about the structure of the text—provides him with a convenient starting point for organizing the text. The schema specifies certain text units, and the reader determines from the text what their labels are for the particular text at hand. In the case of story comprehension, the nature of the schema as well as the required macrostructure operations or summarization rules have been described. The end product of this processing—that is, the final representation of the meaning of a story in the reader's memory—consists then of the propositional microstructure, organized into larger units with macrostructure propositions as labels. The macrostructure represents the gist of the story and is reflected in the way subjects summarize the story; the macrostructure and the microstructure together form the basis for recall.

Clearly, the work reported here is highly tentative and represents only the beginning of the psychological study of the complex processes involved in text comprehension and memory. It shows, however, that such work is possible today, and indeed fruitful. It is also necessary, if cognitive psychology is to become a useful basis for the development of an educational technology. It is not sufficient to study language processing at the level of words and sentences. As was shown above, comprehending and remembering a text, and hence learning from it, introduces a set of problems that simply are not germane to lower level processes. If the material discussed above on schema use and story grammars is not totally misleading—that is, if it is confirmed by further research—it might turn out to be important. Serious educational problems in our society arise from reading difficulties. According to the National Assessment of Educational Progress (1973), many people are poor readers not because they are unable to read words or even sentences but because they are unable to learn from the texts they read. The only way to remedy this situation is to learn more about what is involved in comprehending and remembering texts, and macrostructure organization may turn out to be a crucial concept in this respect.

ACKNOWLEDGMENTS

The research from the Colorado laboratory reported here was supported by Grant MH 15873 from the National Institute of Mental Health. I thank Eileen Kintsch for helping me to prepare this report.

REFERENCES

Anderson, J. R., & Bower, G. H. *Human associative memory.* Washington, D.C.: Winston, 1973.

Baggett, P. Memory for explicit and implicit information in picture stories. *Journal of Verbal Learning and Verbal Behavior,* 1975, **14,** 538–548.

Bartlett, F. C. *Remembering.* Cambridge: University Press, 1932.

Bates, E. *Language and context: The acquisition of pragmatics.* New York: Academic Press, 1976.

Clark, H. H., & Lucy, P. Understanding what is meant from what is said: A study of conventionally conveyed postulates. *Journal of Verbal Learning and Verbal Behavior,* 1975, **14,** 56–72.

Cofer, C. N. Constructive processes in memory. *American Scientist,* 1973, **61,** 537–543.

Crothers, E. J. Paragraph structure description (Tech. Report No. 40, ISIB). University of Colorado, 1975.

Fillmore, C. J. The case for case. In E. Bach & R. T. Harms (Eds.) *Universals in linguistic theory.* New York: Holt, Rinehart, & Winston, 1968. Pp. 1–90.

Frase, L. Prose processing. In G. H. Bower (Ed.), *Psychology of learning and motivation.* Vol. 9. New York: Academic Press, 1976. Pp. 1–47.

Frederiksen, C. H. Representing logical and semantic structure of knowledge acquired from discourse. *Cognitive Psychology,* 1975, **7,** 371–457. (a)

Frederiksen, C. H. Acquisition of semantic information from discourse; Effects of repeated exposures. *Journal of Verbal Learning and Verbal Behavior,* 1975, **14,** 158–169. (b)

Gomulicki, B. R. Recall as an abstractive process. *Acta Psychologica,* 1956, **12,** 77–79.

Gordon, D., & Lakoff, G. Conversational postulates. *Papers from the seventh regional meeting of the Chicago Linguistics Society,* 1971, **7,** 63–84.

Grice, H. P. *The logic of conversation.* William James Lectures, Harvard University, 1967.

Hamilton, W. *Lectures on metaphysics and logic.* Vol. 1. Boston: Gould & Lincoln, 1859.

Harris, R. J., Teske, R. R., & Ginns, M. J. Memory for pragmatic implications from courtroom testimony. *Bulletin of the Psychonomic Society,* 1975, **6,** 494–496.

Haviland, S. E., & Clark, H. H. What's new? Acquiring new information as a process in comprehension. *Journal of Verbal Learning and Verbal Behavior*, 1974, **13**, 515-521.

Hornby, P. A. The psychological subject and predicate. *Cognitive Psychology*, 1972, **3**, 632-642.

Hornby, P. A. Surface structure and presupposition. *Journal of Verbal Learning and Verbal Behavior*, 1974, **13**, 530-538.

James, C. T., Thompson, J. G., & Baldwin, J. M. The reconstructive process in sentence memory. *Journal of Verbal Learning and Verbal Behavior*, 1973, **13**, 51-63.

Keenan, J. M., & Kintsch, W. The identification of explicitly and implicitly presented information. In W. Kintsch (Ed.), *The representation of meaning in memory*. Hillsdale, New Jersey: Lawrence Erlbaum Associates, 1974. Pp. 153-165.

Kintsch, W. Notes on the structure of semantic memory. In E. Tulving & W. Donaldson (Eds.) *Organization of memory*. New York: Academic Press, 1972. Pp. 249-308.

Kintsch, W. *The representation of meaning in memory*. Hillsdale, New Jersey: Lawrence Erlbaum Associates, 1974.

Kintsch, W. Memory for prose. In C. N. Cofer (Ed.), *The structure of memory*. San Francisco: Freeman, 1976. Pp. 90-113.

Kintsch, W., & Keenan, J. M. Reading rate and retention as a function of the number of propositions in the base structure of sentences. *Cognitive Psychology*, 1973, **5**, 257-274.

Kintsch, W., Kozminsky, E., Streby, W. J., McKoon, G., & Keenan, J. M. Comprehension and recall of text as a function of content variables. *Journal of Verbal Learning and Verbal Behavior*, 1975, **14**, 196-214.

Kintsch, W., & Turner, T. Cued and free recall of stories. In preparation.

Kintsch, W., & van Dijk, T. A. Comment on se rapelle et on résume des histoires. *Langages*, 1975, **40**, 98-116.

Kolers, P. A., & Ostry, D. J. Time course of loss of information regarding pattern analyzing operations. *Journal of Verbal Learning and Verbal Behavior*, 1974, **13**, 596-612.

Loftus, E. F., & Palmer, J. C. Reconstruction of automobile destruction: An example of the interaction between language and memory. *Journal of Verbal Learning and Verbal Behavior*, 1974, **13**, 585-589.

Manelis, L., & Yekovich, F. R. Repetition of propositional arguments in sentences. *Journal of Verbal Learning and Verbal Behavior*, 1976, **15**, 301-312.

McKoon, G., & Keenan, J. M. Response latencies to explicit and implicit statements as a function of the delay betwen reading and test. In W. Kintsch (Ed.), *The representation of meaning in memory*. Hillsdale, New Jersey: Lawrence Erlbaum Associates, 1974. Pp. 166-176.

Meyer, B. *The organization of prose and its effect on memory*. Amsterdam: North Holland Publishing Co., 1975.

Minsky, M. A framework for representing knowledge. In P. Winston (Ed.), *The psychology of computer vision*. New York: McGraw-Hill, 1975. Pp. 211-277.

National Assessment of Educational Progress. *Gleaning significant facts from passages* (Report No. 02-R-05). Washington, D.C.: U.S. Printing Office, 1973.

Norman, D. A., & Rumelhart, D. E. *Explorations in cognition*. San Francisco: Freeman, 1975.

Offir, C. E. Recognition memory for presuppositions of relative clause sentences. *Journal of Verbal Learning and Verbal Behavior*, 1973, **12**, 636-643.

Paul, I. Studies in remembering: The reproduction of connected and extended verbal material. *Psychological Issues*, 1959, **2** (Whole issue No. 1).

Riley, D. A. Memory for form. In L. Postman (Ed.), *Psychology in the making*. New York: Knopf, 1962. Pp. 402-465.

Rothkopf, E. Z. Structural text features and the control of processes in learning from written materials. In J. Carroll & R. Freedle (Eds.), *Language comprehension and the acquisition of knowledge*. Washington, D.C.: Winston, 1972. Pp. 315-336.

Rumelhart, D. E. Notes on a schema for stories. In D. G. Bobrow & A. Collins (Eds.), *Representation and understanding*. New York: Academic Press, 1975. Pp. 211-236.

Schank, R. C. Conceptual dependency: A theory of natural language understanding. *Cognitive Psychology,* 1972, **3,** 552–631.

Schank, R. C. SAM - *A story understander* (Tech. Report No. 43). Department of Computer Science, Yale University, 1975.

Searle, J. R. *Speech acts.* Cambridge: University Press, 1969.

Selz, O. *Zur Psychologie des produktiven Denkens und Irrtums.* Bonn: Cohen, 1922.

Sulin, R. A., & Dooling, D. J. Intrusion of a thematic idea in retention of prose. *Journal of Experimental Psychology,* 1974, **103,** 255–268.

Wanner, E. *On remembering, forgetting and understanding sentences.* The Hague: Mouton, 1974.

Winograd, T. Frame representations and the declarative-procedural controversy. In D. G. Bobrow & A. Collins (Eds.), *Representation and understanding.* New York: Academic Press, 1975. Pp. 185–210.

Wulff, F. Ueber die Veraenderung von Vorstellungen. *Psychologische Forschung,* 1922, **1,** 333–373.

Zangwill, O. L. Remembering revisited. *Quarterly Journal of Experimental Psychology,* 1972, **24,** 123–138.

3

Coding Processes in Memory

Neal F. Johnson

The Ohio State University

A rather substantial portion of contemporary cognitive psychology can trace its evolution back to the then-exciting breakthrough into the higher mental processes provided by Ebbinghaus in the late 1800s (Ebbinghaus, 1885). While the decades that have intervened have frequently been dominated by noncognitive and mechanistic constructions of the issues (Hull, 1952; Thorndike, 1932; Watson, 1919), and on occasion there have been digressions into peripheral concerns (Maier & Seligman, 1976), there has been a generally steadfast commitment to Ebbinghaus's original definition of the direction psychology should take in answering these questions (Kausler, 1974). Although this direction was determined to a large extent by the influence of the British Associationists, and the type of naive associationism that eventually evolved was primarily the product of later generations, it was Ebbinghaus who set the original course.

The major area in which this Ebbinghaus influence had an impact was learning and memory, but it also has been evident to a lesser degree in psycholinguistics and human performance. Even some of the more cognitive extensions of associationism apparent in the late 1950s and early 1960s (for example, Horton & Kjeldergaard, 1961) quite clearly fell within the older tradition, although they did represent exciting extensions into new domains. It has only been within the past few years, with the rapid development of information-processing models that we have seen the first break with the Ebbinghaus tradition.

While this long-lasting impact of Ebbinghaus represents an impressive testimonial to his role in defining critical issues, as well as the utility of his analytical system, his major thrust did seem to be toward defining the psyche in terms of "what leads to what." Unfortunately, this legacy has had a rather constraining influence on psychology, and many of the conceptual problems that emerged in the 1960s can be traced to the fact that new issues emerged that went beyond the Ebbinghaus tradition. Issues such as organizational processes in memory and the development of memory codes could not even be construed within the framework of the two-place antecedent–consequent relationship that was the hallmark of Ebbinghaus's associationism.

I. ASSOCIATIONISM

It is tempting to treat associationism as if it were a well-formalized theory that can be tested easily relative to alternative formulations. Unfortunately, not only is that not the case, but it is not even clear that it is a theory. The concept has been tied very closely to what has been termed stimulus–response (S–R) psychology and, as such, it may carry more in the way of methodological commitments than it does theoretical content. Furthermore, the diversity of specific views that have fallen under this umbrella makes it difficult to abstract any single core of assumptions that are common to all. Postman (1968) has provided a description of this variety of views, and they appear to differ from one another about as much as they differ from some of the newer nonassociative views of learning. The result of this diversity is that on occasion data that have been interpreted as being inconsistent with associative views of learning, in reality are only inconsistent with one particular associative view (for example, Greeno, 1970).

Another problem with traditional associative views is that, with a few exceptions (for example, Hull, 1952), there seemed to be a marked resistance to formalizing the positions. Most of the positions were stated vaguely and imprecisely, and they frequently contained so many components that they could explain almost any experimental outcome, regardless of its direction. As such, associationism was more a set of guiding attitudes than a specific theoretical position, and while it may have been useful to the investigator, the position could not be opened to empirical examination.

For these reasons, then, any attempt to define associationism may be questionable, but there do seem to be at least a few components common to many constructions of associative learning. One of these common components, and the one to be examined here, is the commitment to a direct two-place antecedent–consequent relationship as the elementary building block of learning. Association theories from Ebbinghaus (1885) to Hull (1952) were characterized by the explicit or implicit assumption that it is possible to analyze any and all learning states into simple compounds of these two-place relationships, the relationship being a direct connection between the two items, with the items being independently and objectively specified. The question, then, becomes one of determining whether a construct with this definition can account for the domain of data it was designed to handle.

A.   The Forerunners of Doom

Although Gestalt psychology had some impact on early associationism (Tolman, 1932), the influence was quite small, and the theoretical–empirical controversies appeared to focus on details of interpretation rather than on the metatheoretical foundations of the positions. In fact, by the early 1950s, the positions of Tolman and Hull had accommodated one another to the point that it is unlikely there were any remaining formal distinctions between the positions, and the major differences seemed to be in the preferred language of description.

It is also true that there was no great urgency to overthrow naive associationism at that time. Most of the empirical issues being examined could be handled quite nicely under the framework of that position; and as an explanatory mechanism, the concept of an associative link was both parsimonious and elegant. It was a very simple retrieval device; it had convenient and easily understood analogues (that is, the reflex arc and the telephone switchboard); and the mechanism could account for both order and item information. Given these considerations, it is not surprising that new theoretical positions encountered a great deal of resistance.

The primary points of difficulty for naive associationism developed with the increasing analytic capacity provided by the evolution of new conceptual and technical tools. In addition, these difficulties for the traditional view did not seem to arise in exotic new areas of empirical and theoretical endeavor, but rather in the context of the cluster of very simple phenomena that the view was originally devised to explain.

B. Stimulus and Response Learning

While it might be argued that naive associationism was able to account for the way subjects acquire antecedent–consequent relationships in a paired-associate (PA) learning task, there have been some questions on this point (Greeno, 1970; E. Martin, 1971). The issue has focused on the assumption that the antecedent and consequent (stimulus and response) should each have an independent representation in memory along with the association, and there does appear to be some ambiguity as to whether that is the case. That point notwithstanding, however, the concept of an item-to-item link does not seem to provide a very adequate account of either stimulus or response learning within the PA task.

Regarding the stimulus, the major problem has stemmed from the fact that while lists that have highly integrated stimuli (for example, pronounceable nonsense syllables or English words) are learned more rapidly than lists with poorly integrated stimuli (for example, a string of consonants), the nature of the integration process is not at all clear. For example, Postman and Greenbloom (1967) have demonstrated that subjects treat highly integrated stimuli as if they were single units; if just a component of such a stimulus is presented, the subjects' ability to produce the associated response seems to be dependent upon their ability to also recall the other stimulus components. That dependency does not appear, however, if the stimulus is an unintegrated array such as three consonants. On the other hand, the work of Greeno and Horowitz (1968) suggests that the type of learning experience resulting in high degrees of response integration does not result in unitization if the item being learned is to function as a stimulus. In Greeno and Horowitz's experiment, the subjects prelearned the stimuli by either experiencing them as PA responses, or they learned to fill in omitted letters from an array when only some of the letters were presented. Regardless of the type of stimulus pretraining, subsequent performance on a PA task that used these items as stimuli was inferior to a condition that involved no pretraining.

In contrast, Schulz and Martin (1964) have demonstrated that providing subjects with an opportunity to prelearn unintegrated response terms in a free-recall task results in a marked improvement in later learning performance, as compared to providing the same prelearning experience for already integrated responses. However, when the experimental items were to serve as stimuli, prior learning again did not result in a differential facilitation of the previously unintegrated items. As a set, then, these studies would indicate that some type of unitization of a stimulus complex does facilitate learning, but the unitization is somewhat different from that which occurs on the response side, and it does not seem to develop from the formation of simple interitem associations. At least, the conditions that would allow for the formation of such associations seem to have little effect if the item is to function as a stimulus.

There are similar problems with an associative interpretation of response learning. This difficulty was brought out quite clearly in a series of experiments described by Underwood and Schulz (1960). They reported that measures of response integration that take all the components of a response into consideration simultaneously (for example, judgment measures such as association value or ease of pronouncing) result in far better predictions of learning performance than do measures of letter-to-letter associations within the item. In fact, there appears to be little or no relationship between rate of learning and strength of interitem associations within a PA response, and the value of a measure of response integration seems to depend directly upon whether it can assess N-place relationships (where $N > 2$). Furthermore, the fact that these effects become even more pronounced as difficulty increases would seem to be singularly damaging to any view of response learning based on interitem association in that such associations should become increasingly important with increasing response difficulty. It would appear, then, that it is not easy to reduce the knowledge gained during response learning to a set of direct two-place antecedent–consequent relationships, and some alternative construction seems to be necessary.

II. ORGANIZATIONAL PROCESSES IN MEMORY

Although the above issues did not seem to yield important theoretical consequences when they were first reported, the emerging work on organization and memory did have such an immediate effect. In fact, much of that research seemed to be motivated by a direct attack on traditional associationism, and the research was more theoretically oriented than aimed at the empirical mapping of a domain of knowledge. Ironically, as will be noted below, much of the organization research turned out to be far less damaging to interitem association theories than were the problems with S–R learning, and yet it had a considerably greater influence in the development of alternative accounts of learning and memory.

There have been at least two views of the way organization might influence learning and memory, and the distinctions between these views reflect many of the distinctions between associative and nonassociative constructions of learning and knowledge. The first view might be termed "a linear or horizontal conception of organization" and, following the influence of information theory, redundancy is its major construct. Highly organized item sets are those that contain a great deal of contextual constraint, and it is the degree of constraint that defines the organization.

This point can be illustrated by a task in which subjects are presented with either a passage of connected discourse or a passage of equal length that consists of random words. The difference in contextual constraint can be demonstrated by omitting several of the words of each passage and asking subjects to guess the specific words that have been removed. They do considerably better if the passage consists of connected discourse, and the degree of the advantage over some estimate of chance guessing can be used as a measure of the contextual constraint or organization.

The elegance of this conception of organization stems from both the fact that it contains a direct measure of organization (redundancy or reduction in uncertainty), and that it can be construed in terms of the type of two-place antecedent–consequent relationship that can explain the learning and retention of both item and order information.

An alternative view of organization is based on the concept of hierarchical encoding, and its primary emphasis is on the pattern of relationships that exist among items in an organized set rather than on the degree of constraint. For example, if a sequence of words such as *lion, cat, dog, wolf, eagle,* and *falcon* were presented in a free-recall experiment, the linear view would describe the resulting memorial organization in terms of the strength and pattern of interitem associations, while the hierarchical encoding view would describe the organization in terms of the pattern of superordinate categories represented by the items. That is, *lion* and *cat* would be put together as the higher order unit of *felines, dog* and *wolf* as *canines,* and *eagle* and *falcon* as *birds.* At the next level in the hierarchy, *feline* and *canine* would be put together as the superordinate category *mammal;* and at the next level *mammal* could be combined with *bird* to form the highest order category *animal.* Within this characterization of the organization, the items *lion* and *cat* would have a close relationship, as would *dog* and *wolf,* while *cat* and *dog* would not. On the other hand, a linear or contextual constraint view would probably indicate a closer relationship between *cat* and *dog* than between the other two item pairs, reflecting what is probably a stronger interitem association.

In general, then, the linear view would consider a good organization as one with strong preexisting relations among the items, but the hierarchical view would consider a good organization as one in which the relationships were well defined, regardless of their preexperimental strength. In terms of linear sequences of letters, the hierarchical view would see little difference in organization between SBJ FQL ZNG and GEX FUD MOF, because the spaces offer a clear definition of the relationships, and the contextual constraint from the pronounceable sequence's orthographic regularity would add little. On the other hand, the linear view would see SBJ FQL ZNG and SBJFQLZNG as being similarly organized (or unorganized) because the spaces would not modify the contextual constraints (or lack thereof). One way these views differ, then, is whether they emphasize a qualitative or a quantitative description of organizational relationships.

A second, and possibly more important way these positions differ is in terms of whether they view the structure that emerges from an organization as being horizontal (associative) or vertical (hierarchical). A horizontal structure assumes direct interitem relationships among items within a set, and the resulting behavior patterns are viewed as an immediate reflection of these direct relationships. A hierarchical conception of structure, on the other hand, would argue that there are never any direct relationships among items in an organized set, and that all relationships emerge from the fact that items share common coded representations in memory. It is assumed that items are represented in memory by higher order codes, and the relationship between any pair of items is defined in terms of their common pattern of encoding. Therefore, the relationship between two or more items can never be direct, and it arises from a common representation rather than an antecedent–consequent (eliciting?) relationship. The implications of this point will be described in somewhat greater detail below.

A. Organization and Learning

In 1953 Bousfield reported a study that at first appeared to be little more than an empirical exploration of issues raised by a study reported much earlier (Bousfield & Sedgewick, 1944). However, he did demonstrate the rather curious phenomenon that if subjects are asked to recall a presented list of words, and they can do so in any order they choose, there are very gross differences between the order of input and the order of recall. The specific task he used involved a word list that contained several instances of each of several categories (for example, birds or items of furniture), and while the words are presented in random order, the subjects showed a marked tendency to recall the items in category clusters. This grouping effect, and the tendency of the output to have characteristics not present in the input, have been taken as indices of organizational processes in memory.

Most of the measures of subjects' tendency to organize during learning are based on the assumption that materials that are organized together will be recalled both adjacently and in an all-or-none manner. Given that one point of commonality, however, there seems to be a great deal of diversity in the specific nature of the measure, depending upon the specific task. For example, in the case of the free recall of categorized lists, the measure is the tendency to recall the list in category clusters (Bousfield, 1953), while with uncategorized lists the measure is the tendency to recall the list in the same order from trial-to-trial (Tulving, 1962). With serial lists, where order of recall is important, the measure of organization has varied from a correlation between an expected and an obtained pattern of transitional-error probabilities (Johnson,1972a) to the use of various relative error rates for items in the sequence (Fritzen & Johnson, 1969; Martin & Noreen, 1974).

In spite of this wide variation in both the nature of the learning task and the measure of organization, there has been a surprising consistency in the correlation between learning rate and measures of organization. Although all the measures of organization are logically independent of learning rate, the obtained correlations generally fall between .70 and 1.00 and that seems to be the case regardless of whether the sampling units are materials, trials, or subjects.

B. Altered Organization

Another approach to the relationship between organization and learning is the part-to-whole free-recall studies that involve having subjects acquire two free-recall lists, with the second list consisting of all the items in the first list, plus an equal number of new items (Tulving, 1966). If learning these lists involved only the formation of interitem associations, the order in which the common items are recalled should be the same for the two lists, and there would be every reason to expect positive transfer from the first item to the second. That is, one-half of the required interitem associations for the second list already would have been established, and the subjects would have to learn only half as much as subjects who may have had some irrelevant prior-learning task. Unfortunately, the data do not support these expectations, and if the first list is a random selection of items from the final list, there actually appears to be evidence of negative transfer.

One interpretation of these results is that subjects acquire a hierarchical organizational net or structure that can be used for retrieving the words. In that such a structure can be viewed as being both the way in which the items are stored in memory and the mechanism used for generation of the items at the time of recall, it is clear that the structure of organization must be viewed as a critical component of the response itself. If that is the case, the above failure to obtain positive transfer can be explained by noting that the optimally efficient structure for some randomly selected subset of words is unlikely to be the same structure as would be adopted if those items were included within a larger set. Given that the organizations for the two lists would be different, interference would be expected and the net effect should be negative transfer during second-list learning.

This interpretation of the data is further supported by the fact that the negative-transfer effects do not occur if the first-list organization can be used during second-list learning. For example, if the second list consists of instances of several logical categories, and the first list consists of all the instances of half those categories, then there does appear to be marked positive transfer (Birnbaum, 1968, 1969). In addition, there even appears to be positive transfer when the first-list categories appear on the second list, but there is no overlap in specific instances (DeRosa, Doane, & Russell, 1970). This result is particularly damaging to an associative view of learning, because it appears to represent the very condition under which the associative view would have to predict negative transfer (that is, two lists with different items).

A final point is that while DeRosa *et al.* (1970) obtained positive transfer when the two lists had the same categories but different items, Shuell (1968) has shown that these conditions do yield retroactive interference when subjects attempt to recall the first list. The problem this result poses for an associative view is that with interitem association as its only learning construct, it cannot explain how the interaction between two such lists could yield both facilitation through transfer and interference at the time of first-list recall. An organizational view of learning, on the other hand, simply assumes that while the first-list items may be lost during the transfer task, the organization of the list can be retained and used. Furthermore, Shuell has reported data indicating that such retention of the first-list organization does appear to be the case, even when there is a loss of the first-list items.

In general, then, if the first-list experience allows the learner to acquire some information regarding the organization and structure of the second list, then positive transfer will be obtained even when no specific interitem associations could be involved. In fact, the data would suggest that the critical condition for positive transfer in all these situations is the commonality of structure, and any similarity or commonality in overt responses may be irrelevant.

Two rather extreme tests of this hypothesis have been reported by Bower and Winzenz (1969) and Johnson and Migdoll (1971). In the above free-recall experiments, there was always some change in the nature of the response from the first list to the second. At the very minimum, the response was changed by adding items to it, and it might be possible to explain the failures to obtain positive transfer by assuming some unknown disruption of interitem associations coming from the new items. Bower and Winzenz (1969), on the other hand, did not change the overt response. The subjects were presented with a series of letter sequences that were read with a particular rhythm, and they were to recall each sequence immediately after presentation. One particular sequence appeared as every other item in the series of sequences, and for one group of subjects the rhythm in which the sequence was read was changed for each presentation, while the rhythm remained constant for the other subjects. The results indicated that if the rhythm remained constant, there was an improvement in recall with each succeeding occurrence of the critical repeated sequence, but there was no such improvement if the rhythm was changed. That is, even though the overt response sequence remained constant, improvement occurred only when the rhythm-induced organization also remained constant.

Johnson and Migdoll (1971) reported a similar experiment in which subjects memorized three sequences of seven letters each as responses to the digits 1, 2, and 3, and then learned another set of three sequences as responses to those digits. After learning the second list, the subjects attempted to recall both lists.

When the letters were presented for study, they were grouped either as SBJ FQLZ or as SB JFQ LZ, and all three responses for a particular list were similarly grouped. The two factors in the experiment were whether the sequences in the two lists had the same organization and whether they contained the same letters. For the case where the lists had both the same organization and the same letters, second-list learning was just a continuation of first-list learning.

Johnson and Migdoll's (1971) results indicated negative transfer for the subjects who had different organizations on the two lists, and whether the required overt responses for the two lists were identical or totally different seemed to make little difference. Furthermore, in comparison to both a rest-control condition and recall performance on the second list, subjects who used different organizations for the two lists showed significant retroactive interference when attempting to recall the first list, even though the overt responses on first and second list were identical.

If the learning of the sequences in these transfer and retroaction experiments involved the formation of direct interitem associations, and the overt response sequences were the same for the two lists, then the only possible expectation during second-list learning would be massive positive transfer, and subsequent first-list recall should evidence retroactive facilitation rather than interference. Therefore, the basic problem for a theory of interitem association created by these experiments is that a grouping-defined organization seems to be a critical component of the response, and the phenomenon does not appear to be one that can be reduced to simple two-place antecedent–consequent relationships. In fact, the Johnson and Migdoll (1971) data suggest such relationships may be irrelevant.

III. A CODING VIEW OF MEMORY

It would seem that the most straightforward way of handling these difficulties is simply to postulate the reality of N-place indirect relationships, and Miller (1956) has provided a convenient starting point with his concept of a "chunk" of information. Miller was able to demonstrate that immediate memory is not limited in terms of the amount of information it can hold, but does seem to be severely limited in terms of the number of psychological units into which that information can be divided. For example, in an immediate memory task, a subject can retain about as many words as binary digits, yet each word represents many more bits of information than does a binary digit. Similarly, the number of random letters that a subject can retain in short-term memory is quite limited, but the subjects' performance shows a marked improvement if those letters are ordered so that they form words. In fact, the subjects retain about as many words as they do single letters, which would suggest that they may reorganize the letters into words, with the number of units retained being the same regardless of whether the units are single letters or the higher-order letter clusters that form words.

The concept of a chunk, and the idea of recoding information into higher-order units, has been applied to a wide variety of situations with a great deal of success. For example, using stimulus characteristics as the basis of the definition, chunks have been identified with item sets that: (a) form semantic groups, (b) are rehearsed together, (c) are generated by a single rule, (d) lie between some physical marker such as slashes or spaces, or (e) fall within a rhythm pattern during reading. In terms of response characteristics, chunks have been identified with item sets that: (a) cluster in free recall, (b) fall between hesitations, (c) fall within rhythm patterns at recall, (d) fall between points of high error rate, (e) are sorted together, or (f) have high sequential redundancy. However, regardless of whether the chunks are defined in terms of stimulus or response characteristics, or which particular definition is selected, the same orderly relationships between chunking and performance seem to be obtained. That is, performance seems to be a function of both the extent and reliability of a subject's chunking behavior, as well as the number of chunks into which the material is divided. Given these considerations, it is clear that the value and utility of this concept not only comes from the fact that it can accommodate N-place indirect relationships (that is, chunks larger than two items), but there appears to be some empirical base for the general characteristics of the concept.

A. The Nature of Codes and the Representation of Information

Although Miller (1956) provided an exciting concept that fit quite closely with our intuitions regarding how we store and retrieve information, the diversity of the definitions and procedures that followed suggested that some type of formalization might be appropriate. The source of greatest difficulty and ambiguity was the variation in whether the concept was defined in terms of stimulus or response characteristics. With a question such as this left unresolved, the usefulness of the concept suffers a definite limitation.

It would seem desirable, then, to impose some standardization on the definition, and the most convenient way of doing so would appear to be within the context of a general theory of memorial encoding. That is, with a general theory as a base, it would be possible to derive a variety of operational definitions depending upon the task and context in which they were to be used, yet there would be a commonality among the definitions that would allow intertask generalizations.

A necessary preliminary to such a theoretical endeavor is a broad general characterization of the class of phenomena to be covered and, in the present case, the issue seems to resolve to one of abstracting some commonality from the set of stimulus- and response-based definitions described earlier. The abstraction is facilitated by noting that even in the case of stimulus-based definitions, it is their implications regarding subsequent response characteristics that ties them together. Furthermore, it should always be possible to apply a response-based definition, even when the chunks are defined in terms of stimulus characteristics, but the reverse may not be the case.

With these considerations in mind, then, a reasonable candidate for the initial general characterization of a chunk is that it should be defined in terms of response characteristics, and the major response characteristic used by previous investigators is that the items within a chunk have a certain internal integrity that interlocks their fates in a subject's performance. That is, the previous definitions seem to assume that anything influencing the memorial representation of some specific item will also influence any other item within the same chunk. Furthermore, that interdependency also seems to agree with our general intuition regarding the nature of *units* and how they should be reflected in our behavior.

With that as a starting point, the next step is to provide the rough outline of a mechanism that can be used to account for the type of interdependency that is both implied by these definitions and apparent in the data. The simplest mechanism, and the one that seems to have the greatest predictive power, is the assumption that the interdependency arises from the fact that all the information in a chunk has a common memorial representation. That is, some single code is assumed to represent all the information in the chunk, and it is clear that if a set of items are commonly represented in memory, they should be produced both adjacently and on the same response attempt more often than a similar set that is not commonly represented.

1. Functional Properties of Codes

While the primary theoretical property of codes is that they are unitary in the sense that a code is either retrieved or not retrieved, there are a number of other functional properties that codes must have in order to account for the various chunking phenomena that have been demonstrated. One important property is the necessity to maintain a distinction between codes and the information they represent. For example, Cohen (1966) has demonstrated that in the free recall of categorized lists, there are variables that will influence the number of categories a subject can recall (for example, presentation rate), but do not influence the number of words produced from each recalled category. Similarly, Shuell (1968) has demonstrated that one can interfere with a subject's memory for item information from a code and leave his ability to recall the code itself more or less unaffected. Finally, the DeRosa *et al.* (1970) study described above indicated that teaching subjects the nature of the relevant codes facilitated subsequent learning, even when the items in the chunks were not the same in the two tasks.

A second functional property of memory codes is that they appear to function as if they were opaque containers. That would be implied by the assumption that codes are unitary, because if they are unitary there could be no one–to–one correspondence between an aspect of a code and the items of information within the chunk it represents. Given that assumption, having a chunk's code immediately available does not necessarily mean that the information it represents also is immediately available. The information within a code would become available only after it had been decoded, and while the information was in the coded state, it should not be in a form that could be used for making decisions.

A third functional property of codes is that they need to represent all of the information within the chunk, including the order of the information. If the code is the only location for the storage of the chunk's information, then the chunk can have neither item nor order information that is not represented by the code.

The final functional property of codes is that the information they represent can be either individual response items or other codes. For example, if a free-recall list consisted of the items *flower, tree, grass, bear, lion, dog, table, chair* and *lamp,* it would be possible to recode the individual response items into *plants, animals,* and *furniture.* However, it also would be possible to recode the *plants* and *animals* into a higher order code called *living things,* with the list then being retained as *living things plus furniture.*

2. Substantive Properties of Codes

If codes and their contents are assumed to be independent, and codes are viewed as representations of information rather than just an amalgam of the information itself, then codes also should have substantive properties that are independent of the content. Unfortunately, we know very little regarding how codes represent information, other than the fact that it does not appear possible for there to be any one–to–one correspondence between the contents of the chunk and aspects of the code.

One of the most common views of codes is that they are generative routines that can be used for producing the contents of the chunk at the time of recall. That view would allow for the distinction between contents and codes in the same sense that there is a distinction between a cake and the recipe used for making it. In addition, it also can account for the assumption that there are no direct relationships between the items within a chunk, because items would only be related to the generative mechanism and not to one another. That is, an item's immediate antecedent would be a generative step made by the mechanism, rather than the preceding item in the set. Finally, this view can account for the opacity of codes, because having a generative mechanism available does not imply having any immediate knowledge regarding what the mechanism can produce.

Related to this generative view of codes is a potential distinction between two types of codes. While the distinction is not clear, and the data are only suggestive, there may be a certain difference between the codes for chunks that are rule generated and those that are not. This point can be illustrated by pilot data indicating that if subjects attempt to learn a trigram chunk that does not conform to the orthographic structure of English, the resulting unit is inflexible in the sense that it cannot be modified. For example, if they learn SBJ, then are subsequently asked to learn SXJ, they seem unable just to replace the B in the already-learned chunk with the X in the new one. This is evident by the fact that it takes about as long to learn SXJ after learning SBJ as it does to learn an item that shares no letters with the first item. Further, when subjects try to recall the first chunk, the retroactive interference affects the changed and unchanged letters about equally. (These studies will be described in somewhat more detail in Section III.C.1.) Furthermore, the inflexibility seems to be independent of the degree of learning. On the other hand, if the chunk does conform to the orthographic structure of English (for example, GEX), there is an initial inflexibility with a low degree of learning, but it rapidly disappears as learning progresses.

The terms *integrative code* and *representative code* might be used to express the distinction between the codes for rule and nonrule chunks, but the extent to which the distinction is psychologically real remains to be seen. However, it should be noted that the following discussion of response coding will deal exclusively with representative codes. Later the two types of codes will be compared during the discussion of perceptual coding.

A final point concerns the nature of the order information represented by a code and that issue is closely tied to the question of chunk size. While chunks theoretically can be of any size, there is substantial evidence that chunks of about size three are optimum when the task requires ordered recall (Johnson, 1970). There appears to be a very marked deterioration in performance when chunks of size four are used, and chunks of five seem to be beyond the capacity of most subjects. However, the processing limits implied by these observations seem to be confined to those involved with handling order information, for in free-recall tasks, where order is irrelevant, subjects can use chunks that are considerably larger than three. It appears, then, that the system used for representing ordinal position is not only finite, but is severely limited and might be confined to something as simple as *initial–medial–terminal*.

A related point is the apparent need for order and item information to be independently represented within a code. Subjects can retain order (position) information while losing content information, and vica versa, and one suggestion has been that order may be stored as a tag on a content code (Johnson, 1970). On the other hand, if the codes are not order tagged, the subjects can recall them in any order they please. While this point will be expanded below, it should be noted that this assumed independent representation of content and order is a critical distinction between coding and associative views of learning.

B. Coding and Organization

As noted earlier, a coding view of organization entails a hierarchical conception of structure, and the organization can be defined in terms of the hierarchical encoding. For example, a sequence of letters such as SBJFQ would have only one acceptable order of output (that is, the one given), but the encoding pattern or organization used to represent that ordered set in memory could take a variety of forms. One way to organize the sequence would be to have S and B represented by one code; J, F, and Q by a second code; with those two codes then being represented by a yet higher order code that represents the entire sequence. Another possibility might be to represent S, B, and J by the first lower order code and F and Q by the second. A somewhat more complicated structure would be to represent S and B by one lower order code, F and Q by another, and then use a higher order code to represent J together with the code for FQ, with the highest order code providing an integrated representation of the SB code and the J(FQ) code.

By using the coding pattern as the definition of organization, it becomes possible to provide both a quantitative and qualitative description of the relationship between two or more items in a set or sequence. That is, the relationship between the items can be defined as their pattern of common encoding, and the degree and kind of their relationship may be expressed in terms of the amount or level of common encoding.

This point can be illustrated by noting that the major impact of the above changes in organization of adjacent items was in the relationship between J and its neighbors. For example, J was closely related to B in the second organization, but not in the first. Similarly, J and F were quite closely related in the first organization, very distantly related in the second organization, with an intermediate relationship in the third organization. These organizational changes are also reflected in the nonadjacent relationships. For example, J and Q have a relationship that is similar to that of J and F, while the B and F relationship would be the same in the first two organizations, but different and somewhat less in the third. It would seem possible, then, to provide an approximation to an ordinal scale of the organizational relationships between items within a set, and regardless of the basis of the relationship, the scale should be a rough index of interdependency among the items.

The fact that these relationships can be interpreted as interdependencies among the items makes it possible to operationalize this construction of organization on the basis of the conditional probabilities of events in a subject's performance. That is, the closer a relationship, the greater is the likelihood that the items would cooccur in a subject's behavior, and, if allowed by the nature of the task, they also should occur adjacently. Furthermore, the computation of the probabilities is quite straightforward, and the match between expected and obtained patterns of such probabilities can be quite close (Johnson, 1969a). It would appear, then, that this view of organization is both theoretically and empirically fruitful.

C.   Some Empirical Explorations of Coding and Organization in Memory

Much of the early data on coding in learning and memory involved assessing the assumed interdependencies using transitional-error probabilities. For any item-to-item transition within an ordered sequence, the transitional-error probability (TEP) is the likelihood that a subject will make an error on the item following a transition, given that the item immediately preceding the transition was correct. In that the likelihood of cooccurrence of two items represented by the same code should be greater than the cooccurrence of two items from different codes, the TEP between the last item from one chunk and the first item of the next should be greater than the TEPs between items from the same chunk.

This point can be illustrated by an experiment in which subjects learned letter sequences that they were induced to chunk in a particular manner by having spaces left between certain letters (Johnson, 1970). When the sequences were grouped as SBJ FQLZ, the resulting TEP pattern was .10, .11, .31,* .21, .19, and .19. When they were grouped as SB JFQ LZ, the TEP pattern was .07, .30,* .17, .15, .28,* and .05. Quite clearly, the letter–to–letter transitions that reflected code transitions (asterisks) had considerably higher TEPs than did transitions between items that were represented by the same code.

1.   Item Information

The concept of codes being unitary generative mechanisms that are opaque and logically distinct from the information they represent was examined in a series of experiments in which subjects learned physically grouped sequences of letters followed by a second interfering task (Johnson, 1970). They were then asked to reproduce the first set of sequences. In the basic task subjects learned two sequences of letters, such as SBJ FQL ZNG and KTC DMW VHP, and when a sequence was presented for study it contained spaces at certain points in order to induce the subjects to group it in a particular manner. Each sequence was paired with a digit, such as 1 and 2, and the digit was used to signal the subjects as to which sequence they should recall at the time of test. The interfering task involved learning another such pair of sequences, and except for a letter in one or two chunks, they were identical to the first-task sequences. For example, the second-task sequence matching the first sequence above might be SXJ FQL ZNG. The subjects would then attempt to recall the first pair of sequences.

If subjects do attempt to learn the task by using interitem associations, the X in the above example should result in interference when subjects attempt to recall B in the first list, but in that the B is the antecedent for the following items, they should be forgotten as well. The prediction, then, is that the S should be remembered, but B, J, F, Q, L, Z, N, and G should be forgotten at about equal degrees.

The expectation from a coding view is somewhat more complex. If codes are independent of the information they represent, then there would be no reason to expect that any similarity in the contents of two chunks would be reflected in a matching similarity between their codes. In addition, if the code is opaque there would be no way of noting the similarity in content between two chunks while the information was in the coded state. Furthermore, if the code is a unitary generative mechanism, it will produce just those items in the chunk it represents, and a chunk that is different in any way should require an entirely different mechanism.

Given these considerations, if a letter in a chunk is changed, then it is necessary to establish a new chunk using a new code. However, if a new code is learned there should be retroactive interference when subjects attempt to recall the first code, and if the first code becomes unavailable, then all the information it represents also becomes unavailable. That is, not only should the subjects forget the changed letter, but they should show an almost equal loss of the unchanged letters from the chunk. On the other hand, in that items are related to their codes and not to one another, and their necessary antecedent is the code and not the preceding item, there should be no chaining effect. If some chunk is not changed from the first list to the second, there would be no need for a new code and there should be no loss for that chunk, even though some other code from that sequence might be lost. Therefore, the coding view would predict no loss for an unchanged chunk, but both the changed and unchanged letters from a changed chunk should be forgotten.

The results of several related experiments support these expectations from a coding view of learning (Johnson, 1969b, 1970). In addition, if a middle letter from a chunk is changed, the loss of the last letter is no greater than for the first letter, which would suggest no chaining effect. That also seems to hold true at the level of chunks. If the code for the middle chunk in a sequence is lost, there appears to be no greater loss of the last chunk than of the first.

Finally, one of the strongest arguments from a coding view is that there should be no relationship between these forgetting effects and the magnitude of the difference between the two versions of the changed chunk. That is, the effect is assumed to result from the loss of the code (measured by the recall of the unchanged letters in the changed chunk), and any change in the chunk would require a complete change in the code. Therefore, whether one, two, or three letters are changed in a four-letter chunk should have no influence on the recall of the unchanged letters, and that expectation does appear to be confirmed (Johnson, 1970).

As a set, these experiments seem to provide a strong base for arguing that codes are unitary generative mechanisms that are opaque and independent of the information they represent. Furthermore, they provide an unambiguous demonstration of both the internal integrity of chunks, and the view that intrachunk relationships go beyond simple two-place antecedent–consequent relationships.

2. Order Information

The above technique of examining chunk loss in retroactive-inhibition experiments also has been used for studying the nature of order information. The major issue of concern is the assumption that order information must be represented by the code, and that it must be represented independently of the content information. An additional point, however, is that it has been argued that the learning of an organized set or sequence involves learning the position of an item within the organizational net. In the present task that would reduce to learning the sequence, chunk, and intrachunk position of each item, and the issue is whether that is the case and, if so, whether those pieces of order information have separate and independent representations or are a single integrated representation.

The task described above was changed slightly to include a series of memory tests subsequent to second-list learning (Johnson, 1970). After the standard recall task, the subjects were given 18 small cards with one letter from the two sequences on each card. They were to separate them into the nine that were in each sequence, and then order the items within the sequences. This task precluded omissions and extra-list intrusions. The experimenter then took the cards and sorted them into the correct group of 9 for each sequence, and the subjects were to order the items in each sequence. This task precluded intersequence errors. Finally, the experimenter divided each set of 9 letters into the correct 3 groups of 3 letters each for each sequence, and the subjects' task was to put the 3 letters within each group into their proper order and then place the groups into their proper intrasequence position. In this task the subjects could not make either intersequence or interchunk errors, but they could make errors by putting a chunk in its wrong intrasequence position or improperly ordering the letters within a chunk. Across the series of recall tasks, then, the subjects were given increasing amounts of order information, but their performance should have improved only on a task providing specific information that was lost during the interfering task and that should provide a way to determine the exact nature and extent of the loss incurred.

A collection of experiments has been conducted using the procedures of (*a*) replacing letters within chunks, as in the above experiment; (*b*) interchanging the positions of letters within the same chunk; (*c*) interchanging the positions of letters in different chunks that have the same intrachunk position; (*d*) interchanging the positions of letters that have the same chunk and intrachunk positions, but come from different sequences; and (*e*) making the above order changes (*b*, *c*, and *d*) in combinations of two and three (Johnson, 1970).

A summary of the results is that if the second task involved replacing letters, the subjects' performance increased regardless of which of the three scoring comparisons was used; but when order changes were made, the improvement depended upon the task. The loss or retention of sequence information was assessed by noting any improvement in performance from the task with one stack of 18 to the task involving two stacks of 9 in which they were provided with the sequence information. The results indicated that an improvement in performance did occur at that point, but only if the subject was in a condition in which an item had changed sequence from the first task to the second, and the improvement was confined to the change chunk. In addition, the improvement was not influenced by whether some other piece of order information also had been changed (for example, both the sequence of the item and chunk had been changed from the first task to the second).

Retention of chunk information was assessed by comparing a rigid scoring procedure for the final task with one that scored an item correct if it was in its proper intrachunk position, regardless of whether the chunk was properly placed. That is, if the subject retained the chunk-level information for a letter, eliminating the penalty for not recalling that information would not result in an improved score. The results also supported that expectation. If the chunk an item was in was changed from the first list to the second, this scoring procedure resulted in an improvement in score, but the improvement did not occur when this specific position change was not made. Again, the effect seemed to be limited to the changed chunk and was not influenced by whether some other piece of order information also was changed.

Finally, intrachunk-order information was assessed by using a scoring procedure that counted an item as correct if its chunk was properly placed, regardless of the intrachunk position in which it was placed. Again, if subjects had not forgotten intrachunk order, a scoring procedure that did not penalize them for failure to recall that information should not result in an improved score. Again, the results indicated a very specific impact of order changes. An improvement in score occurred only if the subjects had experienced an intrachunk position change for an item, and again the effect was limited to the change chunk and not influenced by any other concomitant changes.

The fact that there was an almost complete loss of all information when an item was replaced, but a very specific loss when order was changed, would argue that the order information is stored with the content, but is independent of it. That is, the order information must be stored with the item if the conditions that result in item loss also result in the loss of all the order information. However, if it is also possible to have a selective loss of specific order information, then it must be the case that not only are item and order information independent of one another, but the specific pieces of order information must be independent of one another.

In a related series of experiments, subjects were asked to memorize two sequences of nine letters with each grouped as SBJ FQL ZNG. After learning the sequences they were shown cards that had two rows of nine dashes, and a single letter appeared on one of the dashes. The subjects' task was to indicate whether the letter was in its proper position, and their reaction time was measured.

In the above example if the J was put in the fourth position (the location of F) or the eighth position (the location of N), there would be a difference in the physical distance, but both changes would involve two pieces of order information (chunk and within-chunk position). If the J was put in the second position (location of B) or in the sixth (location of L) or ninth (location of G) positions, there would be a similar variation in physical displacement, but only one piece of order information would be changed.

The results of the study indicated that the time needed to indicate that an item was improperly placed decreased with both increasing physical distance and increasing numbers of discrepant order tags. That is, both physical and organizational distance had independent influences on decision times.

One way to account for all these effects is to assume that order information is represented in the form of external tags on the codes for chunks and items. A chunk-level code would have an external tag indicating the intrasequence position of the chunk, and when that code was decoded the resulting item codes also would have external tags that would represent their positional information. In that codes are assumed to be opaque, the tags would have to be external because order decisions regarding them need to be made before they are decoded. This view can account for the above results because if a code is lost its order tags would go as well. However, with the tags being external to the code, it should be possible to lose them individually or collectively without interfering with either the other tags or the code itself, and it should be possible to make order decisions without decoding the code.

3. Structural Information

The view proposed here is that the structure of an information set or sequence is defined in terms of its pattern of encoding. An important implication of the assumption is that if the structure is known, then all of the information also should be known. That is, if the codes represent the information, and the pattern of encoding is known, then all the information also must be known.

This idea was partially supported by the Bower and Winzenz (1969) and Johnson and Migdoll (1971) studies mentioned earlier. In those experiments the information remained unchanged when subjects went from one experimental task to another, but if the pattern of encoding was changed, the subjects behaved as if there were no relationship between the two tasks.

A more direct and positive way of examining this issue is to determine whether subjects who form an organization or structure for a set of materials also learn the set. Mandler (1967) was one of the first to report such effects. Subjects were given a set of words that were typed individually on cards, and they were to sort them into groups that, from their point of view, seemed to represent some optimum organization or structure for the word set. They were never told to learn the words, but subsequent to the sorting task were asked to recall as many of the words as possible. Their recall performance was about the same as that of a group of subjects who had the same amount of experience, but had been initially instructed to memorize the words, and they were both superior to subjects that had just put the words into groups without trying to organize or memorize them. It would appear, then, that the instruction to organize was about as effective as the instruction to memorize in terms of inducing subjects to establish a memorial representation of the word list.

An even more direct approach to the issue was used by J. R. Martin (1972). In his experiment he employed a procedure first reported by Keeney (1969). Subjects were presented with a sequence of letters, and they were to learn a set of permutations for the sequence, and the possible permutations defined a hierarchical structure for the sequence. A sequence would be presented with a digit immediately below it, and the subject was to read the sequence in the permutation appropriate for that digit. On the study trial the subject would again see that display, but the appropriate permutation would appear below the digit. For example, if the base sequence was SBJFQ, the digits and their permutations might be (a) 1 - JFQSB, (b) 2 - SBFQJ, (c) 3 - BSJFQ, and (d) 4 - SBJQF. The first permutation identifies SB and JFQ as chunks, and the second permutation indicates that the JFQ code can be decoded into J and FQ. The other two permutations just indicate that the components of the two-letter chunks are the individual letters.

The interesting thing to note about this task is that the subjects can learn the pattern of encoding of the base sequence by learning the pattern of permissible permutations. However, the task never demands that they learn the base sequence itself, because it is presented on every trial, and all the subjects need to do is read the letters in the order appropriate for that permutation cue.

J. R. Martin (1972) compared this standard condition and one in which the digit, but not the base sequence, was presented on a cue trial. Instead of just reading the sequence with the appropriate permutation, it would be necessary for the subject to first recall the base sequence and then read the permutations from memory. While the memory demand in this second task would appear to be considerably greater than in the first task, the organizational view of learning suggests that there should be no difference between them. That is, if subjects learn the organization of the sequence, then they learn the sequence, and the memory demand in the second condition would just involve something they do anyway.

The results of the study indicated that not only did the subjects in the two conditions show equal ability to recall the base sequence after learning the permutations, but the rate at which they learned their permutation sets also was about the same. If they were required to learn the organization for a sequence, requiring them also to learn the sequence seemed to place no additional demand on them, and a reasonable conclusion is that learning the organization entailed learning the organized information.

Another aspect of this coding-as-organization view of learning was examined by Marmurek (1972), who also used a technique based on Keeney's (1969) procedure. If the learning of an item involves learning the item's position within an organizational network, then anything that disrupts a subject's ability to learn a unique organizational position for an item also should seriously disrupt his ability to learn the item set. The type of structural ambiguity Marmurek used can be illustrated by changing the second permutation in the preceding illustration from SBFQJ to FQSBJ. That is, rather than defining the second major unit as consisting of J and FQ, it would indicate that the two major units for the sequence were SBJ and FQ. However, the first permutation (JFQSB) identified the two major units as SB and JFQ. The result would be a structural ambiguity for J and that should be roughly equivalent to the problem a subject experiences in a discrimination task in which the correct response keeps changing.

Marmurek's (1972) results were quite dramatic. Not only was the ambiguity disrupting, but only three of the subjects in the structurally consistent condition performed as poorly as the best subject in the structurally inconsistent condition.

These results indicate that sequence learning does require identifying an unambiguous organizational position for each item. In addition, the order-change and latency studies described above suggest that the positional information is represented in memory by separate and distinct pieces of information reflecting the item's relative position at each hierarchical level in the structure.

D. Organization as a Generative Plan and the Problem of Response Learning

One of the three empirical enigmas with which this discussion began was the fact that knowing the strength of specific interitem associations within a complex response (that is, a response consisting of more than two items) will not allow us to predict the rate at which the response would be learned (Underwood & Schulz, 1960). However, it does appear that this effect can be explained within a coding view of learning. The explanation begins by noting that if the response is a trigram such as SBJ, and the subject is provided with an S–B association and a B–J association, there might be some facilitation from prefamiliarity with the letters, but the subject also might experience the type of difficulty illustrated by the Marmurek (1972) experiment. Prior knowledge of the SB relationship would be in the form of a code representing those items, as would be the case for the BJ relationship, and during the final learning the task would be to form a higher order code to integrate the SB and BJ codes. However, in that B would be represented by two different lower order codes, the structure would produce SBBJ as a response, and the subjects would encounter the same type of structural ambiguity as for the letter J in the above illustration for the Marmurek experiment. Furthermore, if SBBJ was produced, it would be disconfirmed when the correct response SBJ appeared for study, and the previously discussed studies regarding the replacement and deletion of information from chunks indicates that the codes are too inflexible for the subjects to solve the problem by just deleting one of the Bs. Therefore, some type of interference would occur that might reduce or eliminate the value of any prior experience with the specific letters.

The fact that there was a facilitating effect of the prior association when the response consisted of only two letters also is consistent with this view of learning. It would be assumed, however, that the relationship would not be a direct connection between the items, but rather one of being represented by a common code, and no change in encoding would be needed when the items appeared on the final learning task. The issue, then, seems to be whether the prior experience does or does not involve the establishment of the codes to be used on the final task.

1. The Decoding-Operation Model

Given these considerations and data regarding both the nature of codes and organization as an encoding hierarchy, the next issue concerns their function and influence in the generative process. In the case of highly skilled responses, Lashley (1951) has noted that many characteristics of the generative process seem to be quite inconsistent with any view of learning based on direct two-place interitem connections. For example, when someone says the alphabet, the sheer speed with which adjacent letters are produced would preclude any elicitor-elicited relationship between them. Similarly, rule-related responses, such as the finger and hand movements of a skilled pianist, seem to have a structure that goes beyond that which can be expressed in simple antecedent–consequent relationships.

Lashley (1951) suggested that any account of the learning and generative process related to such responses would have to have at least three characteristics. The first is that the functioning of the mechanism cannot rely on any type of sensory feedback from already-executed response components. Clearly, the generative process would be very slow if it were necessary to have feedback from a predecessor before an item could be produced. The second characteristic of the account is that the mechanism must have a way of making a set of items momentarily available, so that a complete memory search is not necessary between each element in a response sequence. Again, if a search were necessary, the response production would be very slow. Finally, the mechanism must have a means for representing all the order information in an efficient manner. Not only must the items be immediately available, but there must be some efficient way of determining which of the available items is next in the sequence.

The decoding-operation model (Johnson, 1970) was designed to account for the way the encoding pattern of a structured sequence might be used at the time of generation, and it seems to include the three characteristics Lashley considered critical. The model has four essential components. First, *whenever a subject recovers a code, he immediately decodes it into the codes for its elements at the next lower level.* Second, *whenever a code is decoded, the resulting element codes are put into a push-down memory store in the order of their occurrence in the sequence, except for the element code that has temporal priority in the sequence, and that code will be further decoded.* It is assumed, consistent with the preceding discussion, that the codes are tagged for order, with the tags being the basis for determining the order in which the codes are put into memory. Third, *whenever a response is produced, the subject returns to the push-down memory store and retrieves the top item, which he can then decode in the same manner.* Finally, *whenever a subject becomes uncertain of a decoding step, he terminates his response attempt at the point the uncertainty is first experienced.*

The generative routine that would result from applying this model to the structured sequence in Figure 1 is illustrated in the 16 steps listed in the figure, with prime markers representing temporal priority tags. In the first step the code for the sequence (X) is elicited, and in the second it is decoded into the codes for the two major units (A and B). In the third step the code for the second major unit (B) is stored in memory while the code A is decoded into its component codes (C and D). In the fourth step the code D is stored in memory and the code C is decoded into its components (E and F). In the fifth step the code for F is stored and E is produced overtly. The subject then retrieves the top item in the push-down memory and decodes it, resulting in an overt occurrence of F. The figure illustrates each step in the decoding process, and indicates which items are in memory at any point.

As has been noted, one of the appealing aspects of an associative view is that it provides a very simple retrieval and generative mechanism, and any alternative view of learning must also have such a component. Not only does the decoding-operation model describe such a generative mechanism, but the mechanism seems to fit quite nicely into the requisite characteristics described by Lashley (1951). For example, regarding the first characteristic, once a generative step has been taken, the mechanism simply goes on to the next step, and feedback would be irrelevant. In fact, once the mechanism has been initiated, it may be impervious to any type of stimulus control, as is illustrated by a speaker who continues on to the end of a sentence even though he has been interrupted and his listener is no longer attending to what he says.

Regarding Lashley's second requisite characteristic, the decoding of a code usually makes a number of elements immediately available to the subject (that is,

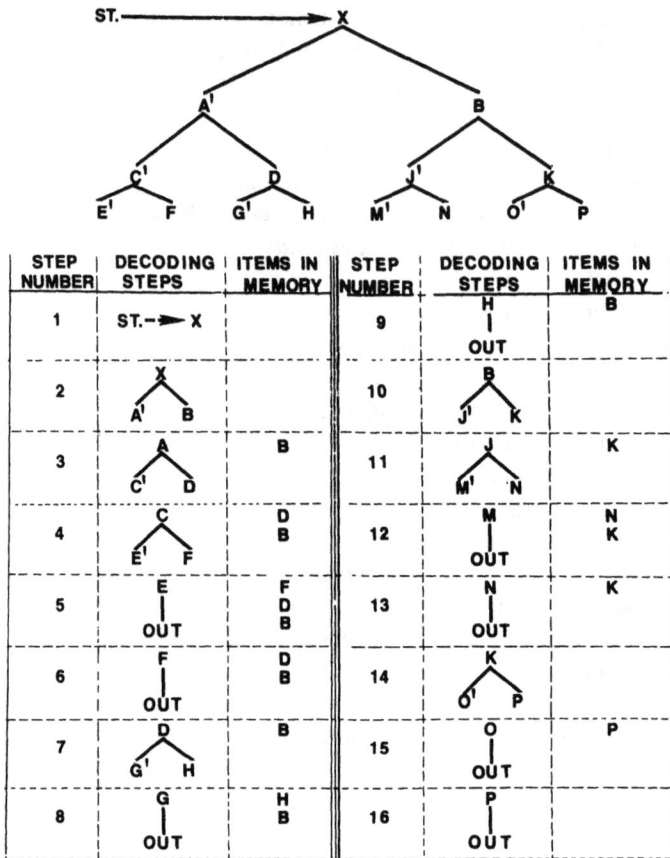

STEP NUMBER	DECODING STEPS	ITEMS IN MEMORY	STEP NUMBER	DECODING STEPS	ITEMS IN MEMORY
1	ST.→ X		9	H → OUT	B
2	X (A¹ B)		10	B (J¹ K)	
3	A (C¹ D)	B	11	J (M¹ N)	K
4	C (E¹ F)	D B	12	M → OUT	N K
5	E → OUT	F D B	13	N → OUT	K
6	F → OUT	D B	14	K (O¹ P)	
7	D (G¹ H)	B	15	O → OUT	P
8	G → OUT	H B	16	P → OUT	

FIGURE 1.

two or more), and the contents of the push-down memory also would be a set of primed and highly available items. Related to this point, it is interesting to note that the optimum size of chunks for ordered recall is about three, but is somewhat larger for free recall. This limit of three might suggest a balance between a facilitating effect from having many items immediately available for generation, and a retarding effect stemming from order confusions. This suggestion is supported by the fact that these two offsetting effects can be seen when subjects try to recall large ordered chunks. That is, while subjects are able to recall the individual items from a sequence without much trouble, they do seem to make a large number of order errors (Wickelgren, 1964, 1967).

Lashley's third requisite characteristic is that the mechanism must provide an efficient means of representing and utilizing order information. The concept of order tags and the properties of a push-down memory seem to fill that requirement. In addition, the structure itself carries a great deal of order information in that it limits the number of items available to the subject for generation at any point in the sequence.

This latter point can be illustrated using the Figure 1 structure. For example, in that E, F, G, and H are represented by a different code than that which represents M, N, O, and P, the two sets of items will not be intermingled in recall. That is, those items ultimately represented by A either must all precede or all follow those represented by B, because the model demands that once subjects begin decoding, the code must be completely decoded before they can even begin on another code at the same level. Similarly, all those items represented by D have to precede or follow immediately those represented by C, and those items represented by K have to precede or follow immediately those represented by J. Therefore, the pattern in which the item information is encoded determines a great deal of the order as well.

The amount of structurally encoded order information can be illustrated by noting that each decoding step in the Figure 1 structure makes two items available to the subject, and all he must decide is which of the two occurs first. If all he knew were the encoding pattern, and at each decoding step he had to guess which of the two items occurred first, there would be about one chance in a hundred that he would produce a correctly ordered sequence of eight items, given the encoding pattern illustrated in the figure. However, if knowing the items did not require that he know the encoding pattern, then when he tried to produce the sequence, he would have to guess among the entire set of eight letters for the first item, among the remaining seven for the second item, etc. Under these circumstances there is only one chance in about 40,000 that he could produce a properly ordered sequence. Clearly, encoding the item information in this manner reduces the amount of additional order information that must be acquired, and that additional order information might be viewed as a tag on one of the items at each decoding step.

One implication of this view is that if subjects are asked to learn an item set of some sort (for example, a random list of words), the organization they impose on the material should severely restrict the order in which they produce the items on any recall attempt, even if the task does not demand ordered recall. This point can be illustrated by an effect first reported by Tulving (1962). The subjects were asked to learn a list of unrelated words, and they could recall them in any order they wished. The results indicated that from trial-to-trial the recall order became increasingly stereotyped, and for any trial or subject, the performance was an increasing function of the degree to which the recall order was stereotyped.

2. Empirical Explorations of the Decoding-Operation Hypothesis

The major approach to examining the decoding-operation model has been through computing the probability that a subject would stop a recall attempt at each item-to-item transition within structured sequences. These are transitional-error probabilities (TEPs) in which the only errors considered are cases in which all the items following a transition are omitted (that is, the subject stopped at that point).

Basically, the decoding-operation model is a description of the location and scope of the generative decisions a subject makes during response production. In addition, it assumes that if a subject is uncertain about some decision, he will terminate his recall attempt at that point. Therefore, it should be possible to determine where particular generative decisions are made during response generation by noting where a subject stops if he has difficulty with the decision.

The most elementary assumption of the model is that subjects completely decode codes into their components before going on to the immediately following decoding step at the next lower level. For example, if a chunk consisted of SBJ, subjects should completely decode the code for the chunk into the codes for the individual letters before going on to the next step of decoding the code for S into an overt response. That would mean that at the beginning of such a chunk the subjects would have as many decoding decisions as there were component codes in the chunk represented by the code, but once those decisions had been made, there would be only one decoding decision as the subject made the letter-to-letter transitions during production (that is, the decision that decoded the letter code into an overt response).

Therefore, with more decisions to make at chunk boundaries than within chunks, the likelihood of becoming uncertain and stopping also should be greater at chunk boundaries. Furthermore, the chance of stopping at a chunk boundary should be an increasing function of chunk size, but the chance of stopping at any point within a chunk should be independent of chunk size. That is, subjects make only one decision at each within-chunk transition regardless of the chunk's size, but at a chunk boundary the number of decisions is equal to the number of elements within the following chunk.

The results of a number of experiments have supported these expectations. In one experiment (Johnson, 1970), the likelihood of stopping at a chunk boundary increased in even steps of .08 from .01 to .25 as the size of the following chunk increased from one to four letters, but there was no reliable variation in within-chunk TEPs related to chunk size.

A subject also makes decisions before he even begins a sequence. For example, if the sequence consisted of SBJ FQL ZNG, and the subject chunked it according to the spacing, at the time of recall he should decode the sequence code into the codes for each of the chunks, store the codes for the two chunks past the first, and then decode the first chunk into its component letter codes. Only then would he attempt to generate the first letter.

Following this decoding plan, then, he would have made the decisions regarding the codes for each of the chunks, and the codes for the components of the first chunk, but he would not have made any decoding decisions regarding the letter codes past the first chunk. This should mean that his tendency to stop before saying the first letter (that is, the tendency to make a complete omission) should be an increasing function of both the number of chunks in the sequence and the size of the first chunk, but it should not be influenced by the size of the chunks past the first. That is, the codes past the first would not have been decoded at that time, and in that they are opaque their contents could not influence the subject's behavior.

The data also seem to provide striking support for this aspect of the model. For example, two groups of subjects learned sequences, but one had their sequence grouped as SBJ FQ LZN, while the other had an SB JFQ LZN grouping (Johnson, 1970). The first group had the largest first chunk, and they had more omissions than the second; but the second group had a larger second chunk, and they had a greater tendency to stop after the first chunk. In addition, the two groups had identical third chunks, and they were equivalent in their tendency to stop after the second chunk. Chunk size, then, seemed to have very specific influences on the subjects' behavior, and those influences were confined to decision loci.

Regarding chunk-level codes, a comparison has been made between conditions in which subjects learn sequences grouped in the form SBJ FQ LZN and a condition in which they learn a SBJ FQLZN grouping (Johnson, 1970). The first condition had more codes and the omission rate was greater, while the subjects in the second condition had an omission rate that was about the same as for subjects in a condition involving sequences such as SBJ FQ. That is, the number of higher order units past the first had an impact on omission rate, but their size and content did not.

A final issue concerns the memory load assumed by this model. The concept of a push-down memory store is the primary mechanism accounting for the way in which a top-to-bottom generative process can result in a left-to-right response production. However, in that this store is assumed to be a working short-term memory, it also should be subject to the standard memory limits, and subjects' performance with a structured sequence should be a decreasing function of the memory load required by the structure. In support of this idea, it is important to note that the concept of memory load within this model is isomorphic with Yngve's (1960) concept of structural depth, and there does appear to be a substantial amount of empirical support for that hypothesis (Martin & Roberts, 1966).

In summary, the decoding-operation model provides a description of the generative process related to a coding conception of organization and learning. It adds very little theoretical baggage to the concept of coding other than noting that the generative process would involve a set of decoding steps. The decoding steps themselves, however, would be just those implied by the original coding, and that also would be true for the order in which the steps occur. The empirical documentation of the model appears to be quite adequate and seems to provide as much support for the general concept as it does for the specific components of the model.

IV. A CODING VIEW OF PERCEPTUAL PROCESSING

Given that information sets are represented in memory by codes, the next question concerns when and how the encoding process occurs. That is, if subjects are asked to learn SBJ as a response unit, there is a point in time at which there is no representing code that would provide an integrated representation of the letter codes, although it would be assumed that the subjects would have preestablished codes for the individual letters. At some later point, after learning is complete, however, a representing code would be established and available and would be elicited by any presentation of SBJ. In addition, all subsequent memorial processing of SBJ should be done in terms of that code.

There are two specific issues raised by this analysis of encoding. The first involves the learning process whereby a code is acquired, and the second issue concerns what happens on a particular presentation, regardless of whether a representing or integrative encoding has been established. That is, although a subject may have a memorized code available for SBJ, a great deal of processing must occur on any given presentation before he can discover the appropriateness of the code and assign it to the display. Therefore, the processing concerns involve both how the codes are established, and, once established, how they are assigned on any given presentation.

A. Encoding as a Memorial Event

A very simple construction of these processes is that the individual items within a chunk are deposited separately within memory on every presentation, regardless of whether an integrative or representative code had been established. Subsequent memorial processing would then determine and assign a code and that also would be done regardless of any prior experience. The place where prior experience would have an influence would be in determining the duration of the active memorial encoding on each presentation, with the assumption being that processing time should decrease as subjects become more experienced with a particular code.

This constellation of ideas was examined by using a modification of the retroactive interference paradigm described earlier. The subjects were given a 6-second presentation of the digit 1 and a nine-letter sequence grouped as SBJ FQL ZNG. Either immediately after that display terminated, or after 24 seconds of counting backward by threes, a second 6-second display occurred that consisted of the digit 2 and a sequence such as SXJ FQL ZTG. That is, the second sequence was identical to the first except one letter was changed in each of two chunks. Then, either immediately after the second sequence, or after 24 seconds of counting backwards by threes, the subjects were shown either the digit 1 or the digit 2 and were asked to recall the appropriate sequence.

If the chunk encoding for the first sequence gradually develops in memory, then the tendency for the changed letters to disrupt recall of the whole changed chunk should increase as the interval between the two sequences increases. If the chunks were not encoded into units immediately after presentation, then only the changed letters should be forgotten if the interference occurred at that point. If the interfering items were presented after memorial processing had progressed, however, there should be a greater tendency for the whole chunk to be forgotten.

Surprisingly, none of these effects were obtained. If the interference occurred immediately after the first sequence had been presented, there was a large loss of both the changed and unchanged letters (but not the unchanged chunks), and the effect did not increase as the intersequence interval increased. It appears that unitization or coding of the chunks was as complete as it was going to be immediately after presentation, and the opportunity for subsequent memorial processing was not needed.

Within the context of this experimental paradigm, it is hard to determine whether the integrative encoding occurs very fast within memory, or whether there is some prememorial process that assigns an integrative encoding to the items prior to their registration in working memory. This issue was examined, however, using a procedure that relied upon the assumptions that codes are opaque and independent of their components. If that is true, then subjects should have to decode a code before they can determine whether it contains a particular component, but determining whether a code matches some other code at the same level should occur quite fast. That is, whether two codes match should be immediately apparent to a perceiver–processor, but deciding that a code has some component could be made only subsequent to some active processing (that is, decoding). The major implication of this analysis is that code-to-code comparison decisions should be faster than code-to-component comparison decisions.

The subjects were asked to memorize a trigram, such as SOF, and then they were presented with a series of trigram displays and were asked to indicate whether each displayed trigram was the same as the predesignated target item. That condition was compared to a condition in which the subjects saw the same series of trigram displays, but their predesignated target was a single letter (S) for example, and they were to determine whether each display began with that item. In both cases the reaction time was measured between the display onset and the occurrence of the response.

In this task it would be assumed that the prememorized target item, regardless of whether it is a trigram or a single letter, would be encoded in memory as a unit and represented by a single code. The displayed trigram, on the other hand, would have to be encoded on each presentation, and the issue is whether the codes for single letters are deposited in memory, and then assigned a unitizing code as a result of memorial processing (the letter-integration model), or the unitizing code is assigned before the information is moved into memory (the pattern-unit model).

The letter-integration model would assume that the code for the first letter would be immediately available for comparison when the information was moved into memory, but active integrative processing would be involved before the chunk-level code would be available. The pattern-unit model, on the other hand, would assume that when the information is moved into memory, the chunk-level code would be immediately available for comparison; but the code for the first letter would become available only after the chunk had been decoded. Therefore, the pattern-unit model would predict that the trigram should be identified faster than the first letter of the trigram, while the reverse would be predicted if the unitizing encoding is the result of memorial processing.

The results of the study were quite clear in demonstrating that subjects can indicate that SOF is SOF faster than they can indicate that it begins with S. Furthermore, the effect seems to hold true regardless of whether the pre-memorized displays are pronounceable (Johnson, 1975) or unpronounceable (Johnson, 1972b; Sloboda, 1976), and there is even a suggestion that a similar effect occurs when the letter arrays are nonlinear (Sloboda, 1976). In general, then, it appears that the encoding of chunks is already relatively complete at the very first point in memorial processing that subjects are able to make either memory comparisons or decisions between items, and that seems to offer support for a pattern-unit type of model.

B. The Pattern-Unit Model

While the problem of chunk encoding involves both the issue of code learning and the issue of when and how codes are assigned, it is only this latter point that is of immediate concern to the pattern-unit model. In addition, the discussion will be confined to the way in which the model would account for the processing of visually presented letter arrays, although it would be assumed that the account given by the model is more general and should be applicable to the processing of any small pattern.

In general, the model is an attempt to account for the processing that intervenes between the time a stimulus pattern first impinges on a perceiver, and the point in processing at which the subject first registers a unitary encoding of the pattern's information within memory (Johnson, 1977). Within this framework the emphasis is on both the nature of the coding process that occurs at each stage, and the nature of the resulting encoded unit, with the latter being the primary focus of the research. That is, the model assumes that as information moves from stage-to-stage during processing, there is a change in both the nature and the scope of the information set that is represented by a single code. Very early in processing there might be a separate code for every feature or aspect of every letter, while at some later point these feature codes for the letters might be integrated into a single higher order letter code. Finally, if the display consists of a word, the individual letter codes can be integrated into a yet higher order word code at some later processing stage. The model, then, is an attempt to both characterize the various points in processing where these unitization effects occur, and describe a possible mechanism whereby the unitization is achieved.

As an overview, the model can be construed as being divided into three broad processing components that are designed to explain (*a*) the development and functional characteristics of the perceptual image, (*b*) the transfer of that perceptual information into working memory, and (*c*) maintenance of the information in working memory so that comparative decisions can be made. Within each of the components, it is assumed that there is a series of processing stages that act as an interface between the form in which the information was encoded when it was first introduced to that component, and the form in which it will be encoded when it is moved on to the next component.

1.   The Perceptual Component.

The model assumes that all perceptual processing is noncognitive and that information is initially encoded in the form of undifferentiated neural activity, with subsequent stages being devoted to differentiating that encoding. While the model makes a number of assumptions regarding the nature of the processing within the perceptual component, the important point for the present issue is that the end state of the processing is assumed to be an uninterpreted, but interpretable, perceptual image. That is, it is assumed that the final perceptual representation is noncognitive and represents only the physical information from a visual array. Any cognitive interpretation of the array must wait until the information is moved on into memory and contact can be made with previously stored information or knowledge.

This point can be illustrated by a nondegraded visual array consisting of the letter X. It is assumed that the perceptual image would faithfully represent all the information needed to identify the display as two crossing diagonal lines, but that should be the only information included within the encoding at that point. The information that X is a meaningful pattern, that it has a name, and that it is a letter from the alphabet could be added to the encoding only after it had been assigned to memory and contact had been made with previously stored information. This view of a perceptual image is very similar to the concept of iconic representations described by Neisser (1967) and Coltheart (1975).

While this view of perceptual processing implies that the perceptual code represents only the physical information in the display, and that there is no elaborative encoding with information from memory, it is assumed that there is a unitization process within the perceptual component. Any small pattern can be viewed as consisting of a set of intersecting components or features, such as short lines and curves, and it is assumed that such intersecting feature sets are assembled and encoded as single units within the perceptual component, just as the above discussion and data suggest that letters can be assembled and encoded into single word units within memory.

This point can be illustrated by the fact that while the letter X would not be encoded as a letter of the alphabet within the perceptual component, the fact that the two diagonals intersect would result in its being encoded as a unit, and the result would be something more than just two diagonal lines. For example, if a subject were asked to indicate whether a display contained a diagonal, he should be able to respond faster to // than to X. That is, the intersection in the X would result in the two diagonals being encoded into a higher order unit, and that unit encoding would have to be decoded before the diagonal features would be available to determine a response. In that the two slashes do not intersect, they would be encoded separately as two diagonals, and there would be no decoding necessary. Finally, the fact that X is also a meaningful pattern could have no influence on this phenomenon, because the contact with memory that would be necessary to detect its familiarity would not have occurred at that point in processing.

To summarize, the product of perceptual processing is assumed to be an uninterpreted perceptual image that only represents the physical information in the display, and within the image the units of encoding are assumed to be bundles of intersecting features. If the display consisted of ANT, it would be assumed that the features that make up each letter would be encoded as a unit, but in that the features from separate letters do not intersect, there would be no higher order encoding of the letters into a word unit. In addition, there would have been no memorial contact that would have allowed unitization in terms of some cognitive code. Given these considerations, then, it would be assumed that the perceptual representation of ANT would be just an array of assembled but uninterpreted small patterns conforming to each letter.

2. The Transfer Mechanism

The next issue concerns the process whereby the perceptually encoded information is transferred into memory. The basic assumption is that the transfer occurs through the assignment of a unifying memorial code to the perceptual image and that the initial attempts to assign an encoding always involve a single unifying encoding for the entire array. That is, subjects initially attempt to represent all the information in the perceptual image within a common memory code, and fractionation of the image into components occurs only after several unsuccessful attempts to assign a unifying encoding. In addition, it is assumed that if the image were to be fractionated, the resulting components would conform to the basic units of the perceptual image (for example, uninterpreted but assembled sets of letter features).

For example, if a display consisted of SAW, the subjects should have a previously learned memorial representation that could be assigned, and the information could be immediately moved on to working memory. For a perceptual display such as SBJ, on the other hand, the subject presumably would not have an available unifying memorial code, and the initial attempts to assign one would be unsuccessful. The subject would then fractionate the perceptual image and process each letter individually, with the item then being moved on into memory in terms of one code for each letter, rather than a single code for the entire array. Given these considerations, then, the difference in processing time for SAW and

SBJ should reflect both the time involved in making the initial unsuccessful attempts to assign a unifying code to SBJ, as well as the additional time needed for its subsequent letter-by-letter processing.

In that it has been assumed that codes are opaque, and do not themselves directly reflect the information they represent, it is clear that it also must be assumed that there can be no one-to-one relationship between characteristics or attributes of the perceptual image and any code used to represent that information within memory. For example, while perceptual images might vary in complexity or number of components, there should be no correlated variations in any attributes of the code. If a letter array such as a word can be assigned a single memorial code, then any variation in number of letters should not be reflected in the code. On the other hand, if the array cannot be assigned a single code, and it must be fractionated, the processing would become more difficult, but the increase in difficulty should stem from the increase in number of to-be-processed codes and not from any difficulty in the handling of any one code.

To summarize, there are two essential characteristics of the transfer mechanism. The first is that subjects always attempt to assign a single unifying memorial encoding to any perceptual image and fractionate the image into components only after some fixed number of unsuccessful attempts to assign such an encoding. The second point is that any assigned code, whether it is a unifying code representing the whole image or one of several codes assigned to each of the components, should not reflect any difficulty or complexity in the material it represents. A code is a code, and there should be no quantitative difference between the code for a word and the code for an individual letter.

3. Working Memory

Once a memory code has been assigned to perceptual information, it is moved on to working memory for any additional cognitive processing. For example, it would be assumed that any analysis of a word's meaning would occur within working memory, as would the eliciting of any associated (related) items. In addition, an important function of working memory stems from the fact that it can hold information for extended periods of time, while the storage capabilities of the perceptual component might be limited to less than a second (Sperling, 1960; Turvey, 1973). As will be noted below, this latter issue becomes important any time the subject's task involves comparing the code for an item with the code for an item that was presented sometime in the past.

4. The Comparison Process

The final issue concerning the pattern-unit model is the assumption that before a decision of any kind can be made regarding a displayed item, there must be some sort of comparison process. If two items are presented simultaneously, their perceptual images would have to be compared in order to determine whether they were the same. If the subject were to search for a predesignated target item, the code for each presented item would have to be compared to that for the target. If the subject's task were to determine the identity of an item, it would be necessary to compare its code with the codes for similar items in memory before the identity determination could be made. In all these cases, then, some code-to-code comparison is needed before the subject could make the decision required by the task.

The model's basic assumption regarding the comparison process is that information must share a common form of encoding (that is, either perceptual or memorial) before it can be compared, but when two items or item sets do share a common form of encoding, the comparison process is more or less automatic. For example, if a subject's task were to determine whether the second of two sequentially presented items was the same as the first, it would be necessary to process the first item into memory so that it could be held until the second one was presented and the comparison could be made. However, in that it had been assigned a memorial code, the second item also would have to be assigned a memorial code before the comparison could be made. On the other hand, if the two items were presented simultaneously, they would share a common form of encoding at all stages of processing, including the perceptual form, and that would allow a comparison to be made before the items had been moved into working memory. The essential point, then, is that comparisons can be made only between two perceptual codes or two memorial codes, and it is not possible to determine whether the information represented by a perceptual code is the same as that represented by a memorial code, or vice versa, without putting them into a common form.

5. A Summary of the Model

As noted earlier, the model is a characterization of the processing events and resulting encodings that occur between the point in time when an array of letters is first presented to the receptors, and the time when the information set is represented in memory in such a form that cognitive processes can be applied. In terms of the current issues, there are four specific aspects of the pattern-unit model that are relevant: (a) the end product of the perceptual component is a set of assembled but uninterpreted letters; (b) the initial attempt to move the information in the perceptual image into memory is always in terms of assigning a single unifying code that represents all the information; (c) if the subject is unsuccessful in assigning a unifying encoding after a fixed number of attempts, he fractionates the display into perceptual components and assigns individual memorial codes to each component; and (d) a comparison can be made between two information sets whenever the two sets share a common form of encoding.

C. Empirical Support for the Pattern-Unit Model

The major focus of the empirical exploration of the model has been on its implications concerning part–whole relationships and length-difficulty relationships. Regarding the length-difficulty relationship, the model assumes that there should be no relationship if the subject has some rule system registered in memory that could be used for assigning an integrating encoding to a display. That is, if a code can be assigned, then the display can be processed with ease and efficiency in terms of the code. If the code cannot reflect any complexity or quantitative variation in the represented material, then those factors could not have any influence on postperceptual processing (for example, identification of the display).

On the other hand, any processing or decision based on comparisons made prior to assigning the unitizing encoding should reflect complexity and quantitative variations in the material. In addition, if a display cannot be assigned a unitary code, and it must be fractionated with each component then being assigned a separate code, there also should be a length-difficulty relationship. Under these circumstances there would be as many codes as there were components in the display, and the number of codes would be an increasing function of the length or complexity of the display.

In terms of letter arrays, it is assumed that single letters and words can be assigned codes, and they should be processed with equal facility. In addition, word length also should have no influence on processing, if subjects can read the word and assign a code to it.

Data seem to support both these expectations. For example, if subjects are given a word target and asked to determine whether it matches some subsequent display, word length does not seem to influence reaction time (Johnson, 1975, 1977), and whether the targets and displays are single letters or words also does not seem to make a difference (Johnson, 1975; Sloboda, 1976). In a similar situation, Terry, Samuels, and LaBerge (1976) found that word length did not influence the time to determine whether a presented word was the name of an animal and that effect also seems to offer support for the model.

While these were cases where no length effects were obtained, both the techniques seem to be quite sensitive and are able to detect length effects in other situations where the model does expect them to occur. For example, an integrative encoding should not be assigned if the display is an unfamiliar consonant sequence, and it does take longer to identify a four-letter consonant sequence than one that contains only three letters. In addition, in the Terry *et al.* (1976) task, there were length effects when the letters were presented in mirror image and had to be identified individually.

Finally, if the target item and the item to be examined are presented simultaneously, as in the standard same–different task, the model would assume that the comparison and decision should be made while the information is still in the form of a perceptual image and before a unifying encoding had been assigned. Under those circumstances the number of needed comparisons would equal the number of letters. Both Eichelman (1970) and Marmurek (1977) have reported data supporting this expectation, and Marmurek further demonstrated that the reaction-time advantage of single letters over words will disappear if there is a 3-second blank interval between the presentation of the target and the appearance of the to-be-examined item. That is, in an otherwise identical task, the length effect disappears if the comparison and decision cannot be made until after the information has been processed into memory.

Regarding the part–whole relationships, it was noted earlier that subjects could accept or reject a presented word as being some predesignated target word much faster than they could indicate whether the word began with some predesignated target letter (Johnson, 1975). At least part of the reason for that effect is assumed to be the fact that the displayed word would have to be decoded before the initial letter could be found and compared to the item in memory, but no decoding would have to occur for the word-level comparison. However, if the display were an unfamiliar consonant sequence, it would have to be fractionated and sent on to memory as a set of separately encoded letters. Under those circumstances the component codes would be immediately available for comparison, and the chunk-level code would become available only after some active memorial processing and that also seems to be the case. That is, subjects can indicate that SBJ begins with S faster than they can indicate it is SBJ, provided they have not been given an opportunity to prememorize a code for SBJ. If they do have a pre-memorized code, however, the reverse seems to be the case (Johnson, 1972b).

Similarly, if the display is a consonant sequence there should be a delay in identifying the first letter, because the subjects should make several attempts to encode the sequence as a unit before giving up and parsing the display. Therefore, a single letter in isolation should be identified faster than a letter within a consonant sequence, even when the consonant sequence contains all the same letter. For example, if subjects are to indicate whether a display contains a B, they should be faster if the display is B than if it is BBBBB, and that also appears to be the case (Johnson, 1977).

As noted by Terry, et al. (1976), effects such as these are very difficult to reconcile with any view of encoding that assumes that the elements of an integratable pattern, such as a word, are themselves encoded into memory prior to the assignment of a word-level code. It simply does not seem to be the case that there is any component-level code that can be used either as a basis for a decision or to determine a response prior to having an available chunk or word-level code. In addition, if component level codes are primed, there appears to be no facilitating effect on processing, but such effects do appear if the chunk or word-level code is primed (Petersen & LaBerge, 1976). The pattern-unit model, then, does appear to be a reasonable approximation to the type of perceptual-memorial processing that occurs when an encodable chunk is presented, as well as accounting for the type of complex processing that seems to be the case with nonencodable arrays.

D. The Problem of Stimulus Learning and Encoding

As noted earlier, the problems of S-R learning and the general effects of organization in memory seem to be the specific points that have caused the most difficulty for traditional associative views of learning. A coding theory has been proposed as an alternative view of learning, and the preceding discussion has illustrated how this alternative can handle both organizational effects in memory and response learning. The issue that remains is to use the theory to account for the way subjects process stimuli.

Within the context of PA learning, the terms *stimulus* and *response* have been used as if they refer to qualitatively distinct events in the real world. That is, the traditional usage has almost implied that there is a class of things that are stimuli and another class that are responses, and a PA item being constructed by picking one of each. Quite obviously, however, an item such as GEX could be either a stimulus or a response. Similarly, the fact that stimuli usually appear on the left and responses on the right cannot be a critical physical distinction, because the situation can be reversed by simply instructing the subjects. Furthermore, when a subject first sees an S-R pair such as GEX-TREE, both of the items are stimuli. The initial question, then, is what makes a stimulus a stimulus and a response a response?

It seems clear that this distinction cannot be drawn in terms of either characteristics of the items or operations under the control of the experimenter, and it appears that the only reasonable basis for differentiating these two classes is in terms of what the subject does with a unit once it has been presented. That is, what makes a unit a stimulus or a response is not an attribute of the unit, but is determined by the particular subset of information processing steps to which it is subjected.

The major functional distinction between a stimulus and a response is that the subject need never reconstruct the stimulus with all its detail, while such perfect reconstruction is necessary if the unit is to function as a response. In addition, there is an important, but not well understood, issue that involves the nature of the requisite memory search and retrieval processes. On every test, the complete stimulus is presented and the subject's task is to then retrieve the response code. Whether this distinction with regard to reconstruction represents just a quantitative difference in the adequacy of the retrieval cue (that is, it is complete and perfect in the case of the stimulus but not in the case of the response), or there is a qualitative distinction with retrieval involved in response processing but not in stimulus processing, seems to be open to question.

1. Stimulus Encoding

The problem presented by the data on stimulus processing stems from the facts that there are clear facilitating effects from having preintegrated stimuli (Hunt, 1959; Postman & Greenbloom, 1967; Sheffield, 1946) and that rule-generated stimuli seem to be treated as integrated units (Postman & Greenbloom, 1967). At the same time, however, the usual conditions that result in response integration (and can be explained by interitem associations) seem to have no impact on subjects' performance if the items are to function as stimuli (Greeno & Horowitz, 1968; Schulz & Martin, 1964).

These effects can be explained within the pattern-unit model if it is noted that a stimulus encoding need not be as complete a representation of the perceptual image as would be needed for a response encoding. That is, an incomplete encoding of a perceptual image would be acceptable if it is to function as a stimulus, provided the encoding could be assigned in a reliable manner, and it would adequately differentiate that stimulus from every other stimulus with which it might be confused. The encoding for a response, on the other hand, would have to be sufficiently complete so as to include a generative mechanism that would allow a perfect reproduction of the perceptual information.

Within this view, the slight advantage of a pronounceable stimulus over a nonpronounceable stimulus (Hunt, 1959; Sheffield, 1946) would stem from the fact that the perceptual image for an unfamiliar and unpronounceable stimulus would have to be fractionated before it could be encoded into memory, while a pronounceable display could be passed on to memory in the form of a single integrated encoding. It is true that subjects do seem to use a component code as the functional stimulus in the case of an unpronounceable array if it is unique to that stimulus (Postman & Greenbloom, 1967), and because of the fractionation, that component code should be as immediately available to the subject as is the integrating code for the pronounceable array. However, in the case of an unpronounceable array, the fractionation also would make several other codes immediately available and that should result in some confusion and increased learning time. This explanation is essentially the same as that given by the encoding-variability hypothesis (E. Martin, 1968).

It also is true that the disadvantage for an unpronounceable stimulus array should not be overcome by an opportunity to integrate the array prior to learning (Schulz & Martin, 1964), as would be the case if the array were to function as the response. It is unlikely that a newly learned chunk-level code would be any more available, efficient, or useful than would be the component-level code for a letter, which would have been the code used if no integrating experience had been provided. For a response, on the other hand, the component-level code would not function as an adequate generative mechanism for the entire chunk, and any opportunity to learn such a mechanism would be helpful.

The Postman and Greenbloom (1967) data also are compatible with this position. Their results indicated that there was a marked tendency for a single component of the array to function as the stimulus if the array were unfamiliar and did not conform to any prelearned rule system. However, if the letter array were rule conforming, the functional stimulus seemed to be some higher order integrated representation of all the letters. Given that the pattern-unit model would imply that the letter codes for SBJ would be more immediately available in memory than a chunk-level code, while the reverse would be the case for an item like MOP, these results make a great deal of sense. In both cases, the code selected would be the one that would not involve any additional memorial processing.

2. Stimulus Learning

The foregoing considerations suggest that the major issue in stimulus learning is to find an encoding for an array that would be both reliable and unique. In the event that the array had no familiar components, as in the case of a random nonsense figure, the subject would devote most of his time to finding some feature set that might be assigned as a code. If no preestablished encoding were available, it would be assumed that early in learning, subjects would fractionate the display into simple features and attempt to pass them on to memory. The subject would then engage in an active process of code construction or discovery using whatever information he had successfully registered in memory. Once that encoding had been established, however, processing should be quite efficient, because there would be no other competing codes that could cause confusions.

A second situation would involve a stimulus for which there was no integrating encoding, but for which there were encodings for each of the components (for example, a consonant trigram such as SBJ). As noted above, in this situation there would be several encodings passed on to memory at the same time, and the subject's job would be to overcome confusion and determine which of the component codes was the most effective. It is likely that the decision would be based on some simple property of the code, such as positional information, and there is substantial support for that hypothesis (Richardson, 1972; Runquist, 1972).

The final situation that would involve stimulus learning would be cases where more than one integrating encoding might be assigned. That could occur either because the feature assigner had more than one encoding available for assignment (for example, cases of ambiguous pronounciation), or it could result when the assigned encoding is further processed within memory (for example, semantically encoded). In the latter situation there might be a variety of semantic representations available, such as would be the case for a homograph, and the subject would have to learn which of the semantic representations to select from memory. In both these situations the subject would have to learn a retrieval mechanism, and his task would be similar to that encountered when attempting to learn a means of retrieving a response code.

In summary, then, the expectations from the model seem quite consistent with the data on both stimulus encoding and stimulus learning. The central issue is that if an array is to function as a stimulus, the subject need not encode all the information, and the functional stimulus should be the encoding requiring the least amount of additional memorial processing. In general, that encoding will be the one first assigned when the information is moved into memory, and performance should be a decreasing function of the number of codes provided simultaneously by the transfer mechanism.

V. SUMMARY AND CONCLUSIONS

This discussion began with a consideration of the adequacy of associative accounts of learning, and it appeared that there were at least three specific areas in which difficulty was encountered. These areas were stimulus and response integration and the general effects of organization in memory. The major difficulty with the associative account seemed to be the fact that, at least in early versions, it was limited to direct two-place antecedent–consequent relationships as the basic explanatory mechanism. An alternative account was given in terms of a coding theory.

The primary distinction between a traditional association and a coding relationship is that the latter is assumed to provide only indirect relationships among a set of empirically related items, and the set size can exceed two. A code is assumed to be a unitary representation of information, distinct from the information, and an organization or structure is defined in terms of a pattern of encoding. This construction of what is learned not only can handle the troublesome issues of response learning and organization, but it also seems to enjoy a considerable amount of additional empirical support.

While the coding theory provides an account of the nature of memorial representations, two additional models were needed to handle the input and output issues. In terms of output, the decoding-operation model represents an attempt to characterize the way in which subjects might utilize the encoding pattern for a response unit or sequence as a generative mechanism. In addition to having a great deal of empirical support, the model is able to account for the speed and efficiency of highly skilled responses, which was a difficult issue for associative accounts of learning.

The pattern-unit model is designed to characterize the prememorial processing of a display and provide an account of the unitization processes. The basic assumption of the model is that for any perceptual array that is rule conforming, or for which there is a previously learned code, there will be a unitizing code assigned prior to moving the information into memory. In the event that there is no available code, the display would be fractionated into its components, with each component being assigned a code before being moved into memory. In terms of the initial issues, this model does seem to provide a means for handling the previously troublesome problems of stimulus learning and integration.

The coding theory and its two attendant input and output models, then, does appear to provide a viable account of the learning process. In addition to being consistent with existing data, it appears to be compatible with contemporary information-processing models of memory and perception. Finally, although the model does seem to be quite elaborate, it is a bit simpler than alternative accounts when they are expanded to provide the same range of general application as a coding theory.

REFERENCES

Averbach, E., & Coriell, A. S. Short-term memory in vision. *Bell System Technical Journal*, 1961, **40**, 309-328.

Birnbaum, I. M. Free-recall learning as a function of prior-list organization. *Journal of Verbal Learning and Verbal Behavior*, 1968, **7**, 1037-1042.

Birnbaum, I. M. Prior-list organization in part–whole free-recall learning. *Journal of Verbal Learning and Verbal Behavior*, 1969, **8**, 836-837.

Bousfield, W. A. The occurrence of clustering in the recall of randomly arranged associates. *Journal of General Psychology*, 1953, **49**, 229-240.

Bousfield, W. A., & Sedgewick, C. H. W. An analysis of sequences of restricted associative responses. *Journal of General Psychology*, 1944, **30**, 149-165.

Bower, G. H., & Winzenz, D. Group structure, coding, and memory for digit series. *Journal of Experimental Psychology Monograph*, 1969, **80**(May, Pt. 2), 1-17.

Clark, S. E. Retrieval of color information from the preperceptual storage system. *Journal of Experimental Psychology*, 1969, **82**, 263-266.

Cohen, B. H. Some or none characteristics of coding. *Journal of Verbal Learning and Verbal Behavior*, 1966, **5**, 182-187.

Coltheart, M. Iconic memory: A reply to Professor Holding. *Memory & Cognition*, 1975, **3**, 42-48.

DeRosa, D. V., Doane, D. S., & Russell, B. The influence of first-list organization on second-list free-recall learning. *Journal of Verbal Learning and Verbal Behavior*, 1970, **9**, 269-273.

Ebbinghaus, H. E. *Memory: A contribution to experimental psychology.* New York: Dover, 1964. (Originally published in 1885 and translated in 1913.)

Eichelman, W. H. Familiarity effects in the simultaneous matching task. *Journal of Experimental Psychology*, 1970, **86**, 275-282.

Fritzen, J. D., & Johnson, N. F. Definiteness of pattern ending and the uniformity of pattern size: Their effects on learning number sequences. *Journal of Verbal Learning and Verbal Behavior*, 1969, **8**, 575-580.

Greeno, J. G. How associations are memorized. In D. Norman (Ed.), *Models of human memory.* New York: Academic Press, 1970. Pp. 257-284.

Greeno, J. G., & Horowitz, L. M. On unitizing a compound stimulus. *Journal of Verbal Learning and Verbal Behavior*, 1968, **7**, 913-917.

Horton, D. L., & Kjeldergaard, P. M. An experimental analysis of associative factors in mediated generalization. *Psychological Monographs*, 1961, **75**, 11(Whole No. 515).

Hull, C. L. *A behavior system.* New Haven: Yale University Press, 1952.

Hunt, R. G. Meaningfulness and articulation of stimulus and response in paired-associate learning and stimulus recall. *Journal of Experimental Psychology*, 1959, **57**, 262-267.

Johnson, N. F. The effect of a difficult word on the transitional error probabilities in sentences. *Journal of Verbal Learning and Verbal Behavior*, 1969, **8**, 518-523. (a)

Johnson, N. F. Chunking: Associative chaining versus coding. *Journal of Verbal Learning and Verbal Behavior*, 1969, **8,** 725–731. (b)

Johnson, N. F. The role of chunking and organization in the process of recall. In G. Bower (Ed.), *Psychology of learning and motivation.* Vol. IV. New York: Academic Press, 1970. Pp. 172–247.

Johnson, N. F. Organization and the concept of a memory code. In A. Melton & E. Martin (Eds.), *Coding processes in human memory.* Washington, D.C.: H. V. Winston & Sons, 1972. Pp. 125–160. (a)

Johnson, N. F. Higher-order encoding: Process or state? *Memory & Cognition,* 1972, **1,** 491–494. (b)

Johnson, N. F. On the function of letter in word identification: Some data and a preliminary model. *Journal of Verbal Learning and Verbal Behavior,* 1975, **14,** 17–29.

Johnson, N. F. A pattern-unit model of word identification. In D. LaBerge & S. J. Samuels (Eds.), *Basic processes in reading: Perception and comprehension.* Hillsdale, New Jersey: Lawrence Erlbaum Associates, 1977. Pp. 91–125.

Johnson, N. F., & Migdoll, D. M. Transfer and retroaction under conditions of changed organization. *Cognitive Psychology,* 1971, **2,** 229–237.

Kausler, D. H. *Psychology of verbal learning and memory.* New York: Academic Press, 1974. Pp. 583.

Keeney, T. J. Permutation transformations on phrase structures in letter sequences. *Journal of Experimental Psychology,* 1969, **82,** 28–33.

Lashley, K. S. The problem of serial order in behavior. In L. Jeffress (Ed.), *Cerebral mechanisms in behavior.* New York: John Wiley & Sons, 1951.

Maier, S. F., & Seligman, M. E. P. Learned helplessness: Theory and evidence. *Journal of Experimental Psychology: General,* 1976, **105,** 3–46.

Mandler, G. Organization and memory. In K. Spence & J. Spence (Eds.), *The psychology of learning and motivation.* Vol. I. New York: Academic Press, 1967. Pp. 328–372.

Marmurek, H. H. C. The relationship between organizing and learning: On the use of hierarchical organizations. Unpublished master's thesis, The Ohio State University, 1972.

Marmurek, H. H. C. Processing letters in words at different levels. *Memory and Cognition,* 1977, **5,** 67–72.

Martin, E. Stimulus meaningfulness and paired-associate transfer: An encoding variability hypothesis. Psychological Review, 1968, **75,** 421–441.

Martin, E. Verbal learning theory and independent retrieval phenomena. *Psychological Review,* 1971, **78,** 413–332.

Martin, E., & Noreen, D. L. Serial learning: Identification of subjective subsequences. *Cognitive Psychology,* 1974, **6,** 421–435.

Martin, E., & Roberts, K. H. Grammatical factors in sentence retention. *Journal of Verbal Learning and Verbal Behavior,* 1966, **5,** 211–218.

Martin, J. R. *The relationship between organizing and learning: The role of structural balance and the necessity to memorize.* Unpublished master's thesis, The Ohio State University, 1972.

Miller, G. A. The magical number seven plus or minus two: Some limits on our capacity for processing information. *Psychological Review,* 1956, **63,** 81–97.

Neisser, U. *Cognitive psychology.* New York: Appleton-Century-Crofts, 1967.

Peterson, R., & LaBerge, D. *The role of letter information in word recognition.* Paper presented at the meeting of the Psychonomic Society, St. Louis, 1976.

Postman, L. Association and performance in the analysis of verbal learning. In T. Dixon & D. Horton (Eds.), *Verbal behavior and general behavior theory.* Englewood Cliffs, New Jersey: Prentice-Hall, 1968. Pp. 551–571.

Postman, L., & Greenbloom, R. Conditions of cue selection in the acquisition of paired-associate lists. *Journal of Verbal Learning and Verbal Behavior,* 1967, **73,** 91–100.

Richardson, J. Stimulus selection in associative learning. In C. Duncan, L. Sechrest, & A. Melton

(Eds.), *Human memory: Festschrift for Benton J. Underwood.* New York: Appleton-Century-Crofts, 1972. Pp. 155–188.

Runquist, W. N. Intralist interference and stimulus similarity. In C. Duncan, L. Sechrest, & A. Melton (Eds.), *Human memory: Festschrift for Benton J. Underwood.* New York: Appleton-Century-Crofts, 1972. Pp. 189–204.

Schulz, R. W., & Martin, E. Aural paired-associate learning: Stimulus familiarization, response familiarization, and pronounciability. *Journal of Verbal Learning and Verbal Behavior,* 1964, **3,** 139–145.

Sheffield, F. D. The role of meaningfulness of stimulus and response in verbal learning. Unpublished doctoral dissertation, Yale University, 1946.

Shuell, T. J. Retroactive inhibition in free-recall learning of categorized lists. *Journal of Verbal Learning and Verbal Behavior,* 1968, **7,** 797–805.

Sloboda, J. A. Decision times for words and letter search: A wholistic word identification model examined. *Journal of Verbal Learning and Verbal Behavior,* 1976, **15,** 93–102.

Sperling, G. The information available in a brief visual presentation. *Psychological Monographs,* 1960, **74**(Whole No. 498).

Terry, P., Samuels, S. J., & LaBerge, D. The effects of letter degradation and letter spacing on word recognition. *Journal of Verbal Learning and Verbal Behavior,* 1976, **15,** 577–585.

Thorndike, E. L. *The fundamentals of learning.* New York: Teachers College, Columbia University, 1932.

Tolman, E. C. *Purposive behavior in animals and men.* New York: Century Co., 1932.

Tulving, E. Subjective organization in the recall of "unrelated" words. *Psychological Review,* 1962, **69,** 344–354.

Tulving, E. Subjective organization and the effects of repetition in multitrial free recall. *Journal of Verbal Learning and Verbal Behavior,* 1966, **5,** 193–197.

Turvey, M. V. On peripheral and central processes in vision: Inferences from an information processing analysis of masking with pattern stimuli. *Psychological Review,* 1973, **80,** 1–52.

Underwood, B. J. & Schulz, R. W. *Meaningfulness and verbal learning.* Philadelphia: Lippincott, 1960.

Watson, J. B. *Psychology from the standpoint of a behaviorist.* Philadelphia: Lippincott, 1919.

Wickelgren, W. A. Size of rehearsal group and short-term memory. *Journal of Experimental Psychology,* 1964, **68,** 413–419.

Wickelgren, W. A. Rehearsal grouping and the hierarchical organization of serial position cues in short-term memory. *Quarterly Journal of Experimental Psychology,* 1967, **19,** 97–102.

Yngve, V. A model and an hypothesis for language structure. *Proceeding of the American Philosophical Society,* 1960, **104,** 444–466.

4

The Word-Superiority Effect: Perceptual Learning from Reading

Jonathan Baron

University of Pennsylvania

Despite the efforts of constructive skeptics, it now seems to be an established fact that our past experience of looking at printed words helps us to see them better in some important sense. This fact is of interest mostly because it might tell us something useful about reading, possibly that this ability to benefit from experience is a prerequisite for fluent reading. In addition, an examination of this effect might also tell us something more general about pattern recognition as an acquired skill.

At the outset, it might be useful to adopt a working definition of the word-superiority effect as a class of results that can be explained by the idea that experience with words helps us perceive something more quickly (or more accurately in a limited time). Some of the results suggest that this "something" is *letters* in words, as opposed to letters in random letter-strings or letters alone. Other results suggest that what is perceived more quickly are the physical features making up the stimuli or possibly even the words (or word-like strings) themselves. It is often hard to distinguish these possibilities. I shall largely ignore this issue from here on and shall assume that what ties all the results together is the kind of experience that is crucial rather than what perceptual unit is facilitated.

In this review, I will first discuss the history of research on this word-superiority effect. This history can be understood largely in terms of a series of efforts to rule out explanations of the effect that would reduce it to some other well-known phenomenon, such as the use of informational redundancy in guessing. The effect has resisted such reduction and must therefore be dealt with as a phenomenon in its own right. In Section II I shall discuss the kind of knowledge we have acquired from reading that is brought to bear in order to produce the effect. It is clear that some of this knowledge must concern general properties of words rather than knowledge of specific words, since the effect can be found for word-like letter strings as well as real words. Section III will be comprised of a discussion of the idea of a hierarchy of codes and the way this idea can help us explain various discrepant results in the literature on the effect. The extent to which the effect depends on the expectations and preparation of the subject will be examined in Section IV. A discussion of how the relevant knowledge is in fact brought to bear to yield the effect will be presented in Section V. There is some evidence suggesting that the effect may depend upon the initial extraction of more features (the lowest level code in the hierarchy) from words than from nonwords. In Section VI I will discuss the relation between the effect and reading. Correlations between the magnitude of the effect and reading skill suggest that the effect actually occurs during reading, but there are other explanations of these results. Finally, in Section VII I will examine word recognition as an example of pattern recognition in general and the extent to which the word-superiority effect can tell us about this more general set of skills.

I. HISTORY: THE EFFECT THAT WOULD NOT GO AWAY

A. Early Studies

The earliest studies of word perception that are still taken seriously were done in the late 19th century in the context of the study of reading. Huey (1908), the standard source on this work, argued that words were perceived as wholes. This claim in itself need not imply that we have benefited in some way from our experience in reading words, since we might also perceive disorganized strings of letters as wholes. Some of the experiments that support this view, however, do suggest that the perception of words is helped by our experience with them. Erdmann and Dodge (cited in Huey, 1908), for example, found that words could be recognized under conditions of exposure in which single letters could not be recognized. This result alone does not establish the superior perception of words. Subjects might have been less willing to *report* a letter on the basis of seeing a fragment of the letter than to report a word on the basis of seeing a string of letter fragments.

The next studies that bear on the issue of interest were not done until about 1950. The revival of interest in the effects of experience on word perception was part of a "new look" in perception, involving emphasis on the idea that perception is influenced by motives and experience. This movement seems to have been a part of the more general effort made by academic psychologists to come to terms with a growing awareness of the general tenacity of prejudice. If it can be shown that learned biases affect even our perception of reality, then it is more understandable that prejudice would not give way to mere contradictory evidence, for the perception of the evidence itself would be distorted (a view clearly implied, for example, by Bruner, 1957). Thus, people may have turned to studies of the effect of experience on word perception not out of an interest in reading, but as a simple way to make the general point that learning can affect perception. A more specific purpose of these studies was to distinguish effects of experience or "habit strength" from those of motives or "drive," the latter being found in studies using "emotional" words. Such effects of experience were found by Howes and Solomon (1951), Solomon and Howes (1951), and Solomon and Postman (1952). It was shown in these studies that words or pseudowords that had been seen more frequently could be recognized at a lower exposure duration in a tachistoscope, thus showing an effect of experience per se. The criterion for recognition in these cases was correct report of the whole word.

In another classic study, Miller, Bruner, and Postman (1954) found that more letters could be reported from a string of eight letters when the sequence of letters resembled the structure of English words (for example, VERNALIT) than when it did not (for example, OZHGPMJJ). This effect cannot be ascribed to knowledge of word frequency alone, since words were not used. The subjects must have learned something about the probable or allowable sequence of letters or about how to convert letter strings into sounds.

B. Guessing and Response-Bias Models

While these studies clearly made the point that learning can influence simple mental processes of the sort that might be involved in making everyday judgments, they did not show so clearly that learning affects *perception*. As pointed out by many others (see Neisser, 1967, Chapter 5, for a review), subjects might have seen the familiar stimuli no better than the unfamiliar ones but might have been able to use their knowledge of the regularities of the language to make an educated guess about the familiar stimuli in the absence of accurate perception.

Different versions of this guessing or response-bias explanation can be found in the literature. The issue hinges on what subjects do when they make an "educated guess." One possibility is that they either see or do not see a stimulus unit (a word or letter, whichever is to be reported) on a given trial, and if they do not see it they guess, picking responses that are likely to occur (or likely to occur in context) as their preferred guesses. This hypothesis is clearly incapable of accounting for the magnitude of the effects observed. The probability of getting a word correct by mere guessing is very low, even for the most frequent words; yet the differences between the probabilities of being correct for high- and low-frequency words is quite large, too large to be accounted for in this way (see Morton, 1968; Neisser, 1967).

The two major remaining possibilities have been called the "criterion bias" and "sophisticated guessing" models, respectively (Broadbent, 1967; Catlin, 1969; Treisman, 1971). According to the criterion-bias explanation, subjects extract the same amount of information from the stimulus regardless of its frequency but require more information to make a low-frequency response than a high-frequency response. When I say that subjects "extract information," I mean simply that the state of the subjects changes as a result of presentation of the stimulus in such a way that they become increasingly likely to make a correct response. In the criterion-bias model, it is assumed that the units of information are small and that a large number must be extracted before recognition occurs. But within that constraint, the units could be percepts of single letters, parts of letters, points of brightness or darkness, edges, etc.; or they could be more abstract increments in the tendency to make certain responses, not reducible to representations of physical characteristics of the stimulus. If we take this abstract view of the units of information, the criterion-bias model has a simple interpretation. Each possible response already has a number of units accumulated in its respective counter before the trial begins. High-frequency words have more units than do low-frequency words. When the stimulus is presented, more units are added to the correct counter (and possibly to counters of other words that resemble the stimulus word). After the trial, the word with the highest count is chosen as the response. If a low-frequency word is presented, more units will be added to its counter, but if the exposure is brief enough, the number of units added might not be enough to make the total higher than the total for some high-frequency response. If a high-frequency word is presented, the same small number of units added would be enough to make the correct response strong enough to be given. Broadbent (1967) and Morton (1969) have shown that certain predictions derived from a version of this model are supported by data from word-recognition experiments.

The sophisticated-guessing model is similar to the criterion-bias model in that it involves no particular assumption about the form of the information extracted from the stimulus. It holds, however, that subjects do not use information to "increment counters" but rather to narrow down the set of possible responses. Basically, the idea is that subjects see part of the word that is presented and then fill in the rest to make their guess. Subjects see just as much of the word regardless of its frequency, but in choosing their response, they tend to fill in the word so as to make high-frequency more often than low-frequency responses and are thus more likely to be correct when a high-frequency word is presented. For example, if the subjects are aware that a word ends in *HE* and has three letters, they will probably choose *THE* as their guess. They will be right if the word was *THE* but wrong if it was *SHE,* the latter being less frequent. Catlin (1969, 1970) has shown that one version of this model is equivalent to the criterion-bias model with respect to the predictions tested by Broadbent (1967) and Morton (1969). Rumelhart and Siple (1974) described a model that has many features of both the sophisticated-guessing and criterion-bias models, again making the point that they may be hard to distinguish.

Furthermore, it is difficult to say which of these two models is more interesting, that is, more consistent with the existence of a real effect of experience on perception. Both models succeed in showing that the failure of the pure-guessing model is not sufficient to rule out all response-bias explanations of the word-frequency effect. Both models can be made consistent with the idea that the favored response is actually what is seen, rather than merely what subjects choose to say; for example, in the sophisticated-guessing model, subjects might "hallucinate" the letters they fill in. It is hard to find any distinction between the models such that one is seen as explaining the word-superiority effect while the other is seen as explaining it away.

In what follows, I will take the position that the best way to distinguish between interesting and uninteresting mechanisms is in terms of their speed of operation. If a mechanism such as sophisticated guessing operates quickly enough to improve performance even when subjects are going as fast as they can on some task, then that mechanism is interesting; insofar as the task resembles anything done during normal reading, we could be sure that the mechanism involved could actually be used to speed up fluent reading. This argument rests on the assumption, which I make henceforth, that the main reason for being concerned with the word-superiority effect at all is an interest in the psychology of reading rather than an interest in showing how learning or expectations influence our perception in general. There are more direct ways of studying the more general effects.

C. Recent Tachistoscopic Studies

Surely, Gibson was largely responsible for the revival of interest in the word-superiority effect as a way of studying reading. Gibson, Pick, Osser, and Hammond (1962) asked whether the superior perception of words is due entirely to word-specific knowledge or whether some contribution is also made by knowledge of general rules of spelling. They found that subjects were as good at reporting letters from tachistoscopically presented pseudowords such as GLURCK as those from real words and that both words and pseudowords were better than nonwords that violated orthographic rules, such as CKURGL. The most interesting possibility to emerge from this study is the idea that at least some, if not all, of the word-superiority effect could be mediated by the use of general rules rather than specific learning of frequent words. It is also of interest that a similar result was found for deaf subjects by Gibson, Shurcliff, and Yonas (1970). This result suggests that the effect was not due to the subjects pronouncing the stimuli as they saw them or even using their knowledge that certain patterns were more pronounceable than others. More likely, the past learning that accounted for this effect was learning that spelling patterns were likely to occur in particular positions of words. However, it should be noted that some deaf readers do seem to pronounce stimuli in much the same way that normal readers do, enough so for them to make acoustic confusions in reporting briefly exposed strings of letters (Conrad, 1971).

All of the effects described so far could be explained in terms of response biases. The subjects might have seen just as much of the nonwords as of the words and pseudowords, but they might have painstakingly made guesses about what they did not see in the case of words and pseudowords.

One way to get around this problem about guessing is to force the subject to make a choice between a few equally likely alternatives after a tachistoscopic exposure rather than leaving him free to guess what the stimulus was. This method was used by Gibson *et al.* (1962), who found that pseudowords such as *GLURCK* were still perceived more easily than nonwords such as *CKURGL,* although the method used to make up the alternatives did not obviously insure that the visual similarity of the items used in one condition would match that in the other. Kempen, Hermans, Klinkum, Brand, and Verhaaren (1969), on the other hand, found no difference between high- and low-frequency words in a forced-choice procedure in which the subjects were given a choice of two high-frequency words or two low-frequency words after each presentation. However, the two alternatives usually differed in all letter positions, so that the subjects needed only one letter in most cases to make the decision; the fact that errors were made at all suggests that too few letters were seen for the context surrounding any given letter to affect its perception.

Reicher (1969) tachistoscopically presented a word such as *WORD,* an anagram such as *OWRD,* or a single letter such as *D* and then gave subjects a choice between two letters that were equally likely to have been presented, such as *D* or *K.* Note that either one of the letters made a word when used in the same position of the word and either made a nonword when used in the same position of the nonword. This control was used uniformly. In addition, the position of each critical letter was constant across subjects. The subjects did better at deciding which of the two letters had been presented when the letters were presented in a word rather than an anagram or even alone. The subjects could not have known beforehand where to look in the word because the critical letter had an equal chance of occurring in any one of the four positions of the four-letter word. Telling the subjects before the trial which two letters they would have to choose between produced the same results. (Strangely enough, however, the subjects did worse in all conditions when they knew beforehand what the choice would be.)

Reicher's (1969) result is usually referred to as "the" word-superiority effect, because it seemed that for the first time an effect of experience had been shown that could not be accounted for by guessing biases of an uninteresting sort. Even the criterion-bias model and the sophisticated-guessing model cannot account for this result without additional assumptions.

While Reicher's (1969) experiment is definitely a great leap forward, it is not immune to all possible uninteresting explanations. Wheeler (1970) found a few ways of explaining away Reicher's result that were indeed possible even though highly implausible, especially in the case of the difference between words and single letters. First, Wheeler noted that the presentation of the alternatives immediately after the display might have interfered with the letters more than the words, by a kind of backward masking. Wheeler solved this problem by delaying the presentation of the alternatives and found that the effect was still strong even with the delay. Second, in Reicher's experiment, the positions of the single-letter stimuli varied, and this uncertainty might have impaired subjects' perception; again, equating letters and words for positional uncertainty failed to make the effect go away. These first two explanations, it should be noted, deal only with the difference between words and single letters, which was Wheeler's main interest. The third explanation was that the subjects might have directed their attention to those places within words in which either of two letters could make a word. Wheeler dealt with this by using words such as *READ* that could be turned into other words by replacing a letter in any position such as *HEAD, ROAD, REND,* and *REAL;* again the effect remained. Fourth, Reicher's results might have been due to response bias if Reicher did not present both possible words of a pair on different trials; the word he presented might have been a more frequent response. Wheeler added this control, and the effect remained. Finally, Wheeler (1970) suggested that "the effect of word frequency need not be limited to a guessing process [p. 64]" and that access to memory "may be easier for more frequent words [p. 64]." It is not clear why Wheeler (1970) considered this to be an uninteresting explanation. In any case, he tested this explanation by looking at performance on the single letters I and A either alone or in words. These letters are in fact high-frequency words. While these letters were perceived better when they were in words, I do not think we can conclude from this that word frequency plays no part in the effect. For one thing the relatively poor perception of the "words" I and A might have been due to sources of stimulus variance other than frequency. We need to show that effects of this sort hold up statistically across stimuli (Baron, 1975; Clark, 1973).

In any case, Wheeler (1970) did show that the artifactual hypotheses he had proposed did not explain the differences between words and letters. Yet there remains the possibility that perception of single letters may be impaired by factors that have nothing to do with our experience with words, for example, the difficulty of localizing a small stimulus before attempts can be made to identify it. In fact, Matthews and Henderson (1971) reported that perception of a letter may be facilitated by imbedding it in a string of other letters that do not make words or pseudowords, and Estes (1975b) found a situation in which free report of single letters is generally worse than that of letters in nonwords, mostly because of failures to report anything at all.

Wheeler (1970) was primarily concerned with the word-*letter* effect because of another objection that can be made concerning the word-*nonword* effect, namely, that the nonwords cannot be pronounced as a single unit and thus might take up more memory capacity. The effect might thus be dependent on the delay between stimulus and response. Baron and Thurston (1973) found a word–

nonword effect for two-letter words and nonwords, and while it is unlikely that two letters are difficult to remember, it is still possible that there is some measurable memory load.

A related difficulty was raised by Mezrich (1973). Perhaps subjects do better at words because they are in the habit of pronouncing them, and a pronouncing response would facilitate the retention of whatever is presented. Mezrich tested this hypothesis by asking subjects to pronounce whatever they saw and found that the word–letter effect disappeared. One explanation of this finding is that pronouncing the letters helped the subjects retain them. But another explanation is that the subjects tended to pronounce letters rather than words no matter what was presented, and the attempt to pronounce single letters when words were presented interfered with the attempt to see all the letters in the words.

D. Redundancy

A more serious difficulty raised by Thompson and Massaro (1973), Massaro (1973), and Bjork and Estes (1973) is, basically, that a form of the original sophisticated-guessing theory, a form locating the effect in memory rather than perception, might still explain the word-superiority effect as demonstrated so far. Let us say that the word *FOLD* is presented, and subjects get enough information to say with confidence that the second letter is a vowel, the last letter is a consonant, and the third letter has a horizontal line at the bottom, which means it must be E, L, or Z. If they now assume that the stimulus is a word—a reasonable assumption to make when they already know that a lot of the stimuli are words— they can now say, with considerable confidence, that the third letter must be an L. In other cases, they may narrow down the possibilities to a small set of letters rather than just one. After they make this decision, we must also assume that they forget the information on which it was based, in particular, that one critical piece of evidence was the horizontal line at the bottom. Now let us say that the alternatives L and R are presented. Clearly, they will make the right response. If the subjects could not use this kind of information about redundancy to help make a decision—and clearly they would not be able to use it to advantage for nonwords such as OFLD—they might have guessed that the horizontal line indicated the letter E rather than L. When presented with the alternatives L and R, they might well decide that the R looked more like an E than the L did and make the wrong response. In general, then, the subjects might use their knowledge of certain kinds of redundancy—the ability to predict the identity of some letters from information about others—to narrow down the set of possible letters before they look at the alternatives (Estes, 1975b, found that subjects did this when the context letters remained present after the critical letter was masked). This process might, however, go on too slowly to be active in fluent reading.

One way to prevent this use of redundancy in tachistoscopic tasks might be to present the letter choices before the display, as Reicher (1969) did, and thus provide an alternative, more useful, way of narrowing down the alternatives. This method does not prevent subjects from using redundancy within the stimulus, but if the effect is still obtained, we can at least say that such redundancy, if used at all, is used fast enough and automatically enough to override the use of prior information about which letters to look for. While Reicher (1969) and Baron and Thurston (1973, Experiments 2 and 4) found word-superiority effects even with prior presentation of the alternatives, Thompson and Massaro (1973) and Estes (1977) did not find such effects. Estes's (1977) experiment is the most careful of these, since he compared presentation orders in otherwise identical conditions. Yet, in spite of his failure to find an effect with prior presentation, it is still true that effects have been found with prior presentation of a small number of alternative letters. (Recently, Spector and Purcell, 1977, have found *no* decrease in the word-superiority effect with prior knowledge of alternatives. They attribute this apparent conflict with Estes' 1975b results to different stimulus materials and display types.)

Another sort of evidence suggesting that the use of redundancy is unnecessary for a word-superiority effect is provided in studies by Smith and Haviland (1972) and Baron and Thurston (1973). These investigators found that the magnitude of the word-superiority effect in tachistoscopic tasks does not appear to decrease after extended practice with the same small set of words and nonwords. This result suggests that the mechanisms behind the effect are automatic enough so that they are not influenced by knowledge of the possible words and nonwords that could be presented.

All of this evidence is not conclusive, however, for the redundancy mechanism may be used automatically enough so that its use is not influenced by knowledge of alternative letters or possible stimuli, even after much practice. It is worthy to note in this context that while Estes (1975b) found evidence of sophisticated guessing from context when the context surrounding a letter remained present after the target letter was masked, such guessing was much less likely if the context was not presented until the target was masked. This result suggests that the use of redundancy in guessing is indeed a fast and automatic process.

More convincing evidence against the necessity of redundancy comes from an experiment in which Estes (1975b) dropped the usual forced-choice procedure and simply asked the subjects to report the identity of a letter in a particular position, indicated after the display. He found that words were superior to nonwords and single letters. A subset of the stimuli was chosen so that the critical letter was either L or R and so that both L and R in the indicated location would always make a word in the word condition and a nonword in the nonword condition. On these trials, if the subjects were using a redundancy mechanism, they would have been more likely to choose L or R on errors when a word was presented than when a nonword was presented, since they would be trying to make a word; but, in fact, they were slightly less likely to choose

L or R on errors when a word was presented, the only time when L or R could make up a word. This direct test of the redundancy explanation thus indicates that a word-superiority effect can be obtained even when redundancy is not used.

E. Reaction-Time Studies

It seems that whatever the critical psychological processes in forced-choice tachistoscopic demonstrations of the word-superiority effect may be, they operate before the alternatives are presented and before the subject can make use of prior information about what the alternatives will be. We can also conclude that the effect is still found when the subject is required to report a single letter rather than to choose between alternatives. However, there might still be some doubt that the mechanisms producing the effect are fast enough to be useful when performance is limited by time, as is the case in fluent reading. In none of the experiments described so far was there any time pressure on the subject. Reaction-time experiments ought to be capable of settling this issue once and for all. In fact, Eichelman (1970) found that words can be compared to one another more quickly than nonwords when the subject has to say whether two adjacent, simultaneously presented, stimuli are the same or different, and Krueger (1970a, 1970b, 1970c) first showed that subjects can search for letters more quickly in words than in nonwords. Finally, Pollatsek, Well, and Schindler (1975) have shown that Eichelman's effect holds even when the task is to compare the physical identity of words that might differ only in the case of a single letter (for example, *WORD–WORd*). One limitation on this set of reaction-time experiments is that they have yet to show anything like a word–letter effect; all of them compare words and nonwords with the same number of letters. However, the main reason for showing the word–letter effect in the first place was to rule out the role of memory in the word-superiority effect. If memory is involved in reaction-time experiments, it is surely the sort of memory that might also be involved in fluent reading.

The existence of a word-superiority effect now seems to be as well established as anything else in psychology. It seems unlikely that anyone can now think of any more uninteresting explanations of this effect that cannot be ruled out on the basis of the evidence now available. Fluent readers have learned something about words, as opposed to random letter strings, that allows words to be perceived more quickly than they would have been if this learning had not occurred.

II. WHAT KNOWLEDGE?

A. The Possibilities

Given that we have learned something about words that allows us to deal with them more quickly than similar forms with which we have had no experience, a question that comes to mind is, what have we learned? There are many properties that distinguish words from nonwords, and learning about any of these properties could help us see words more quickly. It might be helpful to begin with the following rough categorization of the different kinds of knowledge about words that might account for the effect. Each kind of knowledge corresponds to a certain kind of experience we have had with words:

Specific: 1. meaning
2. lexical membership
3. whole-word familiarity
4. word-specific associations with sounds
5. pronunciation rules
General: 6. spelling rules
7. familiarity with spelling patterns

Specific factors require knowledge of particular words, whereas *general* factors characterize pseudowords such as *PAKE* as well as words. Note also that different kinds of knowledge make use of different sorts of representations, loosely categorizable as semantic (1 and 2), phonemic (4 and 5), and visual (3, 6, and 7), which I take to include the use of letter-identity representations.

Knowledge of *meaning* comes from learning to interpret a word in the context of a sentence and to make semantic and grammatical judgments. There may well be several different kinds of knowledge of meaning. (As one illustration, persons with brain damage might be able to distinguish nouns from verbs but not know what the words mean when used in commands they are asked to follow.) However, for our purposes here, they are lumped together. Knowledge of *lexical membership*, resulting from simply being taught to distinguish words from nonwords, is distinct from meaning because its role in the word-superiority effect might be different. Meaning might enrich the perception of the stimulus by adding information to the subjects' representation of what was presented. Knowledge of lexical membership might work by restricting guesses or hypotheses to words, as may occur in the "redundancy" explanation discussed above.

Knowledge of *whole-word familiarity* results from differential exposure to different words. It might affect word perception in still another way: there might be some very general mechanism that allows people to see things more easily simply by virtue of the past experience of seeing them. Whole-word familiarity does not necessarily operate in precisely the same way as does familiarity with common patterns of letters or spelling patterns. While both kinds of knowledge might affect perception in the same way, any effect of whole-word familiarity would depend upon the word preserving its integrity. If the word-superiority effect were found to hold for nonword strings that are similar to words, whole-word familiarity could not account for this generalization. Knowledge of spelling rules, on the other hand, results from learning which letter sequences are possible. It allows a person to say that the only possible letters that could appear in the blank in *BAT__S* are H and the vowels. This sort of knowledge differs from knowledge of lexical membership in that the latter would tell the subject that the only possible letters that could appear in the blank are H and E, and from knowledge of familiarity, which would make H the likely choice.

Knowledge of pronunciation rules is acquired in learning to pronounce new words. It allows a person to translate a string of letters into sounds in a regular way. For example, SH at the beginning of a word is always pronounced the same way. Pronunciation rules must be distinguished, however, from rote associations between words and their sounds. Such associations must be used for words that break the rules of pronunciation, such as *SURE, ONE,* etc., but they may also be used in reading regular words (see Baron, 1977).

This categorization of different kinds of knowledge is rough because each kind of knowledge in the list can be subcategorized still further, and there may be other categories that cut across those mentioned. The main virtues of the list are that some of the distinctions made in the list (unfortunately not always the ones that can obviously be distinguished experimentally) have implications for the mechanism whereby the knowledge is used to improve perception.

B. Specific Versus General Knowledge

The simplest sort of experiment that can begin to distinguish which of these kinds of knowledge are involved is to compare performance on words, unpronounce-able nonwords, and regular pronounceable nonwords that resemble words as much as possible but are not actually words. If the word-superiority effect generalizes to the pseudowords—that is, the stimuli made up to resemble words—and if subjects perceive the pseudowords better than the nonwords, then we can conclude that some subset of the general factors contributes to the effect. Such generalization to pseudowords has been found by all who have looked for it, and this includes a large number of researchers.

Some of these studies have found an even stronger result, namely, that subjects do no better with words than with pseudowords. Baron and Thurston (1973) found this result for forced-choice tachistoscopic recognition, as did Spoehr and Smith (1975) in one of their experiments; Egeth and Blecker (1971) found this equivalence for same–different reaction time, as did Baron (1974a); and Baron (1974a) and Herrmann and McLaughlin (1973) found it for very different kinds of letter-search tasks. In situations where this result is reliably found, we can conclude that factors specific to words do not contribute to the effect at all. In these cases, whatever word-superiority effect is found must be due entirely to properties that characterize pseudowords as well as words.

Others have questioned the generality of this conclusion. Krueger (1970b) had earlier found an effect of word frequency on letter-search speed; and Barron and Pittenger (1974), Spoehr and Smith (1975, Experiment 1), and Manelis (1974), for example, have found differences between words and pseudowords in forced-choice recognition and same–different reaction-time tasks. If these results are robust, they indicate that at least some factors specific to words but not pseudowords are operating in the tasks used. Henderson (1974) has also found that meaningful acronyms such as *FBI* can be compared more quickly than meaningless, but equally un-word-like, strings such as IBF (except in the case of two-letter acronyms, which suggests an involvement of memory in the effect for longer strings.) This finding is of particular interest because it cannot be accounted for by any kinds of knowledge except 1, 2, or 3 above. It differs from the other findings in that it is harder to account for by 4—association of letter groups with sounds—although it is possible to imagine a mechanism by which the effect could be due to the facility acquired in reading acronyms, as strings of letters, more quickly than other strings of letters. Henderson suggests that "meaning" will produce a word-superiority effect only when other factors, such as pronounceability according to rules, are not available. Since "meaning" has not been unconfounded from other factors such as whole-word familiarity, it is appropriate to take Henderson's use of the term to include these other factors.

How can we account for the discrepancy between studies that show effects of word-specific factors and those that do not? While the answer to this question is not yet available, it is possible to point to certain variables that might be involved. The studies that do not show word-specific effects often involve repeated presentations of the same stimuli (Manelis, 1974). Word-specific effects may disappear after the first few presentations of particular words or pseudowords. If word-specific effects do disappear quickly, they may be due to whole-word familiarity. We cannot ascribe such transient effects to any variables that continue to distinguish words and pseudowords regardless of the amount of practice at the task. In particular, transient superiority of words over pseudowords cannot be due to meaning, since pseudowords remain meaningless. So far, it is not clear that repetition is an important variable, since no attempt has been made within a single study to examine the effects of repeated presentation on the difference between words and pseudowords in situations in which such a difference is obtained.

A less interesting factor that might account for some findings of superiority of words over pseudowords (or frequency effects) is a failure to make sure that the pseudowords (or low-frequency words) are in fact as "word-like" as the words. This is surely a problem in studies that attempt to study word-specific effects by manipulating word frequency, since it has repeatedly been noted (for example, Kinsbourne & Evans, 1970) that high- and low-frequency words tend to differ in such general factors as conformity to spelling regularities. Even in studies comparing words and pseudowords, there is no known way to equate the two kinds of stimuli on *all* relevant factors. It is not sufficient, for example, to show that the sets of words and pseudowords used are equal in such measures as the probability of the letter pairs or triples occurring in a sample of English (bigram or trigram frequency), because it might also be relevant where a given group of letters occurs in a word and what else is in the word. To take an extreme example, CKNG might be fairly high in bigram frequency, but it is certainly not very wordlike. Similarly, strings like OTE might appear to be wordlike, and might be high in trigram frequency, but might frustrate the normal operation of a system that looks for vowels in the middle of three letter words, a strategy that might be part of whatever general strategy of analysis accounts for the word-superiority effect.

Aside from these problems in principle, there are problems in fact with the stimuli in all the studies I know of that list the stimuli used and that show a word–pseudoword difference. If we remove the initial consonant cluster from each word or pseudoword beginning with a consonant and then try to make up words by replacing that cluster with other clusters of the same length, we find that more words can be made up from the remainders of words than of pseudowords. This finding indicates that the endings of the words are more productive than those of the pseudowords. In view of this sort of problem, it seems that a good strategy for someone interested in finding a real word-specific effect in a given task would be to use a set of stimuli for which someone else has failed to find such an effect and which otherwise appear well matched, for example, those used by Baron (1974a).

Methodological insensitivity may also be involved in some of the failures to find better perception of words than pseudowords. It turns out that with one or two exceptions (for example, Herrmann & McLaughlin, 1973), the studies that fail to find word–pseudoword differences are also the ones that find relatively small differences between words and nonwords. Possible candidates for factors that make a method sensitive or not (see Manelis, 1974, for further discussion) are the kind of mask used (Johnston & McClelland, 1973), with patterned masks more likely to show a big effect; the frequency of the words used; the mix of stimuli expected (see Aderman & Smith, 1971); the size of the stimuli, with smaller stimuli being better; and the amount of information the subjects have to transmit, with a wider range of alternatives (for example, free report of the letter in a position, as used by Estes, 1975a and 1975b) showing bigger effects. Possibly anything that slows down the speed of analysis will allow more kinds of knowledge to have time to influence the response more strongly. However, except in the case of the Aderman and Smith study—which showed no word–nonword effect when the subjects expected only nonwords—and the Johnston and McClelland study on masking, few studies show that an effect can be made to appear and disappear by manipulating a single variable. Thus, there is no firm basis for saying anything about the other variables. Yet, there is an interesting hypothesis about *why* these kinds of variables should matter, the idea that words are analyzed in a series of processing stages and that different tasks have bottlenecks in different stages. In particular, the tasks that show word-specific effects are influenced by what goes on in fairly late stages, while those that do not rely completely on the output of early stages.

C. Internal Structure Versus Association with Sound

Before discussing this idea in more detail, I should mention some other kinds of experiments that might bear on the issue of the kind of knowledge that accounts for the word-superiority effect. In particular, there have been several attempts to pull apart the effects of knowledge concerning pronunciation, pronunciation rules and word-specific associations, from the effects of knowledge about the internal structure of the stimulus itself, such as familiarity with spelling patterns and knowledge of what spelling patterns are permissible. It turns out to be extremely difficult to get direct evidence bearing on this issue. Some researchers (for example, Spoehr & Smith, 1975) have tried to attack it directly by asking whether conformity to spelling rules or ease of pronunciation is correlated more highly with performance across words; such studies have suggested that both factors are involved.

But the problem here is similar to the one that arises when we try to construct word-like pseudowords. In the absence of full knowledge about how spelling regularities or pronunciation rules might be used to improve perception, it is impossible to know what measure of pronounceability or spelling regularity is the right one to use. Almost all of these kinds of measures, digram frequency, number of phonemes per letter, etc., are themselves correlated across sets of words, and these correlations increase the difficulty of unconfounding their effects.

Other attempts have been made to pull apart the effects of internal constraints on spelling from those of pronounceability per se. As already mentioned, Gibson et al., (1970), found a word-superiority effect in deaf readers, who presumably did not know pronunciation rules; one wishes that there were independent evidence of the lack of knowledge of pronunciation rules, however, and that a procedure less subject to the influence of guessing strategies had been used.

One mechanism whereby pronounceability per se might have an effect on perception is its function in constraining the information subjects have about sound as well as visual appearance of letter strings at the time of decisions. In a task in which they must say which of two words was presented tachistoscopically, or a reaction-time task in which they must say whether two words are the same or different, the subjects might be able to use information about differences in sounds to improve performance, possibly because the visual information from which the sound information was derived is difficult to get at as efficiently at the time of decision.

This particular mechanism has been ruled out, I think, by experiments showing that a comparison of homophones such as *FOUR* and *FORE* is just as efficient as comparison of other word pairs differing in the same letters, such as *SOUR* and *SORE*. Baron and Thurston (1973) got a result of this sort in forced-choice tachistoscopic recognition, and Baron (1974a) as well as Pollatsek et al. (1975) found the same thing in same–different reaction time. One of the problems with these experiments is that the critical comparison was made only on trials in which the right answer was "different," since we would not expect any difference in performance in comparing *SOUR–SOUR* and *FOUR–FOUR*; there may be some unknown reason why extra information about sound would be useful only on "same" trials. Thurston (1974) circumvented this problem by asking subjects to say whether or not two four-letter words had the same final three letters, and he manipulated rhyming orthogonally to similarity versus difference of the last three letters (for example, *SOUR–FORE, SORE–FOUR, SOUR–FOUR,* and *SORE–FORE*). When the words were presented one directly above the other (a display that does yield a word-superiority effect), there was no effect of rhyme on either same or different judgments. When the words were presented side-by-side, however, the "same" judgments were affected by rhyme. As I will discuss later, comparison of side-by-side words might involve the use of processing stages beyond those used in tasks in which the subject may make direct letter-by-letter comparisons between the stimuli.

An interesting feature of Thurston's (1974) experiment was that the two stimuli to be compared (in the one-above-the-other display) were printed in different cases, one in capital letters, the other in small letters. Thus, subjects were forced to compare letter identities rather than visual forms at least some of the time.

The Pollatsek *et al.* (1975) study confirmed in another way the general conclusion that the word-superiority effect in reaction-time tasks is not dependent upon comparison of phonemic codes. Since an effect was found for words that were phonemically identical as a result of their being identical in spelling (*WORD–WORd*), comparison of sounds, or meanings for that matter, could not be used to decide that the words were different.

While these studies rule out the use of phonemic information in comparing two stimuli in some tasks that show a word superiority effect, they do not rule out all possible mechanisms by which pronounceability per se might affect performance on perceptual tasks. Another sort of mechanism is one in which formation of a phonemic representation might facilitate extraction of information from the stimulus, in ways I will discuss later, even when the phonemic representation itself is not used in making a comparison or deciding between alternatives.

On the other side of the coin, some attempts have been made to look for effects of spelling regularities independently of the relation between these regularities and pronunciation. Among these is a study by Baron and Thurston (1973), who looked at performance in a same–different reaction-time task in which the stimuli were correctly or incorrectly spelled chemical formulas, such as *NaBr* and *BrNa,* respectively. Chemists compared the correctly spelled formulas more quickly. This suggests an effect of spelling rules per se, but even if other factors could be ruled out, the situation differs greatly from those that are minimally necessary for the word-superiority effect.

Baron (1974b) tried another approach in looking for an effect of spelling regularities. He made up sets of stimuli that contained various sorts of spelling constraints, formally similar to some of the constraints that actually exist in English spelling, and exposed subjects to stimuli with and without the constraints in forced-choice tachistoscopic tasks of the sort used in earlier demonstrations of the word-superiority effect. The stimuli were consonant pairs, which could not be pronounced at all by the sorts of pronunciation rules that can be applied to words but not to nonwords. If the spelling constraints improved perception, this could not be due to availability of these kinds of pronunciation rules. A constrained set of stimuli could consist of a set like PL and XV, where subjects were given a forced choice between these two pairs. In a corresponding unconstrained set, subjects would be given a forced choice between PL and XV or between PV and XL. (Actually, different, but balanced, sets of letters were used.) In the constrained set, P was always followed by L, just as, for example, in English Q is always followed by U, but in the unconstrained set P could be followed by L or V. Subjects could not use their knowledge of this constraint to improve guessing, since seeing one letter alone was sufficient for them to make a correct choice between the alternatives. Furthermore, each of the possible digrams was presented equally often, so that there were twice as many trials with the unconstrained set because it contained twice as many sets of alternatives; therefore, any effect found in this example could not be ascribed to digram frequency differences, but only to sequential probabilities.

Performance on the constrained set was more accurate, and this superiority persisted for at least a day after the last exposure to the two sets. In another experiment, a persistent effect of digram frequency (or "whole-word frequency," if one wants to look at it that way, since all stimuli contained only two letters) was also found. In still another experiment, an effect of a constraint on order, analogous to the rule that says that T and H must appear only in that order within a syllable, was also found. While this experiment showed that mechanisms exist that are sensitive to certain spelling constraints, it did not show that these mechanisms are brought to bear when other mechanisms, such as those involving pronunciation rules, are available, or when the set of stimuli used is not so small. It might be that such constraints are of no use at all when they are as complex as they are in English.

A study done by Estes (1975b) using real words and nonwords suggests that some sorts of spelling constraints might be much more important than others. Estes asked subjects to report what letter occurred in a position designated after a tachistoscopic presentation. He found that the superiority of words in this task could be accounted for entirely by a reduction of transposition errors, those involving report of a letter in a position other than the one cued, as opposed to intrusion errors in which a letter not in the stimulus at all was reported. This leads naturally to the suggestion that use of constraints on the ordering of letters is sufficient for the effect. While this result shows that ordering is crucial for the word-superiority effect, at least in Estes' situation, it does not help very much in deciding whether spelling or phonemic regularities account for the effect. It might be that the advantage for words in this experiment is a result of knowing how to order phonemes rather than letters, for example.

Brooks (1976) conducted a study bearing more closely on the nature of the relevant word–nonword differences. He made up an artificial alphabet using symbols, such as triangles or squares, to stand for English letters. He then wrote out a number of words in this alphabet and asked subjects to memorize associations between each artificial word and some real spoken word. In the conditions of interest, there was no relation between the artificial word and the response the subjects had to memorize; they simply had to memorize arbitrary associations between each stimulus and a word and then practice responding to the stimuli until they attained considerable speed. While the subjects could not use pronunciation rules, they *were* exposed to the regularities of spelling. After this sort of practice, the subjects were asked to learn new lists of the same sort, except that half of these new lists contained nonwords instead of words written in the artificial alphabet. Even though the associations were still arbitrary, the nonwords were harder to use as stimuli than were the words; response time was longer over the course of learning at least. Since the subjects never learned pronunciation rules for the artificial alphabet, the only thing that can account for this "word-superiority effect" is the spelling regularities contained in the words. These might be rules of spelling or familiarity with common patterns, but whatever it is, it is internal to the stimuli and does not concern their associations with sounds, which were always arbitrary. A problem with this demonstration is its questionable relevance to other measures of the word-superiority effect, regardless of its inherent interest.

A final relevant study is that of Mason (1975), who found that good readers showed an even greater effect for pseudowords than for words when the pseudowords were made up by picking letters that were highly likely to occur in each position. This result supports Estes' (1975b) ideas about the importance of ordering. But it also suggests an effect of spelling regularity over and above any effect of pronounceability, since it is doubtful that the pseudowords were more pronounceable than the words, at least in terms of speed of pronunciation (see Baron, 1977).

Thus, it can be concluded (barring the discovery of as yet unsuspected artifacts in the relevant experiments) that there are some cases in which spelling regularities do affect extraction or use of information from word-like stimuli even when pronounceability per se is controlled. It also seems that the use of artificial materials is at present a more productive way to answer these kinds of questions than correlational studies with real words. More generally, it is clear that general factors such as pronounceability and spelling regularity play a large part in accounting for the word-superiority effect.

III. PROCESSING STAGES IN WORD RECOGNITION TASKS

The idea that there are processing stages strung together in a fixed order can explain many of the apparently discrepant results mentioned above, and it has other attractive features as well. In most discussions based on this idea (for example, Baron, 1974a; Estes, 1975a, 1974b; LaBerge & Samuels, 1974), it is assumed that there are different kinds of representations (codes) that can be activated as the result of presenting a stimulus, given that the subjects have an appropriate set, and that some of these representations require the prior or simultaneous activation of others. The kinds of representations usually talked about are those of physical features of the stimulus such as lines and angles but perhaps including abstract features such as symmetry or repetition as well, letter-identity codes, spelling-pattern codes, abstract word-identity codes, phonemic codes, representations of word groups such as familiar phrases, and various kinds of lexical and semantic representations. It is often suggested that letter codes or spelling-pattern codes depend upon physical codes, and that other codes such as phonemic and word-identity codes depend in turn on letter- or spelling-pattern codes, rather than directly on physical-feature codes.

In some reaction-time tasks, it may be appropriate to assume that only some types of possible codes are used to produce the response. In some cases, as in comparing two simultaneously presented words, extraction of information about visual features might be sufficient. Detection of certain features in both words might permit a correct response. In other cases, letter-identity codes, sounds, or even lexical or semantic representations might be used. It might seem strange to analyze a stimulus up to a fairly high level when a lower level would be logically sufficient, but there are many reasons why it might be advantageous to do so. For example, while extracting visual features might be easier than deriving lexical codes, it might be much faster to compare two unitary lexical codes than a multitude of visual features. It is thus difficult to say a priori what code a subject will use to derive the output for a given task. But we *can* say that performance on a reaction-time task will depend not only on whatever factors influence the stage that provides the output but also on whatever factors influence prior stages on which that final stage depends.

In tachistoscopic tasks, it might be advantageous to have a certain kind of code available before the stimulus effectively disappears. Certain codes, such as feature codes or even letter-identity codes, may be destroyed by the end of the stimulus or the onset of the mask, and it would be necessary to have formed higher level codes by that time to avoid errors. Thus, the speed of formation of the first code that survives the presentation will be crucial for performance, and any factor that influences the speed or accuracy of formation of this code will influence performance.

The usefulness of the idea of stages in explaining the results discussed above, as well as other results, is based on the assumption that different tasks, for whatever reasons, take their output from different stages. For tachistoscopic tasks, this means that the stage in question is the first one to survive the presentation of the stimulus long enough to be used in making a response. To understand the results above, we need to think in terms of, at most, three stages. For purposes of exposition, I will speak of features, letters, and lexical (word) codes, but it should be emphasized that the available data do not allow us to distinguish between different kinds of features, between letter codes and spelling-pattern codes, or even between lexical and phonemic codes. Estes (1975b) provided a stage analysis differing only in details from that proposed here. According to the proposal I am making, tasks that take their output from feature codes do not show a word-superiority effect at all, tasks that take their output from letter codes show a word-superiority effect but do not show specific effects (that is, differences between words and pseudowords), and tasks that take their output from lexical codes do show word-specific effects, as well as effects of phonemic similarity.

There are really only a few cases in which an effect of one of these variables has been found for one task but not for a similar task done in the same laboratory. Johnston and McClelland (1973) found that a word-superiority effect when a patterned mask was used but not when a blank-field mask was used. This result makes sense in terms of the stage idea if we assume that the patterned mask destroys feature codes but the blank field does not, and that the mechanisms responsible for the word-superiority effect are those that construct letter codes from feature codes. In the blank-field condition, errors arise when features are not extracted; if features are extracted, subjects have enough time to construct letter codes before the feature information disappears. In the patterned-mask condition, the speed of constructing letter codes is crucial. Similarly, Estes (1975a, 1975b) has found a situation in which there is no word-superiority effect in a forced-choice situation with prior presentation of alternative letters, but there is an effect when the subject is told what *position* to report after the exposure. Estes similarly suggested that his precue procedure may tap the level of features, while the postcue procedure is limited by construction of letter codes.

In same–different reaction-time tasks, different stages may be used for the output when stimuli are presented side-by-side (for example, by Henderson, 1974) as opposed to one above the other. In the latter condition, the subject can make comparisons letter-by-letter, so that letter codes may be sufficient, but in side-by-side comparison, use of letter codes would require either memory for several letters or switching back and forth, so that a more unitary code such as a lexical or phonemic one becomes more efficient. This idea could explain Thurston's (1974) finding that same–different comparisons of rhyming pairs differed from non-rhymes only in side-by-side comparison.

Baron (1974a) found that when subjects are asked to compare the sounds of words or pseudowords instead of their letters, words are compared more quickly than pseudowords, even though comparing letters in the same situation was not affected by wordness. Presumably, wordness affects a late stage.

The use of different stages in different tasks may also explain why some situations do not show word-superiority effects at all (for example, Estes, 1975b; Massaro, 1973), although it is impossible to say just what factors might have prevented the destruction of feature codes. On the other hand, other unknown factors may encourage the subject to use later stages in certain situations where otherwise unexpected word-specific effects are found. Late stages might be involved in limiting performance when anything is done to slow down performance at all, such as using small letters, letters in an unfamiliar type-face, or low levels of illumination. This may happen because slowing down performance may allow the subject to process different parts of the stimulus at different rates (Baron, 1974a), so that parts of the stimulus may be analyzed to a late stage while other parts are analyzed to an early stage. In such a case, tentative representations at a late stage might have time to influence the formation of codes at an earlier stage in a way that would not occur if processing were allowed to proceed more quickly.

Free-report tasks (as opposed to forced-choice tasks) in which subjects are asked to guess all the letters presented in a tachistoscopic exposure, or to name the word presented, might also involve later processing stages than forced-choice tasks. This would explain why word-specific effects are frequently found in free-report tasks. If this stage hypothesis is correct, an important question is whether the stages used in tachistoscopic free-report tasks are also used in fluent reading, or whether they even limit performance in beginning readers.

Thurston (1974) attempted to test this successive stage idea directly using a number of tasks. He was concerned with two stages, one a phonemic stage that is needed for judging whether two words rhyme and one a letter-identity stage that is needed for deciding whether two words have the same letters (or some of the same letters). In some experiments the two words were presented in different cases, upper or lower. Thurston found that it took no longer to say whether two words rhymed *and* had the same letters than whether they just rhymed, but it did take longer to say whether they rhymed and had the same letters than it took to say whether they just had the same letters. Similarly, as already mentioned, whether the words rhymed did not affect the speed of judging whether they had the same letters (when presented one above the other), but whether they had the same letters did affect the speed of judging whether they rhymed. Most interestingly, specific practice at saying whether a word rhymed with another word had just as much effect on the speed of saying whether that word had the same letters as another word as did specific practice on the letter task itself, but performance on saying whether a word rhymed with another was better when the subject had prior practice with that word in a rhyme task as opposed to a letter task. All of these findings are consistent with the hypothesis that the stage needed for phonemic comparison succeeds that which is needed for letter identity (or spelling pattern) comparison. Also, the findings support the idea that the formation of phonemic information necessarily involves the prior extraction of the kind of information used in the letter tasks (even if the phonemic information is not derived from the letter codes directly), but that letter information can be extracted and used without prior formation of phonemic information. Thurston's results apply only to the two stages he was interested in, but these techniques of analysis might be useful for discovering other stages as well.

It needs to be noted, I think, that we often have no independent definition of a code or kind of representation except that provided by a certain task. Thus, the letter-identity tasks serve to define letter-identity codes (which in Thurston's experiments cannot be distinguished from spelling-pattern codes) and the phonemic tasks define phonemic codes in the sense that the "output" on each task should depend only upon the kind of code in question, even though that code may itself depend on others. This defining of codes in terms of the tasks that measure them may at first seem to be circular in a damaging way. However, when a theory about the sequencing of codes is tested in the way that Thurston tested his proposal, the definition is tested at the same time, and in this way, circularity is no longer a problem.

Another comment is in order about what it means to say that one code precedes another, given that each code can only be defined in terms of the tasks for which it serves as an *output* and given that in a logical sense certain codes must precede others. For example, in a reading task, extraction of visual information must logically precede formation of phonemic information. Is it an empirical question at all whether one code precedes another? I would suggest that it is if we restate the question to ask whether the code that precedes a given code in a given task is exactly the same code that provides the output in some other task. This is why I think Thurston's (1974) transfer experiments are so important. These experiments show that insofar as formation of any codes is subject to practice effects, the code used in the letter tasks is the same as that which precedes the phonemic code in the phonemic tasks. While other methods, such as Sternberg's (1969) additive-factor method, might allow us to say with some certainty that a task involves two stages, these methods do not help us say what those stages are in terms of the tasks for which each stage provides output.

IV. THE ROLE OF VOLUNTARY CONTROL, SET, AND AUTOMATICITY

Some of the most interesting recent findings concerning the word-superiority effect have been those showing that the effect is influenced by preparation and set. Aderman and Smith (1971) led subjects to expect either words or nonwords by presenting a string of words or a string of nonwords in succession in a tachistoscopic task. The word-superiority effect appeared only when the string preceding the critical trial consisted of words, suggesting that the subjects' expectation that words would be presented was necessary for the word-superiority effect. However, these results are suspect because of the lack of a significant interaction between expectation and word vs. nonword.

LaBerge, Petersen, and Norden (1976) have obtained a similar result in a same–different reaction-time task. When the subjects had just been presented with a string of trials using familiar "spelling patterns" (such as CH–CH), these patterns were compared more quickly than control stimuli using the same letters (such as HC–HC), but this spelling-pattern superiority was not found if the patterns were presented after a string of control trials. Further, in one experiment, LaBerge *et al.*, were able to mimic the effects of a string of trials, to some extent, by simply telling subjects which type of stimulus was likely to occur. The magnitude of the spelling-pattern superiority effect was greater when the subjects were told that spelling patterns were likely to be presented than when they were told that control patterns were likely.

Another interesting finding along these lines is that of Johnston and McClelland (1974), who found that perception of letters in words was impaired by telling the subjects where in the word the critical letter would occur. It seems that the position uncertainty encourages the subjects to analyze the word as a whole, that is, to try to see all the letters, and this effort brings into play mechanisms that facilitate word perception.

Still another finding of interest is that of Hawkins, Reicher, Rogers, and Peterson (1976), who found that subjects were able to discriminate nonhomophones (such as SOLD COLD) better than homophones (SENT CENT) in a tachistoscopic forced-choice experiment only when there were few pairs of homophones among the stimuli presented in a block of trials. While not contradicting earlier evidence (Baron and Thurston, 1973) that a word-superiority effect can be obtained without reliance on phonemic information, this result shows that such information can be used under the right conditions.

The general finding that the word-superiority effect is sensitive to set and task demands is also of interest because it contrasts with other findings showing that certain other effects are totally automatized and apparently not subject to control. In the Stroop effect, for example, people seem unable to suppress the activation of a semantic code associated with a word stimulus, as indicated by the finding that the effect is found for associated words as well as color words themselves (Klein, 1964). Similarly, it seems that the mechanisms that produce the word-superiority effect are not modified by the accrual of explicit knowledge about the letters that can occur in particular positions of nonwords. The effect does not disappear even with extended practice on closed sets of redundant nonwords, at least as long as the corresponding words receive similar practice (Baron & Thurston, 1973; Smith & Haviland, 1972). It might eventually be possible to break down performances like those involved in word recognition into units, each of which is brought into play by certain predisposing variables, but each of which functions as an automatized unit, so that no part of the unit can be brought into play without the whole.

V. THE MECHANISMS BEHIND THE WORD-SUPERIORITY EFFECT

The most obvious question about the word-superiority effect is how it works. When many first hear about the effect, it almost seems to them that the perceptual system knows what it is going to see before it sees it. Earlier in this review, I dealt with most of the proposed answers to this question that are uninteresting in the sense of implicating faulty methodology or clearly nonperceptual processes such as guessing biases. Wheeler (1970) proposed three mechanisms that do draw upon perceptual and memorial processes and illustrated each mechanism with a particular example. It is worthwhile to restate Wheeler's basic argument here.

A. Wheeler's Mechanisms

I may interpret the word-superiority effect by saying that subjects have more relevant information about letter identities available at the time of responding for words than for nonwords or single letters, that is, they are more likely to be right in identifying or recognizing a letter in a word at a given time. Wheeler's argument, in essence, is that there are exactly three different ways in which such a state of affairs can come about: (a) The subjects might have extracted *more information* from the words. (b) The subjects might not have extracted more information overall, but might have extracted more relevant information relative to irrelevant information. Wheeler (1970) speaks here of *feature selection* because the features extracted must be selected so that they are more relevant to the decision about letter identities in words than in nonwords. (c) It could be the case that the information from words is preserved in such a way that it is lost less quickly. Thus, Wheeler makes two basic distinctions: between relevant and irrelevant information and between information available immediately and information available only at the time of the response. While the most obvious explanation of the word-superiority effect is that more information is extracted, all we have evidence for is that more relevant information is available at the time the response is made, so we must make these distinctions in enumerating the possible explanations of the effect. Wheeler's classification remains important because practically all other explanations that have been proposed are examples of only one of the three general types and because none of the three can yet be ruled out.

There are, however, several interesting possibilities that have been proposed in one or another of the three categories, and some attempts have been made to test or rule out particular models or even classes of models. For example, Baron (1974b) has attempted to test a class of models that includes Wheeler's simple more-features model in an artificial analogue of the word-superiority effect in which the subject was presented with constrained or unconstrained pairs of letters; in a constrained set the alternatives might always consist of TS vs. JN, while an unconstrained set might consist of alternative sets of PV vs. XL and PL vs. XV. (For another subject, the constrained set would be PV and XL, and the unconstrained set TS, JN, TN, and JS.) The fact that the subjects did better on the constrained sets seems difficult to explain in terms of a more-features model, because each of the six pairs listed above was presented equally often. Any attempt to explain this effect in terms of the extraction of more information from the constrained set would have to explain why the subject came to extract different amounts of information from stimuli presented equally often. While the artificial nature of this task may make it unlike those defining the word-superiority effect in important ways, it does seem to show that there are mechanisms available other than those that would be minimally necessary for the more-features explanation to hold.

Feature-selection mechanisms may be divided into pre-set ones, in which the types of information that will be selectively extracted are determined before the presentation of the stimulus, and contingent mechanisms, which use some information from the stimulus to determine what other information to try to extract. Pre-set selection mechanisms have the same kind of trouble accounting for the results of Baron, 1974b, as the more-features mechanisms; in fact, the distinction between pre-set and contingent mechanisms, where more-features mechanisms are considered pre-set, may be a more useful one in some cases than the distinction between more-features and feature-selection. An example of a pre-set selection mechanism would be one that looks for different features in different positions of a short word, depending on the probability of different letters occurring in each position; the features looked for would be those that best distinguish the letters likely to occur in each position from one another.

Contingent-selection mechanisms may be loosely divided into those that use tentative representations of late-stage codes to facilitate the activation of early-stage codes and those that do not. An example of the latter would be a mechanism using some features of a letter (plus knowledge of redundancies between features; see Smith, 1971) to decide which other features to look for in a given position. For example, a detection of a vertical line on the right side of the second letter of a string might make it worthwhile to look for features that would distinguish C, T, and W from S, A, E, I, O, and U in the first position. If C, T, or W were found in the first position, the second letter would have to be H, and a search for features that distinguish H, N, and M could be avoided. Such a procedure could be based entirely on knowledge of spelling rules and regularities of English words. Another possibility, similar to one proposed by Spoehr and Smith (1973), would use a procedure like this only after another procedure had segmented a word into syllables. Such a two-step mechanism would take advantage of the useful fact that there are more regularities in spelling and pronunciation within syllables than within words. Segmentation may be useful in other cases besides syllables; for example, even within a syllable it might be useful to segment into consonant clusters and vowel clusters, since each type of unit obeys fairly strict rules. A general mechanism that took advantage of the greater regularity within different kinds of segments, but did not use higher level codes, would be formally similar to Winograd's (1972) parser for English grammar with its semantic system removed.

Contingent mechanisms that use higher level codes have a number of such codes available that they might use. Spoehr and Smith (1973) worked out a mechanism that tries to pronounce everything it sees, that is, convert it into a phonemic code according to pronunciation rules. It extracts information about letters only to decide which phonemes to string together, and it makes use of knowledge of pronunciation rules and of constraints on the possible sequence of phonemes to decide what letters to look for. This is the sort of mechanism I talked about in Section II that uses a phonemic code not as the basis for making a response but as a mechanism for getting more visual information from the stimulus. The possibility of this kind of mechanism was the reason that existence of a word-superiority effect for same–different comparison of homophones did not rule out the use of knowledge of pronunciation rules.

Other sorts of units might be used in deciding which features to look for. For example, representations of familiar spelling patterns might act as sufficiently unitary codes to guide the selection of information about letter features, even if letters are coded independently of letter groups. In general, then, the basic idea is that a tentative representation of a small set of high-level codes, such as phonemes or spelling patterns, is formed, and features are sought that would distinguish the possible high-level codes from one another. In this way, assuming that a word has actually been presented, selection of features can be made more efficient. As pointed out by Krueger (1975), this mechanism is similar to one proposed by Bruner (1957) as a general explanation of a variety of perceptual effects. The one difference is that Bruner proposed that the subjects look for *confirming* cues with respect to a tentative categorization. The sort of selection model I am discussing here cannot account for the word-superiority effect unless the subject is assumed to look for *distinguishing* cues with respect to a reduced set of possible categorizations.

Just as several different codes can be used to guide the selection of features in active-selection models of the sort just discussed, there are also several possibilities for the kind of code that might be used in the case of information-loss mechanisms. The "redundancy" mechanism described by Thompson and Massaro (1973), for example, is based on the idea that the subjects choose a set of letter codes for a given position and then lose the feature information on which this choice was based. If the subjects could recover the feature information, this mechanism would not explain the word-superiority effect, since they could use the feature information itself, rather than their guesses about possible letters, to choose between the alternatives in a forced-choice procedure. Thus, this redundancy mechanism is a version of the information-loss explanation. Other versions of this explanation might propose that the subjects constructed a single letter code for each position (rather than a small set of alternatives), letter-group codes, phoneme codes, syllable (phoneme group) codes, or even lexical codes in some cases. For nonwords, it would be more difficult to create these kinds of codes, which are less resistant to interference and decay than the lower level codes that can be created.

B. Evidence about Mechanisms

Information-loss explanations have to be modified to account for word-superiority effects in reaction time for same–different comparison or letter search (see Section I). I must add the assumption that comparison of higher-level codes, in contrast to lower level codes, can speed the required decision. If higher level codes are used, effects on reaction time can be explained in terms of slower extraction of these codes (or their complete absence) for nonwords than for words, the same assumption that was required to make the information-loss explanation work for tachistiscopic tasks. Results showing no effect of phonemic similarity on same–different comparison (Baron, 1974a; Thurston, 1974) are inconsistent with an explanation of the effect in these tasks in terms of comparison of phonemic codes. Further, results showing no difference in the magnitude of the effect for same–different comparison when the different items differ only in the case or in the identity of a letter (*word–worD* or *word–work,* respectively), rule out an explanation of the effect for these tasks in terms of comparison of most kinds of higher level codes. The comparison in these tasks must be made at the level of features, or possibly at the level of letter identities with letter case included as part of the identity or a letter (Pollatsek *et al.,* 1975).

It seems difficult to find other experimental procedures that can distinguish which kind of mechanism (more feature, feature selection, information loss) is operating in a given case. One potentially useful approach is found in a study by Matthews, Weisstein, Williams, and Baron (1976). This study used a tachistoscopic forced-choice procedure, with the third letter of a trigram probed on every trial and with a mask (designed to mask all physical features of letters) presented only before the stimulus. Several different intervals were used between mask and stimulus, allowing the plotting of psychometric functions, percentage correct as a function of mask-stimulus interval. One finding to emerge from these functions was that the magnitude of the word-superiority effect was greater at short mask-stimulus delays than at long ones; that is, the slopes of the functions were steeper for nonwords than for words. The opposite result would seem to follow naturally from a contingent feature-selection explanation. For this explanation, more information would allow the subjects to make more judicious choices about what features to look for next. Thus, conditions that lead to chance performance on nonwords ought to lead to chance performance on words as well.

In fact, there seemed to be cases where performance was at chance on non-words yet substantially above chance on words (a result that was also found for one subject by Baron and Thurston, 1973). Another relevant finding in this study was that the magnitude of the effect was the same when all three letters were masked as when only the critical letter was masked. It would seem most natural for both the information-loss and the contingent feature-selection hypotheses to predict a greater effect when only the critical letter was masked. In this case, there would be more information available either to select relevant features or to form a durable high-level code. The most parsimonious explanation of these results is in terms of more features being extracted for words than for nonwords. These extra features would presumably be those that were relatively unaffected by the particular mask used (a grid of lines). They would contribute more to judgments with short mask-stimulus intervals than with long intervals, where other features would begin to emerge.

In sum, the evidence from this study and from that of Pollatsek *et al.*, (1975) provide suggestive evidence that word-superiority effects occur that cannot be ascribed to information loss or contingent feature-selection. While these experiments are not completely conclusive (because these two explanations could conceivably be modified to account for the results), they do suggest directions for further research. In particular, the use of different kinds of comparisons, the examination of psychometric functions, and the masking of different parts of the stimulus, might shed more light on the way in which knowledge is used to improve perception.

VI. THE WORD-SUPERIORITY EFFECT AND READING

Before moving from the theoretical issues concerning words to more general issues in pattern recognition, it seems appropriate to try to answer a question that was posed at the start: What does the word-superiority effect have to do with reading? This is an important question because much of the interest in the effect, with the exception of the work of the "new look" school, has assumed that the primary reason for studying the effect is that it does have something to do with reading.

I may begin by contrasting two extreme answers to the question. One is that the processes responsible for word-superiority effects are necessary for fluent reading. If beginning readers were somehow to fail to acquire the knowledge and the means of using it that produce the effect, they would be severely hampered in learning to read fluently; at best, reading would be a struggle. The second answer is that since people usually read by actively constructing meanings, the recognition of isolated words has very little to do with reading skill (and that, furthermore, it is ultimately fruitless to try to analyze a complex skill like reading into component subskills).

To knock down the straw man I have set up as the second position, let me point out that it is based on several confusions, mainly a failure to distinguish algorithms and heuristics. Surely in learning to perform any complex skill we learn a number of heuristic shortcuts, like "skimming" in reading, and surely some of us are so good at developing these shortcuts that we can get away with them most of the time. Yet just as surely, there are also algorithms that in a sense define the skill itself; they are procedures that we must fall back on when all shortcuts fail. In reading, for example, it seems obvious that we sometimes have to recognize words. Further, it seems at least plausible that it is very inefficient to try to teach the shortcuts before the algorithms and that, in fact, most of the shortcuts develop spontaneously as a result of repeated practice in situations that at first can be done only with the algorithms. Thus, highly fluent readers may be that way not in spite of their skill at recognizing words but because of it. Mastery of the algorithms leaves them free to develop the heuristics.

If we now accept the view that word recognition may have something to do with reading, we need only show that the word-superiority effect has something to do with word recognition as it occurs in normal reading. It was to this end that I maintained the criterion throughout this review that an explanation of the effect is not interesting unless the critical processes happen *fast enough* to facilitate reading. Yet clearly this is not a sufficient criterion. We need also show that at least some of the mechanisms responsible for the effect are used for normal word recognition, that is, that words are seen better or more quickly during reading for the same reasons that they are in the laboratory. Whether this is true in a given case will depend on the particular mesh of the aspects of recognition and reading involved. For example, let us assume that one mechanism of word recognition in reading involves activation of a semantic code directly from a letter or spelling-pattern code (see Baron, 1973a and 1977, for discussion). On this assumption, if the word-superiority effect were known to depend on the more efficient activation of spelling-pattern codes than random-letter sequences, the effect would be relevant to recognition, for the speeded activation of these codes would facilitate one step in the path to meaning. We would still want to make sure, however, that the codes required for the word-superiority effect, whatever they are, are the same codes as those that form an intermediate link in accessing semantic codes. There might, for example, be different kinds of spelling-pattern codes, one kind involved in the word-superiority effect and the other in accessing meaning.

Despite all these problems, however, one fairly convincing argument for some involvement of the word-superiority effect in reading is the fact that the processes underlying the effect are well practiced enough to operate as efficiently as they do in laboratory experiments. One may well ask how people could come to be so capable in using a mechanism if they did not have experience with it somewhere outside of the laboratory. Thus, it seems likely that the essential processes required for word superiority are part of at least some mechanism of normal word recognition.

There are a few studies that are suggestive about the relation between the word-superiority effect and reading skill. Using a letter-search task, Krueger, Keen, and Rubelevich (1974) found as great a word-superiority effect in fourth-graders as in adults, suggesting that the effect is present before full fluency is reached. Firth (1972), using a tachistiscopic free-report procedure, found a word-superiority effect in first and second graders. He also found that the magnitude of the effect was correlated with reading ability (with IQ scores held constant). Similarly, Mason (1975), using letter search, found a word-superiority effect in good sixth-grade readers but no effect at all in a group of poor readers. These studies still do not resolve the central issue, which is, I think, whether all training or experience that increases the magnitude of the word-superiority effect also improves reading skill. If this question could be answered affirmatively and if we knew what the relevant experience was, we would have a procedure to improve the skill.

A few other points are worthy of mention in the argument about the relevance of the word-superiority effect to reading. On the positive side, the methods developed in studying the effect might be useful in the analysis of clinical deficits. For example, if we knew what knowledge accounted for the effect, we could use the effect as a clinical measure of the possession of this knowledge, although such inferences would have to be made cautiously. Or the kinds of control conditions and sets of stimuli used to analyze the word-superiority effect might be used in other word-recognition tasks, as Brooks (1976) is now doing.

On the negative side, it can be said that, to the extent that we are really interested in normal word recognition as opposed to satisfying our curiosity about the word-superiority effect, we might rely more advantageously on methods that approach normal word recognition more directly. These methods range from the use of artificial materials (Baron, 1977; Brooks, 1976) to the analysis of performance on tasks that actually required semantic analysis for performance (Baron, 1977).

VII. IMPLICATIONS FOR PATTERN RECOGNITION AS A LEARNED SKILL

Aside from telling us something about reading, the word-superiority effect may well tell us something about more general mechanisms of learning to recognize patterns. We learn to recognize many other kinds of patterns besides printed words, for example, spoken words, faces, Chinese characters, electrocardiograms, and letters. If we take pattern recognition to include cases in which the output of the process is not a single categorization but something more like a complex structure, there are also sentences, pictures of forms and scenes, chess positions, mathematical and musical notation, and so on. In fact, even the kind of print used in reading may begin to seem increasingly arbitrary as new technologies of writing and printing are discovered, and new kinds of alphabet systems may be in the offing. From this perspective, the question of the word-superiority effect itself becomes an example of a class of effects having to do with our ability to *learn* to use regularities in our cultural or physical environment to improve our perception of that environment. Investigations of the mechanisms of such learning may lead to principles useful in designing modifications in our environment, for example, inventing new kinds of print. Analysis of the kinds of learning that might be responsible for phenomena like the word-superiority effect can also be useful for other reasons; for example, it may help answer certain more general educational questions, and it may help design adaptive machines that can learn to take over demeaning tasks now done by people.

Speculation about general mechanisms of learning that might induce "superiority effects" in other areas is made less idle by recent investigations that actually demonstrate such effects. Biederman (1972) has shown that according to several different measures of perceptual efficiency, and even with "gestalt" properties such as continuity held constant, scenes that "make sense" are easier to see than scenes that do not. Examples of the latter category would be scenes with objects displaced out of their usual location or given the wrong relative size in the picture. Weisstein, Harris, and Ruddy (1973) have shown that an arrangement of lines that can be interpreted as a folded piece of paper is easier to see than a similar arrangement that cannot be so interpreted. Here the measure of perception was a forced choice between a small number of positions of a given line, chosen so that all the alternatives either did or did not "make sense," a method quite analogous to methods used to demonstrate the word-superiority effect.

In general, we may view pattern recognition as an operation performed on an arrangement of codes. The effect of this operation may be formation of another code, as in word recognition and other "categorization" tasks, or it may be a more complex addition to or modification of an evolving representation, as in parsing sentences (Winograd, 1972) or forming semantic representations of discourse. Pattern recognition may take its input from an earlier stage of processing as well as from some external stimulus.

There are two kinds of knowledge—rules and lexicons—that can be used to operate on an arrangement of codes, although the distinction between them may not always be clear. Pronunciation of printed words provides a good example. Knowledge of rules would be used by carrying out a procedure that would determine the pronunciation from the letters present. Such rules could be applied to pseudowords as well as words. Lexicons seem to be required for exceptions to the rules, such as *ONE*. We could use lexicons for regular words as well, and even for pseudowords if we had a few simple rules for pronouncing by analogy with words already in the lexicon.

Rules themselves may be of two sorts: (*a*) notations to treat certain elements as equivalent for some purpose (category tags) and (*b*) operations, which activate "response" elements under prescribed conditions. As an example of the use of a tag, it is clearly helpful to categorize letters as vowels or consonants. An operation might activate a certain phoneme as a result of the presence of a vowel or consonant nearby. Another example of a tag would be the classification of the series of letters following a vowel in terms of whether the series forces the vowel to have a "long" (for example, P*I*NE) or "short" (e.g., P*I*N) pronunciation. This tag, along with the printed vowel itself, leads to the appropriate response. Tags imply the existence of a sort of lexicon, but the number of categories (for example, the number of parts of speech) in such a lexicon is small compared to the other lexicons considered, and the categories are of no use except insofar as they allow the construction of other codes or structures.

Given this way of looking at things, there seem to be two general kinds of learning that can occur, learning of rules and learning of "rote" connections between arrangements of codes and their associated responses. Most theories of verbal learning have addressed themselves to the learning of lexical associations, and only a few attempts have been made to analyze the acquisition of rules. One type of learning theory that might be able to handle the acquisition of rules of the sort used in pattern recognition is that sketched by Baron (1973b), which analyzes acquisition of operations or strategies in terms of acquisition of their substrategies and attachment of these substrategies to appropriate situations. An example of the kind of substrategy that might be used in pronunciation would be use of the rule mentioned above for deciding whether a vowel was "long" or "short." That substrategy might be acquired first in the case of one vowel and one consonant, and its generalization or transfer to new vowels or consonants at later times would depend both upon the strength of learning of the original instances and on the number of intervening transfer experiences. In some cases a substrategy may be applied in so many situations that it becomes necessary to learn rules for when *not* to apply it. Thus, some strategies or rules may be represented as instructions not to apply other substrategies.

Learning of rules may proceed in phases that are exactly the same as those used for lexical associations. The first phase might consist of the generalization of a substrategy to a new situation or the initial acquisition of a lexical association. Later phases of learning consist of the increasing probability of execution of the correct substrategy or production of the association (except in cases of all-or-none learning), increases in the speed of execution or production, and, finally, as proposed by LaBerge (1974), decreases in the amount of attention required for fast execution or production, to the point at which the substrategy becomes automatic in appropriate situations. Automatized use of rules or associations seems likely to be involved in phenomena such as the word-superiority effect. In the case of the word-superiority effect itself, it seems likely that spelling or pronunciation rules are involved. In other effects, such as the form-superiority effect found by Weisstein *et al.* (1973), other sorts of rules, such as those developed by Guzman (1969) for making sense out of scenes, might be involved.

It should be noted that whether persons first learn to use rules or to use lexical associations for a given purpose might be independent of which method they ultimately adopt. For example, after extensive practice in using rules to pronounce words, people might develop lexical associations for words or syllables that actually work faster than the rules. Conversely, a person who initially learned lexical associations (as the "look–say" approach to reading would encourage), might implicitly "abstract" rules and eventually come to use them automatically. A case in which a lexicon might be formed only after people have learned to use different rules is in association of printed words with their meanings. At first, people might use pronunciation rules to convert print into sounds, and then use a sound lexicon to look up the meanings, the sound lexicon already being available from learning to ta;k. But later people seem to develop a separate lexicon for associating letter strings with meanings directly (Baron, 1973a; Brooks, 1976; Meyer & Ruddy, 1974). Thus, it seems that in principle people may develop lexical associations even when rules are available. The conditions under which people develop new lexicons, as opposed to learning to use rules faster and with less attention, or the converse, have yet to be described.

It should also be noted that the ability to respond to new patterns as though rules were being used need not imply that any particular rules are being used in fact. It is also possible to respond to new patterns on the basis of analogy or similarity with old ones. In this way, the power of a simple lexicon may be extended. This is especially true if there is a general strategy of searching for a number of analogies to a new pattern and then picking only the response consistent with the largest number of analogies. For example, *FUT* may be pronounced "correctly" by analogy with *BUT, CUT, MUT,* etc., even though one analogy, *PUT,* would lead to an incorrect response. (This possibility of errors does not stop real subjects from relying on a single analogy, however; see Baron, 1977, and associated references.) Note that the existence of a pseudoword-superiority effect may in principle also be explained in terms of similarity of pseudowords to real words, rather than the operation of a fixed set of rules in pattern recognition.

In sum, lexical associations, combined with a few highly general strategies for transfer to new patterns, can be as effective in recognizing new patterns as rules. This point has been made previously by those who have been concerned with categorization (for example, Hyman and Frosst, 1974). My present argument is that this point may also be made for pattern recognition that involves more complex relations between stimulus and response.

To summarize these suggestions relating the word-superiority effect to pattern recognition as a learned skill, it would seem that this effect illustrates the automatic and rapid operation of mechanisms used in normal recognition of words. These mechanisms operate only by virtue of extended practice. They may involve either the direct application of rules—whether rules for pronouncing or rules for extracting visual information most rapidly—or they may involve the use of lexical associations between words and some other code, plus a set of general rules for finding similar items in the lexicon.

ACKNOWLEDGMENTS

The preparation of this chapter was supported by a grant from the National Science Foundation. Lee Brooks, William K. Estes, Floyd Glenn, James McClelland, and Paul Rozin provided helpful criticisms of an earlier draft.

REFERENCES

Aderman, D., & Smith, E. E. Expectancy as a determinant of functional units in perceptual recognition. *Cognitive Psychology*, 1971, **2**, 117–129.

Baron, J. Phonemic stage not necessary for reading. *Quarterly Journal of Experimental Psychology*, 1973, **25**, 241–246. (a)

Baron, J. Semantic components and conceptual development. *Cognition*, 1973, **2**, 299–317. (b)

Baron, J. Successive stages in word recognition. In S. Dornic & P. M. A. Rabbitt (Eds.), *Attention and performance V*. New York: Academic Press, 1974. Pp. 563–574. (a)

Baron, J. Facilitation of perception by spelling constraints. *Canadian Journal of Psychology*, 1974, **28**, 37–50. (b)

Baron, J. Stimuli and subjects in one-tailed tests. *Bulletin of the Psychynomic Society*, 1975, **6**, 608–610.

Baron, J. Mechanisms for pronouncing printed words: Use and acquisition. In D. LaBerge & S. J. Samuels (Eds.), *Basic processes in reading: Perception and comprehension*. Hillsdale, New Jersey: Lawrence Erlbaum Associates, 1977. Pp. 175–216.

Baron, J., & Thurston, I. An analysis of the word-superiority effect. *Cognitive Psychology*, 1973, **4**, 207–228.

Barron, R., & Pittenger, J. B. The effect of orthographic structure and lexical meaning on *same–different* judgments. *Quarterly Journal of Experimental Psychology*, 1974, **26**, 566–581.

Biederman, I. Perceiving real-world scenes. *Science*, 1972, **177**, 77–80.

Bjork, E. L., & Estes, W. K. Letter identification in relation to linguistic context and masking conditions. *Memory & Cognition*, 1973, **1**, 217–223.

Broadbent, D. E. Word frequency effect and response bias. *Psychological Review*, 1967, **74**, 1–15.

Brooks, L. E. Visual pattern in fluent word identification. In A. S. Reber & D. Scarborough (Eds.), *Reading: The CUNY Conference*. Hillsdale, New Jersey: Lawrence Erlbaum Associates, 1976. Pp. 143–182.

Bruner, J. S. On perceptual readiness. *Psychological Review*, 1957, **64**, 123–152.

Catlin, J. On the word frequency effect. *Psychological Review*, 1969, **76**, 504–506.

Catlin, J. The word frequency effect: Where it's at. Unpublished manuscript, University of Pennsylvania, 1970.

Clark, H. H. The language-as-fixed-effect fallacy: A critique of language statistics in psychological research. *Journal of Verbal Learning and Verbal Behavior*, 1973, **12**, 335–359.

Conrad, R. The effect of vocalizing on comprehension in the profoundly deaf. *British Journal of Psychology*, 1971, **62**, 147–150.

Egeth, H., & Blecker, D. Differential effects of familiarity on judgments of sameness and difference. *Perception & Psychophysics*, 1971, **9**, 321–326.

Eichelman, W. H. Familiarity effects in the simultaneous matching task. *Journal of Experimental Psychology*, 1970, **86**, 275–282.

Estes, W. K. Memory, perception, and decision in letter identification. In R. L. Solso (Ed.), *Information processing and cognition: The Loyola symposium*. Hillsdale, New Jersey: Lawrence Erlbaum Associates, 1975. Pp. 3–30. (a)

Estes, W. K. On the locus of inferential and perceptual processes in letter identification. *Journal of Experimental Psychology: General*, 1975, **104**, 122–145. (b)

Estes, W. K. On the interaction of perception and memory in reading. In D. LaBerge & S. J. Samuels (Eds.), *Basic processes in reading: Perception and comprehension*. Hillsdale, New Jersey: Lawrence Erlbaum Associates, 1977. Pp. 1–25.

Firth, I. Components of reading disability. Unpublished doctoral dissertation, University of New South Wales, 1972.

Gibson, E. J., Pick, A. D., Osser, H., & Hammond, M. The role of grapheme–phoneme correspondence in the perception of words. *American Journal of Psychology*, 1962, **75**, 554–570.

Gibson, E. J., Shurcliff, A., & Yonas, A. Utilization of spelling patterns by deaf and hearing subjects. In H. Levin & J. P. Williams (Eds.), *Basic studies on reading*. New York: Basic Books, 1970. Pp. 57–73.

Guzman, A. Decomposition of a visual scene into three-dimensional bodies. In A. Graselli (Ed.), *Automatic interpretation and analysis of images*. New York: Academic Press, 1969.

Hawkins, H. L., Reicher, G. M., Rogers, M., & Peterson, L. Flexible coding in word recognition. *Journal of Experimental Psychology: Human Perception and Performance*, 1976, **2**, 380–385.

Henderson, L. E. A word superiority effect without orthographic assistance. *Quarterly Journal of Experimental Psychology*, 1974, **26**, 301–311.

Herrmann, D. J., & McLaughlin, J. P. Language habits and detection in very short-term memory. *Perception & Psychophysics*, 1973, **14**, 483–486.

Howes, D. H., & Solomon, R. L. Visual duration threshold as a function of word-probability. *Journal of Experimental Psychology*, 1951, **41**, 401–410.

Huey, E. B. *The psychology and pedagogy of reading*. New York: MacMillan, 1908. (Reissued by the MIT Press, 1968.)

Hyman, R., & Frosst, N. H. Gradients and schema in pattern recognition. In S. Dornic & P. M. A. Rabbitt (Eds.), *Attention and performance V*. London: Academic Press, 1974. Pp. 631–654.

Johnston, J. C., & McClelland, J. L. Visual factors in word perception. *Perception & Psychophysics*, 1973, **14**, 365–370.

Johnston, J. C., & McClelland, J. L. Perception of letters in words: Seek not and ye shall find. *Science*, 1974, **184**, 1192–1193.

Kempen, G., Hermans, B., Klinkum, A., Brand, M., & Verhaaren, F. The word-frequency effect and incongruity perception: Methodological artifacts? *Perception & Psychophysics*, 1969, **5**, 161–162.

Kinsbourne, M., & Evans, N. Is the word-frequency effect on recognition threshold a function of transition probability? *Psychological Reports*, 1970, **91**, 262–267.

Klein, G. S. Semantic power measured through the interference of words with color-naming. *American Journal of Psychology*, 1964, **57**, 576–588.

Krueger, L. E. Search time in a redundant visual display. *Journal of Experimental Psychology*, 1970, **83**, 391–399. (a)

Krueger, L. E. Effect of frequency of display on speed of visual search. *Journal of Experimental Psychology*, 1970, **84**, 495–498. (b)

Krueger, L. E. Visual comparison in a redundant display. *Cognitive Psychology*, 1970, **1**, 341–357. (c)

Krueger, L. Familiarity effects in visual information processing. *Psychological Bulletin*, 1975, **82**, 949–974.

Krueger, L. E., Keen, R. H., & Rubelevich, B. Letter search through words and nonwords by adults and fourth-grade children. *Journal of Experimental Psychology*, 1974, **102**, 845–849.

LaBerge, D. Acquisition of automatic processing in perceptual and associative learning. In S. Dornic & P. M. A. Rabbitt (Eds.), *Attention and performance V*. New York: Academic Press, 1974. Pp. 50–64.

LaBerge, D., Petersen, R., & Norden, M. J. Exploring the limits of cueing. In S. Dornic & P. M. A. Rabbitt (Eds.), *Attention and performance VI*. Hillsdale, New Jersey. Lawrence Erlbaum Associates, 1977. Pp. 285–306.

LaBerge, D. & Samuels, S. J. Toward a theory of automatic information processing in reading. *Cognitive Psychology*, 1974, **6**, 293–323.

Manelis, L. The effect of meaningfulness in tachistoscopic word perception. *Perception & Psychophysics*, 1974, **16**, 182–192.

Mason, M., Reading ability and letter search time: Effects of orthographic structure defined by single-letter positional frequency. *Journal of Experimental Psychology: General*, 1975, **104**, 146–166.

Massaro, D. W. Perception of letters, words, and nonwords. *Journal of Experimental Psychology,* 1973, **100**, 349-353.

Matthews, M. L., & Henderson, L. Facilitation of foveal letter recognition by metacontrast. *Psychonomic Science,* 1971, **23**, 153-155.

Matthews, M., Weisstein, N., Williams, A., & Baron, J. *The ubiquitous word-superiority effect.* Unpublished manuscript, S.U.N.Y. at Buffalo, 1976.

Meyer, D. E., & Ruddy, M. G. *Lexical-memory retrieval based on graphemic and phonemic representations of printed words.* Unpublished manuscript, Bell Laboratories, Murray Hill, New Jersey, 1974.

Mezrich, J. J. The word superiority effect in brief visual displays: Elimination by vocalization. *Perception & Psychophysics,* 1973, **13**, 45-48.

Miller, G. A., Bruner, J. S., & Postman, L. Familiarity of letter sequences and tachistoscopic identification. *Journal of General Psychology,* 1954, **50**, 129-139.

Morton, J. A retest of the response-bias explanation of the word-frequency effect. *British Journal of Mathematical and Statistical Psychology,* 1968, **21**, 21-33.

Morton, J. Interaction of information in word recognition. *Psychological Review,* 1969, **76**, 165-178.

Neisser, U. *Cognitive psychology.* New York: Appleton-Century-Crofts, 1967.

Pollatsek, A., Well, A. D., & Schindler, R. M. Familiarity affects visual processing of words. *Journal of Experimental Psychology: Human Perception and Performance,* 1975, **104**, 328-338.

Reicher, G. M. Perceptual recognition as a function of the meaningfulness of the material. *Journal of Experimental Psychology,* 1969, **81**, 275-280.

Rumelhart, D. E., & Siple, P. Process of recognizing tachistoscopically presented words. *Psychological Review,* 1974, **81**, 99-118.

Smith, E. E., & Haviland, S. E. Why words are perceived more accurately than nonwords: Inference vs. unitization. *Journal of Experimental Psychology,* 1972, **92**, 59-64.

Smith, F. *Understanding reading.* New York: Holt, Rinehart, & Winston, 1971.

Solomon, R. L., & Howes, D. H. Word frequency, personal values and visual duration threshold. *Psychological Review,* 1951, **58**, 256-270.

Solomon, R. L., & Postman, L. Frequency of usage as a determinant of recognition thresholds for words. *Journal of Experimental Psychology,* 1952, **43**, 195-201.

Spector, A. and Purcell, D. G. The word superiority effect: A comparison between restricted and unrestricted alternative set. *Perception and Psychophysics,* 1977, **21**, 323-328.

Spoehr, K. T., & Smith, E. E. The role of syllables in perceptual processing. *Cognitive Psychology,* 1973, **5**, 71-89.

Spoehr, K. T., & Smith, E. E. The role of orthographic and phonotactic rules in perceiving letter patterns. *Journal of Experimental Psychology: Human Perception and Performance,* 1975, **104**, 21-34.

Sternberg, S. The discovery of processing stages: Extensions of Donders' method. *Acta Psychologica,* 1969, **30**, 276-315.

Thompson, M. C., & Massaro, D. W. Visual information redundancy in reading. *Journal of Experimental Psychology,* 1973, **98**, 49-54.

Thurston, I. *Letter identity and phonemic processing in word comparison: Their relative ordering.* Unpublished doctoral dissertation, McMaster University, 1974.

Treisman, M. On the word-frequency effect: Comments on the papers by J. Catlin and L. H. Nakatani. *Psychological Review,* 1971, **78**, 420-425.

Weisstein, N., Harris, C. S., & Ruddy, M. E. *An object superiority effect.* Paper presented at the meeting of the Psychonomic Society, St. Louis, 1973.

Wheeler, D. D. Processes in word recognition. *Cognitive Psychology,* 1970, **1**, 59-85.

Winograd, T. Understanding natural language. *Cognitive Psychology,* 1972, **3**, 1-191.

5

Speech Perception

David B. Pisoni

Indiana University

I. INTRODUCTION

The fundamental problem in speech perception is to determine how the continuously varying acoustic stimulus produced by a speaker is converted into a sequence of discrete linguistic units by the listener so the intended message can be recovered. This problem can be broken down into a number of specific subquestions. For example, what stages of perceptual analysis intervene between presentation of the stimulus and eventual response? And what types of operations occur at each of these stages? What types of perceptual mechanisms are involved in speech perception, and how do they develop during the course of language acquisition? These are just a few of the broad questions that will be considered in the present chapter.

It should be pointed out here that despite the fact that the speech signal may be of poor quality with many of the sounds slurred or distorted, the perceptual process proceeds quite smoothly. To the naive observer the perceptual process often appears to be carried out almost automatically, with little conscious effort. This is not at all surprising. A good part of the speech-perception process is normally unavailable for conscious inspection. Moreover, some aspects of the process are only partially dependent upon properties of the physical stimulus. As we shall see, the speech signal is so highly structured and constrained that even large distortions in the signal can be tolerated without loss of intelligibility. This is true, in part, because the speech signal is not entirely new for the listener. As a speaker of a natural language, the listener has available a good deal of knowledge about the structure of an utterance even before it is ever produced. For present purposes we assume that the listener has two types of information at his disposal at any time. On one hand, the listener knows something about the context in which a particular utterance is produced. Knowledge of events, facts, and relations about the world can be used by the listener to generate hypotheses and draw inferences from only fragmentary input. On the other hand, the listener has knowledge of his language, including information about syntax, semantics, and phonology that provides the means for constructing an internal representation or percept of the utterance. It is this latter kind of knowledge, especially those aspects dealing with phonetics and phonology, that will be of primary concern in this chapter.

When placed in the context of other communication systems, human language also has certain characteristics that set it apart. First, human language is symbolic and entails a dual patterning of sound and meaning (Hockett, 1958). Second, human language is grammatical, thus permitting an infinite number of meanings to be expressed by the combination of a finite set of elements (Chomsky, 1957). As we shall see, both of these characteristics have placed certain constraints on the types of signals used in speech production and the potential mechanisms available for perceptual analysis.

The present chapter will be concerned with problems and issues in speech perception rather than the details of specific experiments. Extensive literature reviews and interpretations have been carried out recently by Studdert-Kennedy (1976) and Darwin (1976), and the interested reader should consult these for further background. My major goal in this chapter is to present a point of view about the relation between certain attributes of the acoustic signal and various aspects of perceptual analysis of speech sounds. A recurrent theme is that the attributes of sound produced by the vocal mechanism seem to be "matched," in some sense, to mechanisms involved in speech perception. Moreover, from our current knowledge of speech perception and production, there is fairly strong evidence that some portions of the perceptual process may be mediated by specialized neural mechanisms that are either part of the biological endowment of the organism or develop very soon after birth.

II. LINGUISTIC STRUCTURE OF SPEECH

During the normal course of linguistic communication, we are conscious of the words and sentences spoken to us but rarely the speech sounds themselves. Except under special circumstances when, for example, our attention is directed to the sound structure (such as listening to a foreign accent or a child's first words), it is difficult to separate our observations from their subsequent interpretation. For the most part, the earliest stages of speech perception appear to be carried out almost automatically without conscious awareness or control by the listener.

Since most of our awareness of spoken language is based on meanings and not sounds, it is appropriate to discuss some aspects of the sound structure of language, specifically the functional categories that have been developed in linguistic science. Research on speech perception over the last 25 years has generally assumed that these linguistic categories formed the basic objects of perception, and, as a consequence, most of the experimental work was guided by this linguistic analysis.

Although the speech signal that impinges upon the ear of the listener varies more or less continuously as a function of time, the listener, nevertheless, perceives an utterance as consisting of a sequence of discrete segments. The segments that the listener perceives are based on the functional sound categories of the language community—the phonemes. A phoneme is usually defined as the smallest unit of speech that makes a significant difference between two linguistic forms. The phoneme, however, is an abstract concept, since it does not represent a unique instance of a sound (that is, a phonetic segment or phone) but instead refers to some derived or abstract class of sounds that functions in similar ways in a particular language. It has become customary in the literature to represent phones or phonetic segments with square brackets (that is, [x] where x is a particular phone) and phonemes with slashes (that is, /y/ where y refers to an abstract class of sounds). This notation is followed throughout this chapter.

As an illustration of how the phonemic principle works, consider the differences between the words *bin* and *pin*. At the lowest level of linguistic analysis, the phonetic level, the first segment of each word is different. The difference lies both in the way the sound is articulated and in its acoustical properties. Since the phonetic differences between the [b] and [pʰ] serve to distinguish different linguistic forms in English, these segments are assumed to be members of different classes of phonemes, /b/ and /p/. Thus, the phonetic differences between [b] and [pʰ] are retained at a more abstract level, the phonological level, where the linguistically significant information is represented.

The situation is, however, somewhat more complicated in the case of sound segments that are phonetically different but do not serve to contrast different linguistic forms in a specific language. For example, in English the initial [pʰ] in *pin* is phonetically aspirated since it is produced with a brief puff of air when the lips are released, whereas the [p] in *spin* has no aspiration. At the phonetic level, the two p's are represented as distinct phonetic segments, since they are produced differently and accordingly represent acoustically distinct signals. At the phonological level, however, the two sounds are considered to be allophones or variants of the same phoneme class /p/ because the feature of aspiration that distinguishes these two segments does not serve to contrast linguistic forms in English. In some languages, such as Thai, this feature does serve to contrast forms, and in these cases the two phonetic segments [pʰ] and [p] would represent functionally different phonemes.

The symbol /p/ in this example has no unique phonetic status itself; it simply stands for a class of phones having related properties. Some members of the class are in complementary distribution; phonetic segments occur in contexts in which other segments do not appear. For example, the [k] in *keep* is produced further forward in the vocal cavity than the [k] in *coop*, and this difference is predictable in terms of the properties of the following vowel. Members of a class of phonetic segments also have similar articulatory and acoustic attributes. For example, the two k sounds referred to above are both voiceless velar stop consonants, even though they have slightly different places of articulation.

Each utterance of a language can be represented as a sequence of discrete phonetic segments, each of which can be further thought of as consisting of a set of distinctive features. Some idea of the feature composition of various English phonemes can be seen in Table 1. This system is based on the work of Jakobson, Fant, and Halle (1952) in which phonetic segments are described in terms of whether a distinctive feature is present (+) or absent (−). Both phonetic and phonological segments are assumed to consist of bundles of features such as these. The features shown in Table 1 are based on distinctions in both the articulatory and acoustic domains. A brief description of these phonetic features and some of their articulatory and acoustic correlates are given in Table 2. More recent versions of the distinctive-feature theory are based almost exclusively on articulatory descriptions (Chomsky & Halle, 1968).

Thus, there are two distinct levels of linguistic representation, a phonetic level and a phonological level. In modern generative phonology, a phonetic representation of an utterance consists of a distinctive-feature matrix in which the columns represent phonetic segments and the rows indicate their feature specification (Chomsky & Halle, 1968). A phonological representation is more abstract than a phonetic representation. Segments that may be different at the phonetic level are treated as functionally the same at the phonological level when these variations do not serve a distinctive function in the language. However, the distinction between phonetic and phonological levels has little importance for naive listeners who hear speech in terms of the functional categories of their language.

It should be noted here that even the description of speech at a phonetic level is not assumed to be a representation of the actual physical events of speech. A phonetic transcription is neither a physical description of the vocal tract nor a specification of the acoustic signal. At the level of phonetic segments, a great deal of abstraction and categorization has already taken place so that the speech signal is viewed as a sequence of discrete phonetic segments and features.

So far we have discussed only the phoneme that is a meaningless unit. But language also employs meaningful units. Morphemes usually have been considered the smallest meaningful units of language. A free or lexical morpheme, for example, can occur in isolation; it is a word that cannot be analyzed into smaller semantic units. On the other hand, a bound or grammatical morpheme, such as the plural marker /z/ in the word *dogs*, can only occur in context with other morphemes. One important aspect of the dual patterning of human language is the relation between morphemes and phonemes (Hockett, 1958). All morphemes have a complex internal structure that consists of a sequence of phonemes and, in

TABLE 1
Binary Distinctive Feature Representations for some English Phonemes

FEATURES	u	o	ɔ	a	i	e	æ	p	b	m	f	v	k	g	t	d	θ	ð	n	s	z	č	ǰ	š	ž	h
1. Vocalic–Nonvocalic	+	+	+	+	+	+	+	–	–	–	–	–	–	–	–	–	–	–	–	–	–	–	–	–	–	–
2. Consonantal–Nonconsonantal	–	–	–	–	–	–	–	+	+	+	+	+	+	+	+	+	+	+	+	+	+	+	+	+	+	–
3. Compact–Diffuse	–	+	+	+	–	–	+	–	–	–	–	–	+	+	–	–	–	–	–	–	–	+	+	+	+	+
4. Tense–Lax	–	–	–	+	–	–	+	+	–	–	+	–	+	–	+	–	+	–	–	+	–	+	–	+	–	+
5. Voiced–Voiceless	+	+	+	+	+	+	+	–	+	+	–	+	–	+	–	+	–	+	+	–	+	–	+	–	+	–
6. Nasal–Oral	–	–	–	–	–	–	–	–	–	+	–	–	–	–	–	–	–	–	+	–	–	–	–	–	–	–
7. Continuant–Interrupted	+	+	+	+	+	+	+	–	–	–	+	+	–	–	–	–	+	+	–	+	+	–	–	+	+	+
8. Strident–Mellow								–	–	–	+	+	–	–	–	–	–	–	–	+	+	+	+	+	+	–
9. Checked–Unchecked																										
10. Grave–Acute	+	+	+	+	–	–	–	+	+	+	+	+	+	+	–	–	–	–	–	–	–	–	–	–	–	–
11. Flat–Plain	+	+	+	–	–	–	–																			
12. Sharp–Plain																										

TABLE 2

Some Articulatory and Acoustic Correlates of the Distinctive Features [a]

Distinctive feature	Articulatory correlates	Acoustic correlates
1. Vocalic–Nonvocalic	Periodic excitation and open vocal tract vs. narrowed or constricted vocal tract.	Presence vs. absence of a well-defined formant structure.
2. Consonantal–Nonconsonantal	Presence of a constriction or occlusion in the midline of the oral cavity vs. lesser degrees of narrowing in the central path of the oral cavity.	Overall lower energy and presence of a rapid spectrum change at the release of the consonantal configuration vs. higher energy and absence of rapid spectrum change.
3. Compact–Diffuse	Compact sounds have a higher ratio of volume of front cavity to back cavity than diffuse sounds.	Higher vs. lower concentration of energy in the central region of the spectrum as well as an increase vs. decrease of total energy.
4. Tense–Lax	Tense sounds are articulated with greater distinctiveness and oral pressure than lax sounds. For some vowels there is a greater deviation of the vocal tract from its neutral position.	Tense sounds are longer in duration and have greater energy than the corresponding lax sounds.
5. Voiced–Voiceless	Voiced sounds are produced by vibrating the vocal cords whereas voiceless sounds are produced without such vibration.	Presence vs. absence of periodic low-frequency excitation. The spectrum of voiced sounds contains harmonic components of the fundamental.
6. Nasal–Oral	Nasal sounds are produced with lowered velum whereas oral sounds are produced with a raised velum that shuts off the nasal cavity from the rest of the vocal tract.	Nasal sounds have wider spectral peaks and the presence of additional nasal resonances.

172

7. Continuant–Interrupted	Continuants are produced with a vocal tract having no complete closure; interrupted sounds have a complete closure at some point between glottis and lips.	Continuants have smooth envelopes at onset whereas interrupted sounds have an abrupt onset of energy.
8. Strident–Mellow	This feature is restricted to consonantal sounds. Strident sounds are generated by directing an airstream at an obstacle in the vocal tract thus producing greater turbulence of the airstream.	Strident sounds are characterized by turbulent noise well above the intensity of the vowel in the high-frequency range vs. mellow sounds that have much lower intensity.
9. Checked–Unchecked	The airstream is checked by the compression or closure of the glottis.	Checked sounds have an abrupt decay or sharper termination than unchecked sounds.
10. Grave–Acute	Grave sounds are articulated with constriction at the periphery of oral cavity (i.e., labials, velars) vs. acute sounds that are produced in the central region of the oral cavity.	Grave sounds have predominance of energy in lower half of the spectrum whereas acute sounds have predominant energy in upper half.
11. Flat–Plain	Flattening is generated by reduction of the lip orifice by rounding with an increase in the length of the lip constriction and therefore an increase in the overall length of the vocal tract.	Flat sounds manifest themselves by a downward shift of the frequencies of the formants.
12. Sharp–Plain	For sharp sounds, the oral cavity is reduced in size by raising a part of the tongue against the palate. Also known as "palatalization," this feature is made simultaneously with the main articulation of a consonant.	Sharp sounds as compared with plain ones are characterized by a slight rise in the frequency of the second formant and to some extent the higher formants.

ᵃ Adapted from Jakobson, Fant, and Halle (1952).

turn, features arranged in a particular order. Differences between morphemes and hence differences in meanings are expressed by different phonemes or the sequencing and arrangement of phonemes. Therefore, interest in the phoneme as a basic unit of linguistic analysis has been based on the assumption that morphemic relations are ultimately derived from an analysis of the phonological structure of speech.

As noted earlier, the bulk of speech-perception research has assumed the psychological reality of the phoneme and the phonemic principle in linguistic descriptions. The analysis of speech as a sequence of discrete phonetic segments has guided research by providing the basis and the rationale for specifying the appropriate units of linguistic analysis and the objects of perception.

III. ACOUSTIC STRUCTURE OF SPEECH SOUNDS

Speech sounds have certain distinctive properties or attributes that provide the initial acoustic information for the earliest stages of perceptual analysis. In this section we consider some aspects of the way speech is produced by the vocal apparatus and describe several of the distinctive acoustic attributes of speech sounds.

A. Source-Filter Theory

The basic principles of sound production in the vocal tract and the acoustic filtering that is carried out there are now understood in considerable detail (Fant, 1960; Flanagan, 1972; Stevens & House, 1955). The human vocal tract may be thought of as an acoustic tube of varying cross-sectional area that extends from the glottis to the lips. The upper right-hand panel of Figure 1 shows a mid-sagittal outline of the vocal tract during the production of a neutral vowel. An additional tube, the nasal tract, can be connected to the system by lowering the soft palate or velum for the production of nasal and nasal-like sounds.

The overall shape of the vocal tract can be changed rapidly by variations in the position of the lips, jaw, tongue, and velum. The cross-sectional area of the vocal tract at its point of maximum constriction can be varied from complete closure, as in the production of a stop consonant, to about 20 cm^2, as in the production of an open vowel. When the velum is lowered, the nasal tract is also excited and produces changes in the spectral properties of the radiated sound output.

Sound is generated in the vocal tract by either forcing air through the glottis (that is, space between the vocal folds) to produce a quasiperiodic sound source or by creating a noisy turbulence in the vicinity of a constriction in the vocal tract. Both sound sources can be used to excite the vocal tract above the larynx. For some sounds like nonnasalized vowels, there is a direct acoustic transmission

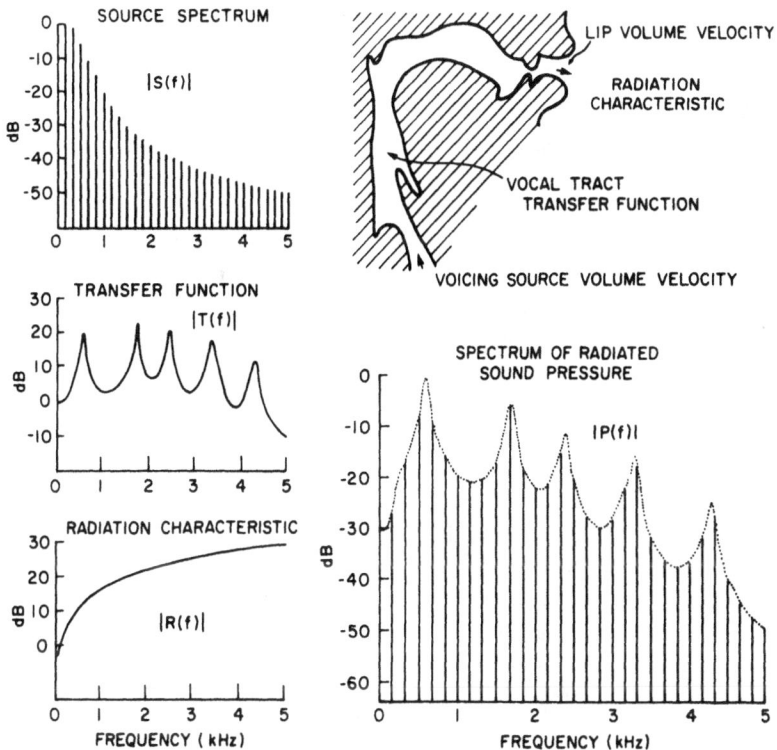

FIGURE 1.   Contribution of source spectrum, vocal-tract transfer function, and radiation characteristic to the spectrum envelope of the radiated sound pressure. (Courtesy of Dr. Dennis Klatt.)

path between glottis and lips; whereas for other sounds such as nasals, there are significant side branches in the transmission path.

The vocal system acts as a time-varying filter with resonant properties that influence the sound waves generated in the tract. The sound pressure radiated from the lips may be thought of simply as the product of the source spectrum $S_{(f)}$, the vocal-tract transfer function $T_{(f)}$, and the radiation characteristic of the vocal tract $R_{(f)}$. The spectrum of the radiated sound pressure $P_{(f)}$ is given by the following equation:

$$P_{(f)} = S_{(f)} \times T_{(f)} \times R_{(f)}.$$

Each of these components is shown separately in the left-hand column of Figure 1. The spectrum envelope ($P_{(f)}$) of the radiated sound pressure that displays the relative distribution of energy at different frequencies is shown in the bottom right-hand corner of the figure. Thus, the speech-production mechanism consists of two relatively independent components: (a) mechanisms that contribute primarily to the generation of sound energy and (*b*) mechanisms that function to modify the sound energy.

For a periodic sound such as a vowel, the sound source consists of a line spectrum with components at multiples of the fundamental frequency ($|S_{(f)}|$ in Figure 1). The amplitude of these components decreases by about 12 dB per octave at high frequencies. When the vocal tract is excited by this source, it acts as a filter to reinforce some frequencies and suppress others. The vocal-tract transfer function shown in the middle panel on the left of Figure 1 can be characterized by a number of natural frequencies or formants that change as the shape of the vocal tract changes from one articulatory position to another. As a consequence, the radiated sound output reflects the resonant frequencies that are favored by the system. These formant frequencies appear as peaks in the spectrum. Finally, the radiation characteristic reflects the relation between acoustic volume velocity at the mouth opening and sound pressure at a distance from the lips. This effect occurs primarily at low frequencies: the slope of the spectrum envelope of the radiated sound pressure drops by about 6 dB per octave as shown in the lower right-hand panel of the figure. The result is to reduce the intensity differences between low- and high-frequency harmonics originally displayed in $|S_{(f)}|$. In summary, the vocal tract acts as a linear time-varying filter that imposes its transmission properties on the frequency spectra of the sound sources generated in the vocal tract. As the vocal tract changes shape during the production of different sounds, the properties of the transfer function change and, accordingly, the sound output changes.

B.   Attributes of Speech Sounds

One method of describing speech sounds is in terms of the degree of vocal-tract constriction employed for their production. This can be ordered along a continuum. At one extreme are the vowels and vowel-like sounds that are produced with a relatively unconstricted vocal tract. Liquids, glides, and fricatives have intermediate constrictions, whereas stop consonants represent the other extreme, with complete closure of the vocal tract at some point of articulation. Figure 2 shows midsagittal outlines of the vocal-tract shapes for the vowels [i], [a] and [u], curves showing the cross-sectional area of the vocal tract as a function of distance from the glottis (that is, area functions), and their respective spectrum envelopes. When the tongue body is high and fronted as in [i], the oral cavity is relatively constricted, whereas when the tongue is low as in [a] and [u], the oral cavity is relatively large. On the other hand, the pharyngeal cavity is relatively large for [i] and [u], but constricted for [a]. The cross-sectional area functions of the vocal tract reflect these differences in position of the tongue body and degree of constriction in the vocal tract as illustrated in the middle panel of the figure. The effect of these differences in vocal-tract shape on the spectra of the sound

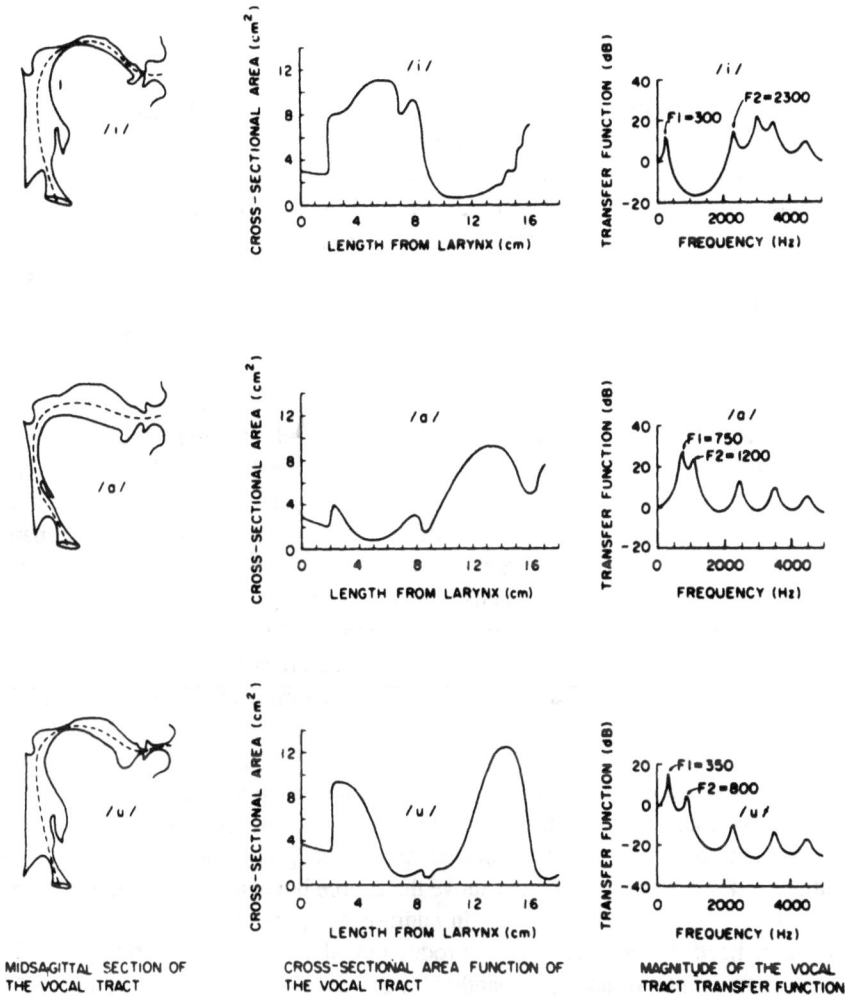

FIGURE 2. Illustrations of the outline shape of midsagittal sections of the vocal tract, cross-sectional area functions, and the corresponding vocal-tract transfer functions for the vowels [i], [a] and [u]. (From Lieberman, Crelin, & Klatt, 1972. Reproduced by permission of the American Anthropological Association from the American Anthropologist 74(3), 1972.)

output is shown by the differences in the spectrum envelopes on the far right of the figure.

The frequency of the first formant (F1) is low for [i] and [u], reflecting, in part, the relatively large pharyngeal cavity compared to [a] where F1 is high. On the other hand, the frequency of F2 is high for [i] due to the narrow oral cavity and low for [u] as a result of lip rounding that increases the overall length of the oral cavity. Although there is a simple relation between formant frequency and cavity affiliation for the vowels [i], [a], and [u], it is not possible to associate a particular formant frequency with a specific cavity resonance. For other vowels, both oral and pharyngeal cavities influence the resonance frequencies of the formants (see Fant, 1960, for further discussion).

The production of speech may be thought of as consisting of a sequence of maneuvers from one idealized articulatory position or target to another. During connected speech the articulatory apparatus frequently moves so rapidly from one position to another that the target positions often are not fully reached. Moreover, instructions for new target configurations often begin to be implemented before a previous target has reached its idealized value. Thus, there is "undershoot" from the ideal articulatory configurations.

As noted above, vowels are produced with a relatively unconstricted vocal tract that generates sounds with well-defined formant structures. From acoustic analysis and synthesis experiments, it has been found that the relative positions of the lowest two or three formant frequencies are sufficient to distinguish different vowels in both production and perception (see Delattre, Liberman, Cooper, & Gerstman, 1952; Peterson & Barney, 1952; Stevens & House, 1955).

In the production of consonants, however, the vocal tract is often highly constricted or even occluded at some point along its length. Consider, for example, the production of a fricative sound in which there is a turbulent noise source generated at the point of a constriction. The spectrum of this noise source is continuous since energy is distributed over all frequencies rather than being restricted to only harmonics of the fundamental. The spectrum of the radiated sound output for a fricative sound is the product of the source function and the vocal-tract transfer function, as was the case with the vowels. However, the sound source for fricatives is located above the glottis: the sound output is influenced not only by structures above the source but also, to a lesser extent, by structures below the sound source in addition to specific properties of the constriction itself. Differences in the production of fricatives are reflected in the relative frequency of noise, its bandwidth and overall intensity. These attributes have been shown to be important perceptual cues for different fricative sounds (Delattre, Liberman, & Cooper, 1964; Harris, 1958; Heinz & Stevens, 1961; Strevens, 1960).

The production of consonantal sounds is characterized by a total or virtual closure of the vocal tract, followed by opening (release). During the closure of a stop consonant no sound is produced and pressure builds up behind the closure. At release—of an initial stop, for example—there is an abrupt change in the vocal tract that results in a rapid spectral change over a very brief period of time as the articulators move toward the position appropriate for the next sound. These rapid transitions affect the rate of frequency change and position of the formant frequencies systematically in terms of the place and type of closure (see Stevens & House, 1956; Delattre, Liberman & Cooper, 1955; Liberman, Delattre,

Gerstman, & Cooper, 1956). Differences in place of articulation among the stop and nasal consonants are cued primarily in terms of the direction and extent of the second and third formant transitions. The liquids, /r/ and /l/, usually have a brief steady-state period that is followed by relatively slow formant transitions into the following vowel. The segment /r/ differs from /l/ in terms of the changes in the third formant transition. The glides /w/ and /j/ are distinguished from the stops in terms of the duration and rate of change of the transitions of the first two formants. These transitions are longer and usually slower for the glides.

The voicing distinction in consonants has received a great deal of attention in the literature. For consonants in final position, voicing can be cued by the duration of the preceding vowel (Denes, 1955; Raphael, 1972). The duration of articulatory closure has been shown to cue voicing differences between stops in intervocalic position (Lisker, 1957). Voice-onset time (VOT), a complex articulatory-timing dimension, has been shown to characterize the voicing distinctions between stop consonants in initial position [b,d,g] versus [p,t,k] (Lisker & Abramson, 1964). Acoustically, VOT involves simultaneous changes in the relative onset of voiced excitation, the amplititude of the F1 transition, and the presence of aspiration in the higher formants during this time period.

While knowledge of the acoustic cues for all segmental phonemes is far from complete, sufficient information is available for reasonably good speech synthesis by rule. With a set of general phonological rules, as well as specific phonetic–acoustic rules, it is possible to take as input some discrete phonemic representation and provide as output a continuous speech signal (Klatt,1975a; Mattingly, 1968).

The acoustical structure of speech can be illustrated by examining a sound spectrogram of an utterance such as the one shown in Figure 3. As customary, time is represented on the abscissa and frequency on the ordinate. The relative concentration of energy at each frequency is shown by the degree of darkness on

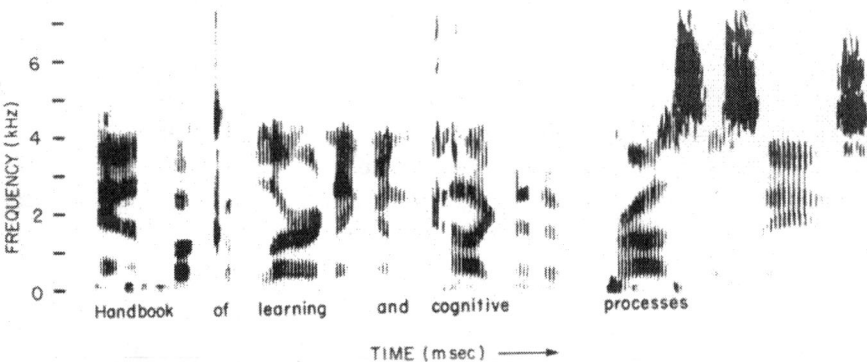

FIGURE 3.   Sound spectrogram of the utterance: "Handbook of Learning and Cognitive Processes."

the trace. The horizontal bars represent concentrations of energy that occur at the natural resonant frequencies of the vocal tract and are called formants. These can most easily be seen in the lower frequency regions during the production of vowel and vowel-like sounds. The closely spaced repetitive striations that occur during vowels and other voiced sounds reflect the presence of individual pulses of air passing through the glottis (that is, glottal pulses), whereas the more randomly structured portions of the spectrogram reflect the presence of turbulance or noise.

Inspection of Figure 3 will reveal that there are some discrete sound segments present in a sound spectrogram, but these acoustic segments do not always correspond to the linguistic segments resulting from perceptual analysis or to larger units such as morphemes. Thus, from this form of analysis, it became quite clear to many investigators that, at the acoustic level, phonetic segments are not represented discretely in time-like beads on a string or bricks in a wall. Instead, phonetic segments are merged together with each other so that there is a complex mapping of acoustic attribute to phonetic segment.

One particularly engaging description of the nature of speech is given by Hockett (1955) in his well-known easter egg passage:

> Imagine a row of easter eggs carried along a moving belt; the eggs are of various sizes, and variously colored, but not boiled. At a certain point, the belt carries the row of eggs between the two rollers of a wringer, which quite effectively smash them and rub them more or less into each other. The flow of eggs before the wringer represents the series of impulses from the phoneme source; the mess that emerges from the wringer represents the output of the speech transmitter. At a subsequent point, we have an inspector whose task it is to examine the passing mess and decide, on the basis of the broken and unbroken yolks, the variously spread out albumine, and the variously colored bits of shell, the nature of the flow of eggs which previously arrived at the wringer [p. 210].

Although this is an amusing analogy to the acoustical structure of speech, our understanding of the relation between phoneme and sound is not as impoverished as it might suggest. For example, some idea of the relation between acoustic cues and phonetic segments can be seen in Figure 4, which shows stylized acoustic patterns[1] for nine consonant-vowel syllables all followed by the vowel [a]. If converted to sound on a pattern playback device (Cooper, Liberman, & Borst, 1951), these patterns produce reasonably intelligible approximations of the intended syllables. As shown in this figure, the acoustic cues that distinguish place, manner, and voicing among these consonants show a systematic relation when the vowel is the same in each syllable. In these syllables, place of articulation is cued by differences in the direction and extent of the F2 transition. Nasals are distinguished from stops by the presence of a low-frequency nasal murmur. The

---

[1]It should be noted here that these are acoustic patterns that listeners interpret as speech sounds. An examination of natural speech utterances will reveal a great deal of additional information that is not shown in these displays and we can presume is employed by listeners in perceiving speech.

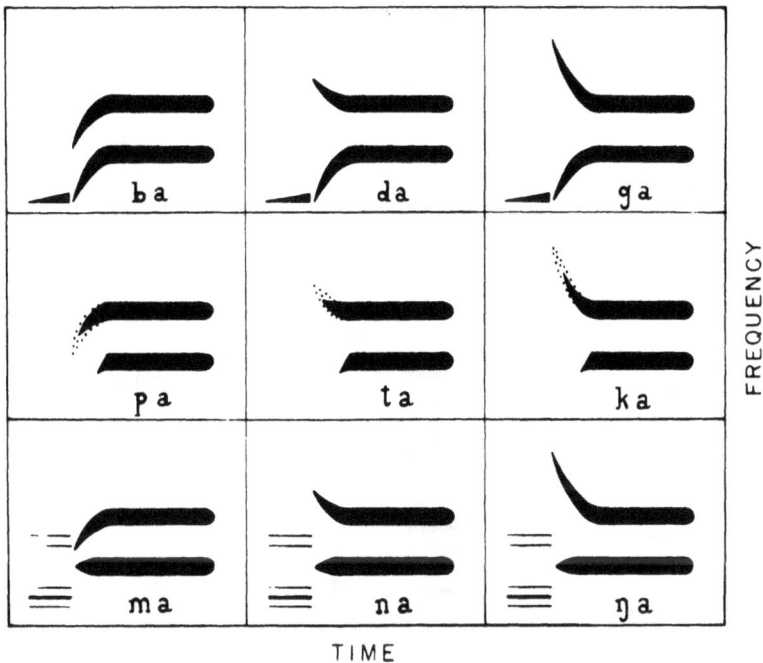

FIGURE 4. Schematized sound spectrograms for nine consonant–vowel syllables illustrating the acoustic cues for place, manner, and voicing. (From Liberman, Ingeman, Lisker, Delattre, & Cooper, 1959, with permission of the authors and publisher.)

voicing differences between [b,d,g] and [p,t,k] are distinguished by the relative onset of F1 to F2.

The situation is, however, more complicated when the vowel context of the syllable changes. As shown in Figure 5, the acoustic cues for a particular consonant—for example, the /d/ segment in the middle panel—vary and are coarticulated[2] with the following vowel and, as a consequence, it has been extremely difficult to find a simple invariant attribute that corresponds uniquely to the same stop consonant in all vowel environments (Cooper, Delattre, Liberman, Borst, & Gerstman, 1952). The results of early synthesis experiments with two-formant patterns such as these, therefore, failed to reveal acoustic invariants for the various places of articulation in stop consonants independently of context.

However, it cannot be concluded from these results that there are no invariant acoustic attributes for stop consonants in natural speech. Rather, a more reason-

[2]There are two types of coarticulation effects in speech, forward and backward. Each results from distinctly different phenomena. Backward effects are due entirely to the noninstantaneous response of the production system due to physical inertia or muscle delay, etc. On the other hand, forward coarticulation effects are assumed to be due to some higher level look-ahead mechanism or anticipation process.

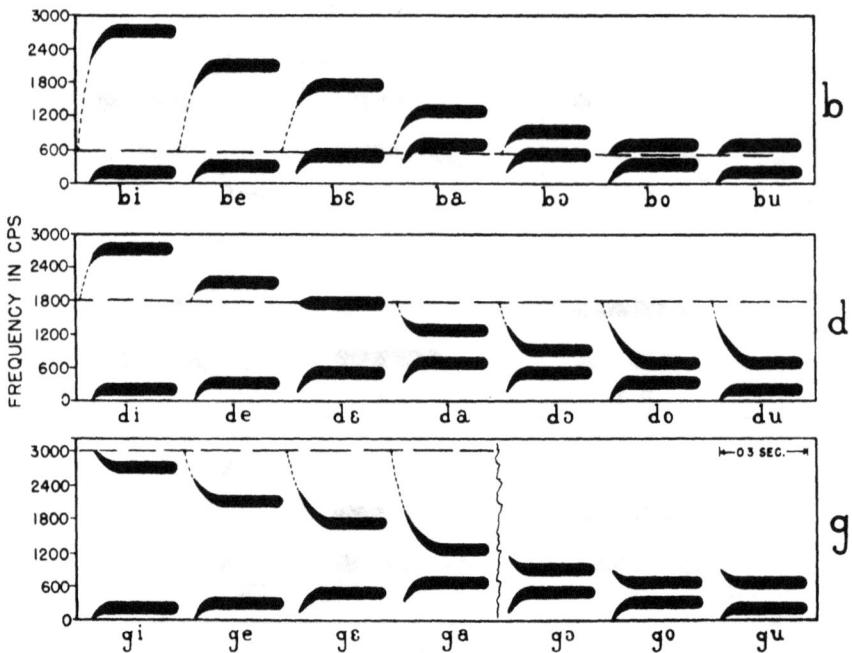

FIGURE 5.   Schematized sound spectrograms showing the formant transitions that are appropriate for the voiced stop consonants [b], [d], and [g] before various vowels. (From Delattre, Liberman, & Cooper, 1955, with permission of the authors and publisher.)

able conclusion, given our current knowledge, is that the invariant attributes are probably not to be found in terms of relatively simple acoustic properties as displayed in a sound spectrogram. Recent work employing somewhat more complex and natural-like synthetic stimuli has, in fact, suggested that there may be rather general properties of the acoustic signal that uniquely specify a particular place of articulation in stop consonants independently of vowel context (Stevens & Blumstein, 1976). The extent to which invariant, context-independent acoustic cues to phonemes can be established has been a topic of some controversy in the speech-perception literature, and is an issue that will be considered again in the next section.

C. Quantal Aspects of Speech Production

What regions of the articulatory space are used to form the phonetic segments and features employed in natural languages? Although the vocal apparatus can theoretically assume a relatively large number of articulatory positions, only a small number of preferred or "natural" regions are actually used in the phonological systems of natural languages. Stevens (1972) has proposed that speech sounds produced in these so-called natural regions have certain quantal properties or attributes that appear to be good candidates for the inventory of phonetic features in a given language. According to Stevens, all phonetic features that occur in languages probably have their basis in acoustic attributes that have such quantal properties: perturbations in articulation at one of these natural regions produce only small changes in the acoustic output. These acoustic attributes are assumed to be well matched to the auditory system (see the categorical perception section below).

The basic line of reasoning behind Stevens' quantal theory of speech production can be illustrated by reference to Figure 6. Assume that one could manipulate some articulatory parameter continuously along a particular dimension. And further assume that one could obtain a measure of some specific acoustic parameter of the speech signal that would be controlled by changes in this articulatory parameter. As the articulatory parameter is varied continuously, one might expect to find continuous changes in the output of this acoustic parameter. However, what seems to happen is shown schematically in Figure 6. There are places where very small changes in the articulatory parameter, as in Region II, produce large variations in the acoustic parameter, whereas in other places, as Region III, large changes in the articulatory parameter produce only small changes in the acoustic output. Relations such as these between vocal-tract shape and sound output have been studied in some detail by Stevens (1972, 1973) and others with the use of computer-simulation models of the vocal tract (see also Liljencrants & Lindblom, 1972; Lindblom & Sundberg, 1969). Small changes have been made

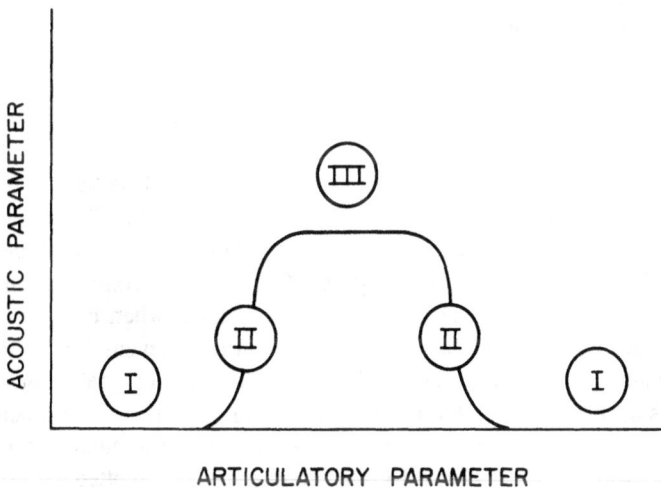

FIGURE 6. Hypothetical quantal relations between a parameter that describes some aspect of articulation and the resulting acoustic parameter of speech. (From Stevens, 1972, with permission of the author and publisher.)

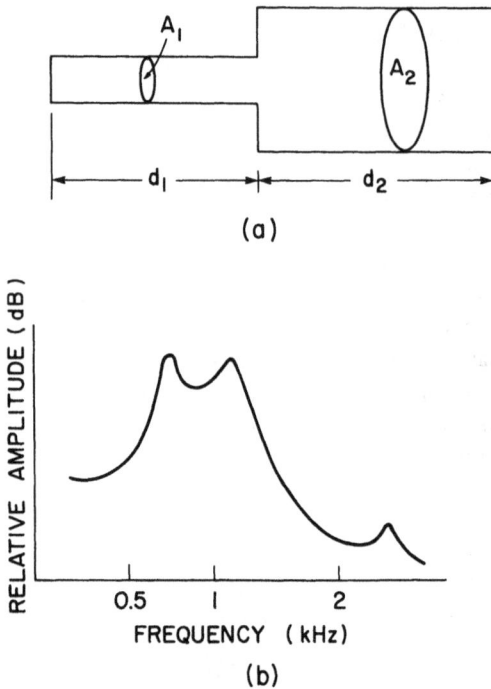

FIGURE 7.   (a) A two-tube resonator approximating the vocal tract configuration for the vowel [a]. A_1 and A_2 represent the cross-sectional areas of the pharyngeal and oral cavities, respectively. (b) An approximation of the spectrum envelope for the vowel [a] produced by the configuration shown above. The peaks in the function represent the center frequencies of the formants. (From Stevens, 1972, with permission of the author and publisher.)

systematically in an articulatory parameter and the resultant effects on the properties of sound output calculated quite precisely.

To see how the simulation was accomplished, it will be helpful to examine briefly the resonance characteristics of the vocal tract. Figure 7 shows an approximation of the vocal-tract shape for the vowel [a] in terms of a two-tube resonator (Fant, 1960). The spectrum envelope produced by this configuration is shown below. The back or pharyngeal cavity is constricted when compared with the front or oral cavity. Using a vocal tract simulation, Stevens (1972) found that, over a wide range, variations in the lengths of the cavities (that is, d_1 and d_2) and the cross-sectional areas (that is, A_1 and A_2) did not affect the formant frequencies of the vowel to any large extent. The results of this simulation are shown in Figure 8, where the calculated formant frequencies are plotted as a function of the length of d_1. Notice that there is an area in the middle of this figure where variations in d_1 produce only small changes in the formant frequencies of F1 and F2. On the other hand, there are regions at the extremes where a small variation

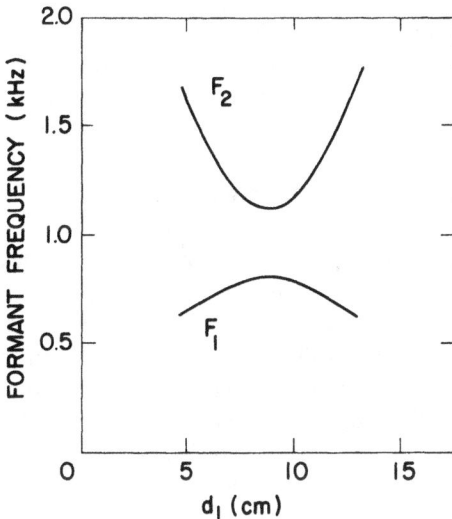

FIGURE 8. Results of a vocal-tract simulation showing the relation between frequencies of the first and second formants (F1 and F2) when the length of the back tube, d_1, is varied between 5 and 15 cm. (From Stevens, 1972, with permission of the author and publisher.)

in d_1 produces a much larger shift in the formant frequencies, especially the values of the second formant.

Stevens (1972, 1973) has employed these simulation techniques to study other vowels as well as several types of consonants. One general conclusion to be drawn from Stevens' work is that there are certain places in the vocal tract that show quantal relations between articulation and the attributes of the sound output. Perturbations in articulation apparently have only small effects on the acoustic signal and, therefore, would presumably affect perception only minimally.

One of the proposals that Stevens has made about these findings is that the sound segments used in languages are selected from a small range of features or distinctive attributes. A careful examination of these attributes reveals that they have a natural basis in terms of certain vocal-tract configurations. These configurations are chosen from precisely those regions where variability in articulation can be tolerated without the sound output being appreciably affected.

Using the same types of simulation procedures, Liljencrants and Lindblom (1972) have studied the vowel systems of a number of languages in order to predict their phonetic structure. Since human vowels represent only a small subset of the possible combinations of formant frequencies, it was of interest to see how the vowels were distributed in acoustic space. Liljencrants and Lindblom found that the vowel systems of quite diverse languages can be described in terms of a simple principle of "maximal perceptual contrast" as defined by the linear distance in mel units between the points representative of two vowels.[3] The whole vowel space for a particular language seems to be organized in terms of sound contrasts that are highly discriminable. This is true of languages having as few as 3 to as many as 12 vowels. These two sets of findings are important because they indicate that the sound systems of natural languages are matched in some sense to attributes of both perception and production.

It should be noted here that not all of the potential distinctive features at the phonetic level are used distinctively at a phonological level in any particular language. Similarly, no natural language has as many phonemes in its phonological system as there are logically possible combinations of utilized distinctive features. The sound systems of language appear to have evolved the way they are for several reasons. First, the distinctions are easily pronounceable for talkers. Second, these articulatory distinctions generate acoustic attributes that are highly distinctive, resulting in sounds that can be identified and discriminated under very poor listening conditions. In the next section, the results of experiments dealing with the perception of speech sounds are considered.

IV. PERCEPTION OF SPEECH SOUNDS

The process of speech production imposes certain well-defined constraints on the resulting acoustic waveform. As noted, these constraints are derived from the anatomy and physiology of the vocal mechanism and the associated resonant properties. Although a good deal of work remains to be done in understanding and modeling the speech-perception process, there are a number of well-established empirical findings that define the problems in the field of speech perception and set it apart from other related areas such as auditory psychophysics and general auditory perception. It is possible to describe the research in speech perception in terms of two general lines of investigation: (a) studies aimed at establishing the acoustic cues to the perception of speech-sound segments and (b) studies aimed primarily at demonstrating the effects of manipulating syntactic and semantic variables on speech perception. The remainder of this chapter will be concerned primarily with experiments that fall into the first class of studies. Four major areas of research dealing with the perception of phonetic segments will be discussed: (a) early research on the acoustic cues for stop consonants, (b) experiments on the identification and discrimination of speech sounds, (c) research on developmental aspects of speech perception in young infants, and, finally, (d) recent work on the role of feature detectors in

[3]A *mel* is a psychophysical unit reflecting equal sense distances of pitch. It is linear at low frequencies and approximately logarithmic at frequencies above 1000 Hz. The scaling of formant frequencies from linear units to mels is based on the assumption that this transformation reflects the response of the auditory system to frequency differences. The mel scale was constructed by Stevens and Volkmann (1940) on the basis of subjective pitch evaluations by naive listeners.

speech perception. The material described in these sections is quite selective in order to focus on some of the major problems and theoretical issues that have been studied in speech perception over the last few years.

The study of speech perception differs in several ways from the study of general auditory perception. First, the signals typically used to study the functioning of the auditory system are simple, discrete, and usually well-defined mathematically. Moreover, they typically vary along only a single dimension. In contrast, speech sounds involve complex spectral relations that vary as a function of time; changes that occur in a single parameter often affect the perception of other attributes of the stimulus (Lane, 1962). Second, most of the research in auditory psychophysics over the last two decades has been concerned with the discriminative capacities of the transducer and the peripheral-auditory mechanism. In the perception of speech, the relevant mechanisms are, for the most part, centrally located. Moreover, experiments in auditory psychophysics have commonly been focused on experimental tasks involving discrimination rather than absolute identification. Differential discrimination is rarely the situation of listeners when they perceive and understand speech. In fact, the listener must almost always attempt to identify, on an absolute basis, a particular stretch of speech. Thus, it is generally believed that a good deal of what we have learned from traditional auditory psychophysics is only marginally relevant to the study of the complex cognitive processes that are involved in speech perception.

In addition to differences in the signal, there are also marked differences in the way speech and nonspeech sounds are processed by listeners. For the most part, when people are presented with speech signals, they respond to them as linguistic entities rather than as auditory events in the environment. Speech signals are categorized and labeled almost immediately with reference to the listener's linguistic background. Moreover, as we shall see, a listener's ability to discriminate certain speech sounds is often a function of the extent to which the particular acoustic distinction under study plays a functional role in the listener's linguistic system.

A. Invariant Acoustic Cues for Stop Consonants

One of the most firmly established findings in the speech-perception literature is that the acoustic correlates of a number of consonantal features are highly dependent on context. This is especially true for the stop consonants (b, d, g; p, t, k) that show the greatest amount of contextual variability. As a result of coarticulation effects, one sound segment often carries information about two or more successive phonemes in an utterance. And, conversely, a single phoneme often exerts an influence on several successive sound segments in the acoustic signal. As noted earlier, listeners perceive speech as consisting of a sequence of discrete segments arrayed in time, although the physical signal often varies continuously. The earliest experimental studies in speech perception were aimed at uncovering the relation or mapping between attributes of the acoustic signal and phonetic units derived from perceptual analysis. The outcome of these initial studies indicated that there were few discrete isolatable and invariant sound segments in the physical signal that correspond uniquely to perceived phonemes. The lack of correspondence between attributes of the acoustic signal and units of linguistic analysis has been, and still is, one of the most important and controversial issues in speech perception. Because of the prominance of this issue, it is appropriate to review first some of the early findings and then briefly discuss some of the more recent attempts that have been made to resolve this issue.

The initial work on the acoustic cues for phonemes involved two related procedures. First, spectrographic analyses were carried out on minimal pairs to identify the potentially important acoustic attributes that distinguished these ut-

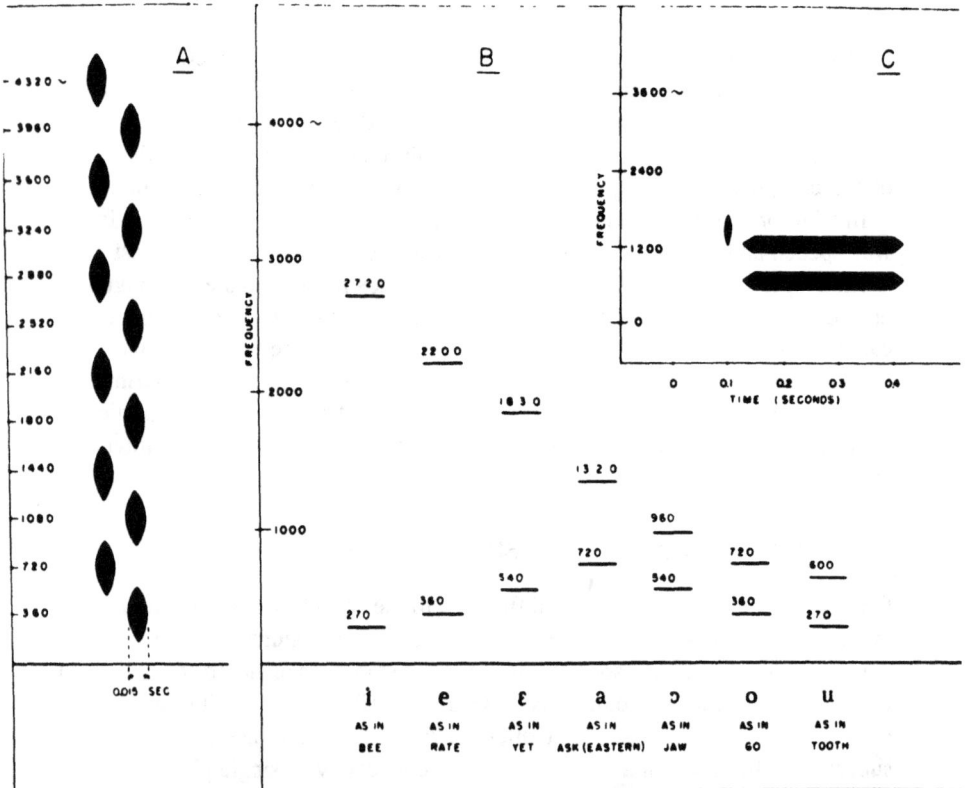

FIGURE 9.   Schematized spectrographic patterns showing the frequency positions of synthetic release bursts (A), the vowel formants (B) and an example of one of the resulting test syllables (C). (From Liberman, Delattre, & Cooper, 1952, with permission of the authors and publisher, The University of Illinois Press. Copyright 1952 by the American Journal of Psychology.)

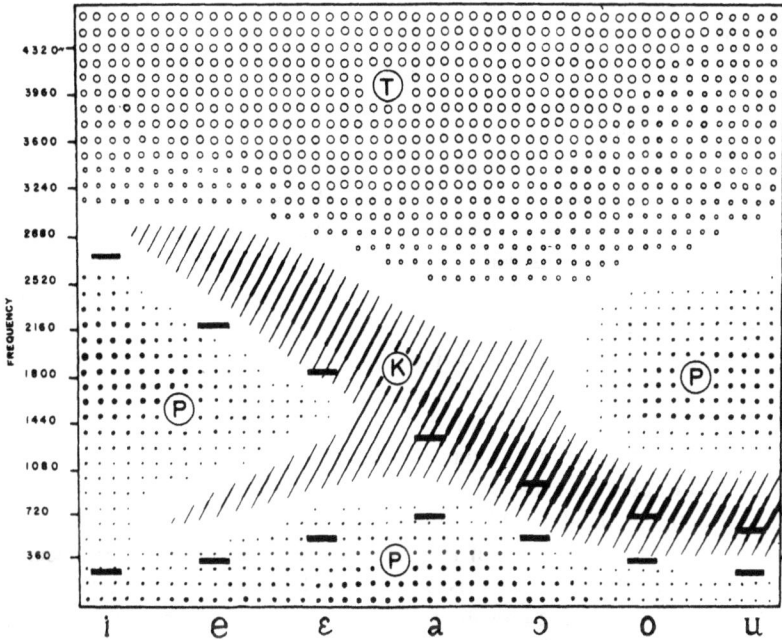

FIGURE 10.   Results showing the distribution of /p/, /t/, or /k/ responses as a function of the burst position and formant frequencies of the vowel. (From Liberman, Delattre, & Cooper, 1952, with permission of the authors and publisher, The University of Illinois Press. Copyright 1952 by the American Journal of Psychology.)

terances. Then synthesis experiments were conducted to verify the significance of these acoustic cues in perception.

In the first study to use these combined methods, Liberman, Delattre and Cooper (1952) examined the relation between the frequency of a noise burst and the perception of the voiceless consonants p, t, and k. An examination of sound spectrograms of real speech showed that the voiceless stops could potentially be distinguished by the frequency of a brief burst of noise, the acoustic counterpart of the articulatory explosion at the release of stop closure. Liberman *et al.* systematically varied the frequency of a synthetic noise burst before a number of different two-formant vowels and observed its effect on perception. The actual stimulus patterns employed in this experiment are shown in Figure 9. An example of one typical stimulus pattern is shown in Panel C of this figure. The stimuli were presented one at a time to subjects who were told to identify each stimulus as either p, t, or k. The results of this experiment are shown in Figure 10. Subjects' identification of a particular stop consonant varied not only according to the frequency of the noise burst but also in terms of the relation of the burst to the vowel with which it was paired. As shown in this figure, high-frequency bursts above 3.2 KHz were heard as /t/ in all vowel environments whereas bursts at other frequencies were heard as either /p/ or /k/, depending on the frequency of the burst in relation to the formant frequencies of the following vowel. Thus, placing the identical burst before two different vowels changes the way in which the burst is perceived by listeners.

The results of this initial study with synthetic speech were replicated with real speech stimuli in a study by Schatz (1954). She found that release bursts spliced from [ki], [ka], and [ku] were perceived as different stops, depending upon the following vowel context. For example, the release burst excised from [ki] is perceived as /t/ when spliced before [a] but is perceived as /p/ before [u]. Therefore, the findings of these two experiments indicate that identification of the consonants does not depend exclusively on the absolute frequency of the burst but rather on the attributes of the burst in relation to the vowel that follows.

Cooper et al. (1952) studied the role of formant transitions in the perception of stop consonants. Variations in the first formant transition were found to provide cues to voicing and manner, whereas variations in the second formant transition were found to provide cues to place of articulation among the stops /b,d,g/ and /p,t,k/. Cooper et al. also studied a range of second formant transitions with the same vowels that were used in the previous burst experiment. Subjects were required to identify the stimuli as b, d, or g. The results indicated that, while most subjects heard rising transitions as /b/ in almost all vowel contexts, perception of the falling transitions as either /d/ or /g/ varied as a function of the following vowel. Thus, as in the previous burst experiments, the perception of the formant transitions as a particular phoneme depended on the following vowel.

Three important conclusions have been drawn from the results of these early perceptual experiments. First, with regard to stop consonants, no invariant acoustic cues could be identified that corresponded uniquely to the same phoneme in all environments. Second, because burst and transition cues depend, to a large extent, on properties of the following vowel, the minimal *acoustic* unit seemed more likely to be about the size of a consonant–vowel syllable than an isolated phoneme. Indeed, as Cooper et al. (1952) remarked, "One may not always be able to find the phoneme in the speech wave, because it may not exist there in free form [p. 605]." Finally, within the context of these experiments that have employed relatively simple synthetic stimuli, it appeared that the acoustic information for a particular phoneme was encoded into the sound stream in a complex way because no one-to-one correspondence could be found between perceived phoneme and acoustic segment.

Although these early findings failed to uncover the invariant acoustic attributes for phonemes (for example, stop consonants) and emphasized a complex relation between acoustic attribute and phonetic unit, numerous investigators have continued to search for a description of the acoustic signal that would reveal invariant attributes for phonemes (Fant, 1960, 1962, 1973; Stevens, 1967, 1973). The experimental literature on this topic during the 1950s and 1960s is extensive and cannot be reviewed here. To illustrate the nature of the problem, however, we consider briefly two different approaches to the invariance issue.

For a number of years, primarily because of their interest in distinctive feature theory and its emphasis on relational invariants, Stevens (1967, 1971, 1973, 1975) and Fant (1960, 1973) have sought to find acoustic invariants for distinctive features. Their argument is that there are well-defined acoustic correlates for the principal places of articulation for consonants, particularly the stops, and that previous research with synthetic speech has tended to obscure some of the important cues found in natural speech. According to Fant and Stevens, these invariant acoustic attributes are contained in the rapid changes in spectral energy that occur during the first 10 to 30 msec after the release. Both investigators emphasize that burst and formant transitions, which previously were assumed to be independent cues, should be regarded as a single integrated stimulus event or cue. Thus, burst and transitions constitute an overall spectral change at onset.

Based primarily on acoustic analyses of consonant–vowel (CV) syllables, Fant (1969) has claimed invariant spectral relations for labials, postdentals, and velars. For labials (that is, [b] and [p]), spectral energy is weak and spread with a major concentration at low frequencies; for postdentals ([d] and [t]), spectral energy is stronger and spread, although the major concentration occurs at high frequencies; for velars ([g] and [k]), the spectral energy is compact and concentrated at mid-frequencies.

Focusing on the rapid spectrum changes that accompany the release of a stop consonant, Stevens (1967, 1973, 1975) has also argued for invariant spectral patterns for place of articulation. According to Stevens, labials can be characterized by low-frequency onsets followed by upward or rising changes in spectral energy, whereas postdentals have high-frequency onsets followed by downward or falling changes in spectral energy. Velars have spectral energy concentrated narrowly in the mid-frequency range at onset followed by spreading of energy to frequencies above and below this region. Some examples of these spectral relations are shown schematically in Figure 11. Stevens (1975) believes that these rapid spectrum changes at onset "identify features of place of articulation without reference to acoustic events remote from this point in time . . . [and that] these cues are absolute properties of the speech signal and are context-independent [p. 319]."

More recently, however, Stevens and Blumstein (1976) have modified this earlier account somewhat and now claim that the invariant properties for stops in initial position involve simply the location and diffuseness of spectral energy at stimulus onset. This position is now closer to Fant's (1969) views summarized above. The main direction of both Stevens' and Fant's position has been to focus on somewhat more complex integrated acoustic attributes of consonants rather than simple isolated cues. By following this strategy, it is assumed that an integrated acoustic pattern will show invariance when each of its components fails to do so when considered separately in isolation.

LABIALS   POST-DENTALS   VELARS

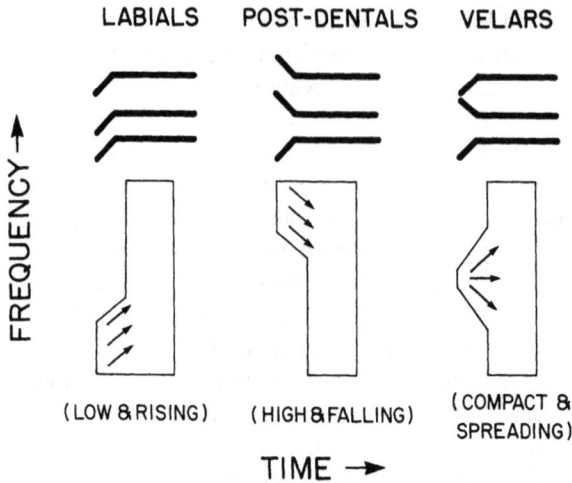

FIGURE 11. Hypothetical invariant patterns for labial, post-dental, and velar stop consonants in initial position. (Adapted from Stevens, 1975.)

The work of Stevens and Fant is important because it represents the only serious attempt to specify the invariants for stops directly in the acoustic signal. It is clear, however, despite Stevens' remark to the contrary, that the types of invariant attributes being proposed here are relational invariants, not absolute invariants that occur independently of context. The patterns that Stevens and Fant describe are derived from examining frequency relations over some short period of time and are, therefore, not absolutely invariant in all contexts (see below).

Although working independently of Fant and Stevens, Cole and Scott (1974a, 1974b) have also argued for context-independent or invariant cues for stop consonants. However, their position is quite different from that of Fant and Stevens. Cole and Scott claim that invariant cues to place of articulation are present in the initial portion of the consonant energy in the release burst. This claim is based on the results of a tape-splicing experiment in which Cole and Scott transposed the initial consonant energy from the six stops between the vowels /i/ and /u/. Their results showed that listeners could identify the original consonants accurately in all cases except when the consonant energy from /ki/ and /gi/ was transposed to /u/.

At first glance these results, as well as the claims made by Cole and Scott, appear to be in sharp conflict with the findings of the earlier experiments carried out by Liberman *et al.* (1952) with synthetic stimuli and Schatz (1954) with natural speech. The discrepancy, however, can be accounted for quite easily and the claims dismissed by a careful examination of the stimuli obtained after the tape-splicing procedure. In these experiments Cole and Scott transposed not only the release bursts, as in the earlier studies, but also the aspirated formant transitions that are, in fact, coarticulated with the following vowel. Thus, it is quite likely that sufficient information was present in these stimuli for subjects to identify the consonant from its original context even before it was transposed to another vowel. Indeed, Schatz (1954) remarked on precisely this point in her tape-splicing experiment some 20 years earlier, stating that "these 'voiceless formants' in the aspiration are prominent enough so that the vowel is easily identifiable even when the entire voiced portion of the syllable has been removed and the voiceless part is heard alone [p. 52]." More recently, Winitz, Scheib, and Reeds (1972) obtained comparable results when listeners were asked to identify only the burst and aspiration portions of /p,t,k/ spoken before the vowels /i,a,u/. Cole and Scott's results, therefore, are not at all in conflict with the previous work by Liberman *et al.* and Schatz. The results and claims have little bearing on the issue of invariance since the burst and aspirated formant transitions vary as a function of the following vowel of the syllable and, consequently, are context-dependent cues.

The arguments advanced in favor of invariant context-independent attributes for stop consonants have recently been reexamined in great detail by Dorman, Studdert-Kennedy and Raphael (1977). In contrast to the views of Fant and Stevens, these investigators argue, based on new perceptual data, that burst and transition cues are highly dependent on context. Dorman *et al.* removed these cues from CVC syllables containing /b,d,g/ spoken before nine different vowels and then recombined them with the same vowels spoken in VC syllables in order to determine whether bursts and transitions were sufficient cues to the three places of articulation. The results indicated that the importance of release bursts and transitions—as cues to place—varied substantially with the particular consonant, the vowel, and the speaker and that no single cue was sufficient for the recognition of a particular place feature in all contexts. In another experiment, Dorman *et al.* transposed the release bursts that were removed from each CVC syllable across all nine VC syllables for a given place of articulation. Although the release bursts were, to a large degree, invariant in their perceptual effect before most vowels, they were sufficient cues to place of articulation in only a small number of cases.

Dorman *et al.* observed in these experiments that the effects of burst and transition were reciprocally related. In some contexts where one cue (for example, the burst) was sufficient for a particular place distinction, the other cue (for example, the transitions) was not and vice versa. For example, the burst was found to be a strong cue for /b/ before rounded vowels (that is, /u/). In this context, however, the formant transitions are brief and served only as weak cues to place. On the other hand, formant transitions were strong cues for /b/ before middle, unrounded vowels such as /a/, whereas the burst was only a weak cue. The isolated burst was an effective cue to place only if its frequency was close to the main formant of the following vowel. When burst frequency differed substantially from the main formant, the transitions were strong cues to place. Thus, as Dorman *et al.* pointed out, burst and transition serve basically similar functions by providing information about the consonantal release and spectral changes into the following vowel.

Based on these more recent findings, Dorman *et al.* (1977) concluded that the sufficiency of each cue varies as a function of context. Thus, any account of the perception of place of articulation for stop consonants, therefore, will have to be relative rather than absolute and, consequently, will require reference to the following vowel.

It is worth pointing out here that the invariance problem in speech perception has, by no means, been resolved yet. The work summarized in this section has been limited to only the stop consonants in initial position in stressed CV syllables. Some idea of the magnitude of the invariance problem in speech perception can be obtained by considering the contextual effects for stop consonants that appear in other phonetic environments such as medial and final position of syllables as well as consonant clusters. Moreover, the problem becomes enormous when we add to it the contextual variability found for other classes of speech sounds, such as fricatives, liquids, nasals, and vowels as well as the inherent variability associated with phonetic context, speaking rate, and individual talker differences.

B.   The Speech Mode and Categorical Perception

The earliest experiments in speech perception showed that listeners respond to speech sounds quite differently from other auditory signals. Liberman and his colleagues at Haskins Laboratories found that listeners perceived synthetic speech stimuli varying between [b], [d], and [g] as members of distinct categories (Liberman, Harris, Hoffman, & Griffith, 1957). When these same listeners were required to discriminate pairs of these sounds, they could discriminate stimuli drawn from different phonetic categories but could not discriminate stimuli drawn from the same phonetic category. The obtained discrimination functions showed marked discontinuities at places along the stimulus continuum that were correlated with changes in identification.

The ideal case of this form of perception, "categorical perception," is illustrated in Figure 12. In an experiment such as this, two or more phonetic segments are selected to represent end points, and a continuum of synthetic stimuli is generated. Subjects are required to carry out two tasks: identification and discrimination. In the identification task, stimuli are selected from the continuum and presented one at a time in random order for labeling into categories defined by the experimenter. In the discrimination task, pairs of stimuli are selected from the continuum and presented to listeners for some discriminative response.

The basic finding of the categorical perception experiments is that listeners can discriminate between two speech sounds that have been identified as different phonemes much better than between two stimuli that have been identified as the same phoneme, even though the acoustic differences are comparable. At the

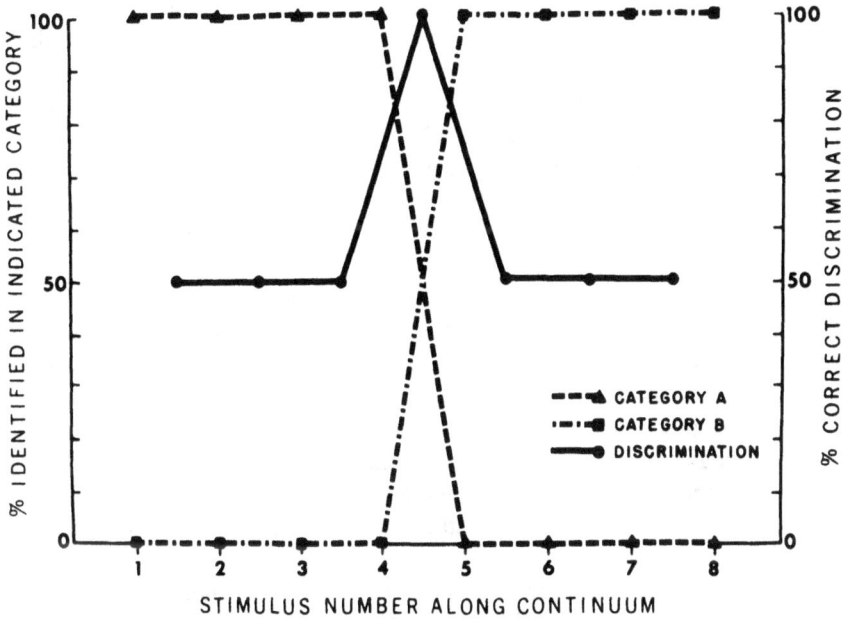

FIGURE 12. Idealized form of categorical perception showing the identification function (left ordinate) and the discrimination function (right ordinate). (From Studdert-Kennedy, Liberman, Harris, & Cooper, 1970. Copyright 1970 by the American Psychological Association. Reprinted by permission of authors and publisher.)

time, the categorical perception results were considered by Liberman and others to be quite unusual when compared with the results typically obtained in most psychophysical experiments with nonspeech stimuli. In general, stimuli that lie along a single continuum are perceived continuously, resulting in discrimination functions that are monotonic with the physical scale. As is well known, there are capacity limitations on information transmission in terms of absolute identification (Miller, 1956). Listeners can discriminate many more acoustic stimuli than they can identify in absolute terms (Pollack, 1952, 1953). However, in the case of categorical perception, the situation is quite different. The listener's differential discrimination appears to be no better than his absolute identification. In the extreme case of categorical perception, a listener's discrimination performance can be predicted from his identification function under the strong assumption that the listener can discriminate between two stimuli only to the extent that these stimuli are identified as different on an absolute basis (Liberman et al., 1957).

These initial findings with stop consonants led to a similar experiment with vowels that varied in acoustically equal steps through the range /I/, /ɛ/ and /ac/. Fry, Abramson, Eimas, and Liberman (1962) reported that these stimuli were perceived continuously, much like nonspeech stimuli. The discrimination functions did not yield discontinuities along the stimulus continuum that were related to changes in identification but were relatively flat across the whole continuum. Moreover, it was observed that vowels were, in general, more discriminable than stop consonants, indicating that listeners could perceive many more intraphonemic differences.

The differences in perception between stop consonants and steady-state vowels have been assumed to reflect two basic modes of perception, a categorical mode and a continuous mode. Categorical perception reflects a mode of perception in which each acoustic pattern is *always* and *only* perceived as a token of a particular phonetic type (Studdert-Kennedy, 1974). Listeners can discriminate between two different acoustic patterns if the stimuli have been categorized into different phonetic categories, but they cannot discriminate two different acoustic patterns that have been categorized into the same phonetic category. Information about the acoustic properties of these stimuli appears to be unavailable for purely auditory judgments as a consequence of phonetic classification. What remains available to the decision process is a more abstract and permanent code based on the listener's interpretation of the stimulus event (see Pisoni, 1971; Pisoni & Tash, 1974).

Although the stimulus generalization as reflected in categorical perception might seem to be a more primitive form of stimulus control, it may provide, on the other hand, a more efficient mode of response for absolute and rapid decisions concerning the presence or absence of particular attributes such as those required in the processing of connected speech. Indeed, the great interest expressed in categorical perception of speech presumably derives from the assumption that listeners do make categorical decisions in listening to continuous speech.

Continuous perception, on the other hand, may be thought of as reflecting an auditory mode of perception where discrimination is independent of category assignment. Although listeners can assign acoustically different stimuli to the same category, they may still discriminate between tokens selected from the same category. Thus, an auditory, nonphonetic basis for discrimination is available to the listener.

For a number of years, the categorical-perception results were assumed to be unique to speech perception and primarily a consequence of phonetic categorization. Indeed, the differences in perception between consonants and vowels has led Liberman (1970a) to argue strongly for a specialized mode of perception, a "speech mode," to characterize the way these stimuli are perceived. Other findings have suggested that a specialized perceptual mechanism, a "special speech decoder," may exist for processing speech sounds (Studdert-Kennedy & Shankweiler, 1970).

The differences in perception between consonants and vowels were originally interpreted as supporting a motor theory of speech perception (Liberman, Cooper, Harris, & MacNeilage, 1963). According to the strong motor theory, reference to articulation is a mediating stage in the perceptual process between the incoming acoustic signal and its recognition. As discussed earlier, stop consonants are produced in a discontinuous way by a constriction at a particular place in the vocal tract, whereas vowels are produced by continuous changes in the overall shape of the vocal tract. The strong version of the motor theory assumed that although the appropriate acoustic cues for consonants could be described by an acoustic continuum, these stimuli were perceived discontinuously (that is, categorically) because the articulations underlying the production of these sounds is essentially discontinuous. In contrast, vowels were perceived continuously because of the continuous changes in the articulators from one position to another. Although the original accounts of the motor theory (Liberman, 1957; Liberman *et al.,* 1963) assumed that articulatory movements and their sensory effects mediate perception, more recent versions of the theory (Liberman, Cooper, Shankweiler, & Studdert-Kennedy, 1967; Studdert-Kennedy, 1974) have placed the reference at the level of the neuromotor commands that activate the articulators.

The major reason for proposing a motor theory was to attempt to resolve the lack of invariance between acoustic attribute and perceived phoneme. According to Liberman (1957), there is a simpler relation between articulation and perception than between acoustic attribute and perception.[4] At that time it was claimed that the articulatory movements and motor commands for a particular phoneme showed less contextual variability than the resultant acoustic manifestation of the phoneme. However, this argument has not found support in the subsequent electromyographic research on speech production (see Harris, 1974; MacNeilage, 1970). If anything, these findings show the ubiquitous nature of variability at all stages of speech production.

The interpretation that categorical perception reflects a specialized mode of perception unique to speech as well as the claims associated with the motor theory have come under strong criticism from a number of directions in the last few years. Several investigators have argued that the differences in perception between consonants and vowels reflect differences in the psychophysical properties of the acoustic cues that distinguish these two classes of speech sounds (Lane, 1965; Pisoni, 1971; Studdert-Kennedy, 1974). For the stop consonants there is a relatively complex relation between phoneme and its representation as sound; the essential acoustic cues are contained in the rapidly changing spectrum at onset (that is, release burst and formant transitions) that is weak, relatively brief in duration (30 to 50 msec), and transient in nature. On the other hand, the cues to the vowels involve changes in the steady-state frequencies of the first

---

[4]With regard to the relation between articulation and acoustics, Liberman (1957) raised the following question: "When articulation and soundwave go their separate ways, which way does the perception go?" and in response replied that "the perception always goes with articulation [p. 121]." Fant (1960) argued that Liberman is wrong since "articulation and sound waves never go separate ways [p. 218]."

three formants that have a relatively long duration and more uniform spectral properties as well as greater intensity. As support for this, Fujisaki and Kawashima (1969, 1970) and Pisoni (1971, 1975) have shown that the differences in perception between consonants and vowels are due, in part, to the duration of the acoustic cues. Vowels of very short duration (that is, 40 to 50 msec) are perceived more categorically than identical stimuli having longer durations.

Other findings have shown that categorical perception is also due, in part, to encoding processes in short-term memory that result from the particular type of discrimination task used in these experiments (Pisoni, 1971, 1973, 1975). The ABX procedure has been used in almost all of the speech-perception experiments demonstrating categorical perception. In this task subjects are presented with three sounds successively, ABA or ABB. A and B are always acoustically different, and the subjects have to indicate whether the third sound is identical to the first or second sound. This is basically a recognition-memory paradigm. In order to solve the discrimination task, the subjects are forced to encode the individual stimuli in temporal succession and then base their decision on the encoded representations that have been maintained in short-term memory rather than to respond to the magnitudes of difference between stimuli within an ABX triad. In a number of experiments, Pisoni (1971, 1973) has shown that differences between categorical and continuous modes of perception are crucially dependent on the memory requirements of the particular discrimination procedure and the level of encoding required to solve the task (Pisoni, 1971, 1973).

Several recent experiments employing nonspeech stimuli have also suggested that categorical perception may not be peculiar to speech sounds or a specialized speech mode as once supposed but may be a more general property of cognitive processes that involve categorization and coding of the stimulus input (see Bruner, 1957). For example, Cutting and Rosner (1974) demonstrated categorical perception effects for nonspeech musical sounds varying in rise-time that could be labeled as a "pluck" or a "bow." Miller, Wier, Pastore, Kelly, and Dooling (1976) have shown comparable categorical perception effects for nonspeech stimuli varying in the onset of a noise preceding a buzz. In another study, Pisoni (1977) has reported similar results for stimuli differing in the relative onset time of two component tones. In each case, these nonspeech experiments showed that discrimination was better for pairs of stimuli selected from different categories than for pairs of stimuli selected from the same category. Moreover, discrimination of stimuli selected from within a category was very nearly close to chance performance, as predicted by the categorical-perception model.

The results obtained with nonspeech stimuli have provided some insight into the underlying basis of categorical perception for speech stimuli. These nonspeech experiments have succeeded in demonstrating categorical perception when previous attempts have failed primarily for three reasons. First, the investigators employed relatively complex acoustic stimuli in which only a single component was varied relative to the remainder of the stimulus complex. In most of the previous nonspeech experiments, only simple stimuli were used. Second, while these complex stimuli may be characterized as varying in linear steps along some nominally physical continuum, on both psychophysical and perceptual grounds, the stimulus continuum that is generated results in several distinctive perceptual attributes or qualities that are present for some stimuli but not others. These perceptual attributes, in turn, define quantal regions along the stimulus continuum that are separated by natural psychophysical boundaries; within these regions sensitivity is low, whereas between these regions it is high. Finally, because the stimulus continuum can be partitioned into several perceptually distinctive classes, subjects can easily employ a set of labels or descriptive categories to encode these signals in short-term memory. These codes can then be assigned to stimuli presented in the subsequent ABX discrimination task.

Therefore, categorical perception of both speech and complex nonspeech signals can be explained, in part, by the presence of well-defined psychophysical boundaries that separate stimuli into distinctive perceptual categories and by the use of verbal labels that can be used to encode these attributes in short-term memory. Thus, this account of categorical perception involves two distinct components, a sensory component and a memory or labeling component. Previous explanations have stressed only the labeling component of categorical perception (Liberman *et al.*, 1967b). If categorical perception were based only on labels and encoding processes in short-term memory as Fujisaki and Kawashima (1969, 1970) and Massaro (1976) as well as others have argued, we would expect to find comparable categorical-like discrimination functions for vowels and other steady-state signals that can be labeled easily. However, the available evidence indicates that while labeling and memory effects may account for some aspects of vowel discrimination, particularly the results obtained with very short vowels, it cannot account for all of the relevant findings. For example, comparable categorical-like discrimination functions have been obtained for stop consonants and nonspeech signals without specific labeling instructions to subjects. While it is possible to argue that subjects did use labels for the speech stimuli in this task, it seems unlikely that they could have used them with the nonspeech signals that also showed marked discontinuities in the shape of the discrimination functions. Thus, these discrimination findings provide support for the presence of a real sensory effect in terms of a well-defined psychophysical boundary and, accordingly, what may be thought of as a perceptual notch in the stimulus continuum at the category boundary (for further discussion see Ades, 1977; Macmillan, Kaplan & Creelman, 1977; Perey & Pisoni, 1977).

But what is the basis for the distinctive perceptual attributes of speech sounds? One approach can be found in the work of Stevens (1972) on the quantal theory discussed earlier. According to Stevens, phonetic features are grounded in a close match between articulatory and auditory capacities. The acoustic attributes common to a phonetic category are determined, in part, by articulatory constraints on speech production and, in part, by the distinctiveness of the resulting acoustic signals in perception. Thus, the strongest evidence for a perceptual match between speech perception and production, according to Stevens, is the categorical-perception findings. The acoustic correlates of certain phonetic features that show quantal properties in production are also precisely those features that show categorical-like discrimination in perceptual experiments.

It should be pointed out, however, that the category boundaries for phonetic features are not inherently fixed perceptual thresholds, since the boundaries and the resulting shifts in sensitivity in this region of the continuum are also a function of linguistic experience. Indeed, as Popper (1972) has suggested, "people who speak different languages may tune their auditory systems dif-

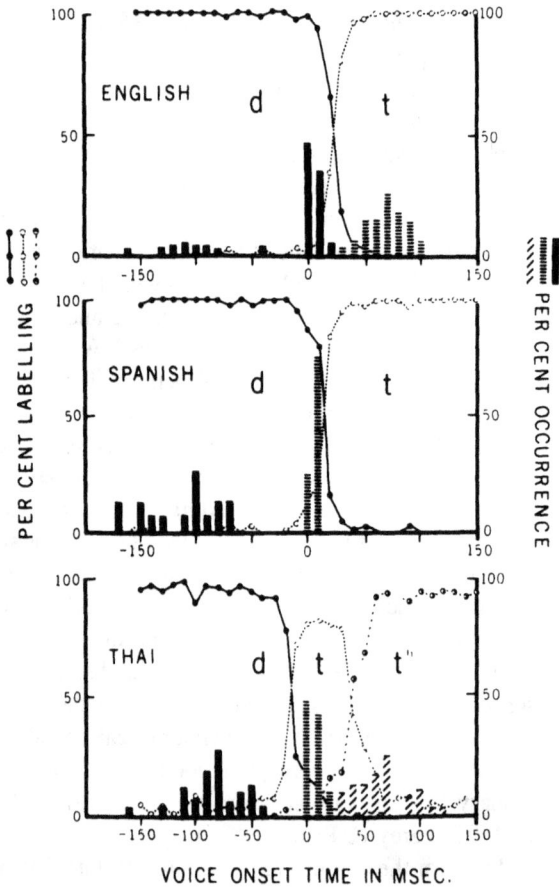

FIGURE 13. Labeling functions for a set of synthetic stimuli varying in voice onset time presented to speakers of English, Spanish, and Thai. (From Abramson & Lisker, 1965, with permission of the authors.)

ferently [p. 218]." Cross-language research has shown, in fact, that the categorizations imposed on synthetic stimuli are based on the acoustic attributes of the stimuli and the linguistic experience of the listener. To take one example, Abramson and Lisker (1965) generated a continuum of synthetic stimuli varying in voice-onset time between /da/ and /ta/ and presented them for labeling to listeners of three different language backgrounds. The labeling functions for English, Spanish, and Thai subjects are shown in Figure 13. As can be seen, these listeners categorized the same stimuli in quite different ways, depending on the phonological structure of their language. The phoneme boundaries are not only placed somewhat differently along the continuum in each case, but the Thai subjects show an additional category. This result was expected, since in Thai a phonological distinction is made between the voiceless aspirated stop [t^h] and the voiceless unaspirated stop [t]. This phonetic difference is not realized phonologically in either English or Spanish and consequently fails to play a role in the listener's identification and discrimination. Therefore, the phonological systems of different languages make use of the acoustic and phonetic distinctions that exist between different speech sounds in somewhat different ways.

In summary, several implications can be drawn from the categorical-perception research. First, the perception of speech sounds appears to have certain quantal properties much like those observed earlier in the production of speech: listeners treat acoustically different sounds as functionally the same. Second, the categorical-perception results can be thought of as representing a phonetic mode of perception in which the listener responds to speech signals in terms of the auditory features deployed in his own linguistic system. The extent to which these perceptual processes are innately determined or modified by the environments has been a topic of great interest in speech perception, as will be seen below.

C. Speech Perception in Infants

Much of what we currently know about the development of language and the acquisition of phonology is based on data obtained in studies of speech production (see Jakobson, 1968; McNeill, 1970; Menyuk, 1971). One conclusion that has been drawn by a number of investigators is that the developmental process proceeds from the general to the specific and gradually involves a greater and greater differentiation of language skills. Within the last 5 years, a number of pioneering studies by Eimas and others have demonstrated that infants as young as 1 month of age are capable of making fine discriminations among a number of the distinctive attributes of speech sounds. These results obviously call into question the validity of the differentiation assumption. While increasing differentiation may very well be true of the development of productive language skills, it may not be true of the perception of speech. The recent evidence from studies of infant speech perception points to a loss of discriminative abilities over time for certain speech sounds if specific experience with these distinctions fails to take place in the local environment.

The procedure used in these speech-perception experiments involved a discrimination paradigm in which the infant was first familiarized with a particular stimulus and then shifted to another stimulus. If the infant showed an increased response rate after the shift, it was assumed that the infant could discriminate the difference between the two stimuli. The actual procedure was a modification of the conjugate reinforcement methodology developed by Siqueland and DeLucia (1969). Each criterion response is reinforced by the presentation of a synthetic speech sound. In the infant speech-perception studies carried out by Eimas, a nonnutritive sucking response was employed (Eimas, 1974, 1975a,b; Eimas, Siqueland, Jusczyk, & Vigorito, 1971). During the course of the experiment, the infant becomes aware of the contingency between the sucking response and presentation of a stimulus pattern. After reaching some asymptote, response rate declines, presumably because the stimulus loses some of its original novel or reinforcing properties. After a period of satiation, a second stimulus is presented repeatedly to the infant under the same contingent arrangement. After the shift, if the infants show a response pattern reliably different from a control group in which no stimulus change was introduced, the results are taken as evidence that the infants can discriminate the difference between the two stimuli.

In the first experiment using this procedure, Eimas et al. (1971) studied the voicing feature that distinguishes [b] from [pʰ]. The stimuli were synthetically produced CV syllables and varied in acoustically equal steps of VOT between [ba] and [pʰa]. The results revealed two important findings. First, infants could discriminate between two speech sounds selected from different phonetic categories. Second, infants could not reliably discriminate between two acoustically different stimuli selected from within the same phonetic category. The latter finding is particularly relevant, since it permitted Eimas and his collaborators to argue that their infants perceived the voicing distinction in a more nearly categorical manner and, therefore, in a linguistic mode comparable to that found in the adult studies.

Other findings have shown that infants can also discriminate between synthetic stimuli varying in place of articulation that is represented acoustically in terms of differences in the second and third formant transitions (Moffitt, 1971; Morse, 1972). In another study, Eimas (1974) has also reported that infants can discriminate between stimuli varying in place of articulation between [b], [d], and [g] and that they do this in a categorical-like manner too. The discrimination data obtained in this study are completely consistent with the three major distinctions found universally for place of articulation in stop consonants.

Two cross-language studies of infant speech perception have also been carried out recently on the voicing distinction using similar synthetic stimuli and methodology. In one study, Lasky, Syrdal-Lasky, and Klein (1975) found that infants from Spanish-speaking environments could discriminate three categories along the voicing continuum. One boundary occurred between +20 and +60 msec and another between −20 and −60 msec. The first boundary is consistent with the discrimination findings of Lisker and Abramson (1970) for English-speaking adults and the previous results of Eimas *et al.* (1971) with infants and suggests a possible innate or sensory basis to the distinction. However, the presence of a second boundary in the discrimination data was of particular interest. Spanish-speaking adults distinguish between only two categories of voicing and, based on the adult discrimination data of Lisker and Abramson (1970), their phoneme boundary does not correspond to the VOT values of either of the two boundaries found with these infants. The implication of these findings is that infants are capable of perceiving three major voicing distinctions in the absence of any specific experience with these particular voicing contrasts in the environment.

In another related study, Streeter (1976) found that Kikuyu infants are capable of discriminating voicing differences between labial stops that are not used phonologically by the adults in their language environment. In Kikuyu, a Bantu language spoken in Kenya, there is only one labial stop with a VOT value in the range of −60 msec (that is, a prevoiced stop). However, the Kikuyu infants could discriminate differences between three voicing categories corresponding roughly to the same ones found in the Lasky *et al.* (1975) study. Thus, the discrimination of these voicing contrasts can also be made in the absence of relevant linguistic experience with the specific sound contrasts. The results of the cross-language experiments suggest that infants may be predisposed, in some sense, to deal with these acoustic attributes with only a very limited exposure to the specific sounds and well before any experience in producing these distinctions.

The developmental course of speech perception, however, may be somewhat different from other forms of perceptual development in which it is assumed that environmental experience serves primarily to sharpen the discriminative capacities of an organism (Gibson, 1969; Gibson & Gibson, 1955). Since the child is capable of making relevant discriminations between the important distinctive acoustic attributes of speech at a very early age, the effects of linguistic experience may be restricted primarily to learning that particular distinctions are not functional within a child's language environment. Thus, the course of development may not involve learning to make finer and finer discriminations among stimulus attributes but may be more analogous to the effects of acquired similarity or equivalence (Gibson & Gibson, 1955; Liberman, Harris, Kinney, & Lane, 1961). As Eimas (1975) has suggested, "the course of development of phonetic competence is one characterized by a loss of abilities over time if specific experience is not forthcoming [p. 346]." Like the adult, if the phonetic distinctions are not used phonologically in the language, sensitivity to the relevant acoustic attributes is lowered, and the child will fail to respond differentially to them. In the next section, one proposal to account for the infant results is considered in terms of a detector system, with feature detectors each sensitive to a restricted range of acoustic information. These detectors are assumed to be available innately to the infant for processing the relevant acoustic attributes of speech, although they can be modified substantially by specific linguistic experience in the environment.

The speech-perception research on infants has also generated a great deal of interest in the types of acoustic attributes that are used for discrimination. As a result, a number of investigators have begun to study other organisms whose peripheral auditory system is similar to humans. Since these organisms have no spoken language and, therefore, lack a phonological system, it has been assumed that their discriminative behavior to speech stimuli would be determined exclusively by the acoustic and psychophysical attributes of the speech signals. For example, in one study, Burdick and Miller (1975) found that with appropriate training four chinchillas could respond differentially to the vowels /a/ and /i/ selected from an ensemble of tokens produced by different talkers at different pitch levels. These results are not surprising, since they demonstrate that common spectral relations characterize similar vowels. As noted earlier, these relations are closely associated with the relative values of the steady-state formant frequencies.

In another study, Kuhl and Miller (1975) reported that chinchillas could learn to respond differentially to the consonants /d/ and /t/ in syllables produced by four talkers in three vowel contexts. Furthermore, the training experience with these stimuli generalized to synthetic speech sounds varying in VOT. Identification functions were obtained for the chinchilla that were quite similar to data obtained with humans for the identical stimulus continuum; the stimuli were partitioned into two discrete categories with a sharp crossover point at the boundary. Thus, these results indicate that there are quantal regions in perception that have well-defined psychophysical properties. In the case of VOT, several changes in the acoustic attributes of these stimuli occur at precisely the region where the boundary between voiced and voiceless stops occur in a number of languages (see Lisker, 1975; Stevens & Klatt, 1974).

The experiments with chinchillas are no doubt of some interest in demonstrating that complex spectral and temporal relations are present in the acoustic waveform and that nonhuman organisms can be trained to respond differentially to them. But what inferences can be drawn from these results with regard to categorical perception? Unfortunately, Kuhl and Miller (1975) did not obtain discrimination data from their chinchillas, so we can only guess at how well they might have done on this task. However, we would expect that chinchillas could probably discriminate between pairs of stimuli selected from within a phonetic category since, presumably, they do not code these sounds phonetically. Accordingly, discrimination should be based on the coding of only lower level acoustic attributes. The results of Morse and Snowdon (1975) and Sinnott (1974), although obtained with monkeys, are consistent with this prediction. Using somewhat different experimental procedures, these investigators found that monkeys could discriminate between pairs of speech sounds selected from within a phonetic category, and they could do this better than would be predicted by the labeling hypothesis derived from the categorical-perception model. Thus, while the chinchilla and monkey can be trained to respond differentially to speech sounds as acoustic signals, unlike humans they do not code these signals as phonetic events having linguistic significance.

D. Property Detectors in Speech Perception

To explain the results of the categorical-like discrimination found in infants, Eimas (1974) proposed an approach to speech perception based on the idea of feature detectors finely tuned to restricted ranges of acoustic information in the speech signal. This particular idea did not originate with Eimas, since a number of other investigators have remarked on the possibility of some sort of feature detecting mechanism in speech perception (see, for example, Abbs & Sussman, 1971; Liberman *et al.*, 1967b; Lieberman, 1970; Stevens, 1972; Whitfield, 1965). However, it was left to Eimas and Corbit (1973) to introduce an experimental paradigm—selective adaptation—to speech perception that could reveal the workings of these hypothesized detectors in some detail (see Cooper, 1975, for an extensive review).

In selective adaptation, repetitive presentation of a stimulus alters the perception of a set of test stimuli. For example, in the initial study, Eimas and Corbit (1973) investigated the voicing feature and showed that adaptation with the syllable [ba] caused the locus of the phonetic category boundary between [ba] and [pʰa] to shift towards the [ba] end of the continuum. Stimuli near the boundary that were identified as [ba] when the listener was in an unadapted state were subsequently labeled as [pʰa] after adaptation with [ba]. Similar findings were obtained when [pʰa] was used as an adaptor; the locus of the phonetic boundary shifted toward the [pʰa] end of the stimulus continuum. Eimas and Corbit also showed that these results were not specific to the syllables or phonetic segments in the test series but were due rather to the presence of a specific attribute or feature in the consonants. This conclusion was based on cross-series adaptation in which the voiceless bilabial stop [pʰa] produced approximately equivalent effects on the identification functions for a series of alveolar stop consonants (that is, [d] and [tʰ]) as it did for the series of bilabial stops (that is, [b] and [pʰ]). In both cases, the locus of the phonetic boundary shifted toward the voiceless end of the continuum. These results are shown in Figure 14 for one of the subjects in the Eimas and Corbit study.

In another experiment Eimas and Corbit (1973) showed that the peak in the discrimination function also shifts after adaptation, suggesting that the shifts in the labeling function are not simply due to a response bias introduced by changing the stimulus probabilities. In a different study, Eimas, Cooper, and Corbit

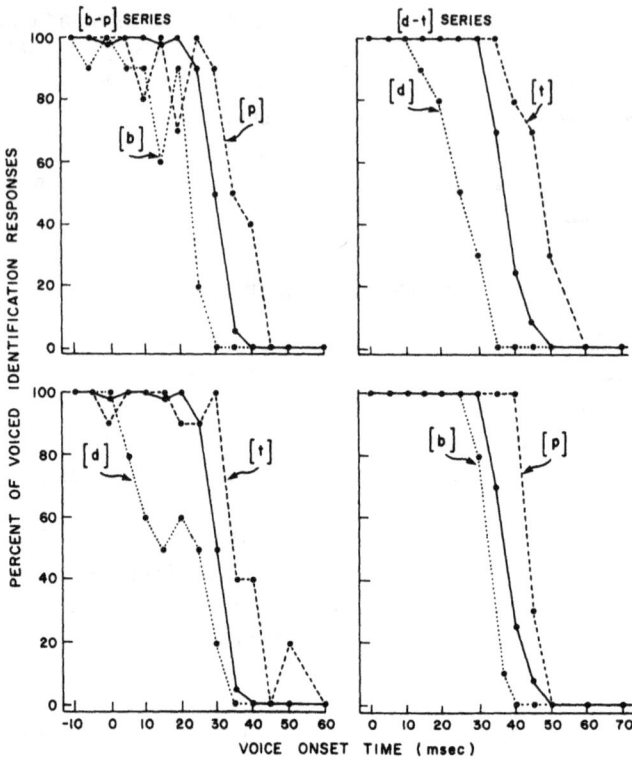

FIGURE 14. Identification functions obtained with and without adaptation for a single subject. The functions for the [b,p] series are shown on the left; the ones for the [d, t] series are on the right. The lower two functions in each panel show the results of cross-series adaptation when the adaptor was not selected from the test series. In each panel, the solid lines show the unadapted identification functions, and the dotted and dashed lines show the functions obtained after adaptation. (From Eimas & Corbit, 1973, with permission of the authors and publisher.)

(1973) showed that the adaptation effects are centrally located, since presentation of the adaptor and test stimuli to different ears still produced large and reliable shifts in the locus of the phonetic boundary.

Eimas and Corbit (1973) interpreted the selective adaptation findings as support for the hypothesis that the perception of voicing involves two distinct types of feature detectors organized as opponent pairs, a voiced detector ($+V$) and a voiceless detector ($-V$). Each detector is assumed to be selectively tuned to a range of partially overlapping VOT values. When a stimulus containing a particular VOT value is presented repetitively, it fatigues the detector most sensitive to that range of the feature and, accordingly, its sensitivity is reduced. After adaptation, the opponent or unadapted detector provides a greater output to the decision process in identification than the adapted detector and, accordingly, produces a shift in the locus of the phonetic-category boundary.

At the time, Eimas and his collaborators argued that the selective-adaptation results provided convincing support for the existence of detectors specialized for processing phonetic features rather than the acoustic attributes that form the basis for these phonetic distinctions. However, their conclusions have been shown to be premature, since more recent work has demonstrated that the adaptation effects are related more to spectral similarity between test series and adaptor than to phonetic identity (see Bailey, 1975; Cooper & Blumstein, 1974; Pisoni & Tash, 1975; Tartter & Eimas, 1975). One of the questions that is currently under extensive investigation is whether the selective-adaptation results are due to fatigue of mechanisms that process the acoustic attributes of speech stimuli, their more abstract phonetic features, or both (see Sawusch, 1977). The specific details of the arguments are intricate and need not concern us here. The important point of the adaptation work is that the perceptual system responds to certain acoustic attributes of speech stimuli, and these attributes turn out to underlie precisely the relevant distinctions made between phonetic segments.

One of the intriguing questions that the infant speech-perception work has raised is the extent to which environmental input determines the development and sensitivity of these hypothesized feature detectors. There is an extensive literature on the role of early experience in the development of the visual system indicating that early environmental experience can modify the selectivity of cortical cells in kittens (for example, Blakemore & Cooper, 1970; Hirsch & Spinelli, 1970). The analogy to this developmental work has already been drawn by Eimas (1978), who argued that the lack of experience with specific phonetic contrasts in the local environment during language acquisition has the effect of modifying the appropriate detectors by reducing their sensitivity. Some detectors originally designed to process certain phonetic distinctions may be captured or subsumed by other detectors after exposure to specific acoustic stimuli from the linguistic environment. Therefore, the nonspecific detectors might assume the specificity for only those attributes present in the stimuli to which they are exposed. The poor within-category discrimination of speech sounds found with adults and infants in the categorical-perception experiments may not only be due to phonetic coding of these signals but may also be a consequence of the modification of the needed discrimination mechanism (that is, a feature detector). This could then account for the troughs found in the discrimination functions.

In considering the infant research, it may well be the case that the general program of development of speech perception abilities is genetically determined, with experience in the environment playing only a role in the tuning and alignment of the system. Moreover, the existence of linguistic universals, particularly in terms of the relatively small number of phonetic features found across many different languages, lends some support to this contention and suggests that at least some of the structural mechanisms underlying speech perception are part of the biological endowment of the organism.

In summary, the work on selective adaptation provides strong evidence for the existence of some type of feature-detecting system in perception. These findings are important since they provide a way of determining precisely to what types of acoustic attributes the system responds and eventually may help to determine how this information is used by the perceptual system. However, the work on selective adaptation and the resulting feature detector models of speech perception as well as the infant perceptual research are still in the very earliest stages of development. Numerous questions still remain to be resolved, such as specifying the locus of adaptation effects and determining whether there are separate classes of detectors that respond to auditory and phonetic feature information, as well as detailing the role of early experience in speech perception. Work on these problems is currently being carried out in a number of laboratories, and a good deal of progress can be anticipated over the next few years.

V. BASIC ISSUES IN SPEECH PERCEPTION

The previous section summarized several of the important empirical findings in speech perception, particularly work dealing with segmental perception. In this section, some of the major issues that have emerged from this work will be reviewed briefly. Emphasis will be placed on the relevance of these issues to theoretical accounts of speech perception that will be considered in the final section of the chapter.

The basic issues in speech perception are, in principle, no different from the problems encountered in other areas of perception. In general, these issues deal with the problems of perceptual constancy to diverse stimulation and of perceptual contrast to identical stimulation and how the physical environment is represented internally (Bruner, 1957).

A. Linearity, Invariance, and Segmentation

One of the most important problems in speech perception is that the speech signal fails to meet the conditions of linearity and invariance (Chomsky & Miller, 1963). As a consequence, the recognition problem becomes quite a complicated task for humans as well as machines. The linearity condition assumes that for each phoneme there must be a particular stretch of sound in the utterance, and if phoneme X is to the left of phoneme Y in the phonemic representation, the stretch of sound associated with X must precede the stretch of sound associated with Y in the physical signal. The invariance condition assumes that for each phoneme X, there must be a specific set of criterial acoustic attributes or features associated with it in all contexts. These features must be present whenever X or some variant of X occurs, and they must be absent whenever some other phoneme occurs in the representation.

As noted in earlier sections, it has been extremely difficult to establish acoustic segments or features that match the perceived phonemes independently of context. As a result of coarticulation in speech production, there is a great deal of contextual variability. Often a single acoustic segment contains information about several neighboring linguistic segments; and, conversely, the same linguistic segment is often represented acoustically in quite different ways, depending on the surrounding phonetic context, rate of speaking, and talker.

The context-conditioned variability between acoustic signal and phoneme resulting from coarticulation also presents enormous problems for segmentation of speech. Because of the failure to meet the linearity and invariance conditions, it has been difficult to segment speech into acoustically defined units that are independent of adjacent segments. Although some segmentation is possible according to strictly acoustic criteria (see Fant, 1962), the number of acoustic segments is typically greater than the number of phonemes in the utterance and, moreover, no simple invariant mapping has been found between these acoustic attributes and perceived phonemes.

The lack of invariance and segmentation problems suggests something peculiar about speech as an acoustic stimulus. Certainly, relations between segments of the acoustic signal and units of linguistic analysis are complex and this, in turn, places certain constraints on the classes of perceptual theories that might be proposed for speech perception. For example, filter or template-matching theories are generally believed to be poor candidates for speech perception, primarily because linguistic segments cannot be defined exclusively by attributes of the acoustic signal. As Chomsky and Miller (1963) have remarked, if both the invariance and linearity conditions were met, the task of building machines capable of recognizing various phonemes in human speech would be greatly simplified. It would surely be a simple enough matter to arrange the appropriate filters in a network in order to construct a recognition device. Although numerous attempts have been made along these lines in the past, the results have been generally unsuccessful because of the inherent variability of the physical signal. Therefore, it is not at all surprising that passive theories of recognition involving template matching and filtering are held in poor regard as potential models of human speech perception.

To deal with the contextual variability of phonemes and the complex relation between acoustic signal and phonetic segment, a number of investigators have proposed models based on specialized feature detectors. It was originally assumed that these complex phonetic feature detectors processed quite diverse acoustic inputs equivalently and thus provided one way to dodge the invariance and segmentation problems. As noted earlier, however, the selective-adaptation results indicate that if there are feature detectors they appear to be quite sensitive to context. Moreover, most of the evidence adduced in support of specific phonetic feature detectors is weak and subject to alternative acoustically based interpretations (Pisoni & Tash, 1975). Other investigators have preferred "active" theories that employ higher level linguistic information in the earliest stages of perceptual analysis. A brief account of this approach will be considered in the next section, which deals with models of speech perception.

B. Articulation and the Internal Representation of Speech

There is good agreement among investigators that speech is represented internally as a sequence of discrete segments and features, although there is somewhat less agreement as to the exact description of these features. Arguments have been proposed for feature systems based on distinctions in the acoustic domain and in the articulatory domain as well as systems that combine both types of distinctions (Chomsky & Halle, 1968; Jakobson *et al.*, 1952; Wickelgren, 1969). The suspicion that articulation may play a role in speech perception goes back to at least the 1600s (Stevens & House, 1972). In this section several reasons for proposing articulatory-motor involvement in speech perception will be considered briefly. Because this has been a controversial topic in the field of speech perception, it is appropriate at this point to review these claims.

The first concern with articulation in speech perception is basically historical. Early acoustic–phonetic work and much of the experimental research on speech perception that followed was guided by the traditional articulatory descriptions developed by phoneticians (Bell, 1867). The acoustic cues underlying the perception of different phonetic segments could be described in terms of the articulatory gestures and dimensions that distinguished these sounds in production (Delattre, 1951). Thus, speech sounds seemed to be naturally arranged in terms of a few simple and relatively independent dimensions that turned out to provide the same distinctions in perception that the articulatory dimensions provided in production and suggested that the two processes might be linked in some yet unknown way.

Ladefoged (1972) has also pointed out the need for some absolute frame of reference in the phonetic description of languages. Articulatory categories such as labial, alveolar, or velar refer to observable phenomena that can be compared across different languages and can be used to express commonalities among attributes used in these languages. Thus, articulatory descriptions could be used to express the similarities and differences among phonetic entities at a common level. Acoustic descriptions of speech were clearly too complex to capture the necessary linguistic distinctions between sounds.

Finally, another motivation for emphasizing the articulatory domain is the view that the speech-production mechanism, which reflects the articulatory capabilities of human talkers, has been the contributing factor in the development of speech-sound systems. For example, Peterson and Shoup (1966) noted that "there is considerable reason to believe that the phonological aspects of speech are primarily organized in terms of the possibilities and constraints of the motor mechanism with which speech is produced [p. 7]." Indeed, speech sounds constitute a highly distinctive class of acoustic signals in the environment. They are produced by a sound source that has well-defined acoustic constraints for the listener (Fant, 1960; Stevens, 1972). In most normal situations, the listener is also a speaker and presumably has access to knowledge of the correlation between vocal tract shape and resulting acoustic output. Thus, although the human auditory system is capable of processing a relatively large number of acoustic signals selected from a wide range of frequencies, only a very small number of distinctive acoustic attributes are actually employed in the phonological systems of human languages. The acoustic properties of these particular attributes are highly constrained by limitations of the production mechanism and not the perceptual mechanism, at least not the peripheral auditory system.

C. Units of Perceptual Analysis

Another important issue in speech perception is the choice of a minimal unit of perceptual analysis. Because of limitations on channel capacity, especially in the auditory system, raw sensory information must be categorized and recoded into some more permanent form that can be used for subsequent analysis. But what is the basic or "natural" coding unit for speech perception? Many investigators have argued for the primacy of the feature, phoneme, syllable, or word as their candidate for the basic perceptual unit. Other investigators, motivated chiefly by early work in generative linguistic theory, have proposed much larger units for perceptual analysis such as clauses or sentences (Bever, Lackner, & Kirk, 1969; Miller, 1962). The current debate over the choice of a perceptual unit can be resolved if a strict distinction were made concerning the level of linguistic analysis under consideration. The size of the processing unit in speech perception apparently varies from feature to segment to clause as the level of linguistic processing changes, and, thus, the question of whether there is one basic or primary unit may be inappropriate.

However, it is worth considering briefly an issue that has received some attention in recent years, namely, the arguments in favor of the syllable as the basic unit of analysis. A number of investigators have proposed that the syllable is a more basic perceptual or linguistic unit than the phoneme (Massaro, 1972; Savin & Bever, 1970). The claim is that phonemes are more abstract entities than syllables because some phonemes cannot exist independently as articulatory and acoustic units whereas syllables presumably can. In support of their claim, Savin and Bever presented reaction times obtained in a target-monitoring task showing that subjects respond faster to syllable targets than phoneme targets. Similar experiments also have been carried out by Foss and Swinney (1973) and McNeill and Lindig (1973), who argued that the reaction-time results are due to the differential speed with which various sized units (that is, phonemes, syllables, words, sentences) can become available to consciousness for a decision and not whether one unit is perceived earlier and, therefore, is more basic than another unit.

Taking a different tact, Massaro (1972) argued that syllables are the basic units of speech perception because phonemes are not represented discretely in the acoustic signal and, accordingly, cannot serve as perceptual units. He also has claimed that by assuming that the syllable is the earliest unit of perceptual analysis, the problems connected with invariance and segmentation could be resolved quite easily. The contextual variability associated with coarticulation, according to Massaro, is restricted to only sequences of phonemes within syllable-sized units.

The controversy over the primacy of syllables as perceptual units is misguided, since most of the arguments have simply failed to consider the role that syllables play in speech. As Studdert-Kennedy (1976) pointed out, the syllable serves a basic perceptual function in speech as the carrier of phonetic information. It creates an acoustic contrast between consonant and vowel, so the listener can recognize the constituent sound segments and features for subsequent operations of the perceptual process. Thus, the syllable is primarily a unit of speech production.

However, it is a totally separate question as to whether the problems of invariance and segmentation can be resolved as simply as Massaro (1972) believes by choosing the syllable as the basic unit of analysis. It is a well-known fact, apparently having escaped Massaro's attention, that there are almost as many problems in defining the syllable acoustically as in defining the phoneme (Malmberg, 1955; Ohman, 1966). It is possible to determine that a syllable has occurred by noting the presence of a high-amplitude peak in the syllable nucleus, but it is more difficult to locate the beginnings and ends of syllables. Although the coarticulation problems may be reduced somewhat by focusing on the acoustic cues for syllables, they still remain, nevertheless, and are subject to precisely the same kinds of contextual effects as the cues for phonemes. Moreover, several findings indicate the presence of overlapping articulatory movements and their acoustic consequences across almost any possible syllable boundary (Daniloff & Moll, 1968; Treon, 1970). As a result, it is almost impossible to provide a definition of the syllable that can account for the diverse coarticulation phenomena found in speech (see also Lindblom, 1963; Ohman, 1966).

A more crucial problem, however, is the fact that syllables are not indivisible units. They have a complex internal structure that must be recovered at some point in the perceptual process. Retrieval of morphemic relations and, in turn, the analysis of meanings is dependent on an analysis of the syllable into its component segments.

Finally, investigators who have argued for the primacy of the syllable have also ignored the issue of economy in psychological representation, as well as linguistic description. Since larger linguistic units such as words and morphemes can themselves be decomposed into smaller units such as phonemes, it follows that the number of different phonemes necessary to describe a sequence will be significantly smaller than a mere listing of the larger units as discrete entities.

One solution to the problems raised about syllables and phonemes as perceptual units is to assume that the perceptual mechanism requires minimal acoustic information distributed over at least a syllable-sized unit in order to analyze the constituent phonetic segments. This assumption says nothing about the size of the earliest perceptual unit but only that the minimal information for a phoneme requires the analysis of acoustic information spread over several adjacent segments.

D. Prosody in Speech Perception

Most of the research in speech perception, as well as the theoretical emphasis, has been concerned with segmental analysis of phonemes. A seriously neglected topic has been the prosodic or suprasegmental attributes of speech that involve differences in pitch, intensity, and duration of segments. At the present time there is a wide gap between the research conducted on isolated segments and features and prosodic factors in speech perception (see Cohen & Nooteboom, 1975). How prosodic factors might be used in perception has not been considered in detail, although it is clear that this information serves as a possible link or interface between phonetic segments and features on the one hand and grammatical processes at higher levels on the other (see Huggins, 1972a, for a review).

There is evidence that differences in fundamental frequency provide important cues to segmentation of speech into constituents that are suitable candidates for syntactic analysis. Lea (1973) has found from acoustic analysis of connected speech that a decrease in fundamental frequency (F_0) usually occurred at the end of each major syntactic constituent in a sentence, and an increase in F_0 occurred near the beginning of the following constituent. Thus, prosodic cues may be used to cue syntactic structures. Lindblom and Svensson (1973) and Svensson (1974) have carried out investigations on the role of prosody in identifying various syntactic structures in the absence of segmental cues. Their findings indicate that a good deal of information about the surface syntactic structure of an utterance may be conveyed by prosodic features and that unambiguous identification can take place even with an incomplete specification of the acoustic properties of the phonetic segments.

Other evidence from studies on the acoustic analysis of speech indicates that the durations of phonetic segments vary in stressed and unstressed syllables as well as in various syntactic environments. For example, Oller (1973) has found substantial lengthening effects for both consonants and vowels in a number of environments, including utterances with various intonation patterns, word-final and phrase-final positions, as well as utterance-final position. Klatt (1974) has shown that the duration of the segment [s] is longer in prestressed position and shorter before unstressed vowels and in word-final position. In another study, Klatt (1975b) also found that vowel-lengthening effects occur at the end of major syntactic units, such as the boundary between a noun phrase and a verb phrase.

It is clear that durational effects such as these argue against uncovering invariant acoustic attributes for phonemes that are identical in all phonetic environments. More importantly, however, these systematic lengthening effects may provide additional cues to the higher order syntactic structure of the sentence. Much research remains to be done on this particular problem. It would be of interest to know, for example, the extent to which syntactic and semantic variables influence the durations of phonetic segments and the precision with which listeners can and do use this information in the recognition process (see Cooper, 1976; Huggins, 1972b; Klatt & Cooper, 1975).

E.   Higher Level Contributions to Speech Perception

A well-documented finding in speech perception is that words presented in sentential context are more intelligible than the same words presented in isolation (Miller, Heise, & Lichten, 1951; Pollack & Pickett, 1964). The usual interpretation of these findings is that syntax and semantics serve only to narrow down the number of possible response alternatives available to the listener (Miller, 1962). It is assumed that phonetic segments and features are recognized more or less directly from a set of physical properties in the sound wave and that processing proceeds serially on the basis of independent decisions about individual speech segments at each successive level (Halle & Stevens, 1962; Licklider, 1952).

But what role does syntax and semantics serve in speech perception? Chomsky (1964) has argued that it is not possible to describe a language adequately by starting with only a description of the sound system without reference to the function of these sounds as linguistic entities. That is, more information than a phonetic sequence is necessary to establish the identity of a phoneme. This information presumably involves the contribution of syntactic and semantic variables to the recognition process.

In several recent studies this problem has been examined experimentally. For example, Shockey and Reddy (1974) determined how well phonetically trained listeners could recover the correct phonemes in the absence of higher order information such as syntax and semantics. To accomplish this, they presented listeners with recorded utterances of sentences taken from unfamiliar languages and required them to provide a phonetic transcription. The only basis for segmentation and recognition of these phonemes, therefore, was the information contained in the physical signal, since higher level information was eliminated. The results of Shockey and Reddy's experiment are interesting. The transcription task was quite difficult; only about 56 percent of the segments in the original utterances could be identified correctly. With an accuracy in this range, it can be concluded that higher levels of linguistic information must provide a good deal of additional information even to the earliest stages of perceptual analysis.[5]

In a similar experiment, Klatt and Stevens (1973) attempted to recognize a set of unknown sentences by visual examination of sound spectrograms along with a machine-aided lexical look-up program that was implemented on a computer. Although the syllable structure of an utterance could be identified reasonably well from a spectrographic representation, only 33 percent of the segments could be transcribed correctly whereas only another 40 percent of the segments could be partially transcribed. Klatt and Stevens emphasized that the problem of recognizing segments in sentences from spectrograms is more difficult than in isolated words because in sentences, word boundaries are not as clearly marked and coarticulatory effects occur between adjacent words. Moreover, the duration of a segment is shorter in sentences than in isolated words and there is more vowel reduction. All these observations led Klatt and Stevens to conclude that it is doubtful whether accurate recognition from spectrograms can be carried out in the absence of higher level constraints. They suggested that these constraints can be used to verify decisions about segments and predict missing or distorted information based on the previous generation of some hypothesis or search set.

In another study, Marslen-Wilson (1975) found more direct evidence for the use of higher levels of processing in speech perception. Subjects shadowed sentences in which specific changes were made in the syntactic, semantic, or phonetic structure. Analysis of the restoration of disrupted words to their original form was shown to be dependent on the semantic and syntactic context variables. According to Marslen-Wilson, the listener analyzes the incoming information at all levels of analysis so that decisions at any level can affect processing at other levels.

The results of these studies as well as the findings on prosody indicate that the perception of connected speech does not rely exclusively on the analysis and recognition of segmental acoustic features. When speech perception is viewed only from the vantage point of the acoustic signal and the phoneme, the task of finding invariant attributes becomes the primary focus. However, if prosodic information and higher order variables are included in the perceptual process, the scope of the potential models widens appreciably.

F.   Speech Perception as a Specialized Process

For a number of years, Liberman and others have argued that speech perception is a specialized process requiring the postulation of specialized neural

[5]It should be pointed out here that exotic languages were deliberately used in this study. A better test might have been to require the phoneticians to transcribe nonsense-syllable sentences that had appropriate intonation. In this case, they would surely have done very much better. Phonetic-inventory size as well as familiarity were factors that were not controlled in this experiment.

mechanisms and processes for perceptual analysis (Liberman, 1970a). But what is the evidence for a specialized mode of perception unique to speech? Some of the original support for this view came from the early categorical-perception experiments with synthetic speech sounds. As noted in previous sections, this form of perception was thought to be unique to only certain types of speech sounds, namely, stop consonants. Recent findings, however, have shown comparable categorical effects for complex nonspeech signals, suggesting that the original interpretation of categorical perception was probably wrong and that the findings are a special case of a more general phenomenon involving the coding of complex acoustic signals.

Other evidence adduced in support of a specialized neural mechanism has come from dichotic listening experiments in which laterality effects have been demonstrated for competing acoustic signals (Studdert-Kennedy & Shankweiler, 1970). These results have been interpreted as evidence for hemispheric specialization in the perception of speech signals and processing of linguistic information. It has been known for over 100 years that the left hemisphere of most right-handed adults is the language-dominant hemisphere, specialized for linguistic analysis. The dichotic-listening results provide behavioral support for this asymmetry even at the phonetic-feature level and have been used as strong evidence for the assumption of a specialized neural mechanism for processing speech. Unfortunately, little is currently known about the specific types of processes or operations that the left hemisphere performs in perceiving speech and language other than that it is clearly different from the processing carried out in the right hemisphere.

The recent findings on infant speech perception have also been interpreted as supporting the view that some aspects of perceptual analysis of speech are innately determined and, therefore, may be due to some specialized neural process. The experiments demonstrating categorical-like discrimination with infants are, however, subject to precisely the same criticisms as the categorical-perception experiments with adults. The discrimination findings may not be due exclusively to phonetic coding and linguistic processing as Eimas has argued, but may be the result of the specific psychophysical properties and memory representations of the specific speech signals employed. The cross-language experiments with infants as well as the labeling results obtained with the chinchilla provide additional support for this conclusion. Young infants may be predisposed in some sense to respond to speech signals in a phonetically relevant manner, but alternative explanations based only an auditory-processing capabilities have not yet been adequately ruled out. Moreover, our understanding of the exact contribution of the linguistic environment to the course of phonetic development, as well as the developmental process itself, is still quite meager at the present time. Thus, the infant speech-perception findings, while important in their own right, are somewhat ambiguous with regard to providing convincing support for the speciality issue.

Finally, additional support for the speciality of speech has come from rational and logical considerations dealing with attempts to communicate language by sounds other than speech. It has been argued by Liberman and his colleagues that speech sounds are uniquely efficient vehicles for transmitting phonemic information in language primarily because speech represents a complex code rather than a simple cipher or alphabet. The rate at which phonemic information can be perceived in speech is known to be well above the temporal resolving power of the ear if listeners had to process only isolated acoustic segments that stood in one-to-one relation with phonemes (Liberman *et al.*, 1967a, 1967b). Liberman argued, however, that speech sounds are a code, since they represent a substantial restructuring of phonemic information in the acoustic waveform.

It is reasonable to conclude that while there is some evidence for a specialized neural mechanism in speech perception, the exact nature of its operation and course of its development remain somewhat elusive problems at the present time. The blanket assertions of speciality have been shown to be generally inadequate as explanatory principles as more and more becomes known about the psychophysical and perceptual aspects of speech signals and the physiological mechanisms involved in speech production. Future work should be directed towards determining in precisely what ways speech perception conforms to general perceptual processes, regardless of modality and in what ways speech perception will clearly require the postulation of additional specialized explanatory theories and mechanisms for perceptual analysis.

VI. LEVELS OF PROCESSING AND THEORIES IN SPEECH PERCEPTION

Current theories of speech perception are quite general and vague and, for the most part, not terribly well developed, at least by the standards in other areas of experimental psychology. Indeed, it is not unreasonable to characterize these theories as only preliminary attempts at specifying what a possible model of human speech perception might entail. A few quotes should make this point clear:

> Since this symposium is concerned with models, we should say at the outset that we do not have a model in the strict sense, though we are in search of one. (Liberman, Cooper, Harris, MacNeilage, & Studdert-Kennedy, 1967, p. 68)

> Any attempt to propose a model for the perception of speech is deemed to become highly speculative in character and the present contribution is no exception. (Fant, 1967, p. 111)

> Since we are still far from an understanding of the neurophysiological processes involved, any model that can be proposed must be a functional model, and one can only *speculate* on the relation between components of the functional model and the neural events at the periphery of the auditory system and in the central nervous system. (Stevens & House, 1972, p. 47)

We have no models specified in enough detail for serious test....(Studdert-Kennedy, 1976, p. 254)

In this section I summarize first the most widely accepted views of the levels of processing in speech perception as they have developed over the past few years and then discuss several prominent theoretical views that have influenced current thinking about models of the perceptual process.

A. Speech Perception as a Process

It has become common in recent years to think of speech perception as a process involving a series of levels between the initial acoustic waveform that impinges upon the ear and its final conceptual representation in the mind of the listener (Studdert-Kennedy, 1974, 1976). Most investigators assume that these levels are hierarchically organized, although the exact relation to a definite sequence of processing stages is still a matter of some controversy. One view of these levels of processing is shown in Figure 15. At the very lowest level of analysis in this figure is the acoustic structure of an utterance that may be thought of as the

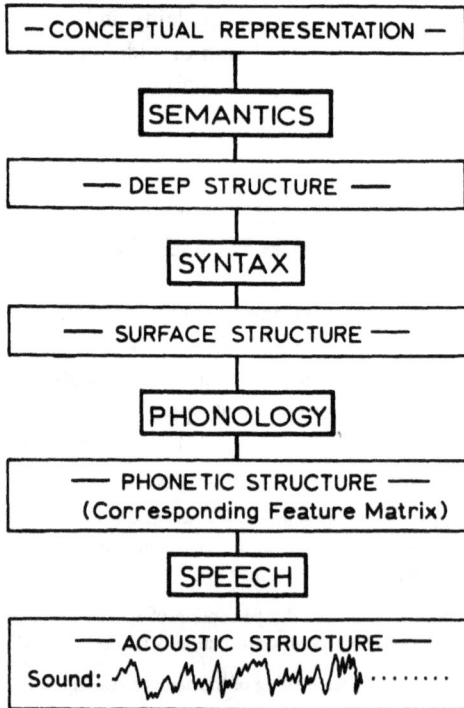

FIGURE 15. Hierarchial organization of levels of processing in speech perception. (Adapted from Liberman, 1970b.)

time-varying acoustic waveform. At the highest level is the conceptual representation of the utterance as a linguistic object. Such a representation is constructed from the listener's knowledge of events, relations and facts about the world that are present in long-term memory, as well as his specific linguistic knowledge. These two levels, corresponding to sound and meaning, respectively, are linked by a number of intermediate levels of analysis that serve to transform and recode the initial acoustic input into successively more abstract and often more elaborated representations.

B. Levels of Processing in Speech Perception

The view of speech perception suggested in Figure 15 assumes that speech is processed through a series of independent stages corresponding to the levels identified in the figure. Although the specific levels have been derived from rational principles and linguistic considerations, the arrangement of the processing stages and their specific function is still a topic of current investigation (see Pisoni & Sawusch, 1975). As such, we focus primarily on some of the levels of analysis that have been identified and are generally agreed upon and postpone a discussion of processing stages until the end of this section.

1. Auditory Level

The auditory level is assumed to be the first and earliest stage in the perceptual analysis of speech. At this level the acoustic waveform is transformed or recoded into some neural representation in the nervous system. Acoustic information about spectral structure, fundamental frequency, overall intensity, and duration of the signal as well as amplitude onsets and offsets is extracted and coded by the auditory system. These properties are assumed to be preserved in sensory memory for a brief period of time until subsequent operations can be carried out to recode this information into a more permanent form in short-term memory.

2. Phonetic Level

The phonetic level is assumed to be the next stage of analysis. Here features and segments necessary for phonetic classification are abstracted or derived from the auditory representations of the acoustic signal at the previous stage and placed in short-term memory. As discussed earlier, there is a many-to-many mapping of the auditory attributes derived from the previous level and the phonetic features identified at this level. Phonetic features may be thought of simply as abstract perceptual and memory codes that stand for combinations of both specific acoustic attributes on the one hand, and their articulatory antecedents on the other. However, it has been convenient to describe these features in terms of articulatory descriptions and labels primarily since this notation captures linguistically relevant distinctions at a phonetic and phonological level. The description of speech at this level consists of a phonetic matrix in which the columns represent discrete phonetic segments and the rows indicate the phonetic feature composition of each segment (Chomsky & Halle, 1968). At this level, segmentation must have already been assumed to take place. Segments and juncture boundaries are indicated in the matrix representation.

3. Phonological Level

At this level the phonetic segments from the previous level are converted into phonological segments or phonemes. The phonological component provides information about the sound structure of a given language that is imposed on the phonetic matrix to derive a phonological matrix. Thus, the phonological rules that are applied to the phonetic input at this level determine the extent to which the phonetic segments function as distinctive elements in the language and the extent to which these attributes may be predicted from either language-specific rules or language universal principles. Thus, predictable and redundant phonetic details can be accounted for systematically at this level. And it is also at this level that allophonic variations present at the phonetic level are eliminated and only phonologically distinctive information is coded for subsequent processing.

4. Higher Levels of Analysis

There are also several additional levels of analysis involving lexical search, syntactic analysis, and semantic interpretation of the original input. These higher levels serve to generate the structure into which the phonological segments are placed as well as specifying the grammatical organization of the input. Since the primary concern in this chapter has been with the lower levels of speech perception, these higher levels of analysis will not be considered any further in this discussion. However, the reader should not be led to believe that their contribution to the lower levels of perceptual analysis is unimportant. As noted earlier, the information generated at these levels may be used to constrain phonetic and phonological interpretations as well as to guide lexical search and subsequent word-verification processes.

C. Models of Speech Perception

Historically, models of speech perception were derived from the taxonomic principles of segmentation and classification. It was generally assumed that the level of linguistic structure corresponding roughly to the phoneme could be discovered entirely by the use of these cataloguing procedures applied automatically to a corpus of data. Moreover, according to this view, a separate level of phonological structure could be described independently of higher-level grammatical and syntactic considerations. The process of phoneme recognition was assumed to take place passively by means of successive filtering of the acoustic signal or by template matching of the acoustic input against stored representations in memory.

More recent models, developed primarily under the impetus of generative linguistic theory, have stressed a much more active or dynamic view of the recognition process. Models proposed along these lines assume that phoneme recognition is carried out by matching some representation of the input signal against an internally generated representation. The presence of active feedback loops in the system permits the recognition of a wide variety of diverse signals, since the parameters can be adjusted continually over time. In this final section we consider briefly a number of the prominent theories in speech perception and discuss several aspects of their approach to the major problems raised earlier in the chapter.

1. Motor Theory of Speech Perception

The basic assumption of the motor theory as described by Liberman *et al.* (1967b) is that "speech is perceived by processes that are also involved in its production [p. 452]." This view of speech perception was motivated by the observation that the listener is also a speaker, and it would be more economical to assume that the speaker–hearer uses only one common process for language processing rather than two separate processes. As mentioned earlier, one of the central problems in speech perception at the phonemic level and the major reason for postulating a motor theory is the issue of the lack of invariance between the acoustic signal and its phonemic representation. Advocates of the motor theory argue that one possible way of resolving the invariance problem is to assume that the same perceptual response to widely differing acoustical signals arises because the intended pattern is produced by the same articulation or underlying motor commands to the articulators. Similarly, different perceptual responses to fairly similar acoustic signals arise from different underlying articulations or motor commands.

Although the motor theory has occupied an overwhelmingly dominant place in contemporary accounts of speech perception, the link between empirical data and theory has not been very strong. Indeed, much of the early support for the motor theory was based on recurrent demonstrations of the same experimental outcome using near identical techniques and a very restricted set of stimuli. As discussed earlier, the primary data used to support the early versions of the motor theory came from perceptual experiments that found differences between synthetic stop consonants and steady-state vowels. If we set aside the consonant and vowel differences that may be due to other factors, there seems to be very little direct empirical support for some active mediation of articulatory knowledge or information during perceptual processing. Most of the current arguments for motor theory rest on parsimony, logic, and faith rather than a firm empirical foundation. The most serious problem for the motor theory rests on the failure to specify the level of perceptual analysis where articulatory knowledge is employed in recognition.

2. Analysis-by-Synthesis

The analysis-by-synthesis model proposed by Stevens is much more explicit than the motor theory (Stevens, 1960; Stevens & Halle, 1967; Stevens & House, 1972). The basic assumption of the model is similar to the motor theory: close ties exist between the processes of speech production and perception, and there are components and operations common to both. According to Stevens, the perceptual process begins initially with peripheral processing of the speech signal to yield a description in terms of auditory patterns. In cases where phonetic features are not strongly context dependent, the auditory pattern will provide a relatively direct mapping of those features during preliminary analysis. The output of preliminary analysis is a rough matrix of phonetic segments and features that is then transferred to a control system. Recognition of some features is thus assumed to take place by relatively direct operations on the acoustic information output from peripheral analysis. However, when there are no invariant attributes to identify a phonetic feature, additional processing is required. In analysis-by-synthesis, a hypothesis concerning the representation of the utterance in terms of phonetic segments and features (that is, an abstract distinctive-feature matrix) is constructed. This representation then forms the input to a set of generative rules that produce candidate patterns that are subsequently compared against the original patterns. Results of this match are sent to a control component that transfers the phonetic description to higher stages of linguistic analysis. Analysis-by-synthesis is simply a more carefully specified version of the motor theory, except that the comparison process takes place at the neuroacoustic level rather than the neuromotor level. Analysis-by-synthesis, like the motor theory, is quite abstract, and little direct experimental evidence has been found to support this view.

3. Fant's Auditory Theory

Fant's theory of speech perception is not terribly well developed. He objects strongly to the "active" motor-type theories on the grounds that the evidence used to support them is not conclusive (Fant, 1967). Fant claims that all the arguments brought forth in support of the motor theory would fit just as well into sensory-based theories, in which the decoding process proceeds without postulating the active mediation of speech-motor centers. The basic idea in Fant's approach is that the motor and sensory functions become more and more involved as one proceeds from the peripheral to central stages of analysis. He assumes that the final destination is the concept of a "message" that comprises brain centers common to both perception and production. However, according to Fant, there are separate sensory (auditory) and motor (articulatory) branches, although he leaves the possibility of interaction between these two blocks open. Auditory input is first processed by the ear and subject to some primary auditory analysis. These incoming auditory signals are then submitted to some kind of direct encoding into distinctive auditory features (Fant, 1962). Auditory features are then combined together in some unspecified way to form phonemes, syllables, morphemes, and words. Although much of Fant's concern has been on continued acoustical investigations of distinctive features of phonemes, the model is much too gross to be tested in any serious way. Moreover, the problems of invariance and segmentation that are central issues in speech perception still remain to be resolved by the model.

4. Stage Theories

In line with a number of other investigators, Bondarko, Zagorujko, Kozhevnikov, Molchanov, and Chistovich (1970) have proposed a model containing a series of hierarchically organized stages of perceptual analysis. The following stages are proposed: (a) auditory analysis, (b) phonetic analysis, (c) morphological analysis, (d) syntactic analysis, and (e) semantic analysis. Only the first two stages in their model will be considered here. The first stage involves auditory analysis of the signal and provides a description of the stimulus in terms of "auditory features." Some form of spectral analysis is assumed to take place at this stage, although the presence of auditory-feature detectors that respond differentially to specific acoustic attributes is also considered a possibility. Thus, some low-level and auditory-feature analysis may take place relatively close to the periphery. The second stage in the model involves phonetic analysis. The output of this stage is abstract and may be either an acoustic or articulatory representation of the speech signal. The representation of the information at this stage is thought to be based on phonetic segments or distinctive features. Provision is also made for the use of various types of normalization routines so that variability from different talkers can be reduced for subsequent processes of recognition. The model deals with the invariance problem by assuming that multiple decisions can be made on the basis of outputs from a number of auditory-feature detectors. Thus, the model is designed to process multiple cues simultaneously and in parallel rather than to focus on only isolated auditory features (that is, acoustic cues).

5. A Novel Theory of Speech Perception

Chomsky and Miller (1963) and Chomsky and Halle (1968) have proposed a "novel theory of speech perception" that also merits some attention. According to these authors, speech perception is an "active process" in which acoustic information is utilized to form hypotheses about the structure of sentences. These hypotheses, which are based, in part, on expectations and knowledge of the language, are then subsequently used to generate syntactic structures that can be compared against the original input. In this way, the listener uses knowledge of phonological principles to determine the phonetic properties of the sentence. Chomsky and Halle (1968) have described the perceptual process as follows:

> The hearer makes use of certain cues and certain expectations to determine the syntactic structure and semantic content of an utterance. Given a hypothesis as to its syntactic structure—in particular its surface structure—he uses the phonological principles that he controls to determine a phonetic shape. The hypothesis will then be accepted if it is not too radically at variance with the acoustic material. . . . Given acceptance of such a hypothesis, what the hearer 'hears' is what is internally generated by the rules. That is, he will 'hear' the phonetic shape determined by the postulated syntactic structure and the internalized rules [p. 24].

This view of the perceptual process is, of course, a version of the analysis-by-synthesis theory summarized earlier, although the comparison process takes place at the phonological and syntactic levels rather than the neuroacoustic level. While this theory is very abstract, it emphasizes an important point that has often been overlooked in speech-perception work. A listener's final interpretation of a speech signal depends upon a number of variables, including the listener's linguistic knowledge as well as many extragrammatical factors that determine what the listener expects to hear in a given situation.

One preliminary account of speech perception based on this approach is illustrated schematically in Figure 16. Processing stages corresponding to syntactic, lexical, and semantic levels are assumed to be arranged more or less in parallel. Auditory input first enters the system and is processed by the peripheral-auditory mechanism. Sensory information is then passed on to several intermediate stages shown as the "recognition device" in this figure. Various operations associated with the feature detection and recognition process are assumed to be carried out

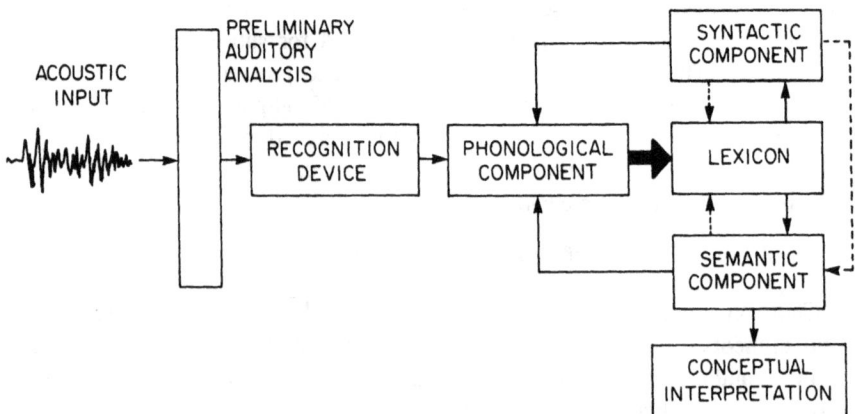

FIGURE 16. Tentative organization of some processing stages in a functional model of speech perception.

here in a relatively automatic fashion. The output of the recognition device is a rough and tentative classification of the features and some of the segments in the input. Some features can be recognized by fairly straightforward operations on the input signals, whereas other features may be analyzed in only a very gross way, pending additional information about the phonological and syntactic structure of the sentence. The output of the recognition device is then passed on to the phonological component where phonological decoding rules are employed in conjunction with syntactic and semantic information to derive a lexical representation. At this stage, information about segments, stress assignment, duration of each segment, and fundamental frequency is used to arrive at a tentative representation of the lexical items in the input sentence. In this model, the word-recognition process is thought to allow considerable ambiguity pending information from higher levels.[6]

The earliest stages of speech perception are assumed to occur relatively automatically and are not under the conscious control of the listener. There is a good deal of uncertainty about the exact composition of the features and segments of the input, the placement of word boundaries and the specific syntactic structure of the utterance. Although very little information is generally available in the waveform about the exact phonological or syntactic structure of the input, some initial acoustic information is necessary to formulate hypotheses for generating a syntactic structure. This initial structure provides the necessary information for specifying the segments and features of the phonological representation. One consequence of this view is that feature recognition and segmentation may result from similar processing operations. Similarly, word-boundary placements may be determined simply as a by-product of a listener's solution to the word-recognition problem.

The approach to speech perception proposed here is rather speculative and in need of empirical support. Nevertheless, it is consistent with the emphasis of other active approaches to perception in which the structure is imposed on the input by the listener during the perceptual process (Neisser, 1967). Thus, the listener does not identify speech feature-by-feature or phoneme-by-phoneme in some strictly serial order from bottom-to-top; rather, a gross and tentative analysis is performed initially with the final decision delayed until information from higher levels is available.

One common property of the diverse theoretical approaches reviewed in this section is that they are all quite general and vague and not easily tested empirically, at least in any obvious way. Because speech perception is a complex

---

[6]We should note here that some investigators have argued that the word-recognition process can take place in the absence of, or at least prior to, syntactic analysis (see Cairns & Kamerman, 1975). Given the comments made by Chomsky (1964) on the role of syntactic descriptions in phonological analysis, it is hard to see the rationale behind the claims for a strictly autonomous level of lexical analysis.

process involving several interrelated components, it has been difficult to formalize all relevant aspects of the process into a coherent model. The goal of future research in speech perception over the next few years is, however, quite clear; a global theory with a specific model should be developed that is on the one hand rich enough to account for the relevant phenomena in speech perception, yet, on the other hand, precise enough to be subject to empirical test and modeling.

ACKNOWLEDGMENTS

Preparation of this chapter was supported, in part, by NIMH Grant MH-24027 and NIH Grant NS-12179 to Indiana University and, in part, by NIH Grants NS-07040 and NS-04332 to the Research Laboratory of Electronics, Massachusetts Institute of Technology, where the final manuscript was completed. I thank Professor Kenneth Stevens and Dr. Dennis Klatt for their advice and kind hospitality at M.I.T., Professors Michael Studdert-Kennedy and Peter Eimas for their comments and criticisms on an earlier draft of the chapter and Professor W. K. Estes for his patience and thoughtful suggestions during the time this chapter was being completed.

REFERENCES

Abbs, J. H., & Sussman, H. M. Neurophysiological detectors and speech perception: A discussion of theoretical implications. *Journal of Speech and Hearing Research,* 1971, **14,** 23–36.

Abramson, A. S., & Lisker, L. Voice onset time in stop consonants: Acoustic analysis and synthesis. *Proceedings of the 5th International Congress of Acoustics* (Liege), 1965.

Ades, A. E. Vowels, consonants, speech and nonspeech. *Psychological Review,* 1977, **84,** 524–530.

Bailey, P. J. Perceptual adaptation in speech: Some properties of detectors for acoustical cues to phonetic distinctions. Unpublished doctoral dissertation, University of Cambridge, 1975.

Bell, A. M. *Visible speech and the science of universal alphabetics.* London: Simpkin, Marshall, & Co., 1867.

Bever, T. G., Lackner, J., & Kirk, R. The underlying structures of sentences are the primary units of immediate speech processing. *Perception & Psychophysics,* 1969, **5,** 225–231.

Blakemore, C., & Cooper, G. F. Development of the brain depends on the visual environment. *Nature,* 1970, **228,** 477–478.

Bondarko, L. V., Zagorujko, N. G., Kozhevnikov, V. A., Molchanov, A. P., & Chistovich, L. A. A model of speech perception in humans (Tech. Report 70-12). *Working Papers in Linguistics No. 6.* Columbus: Ohio State University, Computer & Information Science Research Center, 1970.

Bruner, J. S. Neural mechanisms in perception. *Psychological Review,* 1957, **64,** 340–358.

Burdick, C. K., & Miller, J. D. Speech perception by the chinchilla: Discrimination of sustained /a/ and /i/. *Journal of the Acoustical Society of America,* 1975, **58,** 415–427.

Cairns, H. S., & Kamerman, J. Lexical information processing during sentence comprehension. *Journal of Verbal Learning and Verbal Behavior,* 1975, **14,** 170–179.

Chomsky, N. *Syntactic structures.* The Hague: Mouton, 1957.

Chomsky, N. Current issues in linguistic theory. In J. A. Fodor, & J. J. Katz (Eds.), *The structure of language.* Englewood Cliffs, New Jersey: Prentice-Hall, 1964. Pp. 50–118.

Chomsky, N., & Halle, M. *The sound pattern of English.* New York: Harper & Row, 1968.

Chomsky, N., & Miller, G. A. Introduction to the formal analysis of natural languages. In R. D.

Luce, R. Bush, & E. Galanter (Eds.), *Handbook of mathematical psychology.* Vol. 2. New York: John Wiley & Sons, 1963. Pp. 269-321.

Cohen, A., & Nooteboom, S. (Eds.). *Structure and process in speech perception.* Heidelberg: Springer-Verlag, 1975.

Cole, R. A., & Scott, B. The phantom in the phoneme: Invariant cues for stop consonants. *Perception & Psychophysics,* 1974, **15**, 101-107. (a)

Cole, R. A., & Scott, B. Toward a theory of speech perception. *Psychological Review,* 1974, **4**, 348-374. (b)

Cooper, F. S., Delattre, P. C., Liberman, A. M., Borst, J. M., & Gerstman, L. J. Some experiments on the perception of synthetic speech sounds. *Journal of the Acoustical Society of America,* 1952, **24**, 597-606.

Cooper, F. S., Liberman, A. M., & Borst, J. M. The intervonversion of audible and visible patterns as a basis for research in the perception of speech. *Proceedings of the National Academy of Sciences,* 1951, **37**, 318-325.

Cooper, W. E. Selective adaptation to speech. In F. Restle, R. M. Shiffrin, N. J. Castellan, H. Lindman, & D. B. Pisoni, (Eds.), *Cognitive theory.* Vol. 1. Hillsdale, New Jersey: Lawrence Erlbaum Associates, 1975. Pp. 23-54.

Cooper, W. E. *Syntactic control of timing in speech production.* Unpublished doctoral thesis, M.I.T., 1976.

Cooper, W. E., & Blumstein, S. E. A "labial" feature analyzer in speech perception. *Perception & Psychophysics,* 1974, **15**, 591-600.

Cutting, J. E., & Rosner, B. S. Categories and boundaries in speech and music. *Perception & Psychophysics,* 1974, **16**, 564-570.

Daniloff, R., & Moll, K. Coarticulation of lip rounding. *Journal of Speech and Hearing Research,* 1968, **11**, 707-721.

Darwin, C. J. The perception of speech. In E. C. Carterette & M. P. Friedman (Eds.), *Handbook of perception.* New York: Academic Press, 1976. Pp. 175-226.

Delattre, P. The physiological interpretation of sound spectrograms. *Publication of the Modern Language Association,* 1951, **66**, 864-875.

Delattre, P. C., Liberman, A. M., & Cooper, F. S. Acoustic loci and transitional cues for consonants. *Journal of the Acoustical Society of America,* 1955, **27**, 769-773.

Delattre, P. C., Liberman, A. M., & Cooper, F. S. Formant transitions and loci as acoustic correlates of place of articulation in American fricatives. *Studia Linguistica,* 1964, **18**, 104-121.

Delattre, P. C., Liberman, A. M., Cooper, F. S., & Gerstman, L. J. Observations on one- and two-formant vowels synthesized from spectrographic patterns. *Word,* 1952, **8**, 195-210.

Denes, P. Effect of duration on perception of voicing. *Journal of the Acoustical Society of America,* 1955, **27**, 761-764.

Dorman, M., Studdert-Kennedy, M., & Raphael, L. Stop consonant recognition: Release bursts and formant transitions as functionally equivalent context-dependent cues. *Perception & Psychophysics,* 1977, **22**, 109-122.

Eimas, P. D. Auditory and linguistic processing of cues for place of articulation by infants. *Perception & Psychophysics,* 1974, **16**, 513-521.

Eimas, P. D. Speech perception in early infancy. In L. B. Cohen & P. Salapatek (Eds.), *Infant perception.* New York: Academic Press, 1975. Pp. 193-231. (a)

Eimas, P. D. Auditory and phonetic coding of the cues for speech: Discrimination of the r-l distinction by young infants. *Perception & Psychophysics,* 1975, **18**, 341-347. (b)

Eimas, P. D. Developmental aspects of speech perception. In R. Held, H. Leibowitz, & H. L. Teuber (Eds.), *Handbook of sensory physiology: Perception.* New York: Springer-Verlag, 1978. Pp. 365-382.

Eimas, P. D., Cooper, W. E., & Corbit, J. D. Some properties of linguistic feature detectors. *Perception & Psychophysics,* 1973, **13**, 2, 247-252.

Eimas, P. D., & Corbit, J. D. Selective adaptation of linguistic feature detectors. *Cognitive Psychology*, 1973, **4**, 99–109.

Eimas, P. D., Siqueland, E. R., Jusczyk, P., & Vigorito, J. Speech perception in infants. *Science*, 1971, **171**, 303–306.

Fant, G. *Acoustic theory of speech production*. The Hague: Mouton, 1960.

Fant, G. Descriptive analysis of the acoustic aspects of speech. *Logos*, 1962, **5**, 3–17.

Fant, G. Auditory patterns of speech. In W. Wathen-Dunn (Ed.), *Models for the perception of speech and visual form*. Cambridge: M.I.T. Press, 1967. Pp. 111–125.

Fant, G. Stops in CV-syllables. *Speech Transmission Laboratory Quarterly Progress and Status Report No. 4*, 1969, 1–25.

Fant, G. *Speech sounds and features*. Cambridge: M.I.T. Press, 1973.

Flanagàn, J. L. *Speech analysis, synthesis and perception*. (2nd ed.) New York: Academic Press, 1972.

Foss, D. J., & Swinney, D. A. On the physiological reality of the phoneme: Perception, identification and consciousness. *Journal of Verbal Learning and Verbal Behavior*, 1973, **12**, 246–257.

Fry, D. B., Abramson, A. S., Eimas, P. D., & Liberman, A. M. The identification and discrimination of synthetic vowels. *Language and Speech*, 1962, **5**, 4, 171–189.

Fujisaki, H., & Kawashima, T. On the modes and mechanisms of speech perception. *Annual Report of the Engineering Research Institute, Vol. 28*. Tokyo: University of Tokyo, Faculty of Engineering, 1969. Pp. 67–73.

Fujisaki, H., & Kawashima, T. Some experiments on speech perception and a model for the perceptual mechanism. *Annual Report of the Engineering Research Institute, Vol. 29*. Tokyo: University of Tokyo, 1970. Pp. 207–214.

Gibson, E. J. *Principles of perceptual learning and development*. New York: Appleton-Century-Crofts, 1969.

Gibson, J. J., & Gibson, E. J. Perceptual learning: Differentiation or enrichment? *Psychological Review*, 1955, **62**, 32–41.

Halle, M., & Stevens, K. N. Speech recognition: A model and a program for research. *IRE Transactions of the Professional Group on Information Theory*, 1962, **IT-8**, 155–159.

Harris, K. S. Cues for the discrimination of American English fricatives in spoken syllables. *Language and Speech*, 1958, **1**, 1–7.

Harris, K. S. Physiological aspects of articulatory behavior. In T. A. Sebeok (Ed.), *Current trends in linguistics*. Vol. 12. The Hague: Mouton, 1974. Pp. 2281–2302.

Heinz, J. M., & Stevens, K. N. On the properties of voiceless fricative consonants. *Journal of the Acoustical Society of America*, 1961, **33**, 589–596.

Hirsch, H. V. B., & Spinelli, D. N. Visual experience modifies distribution of horizontally and vertically oriented receptive fields in cats. *Science*, 1970, **168**, 869–871.

Hockett, C. F. Manual of phonology. *Indiana University Publications in Anthropology and Linguistics*, 1955, No. 11.

Hockett, C. F. *A Course in modern linguistics*. New York: MacMillan, 1958.

Huggins, A. W. F. On the perception of temporal phenomena in speech. *Journal of the Acoustical Society of America*, 1972, **51**, 1279–1290. (a)

Huggins, A. W. F. Just noticeable differences for segment duration in natural speech. *Journal of the Acoustical Society of America*, 1972, **51**, 1270–1278. (b)

Jakobson, R. *Child language, aphasia and phonological universals*. The Hague: Mouton, 1968.

Jakobson, R., Fant, G., & Halle, M. *Preliminaries to speech analysis* (Tech. Report No. 13). Cambridge: M.I.T. Acoustics Laboratory, May 1952.

Klatt, D. H. The duration of (s) in English words. *Journal of Speech and Hearing Research*, 1974, **17**, 51–63.

Klatt, D. H. Structure of a phonological rule component for a synthesis-by-rule program. Paper presented at the Acoustical Society of America, San Francisco, November 1975. (a)

Klatt, D. H. Vowel lengthening is syntactically determined in a connected discourse. *Journal of Phonetics*, 1975, **3**, 129-140. (b)

Klatt, D. H., & Cooper, W. E. Perception of segment duration in sentence contexts. In A. Cohen & S. Nooteboom (Eds.), *Structure and process in speech perception*. Heidelberg: Springer-Verlag, 1975. Pp. 69-86.

Klatt, D. H., & Stevens, K. N. On the automatic recognition of continuous speech: Implications from a spectrogram-reading experiment. *IEEE Transactions on Audio and Electroacoustics*, 1973, **AU-21**, 210-217.

Kuhl, P. K., & Miller, J. D. Speech perception by the chinchilla: Voiced-voiceless distinction in alveolar plosive consonants. *Science*, 1975, **190**, 69-72.

Ladefoged, P. Phonetic prerequisites for a distinctive feature theory. In A. Valdman (Ed.), *Papers in linguistics and phonetics to the memory of Pierre Delattre*. The Hague: Mouton, 1972. Pp. 273-285.

Lane, H. L. Psychophysical parameters of vowel perception. *Psychological Monographs*, 1962, **76**(44, Whole No. 563).

Lane, H. L. The motor theory of speech perception: A critical review. *Psychological Review*, 1965, **72**, 275-309.

Lasky, R. E., Syrdal-Lasky, A., & Klein, R. E. VOT discrimination by four to six and a half month old infants from Spanish environments. *Journal of Experimental Child Psychology*, 1975, **20**, 215-225.

Lea, W. A. An approach to syntactic recognition without phonemics. *IEEE Transactions on Audio and Electroacoustics*, 1973, **AU-21**, 249-258.

Liberman, A. M. Some results of research on speech perception. *Journal of the Acoustical Society of America*, 1957, **29**, 117-123.

Liberman, A. M. Some characteristics of perception in the speech mode. In D. A. Hamburg (Ed.), *Perception and its disorders, Proceedings of A.R.N.M.D.* Baltimore: Williams & Wilkins, 1970. Pp. 238-254. (a)

Liberman, A. M. The grammars of speech and language. *Cognitive Psychology*, 1970, **1**, 301-323. (b)

Liberman, A. M., Cooper, F. S., Harris, K. S., & MacNeilage, P. F. A motor theory of speech perception. In G. Fant (Ed.), *Proceedings of the speech communication seminar*. Stockholm: Royal Institute of Technology, Speech Transmission Laboratory, 1963.

Liberman, A. M., Cooper, F. S., Harris, K. S., MacNeilage, P. F., & Studdert-Kennedy, M. Some observations on a model for speech perception. In W. Wathen-Dunn (Ed.), *Models for the perception of speech and visual form*. Cambridge: M.I.T. Press, 1967. (a)

Liberman, A. M., Cooper, F. S., Shankweiler, D. P., & Studdert-Kennedy, M. Perception of the speech code. *Psychological Review*, 1967, **74**, 431-461. (b)

Liberman, A. M., Delattre, P. C., & Cooper, F. S. The role of selected stimulus variables in the perception of the unvoiced stop consonants. *American Journal of Psychology*, 1952, **65**, 497-516.

Liberman, A. M., Delattre, P. C., Gerstman, L. J., & Cooper, F. S. Tempo of frequency change as a cue for distinguishing classes of speech sounds. *Journal of Experimental Psychology*, 1956, **52**, 127-137.

Liberman, A. M., Harris, K. S., Hoffman, H. S., & Griffith, B. C. The discrimination of speech sounds within and across phoneme boundaries. *Journal of Experimental Psychology*, 1957, **54**, 358-368.

Liberman, A. M., Harris, K. S., Kinney, J. A., & Lane, H. L. The discrimination of relative onset time of the components of certain speech and non-speech patterns. *Journal of Experimental Psychology*, 1961, **61**, 379-388.

Liberman, A. M., Ingemann, F., Lisker, L., Delattre, P. C., & Cooper, F. S. Minimal rules for synthesizing speech. *Journal of the Acoustical Society of America*, 1959, **31**, 1490-1499.

Licklider, J. C. R. On the process of speech perception. *Journal of the Acoustical Society of America*, 1952, **24**, 590-594.

Lieberman, P. Towards a unified phonetic theory. *Linguistic Inquiry*, 1970, **1**(3), 307–322.

Lieberman, P., Crelin, E. S., & Klatt, D. H. Phonetic ability and related anatomy of the newborn and adult human, Neanderthal man, and the chimpanzee. *American Anthropologist*, 1972, **74**(4), 287–307.

Liljencrants, J., & Lindblom, B. Numerical simulation of vowel quality systems: The role of perceptual contrast. *Language*, 1972, **48**, 839–862.

Lindblom, B. E. F. Spectrographic study of vowel reduction. *Journal of the Acoustical Society of America*, 1963, **35**, 1773–1781.

Lindblom, B., & Sundberg, J. A quantitative model of vowel production on the distinctive features of Swedish vowels. *Speech Transmission Laboratory, Quarterly Progress and Status Report*, 1969, No. 1, 14–30.

Lindblom, B. E. F., & Svensson, S. -G. Interaction between segmental and nonsegmental factors in speech recognition. *IEEE Transactions on Audio and Electroacoustics*, 1973, **AU-21**, 536–545.

Lisker, L. Closure duration and the intervocalic voiced–voiceless distinction in English. *Language*, 1957, **33**, 42–49.

Lisker, L. Is it VOT or a first-formant transition detector? *Journal of the Acoustical Society of America*, 1975, **57**, 6, 1547–1551.

Lisker, L., & Abramson, A. S. A cross language study of voicing in initial stops: Acoustical measurements. *Word*, 1964, **20**, 384–422.

Lisker, L., & Abramson, A. S. The voicing dimension: Some experiments in comparative phonetics. In *Proceedings of the Sixth International Congress of Phonetic Sciences, Prague*. Prague: Academia, 1970. Pp. 563–567.

Macmillan, N. A., Kaplan, H. L., & Creelman, C. D. The psychophysics of categorical perception. *Psychological Review*, 1977, **84**, 452–471.

MacNeilage, P. F. Motor control of serial ordering of speech. *Psychological Review*, 1970, **77**, 182–196.

Malmberg, B. The phonetic basis for syllable division. *Studia Linguistica*, 1955, **9**, 80–87.

Marslen-Wilson, W. D. Sentence perception as an interactive parallel process. *Science*, 1975, **189**, 226–228.

Massaro, D. W. Perceptual images, processing time, and perceptual units in auditory perception. *Psychological Review*, 1972, **79**, 124–145.

Massaro, D. W. Auditory information processing. In W. K. Estes (Ed.), *Handbook of learning and cognitive Processes*. Volume 4. Hillsdale, New Jersey: Lawrence Erlbaum Associates, 1976. Pp. 275–320.

Mattingly, I. G. Synthesis by rule of general American English. *Supplement to status report on speech research*. New York: Haskins Laboratories, 1968.

McNeill, D. *The acquisition of language*. New York: Harper & Row, 1970.

McNeill, D., & Lindig, L. The perceptual reality of phonemes, syllables, words and sentences. *Journal of Verbal Learning and Verbal Behavior*, 1973, **12**, 419–430.

Menyuk, P. *The acquisition and development of language*. Englewood Cliffs, New Jersey: Prentice-Hall, 1971.

Miller, G. A. The magic number seven plus or minus two: Some limits on our capacity for processing information. *Psychological Review*, 1956, **63**, 81–97.

Miller, G. A. Decision units in the perception of speech. *IRE Transactions on Information Theory*, 1962, **IT-8**, 81–83.

Miller, G. A., Heise, G. A., & Lichten, W. The intelligibility of speech as a function of the context of the test materials. *Journal of Experimental Psychology*, 1951, **41**, 329–335.

Miller, J. D., Wier, C. C., Pastore, R., Kelly, W. J., & Dooling, R. J. Discrimination and labeling of noise-buzz sequences with varying noise-lead times: An example of categorical perception. *Journal of the Acoustical Society of America*, 1976, **60**, 410–417.

Moffitt, A. R. Consonant cue perception by twenty to twenty-four week old infants. *Child Development*, 1971, **42**, 717–731.

Morse, P. A. The discrimination of speech and nonspeech stimuli in early infancy. *Journal of Experimental Child Psychology*, 1972, **14,** 477–492.

Morse, P. A., & Snowdon, C. T. An investigation of categorical speech discrimination by rhesus monkeys. *Perception & Psychophysics*, 1975, **17,** 9–16.

Neisser, U. *Cognitive psychology.* New York: Appleton-Century-Crofts, 1967.

Ohman, S. E. G. Coarticulation in VCV utterances: Spectrographic measurements. *Journal of the Acoustical Society of America*, 1966, **39,** 151–168.

Oller, D. K. The effect of position in utterance on speech segment duration in English. *Journal of the Acoustical Society of America*, 1973, **54,** 1235–1247.

Perey, A. J., & Pisoni, D. B. Dual processing vs. response-limitation accounts of categorical perception: A reply to Macmillan, Kaplan and Creelman. *Journal of the Acoustical Society of America*, 1977, **62,** S1, 60–61.

Peterson, G. E., & Barney, H. L. Control methods used in a study of the vowels. *Journal of the Acoustical Society of America*, 1952, **24,** 175–184.

Peterson, G. E., & Shoup, J. E. A physiological theory of phonetics. *Journal of Speech and Hearing Research*, 1966, **9**(1), 5–67.

Pisoni, D. B. On the nature of categorical perception of speech sounds. *Supplement to status report on speech research*, SR-27. New Haven: Haskins Laboratories, November 1971. Pp. 1–101.

Pisoni, D. B. Auditory and phonetic memory codes in the discrimination of consonants and vowels. *Perception & Psychophysics*, 1973, **13,** 253–260.

Pisoni, D. B. Auditory short-term memory and vowel perception. *Memory & Cognition*, 1975, **3,** 7–18.

Pisoni, D. B. Identification and discrimination of the relative onset of two component tones: Implications for voicing perception in stops. *Journal of the Acoustical Society of America*, 1977, **61,** 1352–1361.

Pisoni, D. B., & Sawusch, J. R. Some stages of processing in speech perception. In A. Cohen, & S. Nooteboom (Eds.), *Structure and process in speech perception.* Heidelberg: Springer-Verlag, 1975. Pp. 16–34.

Pisoni, D. B., & Tash, J. B. Reaction times to comparisons within and across phonetic categories. *Perception & Psychophysics*, 1974, **15,** 285–290.

Pisoni, D. B., & Tash, J. B. Auditory property detectors and processing place features in stop consonants. *Perception & Psychophysics*, 1975, **18,** 401–408.

Pollack, I. The information in elementary auditory displays. *Journal of the Acoustical Society of America*, 1952, **24,** 745–749.

Pollack, I. The information in elementary auditory displays II. *Journal of the Acoustical Society of America*, 1953, **25,** 765–769.

Pollack, I., & Pickett, J. M. The intelligibility of excerpts from conversation. *Language and Speech*, 1964, **6,** 165–171.

Popper, R. D. Pair discrimination for a continuum of synthetic voiced stops with and without first and third formants. *Journal of Psycholinguistic Research*, 1972, **1,** 205–219.

Raphael, L. J. Preceding vowel duration as a cue to the perception of the voicing characteristic of word-final consonants in American English. *Journal of the Acoustical Society of America*, 1972, **51,** 1296–1303.

Savin, H. B., & Bever, T. G. The nonperceptual reality of the phoneme. *Journal of Verbal Learning and Verbal Behavior*, 1970, **9,** 295–302.

Sawusch, J. R. Peripheral and central processes in selective adaptation of place of articulation in stop consonants. *Journal of the Acoustical Society of America*, 1977, **62,** 738–750.

Schatz, C. The role of context in the perception of stops. *Language*, 1954, **30,** 47–56.

Shockey, L., & Reddy, R. *Quantitative analysis of speech perception: Results from transcription of connected speech from unfamiliar languages.* Paper presented at the Speech Communication Seminar, Stockholm, Sweden, August, 1974.

Sinnott, J. M. *A comparison of speech sound discrimination in humans and monkeys.* Unpublished doctoral dissertation, University of Michigan, 1974.

Siqueland, E. R., & DeLucia, C. A. Visual reinforcement of nonnutritive sucking in human infants. *Science*, 1969, 165, 1144–1146.

Stevens, K. N. Toward a model for speech recognition. *Journal of the Acoustical Society of America*, 1960, **32**, 1, 47–55.

Stevens, K. N. *Acoustic correlates of certain consonantal features*. Paper presented at Conference on Speech Communication and Processing, Cambridge, November 1967.

Stevens, K. N. Airflow and turbulence noise for fricative and stop consonants: Static considerations. *Journal of the Acoustical Society of America*, 1971, **50**, 1180–1192.

Stevens K. N. The quantal nature of speech: Evidence from articulatory-acoustic data. In E. E. David, Jr., & P. B. Denes (Eds.), *Human communication: A unified view*. New York: McGraw-Hill, 1972. Pp. 51–66.

Stevens, K. N. Further theoretical and experimental bases for quantal places of articulation for consonants. *Quarterly Progress Report No. 108*. Cambridge: M.I.T., Research Laboratory of Electronics, 1973. Pp. 247–252.

Stevens, K. N. The potential role of property detectors in the perception of consonants. In G. Fant & M. A. A. Tatham (Eds.), *Auditory analysis and perception of speech*. New York: Academic Press, 1975. Pp. 303–330.

Stevens, K. N., & Blumstein, S. E. *Context-independent properties for place of articulation in stop consonants*. Paper presented at the 91st meeting of the Acoustical Society of America, Washington, D.C., April 1976.

Stevens, K. N., & Halle, M. Remarks on analysis by synthesis and distinctive features. In W. Wathen-Dunn (Ed.), *Models for the perception of speech and visual form*. Cambridge: M.I.T. Press, 1967. Pp. 88–102.

Stevens, K. N., & House, A. S. Development of a quantitative description of vowel articulation. *Journal of the Acoustical Society of America*, 1955, **27**, 484–493.

Stevens, K. N., & House, A. S. Studies of formant transitions using a vocal tract analog. *Journal of the Acoustical Society of America*, 1956, **28**, 578–585.

Stevens, K. N., & House, A. S. Speech perception. In J. Tobias (Ed.), *Foundations of modern auditory theory*. Vol. 2. New York: Academic Press, 1972. Pp. 1–62.

Stevens, K. N., & Klatt, D. H. Role of formant transitions in the voiced–voiceless distinction for stops. *Journal of the Acoustical Society of America*, 1974, **55**, 653–659.

Stevens, S. S., & Volkmann, J. The relation of pitch to frequency: A revised scale. *American Journal of Psychology*, 1940, **53**, 329–353.

Streeter, L. A. Language perception of 2-month-old infants shows effects of both innate mechanisms and experience. *Nature*, 1976, **259**, 39–41.

Strevens, P. Spectra of fricative noise. *Language and Speech*, 1960, **3**, 32–49.

Studdert-Kennedy, M. The perception of speech. In T. A. Sebeok (Ed.), *Current trends in linguistics*. Vol. XII. The Hague, Mouton, 1974. Pp. 2349–2385.

Studdert-Kennedy, M. Speech perception. In N. J. Lass (Ed.), *Contemporary issues in experimental phonetics*. New York: Academic Press, 1976. Pp. 243–293.

Studdert-Kennedy, M., Liberman, A. M., Harris, K. S., & Cooper, F. S. Motor theory of speech perception: A reply to Lane's critical review. *Psychological Review*, 1970, **77**, 234–249.

Studdert-Kennedy, M., & Shankweiler, D. Hemispheric specialization for speech perception. *Journal of the Acoustical Society of America*, 1970, **48**, 570–594.

Svensson, S.-G. Prosody and grammar in speech perception. *Monographs from the Institute of Linguistics University of Stockholm*, Institute of Linguistics, Stockholm, Sweden, 1974.

Tartter, V. C., & Eimas, P. D. The role of auditory feature detectors in the perception of speech. *Perception & Psychophysics*, 1975, **18**, 293–298.

Treon, M. A. Fricative and plosive perception-identification as a function of phonetic context in CVCVC utterances. *Language and Speech*, 1970, **13**, 54–64.

Whitfield, I. C. "Edges" in auditory information processing. In *Proceedings of the XXIII International Congress of Physiological Sciences*. Tokyo, September 1965. Pp. 245-247.

Wickelgren, W. A. Auditory or articulatory coding in verbal short-term memory. *Psychological Review*, 1969, **76**, 232-235.

Winitz, H., Scheib, M. E., & Reeds, J. H. Identification of stops and vowels for the burst portion of /p,t,k/ isolated from conversational speech. *Journal of the Acoustical Society of America*, 1972, **51**, 1309-1317.

6
On the Organization and Core Concepts of Learning Theory and Cognitive Psychology

W. K. Estes

Rockefeller University

In the *Foreword* to the first volume of this *Handbook,* we raised the question of whether it is "possible at present to identify a core cluster of theoretical ideas, concepts, and methods with which everyone working in the area of learning and cognition needs to be familiar . . . to make explicit the relationships that we feel do or must exist among the various subspecialties, ranging from conditioning through perceptual learning and memory to psycholinguistics" (p. ix) in a way that might help both investigators of learning and cognition and interested outsiders to relate particular lines of research to the broader spectrum of activity.

Presumably, the answer to this question is imbedded in the six volumes of the *Handbook,* where those students of our discipline strongly enough motivated to make the effort can extract the materials for their own assemblage of core concepts and principles. Though with no illusion that my assemblage will come close to a concensus, I propose in the following pages to present it in the hope that the essay may find some uses, if only to provoke others into doing better.

I. CONSIDERATIONS OF CONTENT AND STRUCTURE

A. Scope and Dimensions of the Research Literature

In Volume 1 of this *Handbook,* we noted that present-day cognitive psychology presents an almost unmanageable volume and heterogeneity of research and that, consequently, one of the greatest challenges facing us is that of finding effective means of organizing this material for purposes both of theoretical development and of application. A scan of the six volumes would seem to confirm this impression. In Table 1, we present a by no means exhaustive outline of topics covered, together with volumes in which principal references are to be found.

TABLE 1
Research Topics

Topic	Volumes
General theoretical issues	1
Conditioning and reinforcement theory	2, 3
Methodology	2
Excitatory and inhibitory processes	2
Operant conditioning	2
Choice behavior	2
Stimulus selection and generalization	2
Behavior modification	3
Discrimination and concept learning	1, 3
Discrimination models	1, 3
Hypothesis models	1
Perceptual learning	4
Verbal learning and retention	3
Methodology	3
Interference theory	3
Probability and sequence learning	3
Spacing and frequency	3
Perception	
Pattern recognition	1
Auditory processing	4
Visual processing	5
Speech	6
Role in reading	4, 6
Attention and memory	
Selective attention	3, 4
Capacity limitations	4
Short-term memory	4
Primary memory	4
Working memory	4
Coding	4, 6
Retrieval	4
Long-term memory	3, 5, 6
Coding	4, 6
Search and retrieval	4, 5, 6
Propositional vs. analog storage	5
Network models	1, 5, 6
Memory for text	6
Cognitive development	
Theoretical approaches	5
Developmental aspects of learning	1, 3
Language	5, 6
Speech	6
Representations of meaning	5, 6
Comprehension	6
Cognitive aspects of motivation	1, 3
Problem solving	5
Individual differences and comparative approaches	1
Applications in education and psychotherapy	3, 5

One's predominant impression on scanning the accumulated list of topics may well be one of diversity. Further, there is little superficial appearance of any rational order, even though the topics are organized much as they would be in a course outline. However, with a few conspicuous exceptions, one embarking on a systematic study of cognitive psychology would do well to start at the beginning of the topical outline and work through. The sequencing is correlated with a number of major dimensions that can be used to impose some order on the enormous literature.

1. *Phylogenetic sequence*

Processes or mechanisms associated with the first listed topics, habituation and conditioning, are found in all organisms but appear in the simplest forms and are studied most often in lower animals. The conception of conditioned responses or similar units as the building blocks of higher cognitive activity, conspicuous in some of the early writings of Hull (1930, 1931) and other learning theorists, simply has not worked out. Nor does there turn out to be much to be said for the idea of sharp discontinuities in the sequence. Rather, there is much evidence for continuity in the sense that such processes as habituation and conditioning, which apparently constitute the entire cognitive life of the lowest organisms, still occur in higher organisms, but there are mainly identifiable in relatively autonomous subsystems (defense reflexes, vegetative processes) and are subject to domination by later appearing, predominantly verbal processes or mechanisms (Estes, in press; Pavlov, 1927; Ross & Ross, 1976; White, 1965).

2. *Developmental Sequence*

Similarly, the first listed topics refer to processes readily identifiable in younger organisms (in the case of human beings even in infants), but tending to be overlaid in the course of development by more complex processes. The transition has been perhaps most carefully worked out in the case of discrimination learning and classificatory behavior (see, for example, Kendler & Kendler, *Handbook,* Vol. 1, Chapter 6; Medin, Vol. 3, Chapter 4).

3. *Complexity*

The term *complexity* is not a very descriptive label, for complexity of phenomena is primarily a function of the depth of analysis that has been achieved. Classical and operant conditioning are traditionally considered simple and human memory complex. Yet current models for aspects of conditioning (as Gibbon, 1977; Rescorla, 1972) seem fully as complex as some models of human memory (as Atkinson & Shiffrin, 1968; Wickelgren & Norman, 1966), perhaps a consequence of the fact that more detailed analyses are being attempted.

The dimension we associate with complexity may have to do with remoteness of the process under study from initiating stimuli, in the sense of the depth or stage of processing or the degree of encoding, the flexibility of coupling of cognition and action, and the richness of structure. As the terms are customarily used, *conditioning* and *learning* usually refer to research dealing with situations in which the behavior of an organism is progressively modified in the direction of some criterion as a function of experience, whereas *memory* refers to research in which information an organism stores as a consequence of some experience may not be manifest until much later and often under very different test conditions. With regard to structure, concepts of conditioning typically refer to simple stimulus–response relations, whereas research on memory and information processing deals with more elaborate networks of associations that are connected to action via decision processes, strategies, or plans.

B. An Effort toward Organization

1. Structural Interconnections among Research Clusters, Ideas and Disciplines

In the case of individuals having relatively extensive experience with the field of learning and cognition, we should expect their mental pictures of the field to be rather more structured than the linear sequence of the topical outline presented in Table 1. Taking a cue from current models of memory, we might speculate in terms of something like the tree structure of Figure 1. In this schematization, specific research topics are aligned along the bottom row, the clustering corresponding to what typically goes together in the same journals or the same laboratories. But also, topics close together on the horizontal axis tend to be interpreted by common concepts or theories at a somewhat higher or more abstract level, and these in turn are ordered in terms of still more abstract or general sets of ideas as one traces the connections upward.

The vertical dimension thus simultaneously represents the main line of chronological development, predominant lines of influence, and the dimension of generality–specificity. We might also add durability, since, in the nature of things, concepts and presumed facts at the lowest level are continually under renewal, whereas the higher level, more abstract ideas and viewpoints tend to be influential over relatively long periods and relatively unsusceptible to modification by specific empirical developments.

To trace just one set of branchings, we recall from every history of psychology that a combination of philosophy and naturalistic observation gave rise to the association theory that was the predecessor of all current theories of learning and memory. Hence, in Figure 1 the concepts of association theory, together with inputs from research in biology, lead downward in one direction to theories of conditioning; but the same concepts, together with inputs from laboratory studies of learning and memory, lead to the body of more empirically grounded association theory identified with what Hilgard (1948) termed *current functionalism* (not

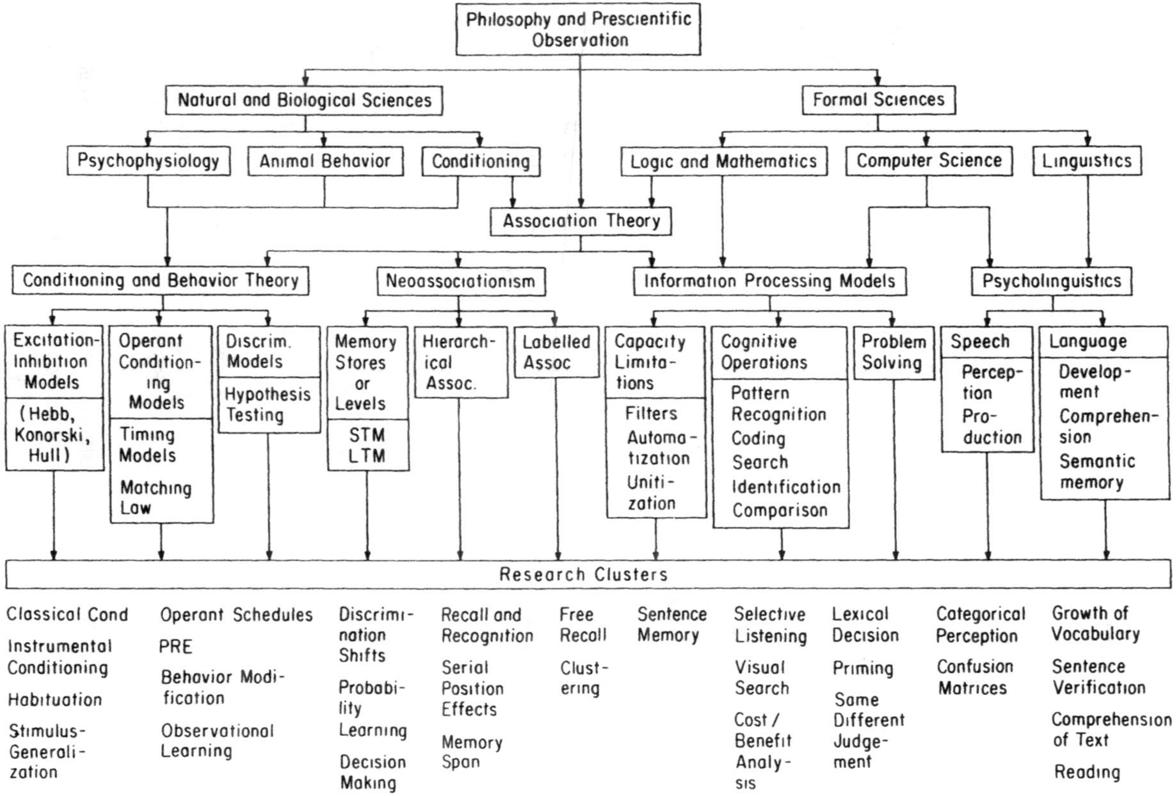

FIGURE 1. A schematization, in the manner of semantic memory models, of lines of influence (denoted by arrows) flowing from higher order, or longer established, to lower order, or more recently emergent, bodies of theory, and then in turn to clusters of research activity. STM = short-term memory. LTM = long-term memory. PRE = partial reinforcement effect.

identified in the figure). This body of theory has, on the one hand, together with inputs from linguistics and the emerging discipline of psycholinguistics, led to a newer body of theory that may be termed *neoassociationism* (for example, Anderson & Bower, 1973; Collins & Quillian, 1972; Estes, 1972a, 1976; Feigenbaum, 1963), but has on the other, together with inputs from emerging disciplines of computer science and communication theory, led to the currently extremely influential development associated with information-processing models.

The left–right dimension, like the sequencing of the topical outline, is correlated both with phylogenetic and ontogenetic development and with the various senses of complexity. However, the tree diagram is more helpful than the linear outline in making understandable the relative isolation and lack of direct influence among investigators and concepts associated with topics much separated along the left–right axis. Those research topics closer together on the latter dimension are related via common predecessors or higher order concepts rather than by direct lines of communication.

Not apparent at all in Figure 1 are theories whose lines of influence run along the left–right rather than the top–down dimension, that is, theories that are developmental rather than cross-sectional in character. These would be hard to portray, for there are no general developmental theories but rather a number of relatively limited theories that have grown up in connection with research within major clusters. Most conspicuous among these are the models growing out of learning and perceptual theory (Estes, 1970; Gagne, 1968; Gibson, 1969; Kendler & Kendler, 1975; Stevenson, 1972) and the stage models of the emergence of cognitive processes and operations. The latter subdivide again into the relatively autonomous but extremely influential theory of Piaget and his followers (see, for example, Flavell, 1963) and a more recently emerging line of theoretical development associated with information-processing theory (Klahr & Wallace, 1976; Neimark, 1970).

Ideally, we would like also to be able to add a body of comparative theory exerting its lines of influence along the left–right dimension. Unfortunately, this class of theories is still virtually empty. However, the lack is not escaping attention of current investigators, and there is research in progress that might lead to the emergence of some truly comparative theory (Medin & Cole, *Handbook*, Vol. 1, Chapter 4).

Also missing from the diagram in Figure 1 are important feedback loops that should be added in a more elaborate portrayal. These feedback loops would represent the way in which facts generated by research on specific topics at the bottom of the tree feed upward to modify concepts at higher levels and, hence, indirectly influence research in other clusters. For example, current research on conditioning has importantly modified the models of conditioning and learning associated with the learning theorists of the 1940s and 1950s, and the revised conditioning theories have in turn generated lines of influence downward upon research topics primarily falling under the rubric of neoassociationism (Estes, 1973; Rudy, 1974).

2. Lines of Influence and Development

In view of the complexity of these dynamics, it seems worthwhile to try to add a bit more life to our static portrayal of the hierarchical structure of cognitive theory by considering briefly how the evolution and differentiation of some important concepts relate to influences that can be traced from the higher to the lower levels.

In the earliest association theories, one finds the progenitors of modern concepts of stages and levels of information processing in the sensation–perception–memory distinction and those of neoassociation and conditioning models in the concepts of the memory trace and associative connections or bonds. It was apparent even before there were experimental methods to provide objective documentation that cognitive operations do not deal with literal records of the stimuli that have impinged on one's sensory apparatus; rather, the immediate consequences of stimulation ("sensations") interact with the contents of memory to yield percepts, which then may be remembered and enter into associations with the consequences of other experiences. The primitive unit of memory was conceived in terms of the memory trace or engram—a record in the brain of what was perceived as a consequence of a sensory experience or of an internally generated idea—and in either event having the important property that engrams laid down in close temporal succession are connected by associative bonds, so that later reactivation of one leads more or less automatically to reactivation of the other. One spoke of *redintegration* if the later recurrence of a portion of an earlier perceived sensory pattern led to reinstatement of the whole in memory and of associative memory if the latter event in turn led to reactivation of other engrams and, therefore, recall of other experiences.

Although there has been some variation in the detailed properties assumed, the concept of the memory trace has been one of the most durable in psychology. In current theoretical efforts, much attention is devoted to the problem of explicating the structure of the memory trace and developing a picture of the levels of complexity of structure that result from different amount and kinds of processing of the original stimulus input that go into the generation of a particular trace (Anderson, 1973; Estes, 1976). The currently prevalent view is that a sensory experience is not simply recorded in memory like an image on a photographic plate but, rather, undergoes systematic analysis by systems of analyzers (Sutherland & Mackintosh, 1971) or feature detectors, with the resultant trace taking the form of a multidimensional vector– in effect, a listing of the distinctive features that were present in a stimulus or the values of the stimulus on a number of critical dimensions (Bower , 1967).

In the neoassociation theories, one finds a preoccupation with the structure of memory and with the successive levels of encoding and recoding of stimulus information that give rise to structure. The original idea of simple chain associations between memory traces at a single level has proved to be inadequate and has been replaced by the now popular conceptions of hierarchies of associations. These take various particular forms, but all have some of the properties of the schema of Figure 1 in that memorial units at a given level are associated not by inter-item connections at that level but rather by higher order nodes (Anderson & Bower, 1973) or control elements (Estes, 1972a, 1976). Further, there is increasing attention to the dynamics of the associative network. In order to predict or account for recall, one takes account not only of what is connected in the network but of which nodes or pathways have been recently activated, on the supposition that these will be more readily excited by new inputs, thus the extensive current literature on "priming" in semantic memory (Collins & Loftus, 1975).

In the models of conditioning and behavior theory, from Pavlov through Hull and Tolman and down to the recent formulation of Rescorla and Wagner (1972), structure and process have not been so sharply distinguished and for the most part a stimulus, or the representation of a stimulus, continues to constitute the unit conceived to enter into associations. Only with the very current beginnings of some infiltration of the idea of human memory theories into the sphere of conditioning has the notion taken root that the stimulus in conditioning and animal-learning situations may similarly be best represented in terms of a multidimensional vector of attribute values (Spear, 1976). But whereas theorists of conditioning have been much less concerned with problems of organization and structure than have the neoassociationists, they have been much more attentive to the conditions responsible for the formation of associations and to the distinction between learning and performance.

In the traditional approaches to human learning and memory, it has generally been assumed that questions of what experiences leave traces in memory and what traces become associated can be almost entirely answered if one can specify the events and relationships to which the individual attends. In contrast, within the tradition of conditioning and animal learning, it has been assumed that one of the necessary conditions for the formation of associations is that the organism's response to a stimulus leads to consequences of some motivational significance. The once widely held view that learning occurs only if a consequence of an action is the satisfaction of some drive or motive has waned somewhat over the years. In place of the rather simplistic drive-reduction concept, we now find considerable agreement on one form or another of the idea that memory traces or representations of stimuli to which an organism attends are formed automatically but that associations among these develop only when at least one of the constituent elements has some informational significance relative to the organism's motivational state (Kamin, 1969; Konorski, 1967; Rescorla & Wagner, 1972).

In both the early association theories and the early theories of conditioning, there was no sharp distinction between learning and performance. In the association theories, the issue scarcely arose, with the tacit assumption prevailing that an individual can directly report the contents of memory. In conditioning theory the distinction between learning and performance received much more attention, but for a long period the dominant view was that of direct associative connections between stimuli and responses. In both cases the trend over a number of decades has been toward a sharper distinction and looser coupling between cognitive and performance variables.

In association theories of human memory, the break came with the impact of signal-detection theory and the concept of the criterion (see, for example, Heinemann & Chase, *Handbook,* Vol. 2, Chapter 8; and Murdock, *Handbook,* Vol. 4, Chapter 2). In the case of conditioning and animal learning, the long-term trend has been a progressive elaboration and refinement of the concept of expectation. First, incorporated into a systematic body of behavior theory by Tolman (1932), expectation has more recently been coupled with systematic treatments of learning relative to contingencies and feedback models of the mechanisms whereby information concerning disparities between expectations and actual experiences feeds back to modify ongoing performance (Estes, 1962, 1972b; Irwin, 1972).

The theories associated with the information-processing approach are somewhat complementary to the neoassociation theories in their emphases and core concepts. The latter have focused on problems of structure of memory, the former on the analysis of the course of information processing with special reference to stages and levels at which various cognitive operations come into play, the time required for these operations, and such questions as whether they operate in serial or in parallel.

Whereas modern learning theory and neoassociationism have fanned out from common origins, information-processing psychology represents rather a combination or confluence of ideas from quite different sources, including, on the one hand, association psychology and on the other the flourishing science of inanimate information-processing systems and, in particular, the computer metaphor. Digital computers were built to solve the same kinds of problems that people do, but faster and sometimes more accurately. Then the computer itself and its potentiality became a favorite object of study: Can computers play chess? Can they learn? Will they overtake man at reasoning and thinking?

In turn, analyses of the functions of computers and comparisons with the performance of human beings led indirectly to developments that helped free human cognitive psychology from some of the stereotypes in its intellectual approach that may have persisted through sheer inertia. It became clear that one could study the performance of a computer, in terms of the flow of information, without regard to the hardware of the machine (analogous to the physiological substrate of the human processer), without recording correlations of specific inputs and outputs (analogous to stimulus–response descriptions), and without worry over questions as to whether the computer is aware of what it is doing.

Further, the heuristic value of programming sequences of operations to be carried out by a computer in the course of solving a problem suggested the possibility of simulating human problem solving in terms of sequences of similar operations, an idea realized in the simulation models of Newell and Simon (1972) and leading more indirectly into the currently highly active line of research associated with the additive factors method and the tracing of cognitive and linguistic operations by means of reaction times (Chase, *Handbook*, Vol. 5, Chapter 1).

Psycholinguistics similarly represents a convergence of many lines of influence, most of them somewhat remote from the origins of the mainstream of cognitive psychology. Among the forebears must be listed, I suppose, the extensive but almost purely empirical studies of statistical properties of language and of the growth of vocabulary in the child (reviewed by Miller, 1951), but it is hard to see a strong intellectual connection with the work now associated with psycholinguistics. More direct lines of influence could be traced, I should think, from the work of the linguists interested in the psychological and behavioral side of linguistics, perhaps most notably Bloomfield (1933).

Just as *learning theory* took on a special identity in the minds of most psychologists only with the appearance of Hilgard's book in 1948, the same is perhaps true of *psycholinguistics* and Miller's (1951) volume on language and communication, evidently sparked by a conjunction of ideas from the linguist–psychologists and from the communication and information theory that began to flourish in the late 1940s. The portions or aspects of psycholinguistics that most clearly intersect cognitive psychology have continued to be catalyzed by inputs from areas and traditions, notably speech perception and production (well reviewed by Pisoni in this volume), reading, modern theories of grammar (Chomsky, 1965) and, more recently, case grammars (Fillmore, 1969), and, finally, the currently rapidly expanding study of the more complex aspects of semantic memory and comprehension of text (for example, Kintsch, 1974). It seems scarcely an exaggeration to say that persons interested in pursuing cognitive psychology or any of its branches are well advised to master some specialty in addition to their own, for almost any choice may turn out to be highly relevant and the only great hazard seems to be that of narrowness or insulation from the catalyzing effects of inputs from other disciplines.

II. CORE CONCEPTS AND PRINCIPLES

Although there may prove to be no sharp boundaries or discontinuities at a deep *conceptual* level within the broad area of learning and cognitive processes, in practice one can scarcely avoid recognizing some fairly rigid compartmentalizations. In particular, we must for the most part deal separately with three major bodies of research and theory having to do with conditioning and learning, information processing, and psycholinguistics. Not only are the corresponding groups of investigators largely disjoint, but, more importantly, the research orientations and theoretical ideas have quite different origins.

The study of conditioning and learning, as conventionally conceived, has its origins in observations of the behaviors of animals and people in their ordinary habitats; in turn these provide the basis for research and theory dealing with the processes whereby organisms profit from their individual experiences in ways that improve their abilities to adjust to their environments. The subdiscipline currently dubbed *human information processing*, in contrast, arises largely from considerations of analogies between specific categories of human cognitive activity and the operation of inanimate information-processing systems. The concern is with the specific ways in which people extract and perform various cognitive operations on information obtained from stimulus inputs, usually of a symbolic character, with little concern as to how the information serves any functions of adjustment or adaptation to the physical or social environment. The third member of the triumvirate, psycholinguistics, deals as much with the study of the properties of language itself as with data arising from observations of the behavior of people who use it. Some aspects of psycholinguistics can at present be related in reasonably specific and meaningful ways to other strains of cognitive psychology whereas some cannot; as anyone who has read this far in the *Handbook* will have observed, we have been able to attempt some coverage only of the former aspects.

A. Levels of Learning Processes

Beyond the obvious correlation between complexity of learning processes and age and phylogenetic status of the organism, perhaps the most conspicuous overall trend is that for learning processes or mechanisms that constitute a major part of the adaptive repertoire of lower organisms to continue to appear in higher organisms in much the same form but progressively constricted and overlaid with other, usually more complex, processes. The same trends appear to some extent in the ontogeny of higher organisms. These relationships can be most fully documented in the case of habituation and classical conditioning.

1. Habituation

Perhaps the most ubiquitous of all learning processes is the progressive decline in responsiveness to repeated stimuli termed *habituatory decrement*. Investigations ranging over the entire phylogenetic scale, and often using similar or even identical stimuli, demonstrate very similar properties for habituation from one-celled organisms to man (see, for example, Harris, 1943; Peeke & Herz, 1973).

There is, however, no reason to think that the neural basis is the same in organisms at very different levels. Rather, functional properties appear to be those demanded by requirements of adaptation. Evidently, even the lower organisms that operate almost entirely by means of genetically programmed behavioral routines must have some means of avoiding "capture" by continuing or repetitive stimulation. It seems adaptive enough for any organism to exhibit a startle response to a novel stimulus; but if the stimulus continues to recur repetitively, adaptation must nearly always require further that repetition of the same response give way to variation in order that a route to escape may be found, if escape is needed, or that other needs of the animal can be served. Adaptation of sense organs and fatigue of effectors provide partial solutions, but it would be hazardous for organisms to rely on these alone, for an adapted sense organ does not respond properly to a new stimulus in the same modality, and fatigued muscles are not ready to cope with the demands of changes in the environmental situation. It is necessary, in fact, for the organism in many instances to be protected from adaptation or fatigue.

The answer to these various requirements on the part of all forms of animal life is a central mechanism of habituation. The most notable property is progressive decrement of response to uniformly repeated stimuli. Responsiveness recovers with rest, or upon "disinhibition" by new stimuli, but in either case habituation progresses more rapidly upon a new sequence of occurrences of the same stimulus. Further, habituation is reduced, sometimes to the point of being almost unobservable, if the organism's response to repetitive stimulation produces rewarding feedback. From a behavioral engineering standpoint, the combination of properties seems admirably contrived to make the organism always as well prepared to respond to changes in stimulation as the demands of its current situation permit.

In contrast to the relative invariance of its properties, the part played by habituation in the life of an organism varies greatly over ontogenetic and phylogenetic levels. In the lowest organisms studied experimentally (for example, stentor, amoeba), the only form of learning clearly demonstrable is habituation to repeated mechanical stimulation (Humphrey, 1933). From the standpoint of the experimental psychologist, at least, much the same seems to be true of the newborn human infant. Although other forms of learning may already be in progress, much of what can be observed falls under the category of habituation and with quantitative properties generally similar to those observed even in the adult (Graham, 1973).

At the higher phylogenetic levels and in the mature organism, including the adult human being, habituation of various reflexes appears to be very similar to that observed in lower forms and may even be mediated by similar neural mechanisms. However, this reflex-level habituation is demonstrable only under rather special circumstances, and these circumstances rarely obtain outside of the laboratory, except perhaps for the orienting reflex, much studied as a possible index of selective attention (for example, Sokolov, 1963). Nonetheless, decremental processes with properties similar to those of habituation can be observed even with molar behaviors far above the reflex level, for example, responses of human beings to symbolic and even verbal stimuli (Sokolov, 1963; Syz, 1926).

Although the term *habituation* has customarily been used to denote a behavioral process with common functional properties, the usage may change, for in the most comprehensive theory so far advanced (Groves & Thompson, 1973), it refers to only one of two inferred processes associated with repetitive stimulation. At least in the case of the orienting response, the stimulus, upon successive repetitions, is assumed simultaneously to generate an habituating process with respect to the specific stimulus–response association and a sensitization of the general state of arousal. The observed course of response decrement is conceived to be a resultant of these opposed processes, which have different time courses.

2. Classical Conditioning

Processes at least phenotypically similar to conditioning have been observed even in some of the lowest invertebrates, notably paramecia (Gelber, 1952) and planaria (Kimmel & Yaremko, 1966) and indeed the latter study exhibits phenomena going beyond mere anticipatory responding and including an analog of the partial reinforcement effect. It is, of course, unlikely that the neural or biochemical basis is similar in lower and higher organisms. As with habituation, it seems most plausible that the functional similarities are dictated by adaptive requirements. Just as every organism needs some means of avoiding capture by repeated stimuli, organisms with any appreciable capacity to vary their behavior certainly need some means of anticipating coming events so that appropriate preparatory responses can be selected.

This signal function appears in its simplest and clearest form in classical conditioning. Conditioning is fastest and surest in the case of the most intense unconditioned stimuli (hence the most traumatic or dangerous events) or, in appetitive cases, at high-drive levels. Likelihood and speed of conditioning likewise prove directly related to the information value of the unconditioned stimulus (Rescorla, *Handbook*, Vol. 2, Chapter 1). If the contingency between the signaling and the signaled stimulus is broken, the tendency to anticipate the latter, as manifest in anticipatory responding, decreases (experimental extinction) but upon reinstatement of earlier contingencies relearning and reextinction proceed more rapidly; that is, if it has been necessary to anticipate an event once, the organism exhibits increasing proficiency at learning about it in the future.

Although phenomena with very similar properties to classical conditioning occur in nearly all organisms, in the higher organisms conditioning is identifiable mainly with respect to visceral functions (for example, glandular secretion) and very restricted classes of reflex movements. For the most part, conditioning involving instrumental or operant behavior comes to be overlaid by more complex, largely verbal processes. Associative learning in higher organisms, including the human being, is similar in some respects to conditioning (hence, the frequently noted analogy between paired-associate learning and conditioning, see, for example, Nelson, 1971; Rudy, 1974), but it is probably not fruitful to press the analogy too far.

Like habituation, conditioning is coming to be interpreted by many investigators in terms of processes of memory and response selection rather than as an automatic strengthening of connections by virtue of repeated occurrences (for example, Estes, 1973; Konorski, 1967; Whitlow, 1976). In its classical form, that is, as it appears nearly always in the lower organisms and for restricted reflex preparations in the higher organisms, conditioning can be most simply interpreted as a matter of stimulus substitution. Some unconditioned stimulus, usually a biologically significant one, originally elicits a preprogrammed response, and upon paired presentations of this unconditioned stimulus with a preceding signal stimulus, the latter comes to evoke the same response or one very similar to the unconditioned reaction. In these instances, a translation into the terminology of memory would seem gratuitous. However, in some instances even in subhuman vertebrates (notably, the conditioned emotional response, or CER, Estes, 1973; Estes & Skinner, 1941) and in nearly all instances of conditioning in human beings involving striate musculature (Ross & Ross, 1976), the behavior taken to index conditioning, hence, the "conditioned response," bears little resemblance to any behavior identifiable as an unconditioned response. Since the experience of paired presentation of a conditioned stimulus (CS) and an unconditioned stimulus (US) in these instances yields evidence of learning by way of very different behaviors under very different conditions, it may be the description in terms of concepts of memory that comes to have the greatest theoretical economy. That is, as a consequence of paired presentations, a CS comes to evoke memory of the US that followed it, and, further, of the response made to the US in a particular context. The same information retained in memory concerning the relation between CS and US may then yield quite different behavioral manifestations if the context changes.

With regard to age trends, in the case of the human being, rudimentary evidence of conditioning has been obtained even in the fetus (Wickens & Wickens, 1940) and many of the principal phenomena of conditioning in infants as young as it is feasible to study (Kimble, 1961). Beyond early infancy, constancy rather than variation with age is the conspicuous generalization. Over most of the life span of human beings, speed and other quantitative properties of conditioning in the case of glandular, smooth muscle, and simple reflex responses have proved virtually invariant with age, and, further, with measures of mental development or mental retardation (Estes, 1970). In most other cases, both in and out of the laboratory, and most certainly in the instance of that favorite of American investigators, eyelid conditioning, the phenomena observed in human beings under the experimental arrangements of conditioning clearly represent mixtures of conditioning in the classical sense and verbally mediated processes (Grant, 1972; Hilgard, 1938; Ross & Ross, 1976).

As a consequence of the enormous range of guises in which phenomena akin to conditioning appear, it is not surprising that one can find almost commensurate variability in usage of the term *conditioning* in the literature, ranging from extremely strict constructions (Gormezano & Kehoe, 1975) to identification of conditioning with any form of associative learning. I am in no better position than most anyone else to legislate commonality, but I would suggest that one will encounter little ambiguity throughout the volumes of the present *Handbook* and avoid some unnecessary confusion in other contexts if one reserves the term *conditioning* to refer to learning that depends on relations of temporal succession and contingency between conditioned and unconditioned stimuli and on the intensity relations of both to the background context in the manner characteristic of classical Pavlovian conditioning. Although at one time I used such terminology as *verbal conditioning* as often as anyone (for example, Estes, 1964), I no longer do so.

3. *Higher Forms of Learning*

Although textbooks on learning almost universally distinguish "lower" from "higher" learning phenomena or processes, the terms are used in several rather different senses. Within the sphere of conditioning, lower and higher refer to the remoteness of a learned association from the original unconditioned or reinforcing stimulus. Thus, in classical conditioning, a CS that has been paired with a US can subsequently itself be used in the role of a US, the learning that results being denoted *higher order conditioning*. Similarly, in operant conditioning, a stimulus that has preceded reward is found to take on the properties of a secondary reward and can be used to shape performance when it in turn is made contingent on the occurrence of some action or action sequence. In the operant domain, especially, this chaining can be continued and, even in what are commonly termed lower organisms, can lead to rather complex learned behavior sequences. In theories of conditioning, from Pavlov (1927) to Rescorla (1973), the prevailing view seems to be that these higher order phenomena do not involve any genuinely new principles but rather may be regarded as a pyramiding or cascading of processes and mechanisms that can be studied in simpler forms in the basic conditioning experiments.

Still further removed from, or less dependent on, the basic operation of pairing specific responses and reinforcements are forms of learning termed *observational learning* and *hypothesis selection*. In the former, the organisms, usually children in the extensive research of Bandura (1971) and his associates, have an opportunity to obtain information concerning relationships between actions and rewards by observing models (that is, other individuals) and to use this information to modify their own behaviors in later test situations so as to increase the likelihood of reward. The fact that this form of learning occurs so ubiquitously in human beings and can quite clearly be demonstrated even in some subhuman animals has been taken as one source of evidence that, in general, the function of reinforcement in learning can be dissociated into at least two aspects: the acquisition of information concerning relations between situations and reinforcing events and the control of decisions or choices by feedback from such information (Bandura, 1977; Estes, 1969a, 1972b).

The basic premise of hypothesis-selection models, especially as developed by Levine (1975), is that in most learning by human beings and higher animals that goes on outside the laboratory, single responses are too small a unit for fruitful analysis. Rather, it is assumed that the individual develops a repertoire of hypotheses or strategies, each of which governs a family of specific actions and that most trial-and-error learning can best be described in terms of the selection of an appropriate member of a set of hypotheses or strategies rather than the selection of a particular response. The viewpoint that I have previously advanced (Estes, 1971) concerning learning by hypothesis selecting is that it does not necessarily involve new principles of learning or memory but, rather, may yield to analysis in terms of the same principles that have been worked out in studies of simpler forms of conditioning and learning, the principles now being applied to higher order response units or organizations.

It needs to be recognized, however, that although it may be useful for some investigators of learning to proceed on the working hypothesis that such higher forms of learning as observational learning and hypothesis selection may be ultimately analyzable in principle into constituent associations between stimulus and response units, in actuality there are almost no examples of such analyses being carried through, and efforts to do so have not to date generally proved rewarding. Rather, progress toward useful interpretations of these ubiquitous forms of human learning has occurred largely within the framework of concepts of memory and information processing.

The question whether such "cognitive" concepts as memory and perception should be held to fall higher on some scale of mental development or complexity than concepts of conditioning is again difficult to answer if one demands evidence and not simply opinion. What can be said is that at one time the prevailing answer among psychologists was certainly affirmative but that there has been some erosion of that view with the advances of information-processing theories. An alternative viewpoint is that memory, for example, may in a sense be a more fundamental concept than either learning or conditioning, memory processes and structures being involved in all forms of learning. This idea is not peculiar to those who would be called cognitive psychologists. For example, Konorski (1967) presents the view that conditioning is simply a special case of associative memory, the conditioned reflex being not a lower form of learning but simply an experimentally privileged instance of association, privileged in that there is a

built-in indicator, the conditioned response, that serves as an especially convenient "tracer" of changes in the organism's memory for experiences with the
conditioned and unconditioned stimuli. The study of conditioning cannot be held
to deliver in any meaningful sense the units of which higher forms of learning are
built, but it does offer special advantages for revealing functional properties that
are common to all varieties of learning, although easier to discern and quantify in
simpler preparations.

B. Functional Properties of Conditioning and Learning

The vast amount of research on conditioning has often been justified in part in
terms of the value of the simplified conditioning situation in facilitating the
analysis and explication of basic principles that may pervade all forms of learning. How has this expectation fared? In one sense not well, for one finds in the
current literature numerous expressions of dissatisfaction, ranging from the mild
regret that progress has not been as fast as one might wish to strong claims
regarding the impossibility of general laws of learning (for example, Seligman,
1970). The point of view on this issue to which one seems to be led by the
discussion in the preceding section and the firmer documentation in Volumes 1
and 2 of the *Handbook* is that some goals have proved unrealistic, but others,
perhaps equally valuable, still offer promise of attainment.

   On the first tack, it surely becomes ever clearer that even apparently similar
learning mechanisms are based on very different neurobiological processes and
structures in different species and that there is little reason for optimism with
regard to very general explanatory theories. But on the second tack, it has at the
same time become clear that many functional properties of learning and memory
are very similar across wide variations in situations and biological categories.
Even organisms widely separated in the phylogenetic scale face similar problems
of adaptation to a common physical environment, and, consequently, one should
perhaps not be surprised at the emergence of functionally similar learning processes just as has been the case with respiration, reproduction, and other adaptive
functions. The importance of understanding the diversity of species-specific
behavioral organizations and modes of adjustment has deservedly received increasing emphasis during recent years in the literature of ethology, comparative
psychology, and even learning theory (Bolles, 1975; Hinde, 1973; Stevenson-
Hinde, 1973). Here I propose to highlight the other side of the picture by
summarizing some of the well-established functional principles of learning, with
brief indications regarding their continuity in form from conditioning through
human learning and information processing.

1. Temporal Contiguity

In neurophysiological theories of conditioning (for example, Hebb, 1949;
Konorski, 1967), it seems almost universally to be assumed that the central

events corresponding to the stimuli or responses that are to be associated must occur in temporal contiguity in order to enable the contact at the electrophysiological or biochemical level that makes learning possible. Whether or not this assumption is correct, it seems clear that organisms almost universally operate functionally on the principle that the best predictor of a significant event is usually to be found among its closest temporal predecessors. Thus, degree of temporal contiguity is nearly always found to be a strong determiner of the probability or speed of learning, with usually some optimal interval short of simultaneity, and with the steepness of the gradients around the optimum point depending on other variables such as the degree of isolation from distractor events at the time of the learning experience. Not surprisingly, human beings, especially in learning situations involving language, are even more adept than are lower organisms at detecting correlations between events separated in time, and here one typically finds less steep gradients of temporal contiguity. However, even so, when events to be associated are separated in time of occurrence, their central representations evidently have to be brought together by means of rehearsal if retrievable associations between them are to be established in long-term memory.

2. Contingency

The concept of contingency has come into its own in the recent literature (for example, Rescorla, 1967; Staddon, 1975) as a factor fully as important as temporal contiguity for the interpretation of conditioning. Many facts that would otherwise seem unrelated are brought together and enlightened by the principle that the behavioral effects of a sequence of conditioning trials depend on the organism's having an opportunity to learn not just that a CS follows a US, but that the probability of the US is higher immediately following a CS than at other times in the same context. More formally, if B is any reinforcing stimulus and A is any signalling stimulus (a CS or discriminative stimulus), then, functionally, conditioning involves the acquisition of information concerning the difference between the probability of B given A ($P(B|A)$), and the probability of B given the absence of A ($P(B|\bar{A})$), with behavioral evidence of conditioning ordinarily appearing only if conditions are such that the probability of B given A is greater than the probability of B given the absence of A.

An extreme example of the importance of differential contingencies is given in a study by Rescorla (1968) in which a given number of paired occurrences of a CS followed by shock in a CER conditioning paradigm yielded results varying from strong evidence of conditioning to no evidence of conditioning, depending on the frequency with which shocks occurred unpaired with the CS in the same situation. Similarly, in human trial-and-error learning situations, it is easy to show that information concerning differential contingencies almost completely outweighs the presumably satisfying effects of actually receiving rewards for correct responses (Estes, 1969a, 1972b).

It should be understood that the important role of differential contingencies over sequences of trials or experiences does not necessarily rule out the possibility of "one-trial conditioning." However, the concept of contingency is relevant to the conditions under which evidence of one-trial conditioning is likely to be obtained. Thus, if the first occurrence of an unconditioned stimulus in a novel context were preceded by a CS, conditions would be conducive to one-trial conditioning, for substantial information would be obtained on the one trial that the probability of the US is higher in the presence of the CS than in its absence in the given context. But if, as is often done, unpaired presentations of a CS and a US were given in the conditioning situation prior to the first paired presentation, then the one conditioning trial would provide very little information regarding differential contingencies, and one would expect the likelihood of one-trial conditioning to be small. In earlier literature (for example, Harris, 1941), presentations of the CS or the US or both separately prior to conditioning have been interpreted in terms of nonassociative factors, or as evidence for special processes such as latent inhibition (Lubow, 1973). However, whatever turns out to be the case with regard to underlying mechanisms, manipulations of this sort all lend themselves to a coherent interpretation in terms of differential contingencies.

3. Information Value

Since the first learning curves were plotted by the early experimenters on conditioning and learning, it has been apparent that a ubiquitous property is a diminishing returns characteristic. That is, as the sequence of learning trials proceeds under any given condition, learning functions show the greatest gains at first and progressively less as a final limit is approached. Major efforts to interpret this characteristic in terms of more primitive notions had in common the basic idea that as learning of the relation between any two events, A and B, proceeds and the predictability of B increases, less remains to be learned, and, consequently, the increments in information obtained from succeeding experiences are progressively smaller (Estes, 1950, 1959; Thurstone, 1930).

Another aspect of the role of information value has to do with the obvious fact that any event, A, that recurs in an organism's experience does not do so under exactly the same conditions of background context and that events or processes in the background will sometimes be relevant to the predictability of a subsequent event, B. Consequently, it must usually be the case that repeated trials will be needed in order for an organism to obtain adequate information that A is actually a valid predictor of B. Further, it is most often the case that appreciable time is required for properties of the background context to change. As a consequence, repeated learning trials too close together in time provide redundant samplings of the context, and, therefore, distribution of learning trials in time must generally be expected to yield the most efficient acquisition of information (Estes, 1955a, 1955b; Guthrie, 1933).

In an important recent extension of these ideas, Rescorla and Wagner (1972) have added the idea that when the signalling stimulus preceding some event, B, is a compound, say A_1A_2, the predictability of B from knowledge of its correlation with the compound at any point determines the amount of learning that occurs relative to the constituents. That is, as the organism's tendency to anticipate B upon occurrence of the compound A_1A_2 increases, the amount of learning that will occur on any trial relative to either A_1 or A_2 separately decreases. This idea accounts nicely for the phenomenon Kamin (1969) has termed *blocking of conditioning*, together with other effects that other investigators have attributed to selective attention or other processes (see, for example, Mackintosh, 1975; Rudy & Wagner, 1975).

4. Readiness

The conspicuous fact that relations between various pairs of events are not equally easy to learn for a given organism has given rise to various concepts having to do with "readiness" for conditioning or learning. Konorski (1948) has, for example, offered the generalization that conditioning is always a matter of realizing potential connections. Thus, with respect to associative connections that might be formed, pairs of stimuli or events can be ordered from those between which strong unconditioned, in some instances presumably innate, associative connections exist through pairs of stimuli that are not innately connected but for which associations are easily learned to combinations of stimuli that are very difficult to associate. The studies of Garcia and his associates (for example, Garcia & Koelling, 1966), showing that conditioned associations between gustatory stimuli can readily be formed at very long time intervals whereas the same is not true of associations between, say, gustatory and visual stimuli, have been taken to support the idea that this form of readiness has to do with the innate biological substrate of the organism. Whatever the interpretation, the fact is clear that conditioning, or indeed any form of associative learning, depends strongly on the particular stimuli or events involved and their relationships to the biology and ecology of the organism (Bolles, 1975; Seligman, 1970; Shettleworth, 1972).

Even in human verbal learning it is found that the formation of durable associations in memory between words or concepts is greatly facilitated if these are connected prior to the given learning experience by some chain of associations (for example, "natural language mediators," Prytulak, 1971). Further, there has been much interest in the possibility that states of special readiness for particular forms of learning characterize particular points of an organism's lifespan. However, except for some reasonably convincing demonstrations in the cases of imprinting and the learning of bird songs (see, for example, Brown, 1975), firm evidence is largely lacking. There is little doubt that functionally the conception is well founded, but it may be that, for the most part, states of readiness for particular forms of learning depend mainly on prior learning rather than on age per se.

5. *Motivational Relevance*

Another almost ubiquitous observation at a functional level is that associations are more easily formed and more likely to be durable if they are relevant to a motivational state of the organism or to some ongoing activity (which may come down to the same thing, since ongoing activities are presumably motivated). In the case of conditioning, Konorski (1967) included as a basic premise of his general theory the assumption that formation of an association between the neural units corresponding to any two stimuli depends on the activation of the recipient unit by an emotive or drive system. The well-known importance of intensity of an unconditioned stimulus would, for example, be presumably derivative to this general principle, since intense unconditioned stimuli would always be assumed to activate emotive or drive systems.

In human learning the efficacy of reinforcing events in the sense of rewards and punishments depends strongly on their relation to ongoing activities. For example, Nuttin and Greenwald (1968) classified learning situations into *closed* vs. *open* tasks, with the major assumption that rewards or punishments occurring in closed tasks have little or no effect on the individual's tendency to repeat actions that occur during the task on future occasions, whereas the same rewards or punishments occurring in open tasks do lead to increased tendencies to repeat the constituent actions. A rather similar conception has been presented by Estes (1972b). The common idea is that in some situations, corresponding to the closed tasks of Nuttin and Greenwald, the individual has no information indicating that reinforcement contingencies obtaining within the given situation will hold outside it, whereas in the other cases, the open tasks, the individual does have information available indicating that the contingencies observed during the particular learning experience will obtain on future occasions and perhaps in different situations.

6. *Limited Availability*

An aspect of the concepts of information value and diminishing returns that has been important enough to merit special attention might be termed the *principle of limited availability*. This concept has to do with the fact that not all of the units or subsystems involved in an organism's processing, storage, and retrieval of information from any learning experience are simultaneously maintained in a state of maximum availability. Rather, as a consequence of the continual fluctuations in stimulus input from the environment and in an organism's internal state, the availability of various units and subsystems for participation in a task fluctuates over time. The implications of this idea for learning and retention at the level of conditioning have been developed in the concept of stimulus fluctuation (Estes, 1955a, 1955b) and at the level of human memory in encoding variability (Martin, 1971).

Since the availability of perceptual and memory units for participation in a task fluctuates, it follows that if all of the units of a given kind that might potentially contribute to a task are to be recruited, sufficient time must be allowed so that all will have opportunity to fluctuate into the state of availability at some point. Further, massing learning experiences close together in time will limit the opportunities for fluctuation and, therefore, will tend to be inefficient from the standpoint of recruiting the maximum number of participatory units.

The other side of the coin is that units in a state of high availability at a particular time are likely to remain so a short time later. Thus, it follows that very short-term retention will be favored if learning experiences or trials have been massed closely together in time so that all of the units potentially available at the given time have been sampled, whereas long-term retention will be favored if learning trials are distributed so that as many as possible of the units that might be available at a later time will have been sampled during the learning series.

7. Context

One of the most firmly established principles in the psychology of memory is that retrieval of a stimulus-response association or any other item of information stored in memory depends directly on the degree to which the original context is reinstated at the time of a retention test (see, for example, McGeoch & Irion, 1952; Murdock, 1974; Tulving & Donaldson, 1972). In classical conditioning the contextual factor is most apparent in the effects of changing the experimental background. For example, Konorski (1967) presented a number of studies showing not only that probability of occurrence of a conditioned response (CR) depends on the intactness of the original experimental background, but even more strikingly that if responses are conditioned to two different stimuli in two different backgrounds and then the combinations of stimulus with background are shifted, it is generally the background rather than the CS that is dominant in determining the transfer response. Another manifestation of context in conditioning is to be found in the phenomenon of "state dependence," observed in connection with the changes of internal state of the animal produced by drugs (for example, Spear, 1976).

In studies of human memory, changes in general background context can be shown to have measurable effects, but much more important is the role played by more local contexts. Thus, in one of the most influential treatments of retrieval processes in recall, Tulving (1968) has introduced the concept of a *retrieval cue*. This term refers to some specific element of the local context accompanying a to-be-remembered word or concept (the retrieval cue often being itself a word) that is stored in memory together with the to-be-remembered item and serves later as a facilitator of recall. In a more formal quantitative model intended to apply both to animal discrimination learning and to human discrimination and conceptual learning, Medin (1975) has developed numerous implications, with supporting evidence, for the assumption that the inputs from discriminative cues and contexts combine multiplicatively in the determination of retrieval.

8. Stimulus Functions: Salience, Encoding, Dimensionality

Few concepts enter so pervasively into the study of behavior but so lack a commensurate associated body of theory as that of stimulus salience or distinctiveness. The disparity perhaps owes to the earlier tradition in experimental psychology of proceeding on the assumption that laws of conditioning and learning apply almost independently of the nature of the particular stimulus involved. As a consequence the individuals who were developing more formalized theories of conditioning and learning (as Hull, 1943; Skinner, 1938; Spence, 1937; Tolman, 1932) made no formal provision for a concept of salience, thus paving the way for an overreaction to such recent events as the "Garcia phenomenon." The course of events was quite different in ethology, where a great deal of research and a great deal of literature was focused on working out in detail the properties of stimuli that prove salient (that is, which readily gain control of behavior or enter into learning) for a large variety of animal species and relating these properties to the biology and ecology of the organisms.

At the present time it seems safe to say that psychologists generally, regardless of their theoretical attachments, are well aware that at all ontogenetic and phylogenetic levels and in all types of situations, the properties subsumed under the notion of salience or distinctiveness of stimuli are among the most potent determiners of speed and durability of learning. Further, there is probably fairly general agreement on the distinction introduced formally by Lovejoy (1968) between a relatively fixed component of salience, presumably a function of innate organization, and a variable component. Little of a general character can be said about the fixed component except that it is usually to some extent a function of stimulus intensity and that the relative saliences of the different stimuli that may be operative in a situation always need to be evaluated before specific predictions can be made regarding rates of conditioning or learning.

The variable component, first clearly recognized in Lawrence's (1949) conception of acquired distinctiveness of cues, is of special importance for analyses of discrimination learning in higher animals and man. Stimuli or stimulus attributes that have been associated with rewarding outcomes in a given learning situation not only tend to gain control of the immediately rewarded behaviors but also manifest increased capability of entering into associations for the given organism if characteristics of the situation and response requirements change.

Although investigators often, for brevity, speak of associations between stimuli and responses or between stimuli and other stimuli, it is no longer assumed in any influential theory that representations of physical stimulus patterns per se are what enter into associations with responses or into other forms of memory storage. Rather, conditioning and learning, memory storage, and retrieval are assumed to occur with respect to stimuli as encoded by attentional and perceptual processes. Even in classical conditioning, Konorski (1962) has emphasized that conditioning occurs relative to a stimulus as perceived in some sense and that the properties to which the organism responds may vary as a function of contingencies in a learning situation even though the physical stimulus input does not vary.

In the case of discrimination learning, Lawrence (1963) first made fully explicit the idea of learning relative to stimuli as encoded, and this concept was implemented in the mechanism of analyzers in the more formal treatment of discrimination learning by Sutherland and Mackintosh (1971). Analyzers are presumed to be part of the innate equipment of the organism with the function of analyzing stimulus inputs and yielding as their outputs values of the stimuli on important sensory dimensions, these values then entering into processes of discrimination and generalization. In still more formally developed discrimination theories, for example those of Zeaman and House (1963) and of Lovejoy (1968), it is further assumed, with much supporting evidence, that reinforcing events in discrimination learning situations have as one of their important effects the selective strengthening of tendencies to respond to relevant and to ignore irrelevant stimulus dimensions. Much the same conception is represented in Trabasso and Bower's (1968) treatment of selective attention in adult human discrimination learning. The increasing centrality of the role of stimulus dimension in discrimination-learning theories parallels rather strikingly the increasing tendency for theories of human memory storage to be formulated in terms of the conception that representations of stimulus patterns or sensory experiences in memory take the form of lists or vectors of attribute values (Bower, 1967; Estes, 1976; Norman & Rumelhart, 1970; Spear, 1976; Underwood, 1969).

9. Stimulus Generalization

A stimulus function as ubiquitous in the practical control of behavior as salience but better represented in formal theories and models is stimulus generalization, or generalization decrement. Whenever a response has been conditioned or learned in any situation, one can expect that the probability or speed of evocation of the response will be reduced if the situation changes. One speaks of stimulus generalization if the change is in the conditioned stimulus or discriminative stimulus specifically associated with the reference response and of contextual effects if the change is in nonspecific background stimulation, whether external or internal to the organism.

The concept of stimulus generalization in the theories of Hull (1943) and Spence (1937) differs only in detail from Thorndike's (1913) interpretation of transfer in terms of proportion of identical elements between training and transfer situations. For both Hull and Spence, and indeed virtually all other learning theorists of the same period (including, for example, Atkinson & Estes, 1963; Bush & Mosteller, 1951; Restle, 1961), the heart of a theory of generalization was a suitable mathematical function relating training to test stimuli along relevant sensory dimensions. In the more recent approach of Heinemann and Chase (1975), the concept of generalization is brought into closer relation to other current work in cognitive psychology with the introduction of the concepts of signal-to-noise ratio and the decision criterion. In the model developed by Heinemann and Chase, it is recognized that, as a consequence of noise both in the environment and in the organism, a series of administrations of any given stimulus to an organism must give rise to a distribution of sensory states. Further, any two stimuli that are physically similar will give rise to distributions of states that overlap; consequently, the occurrence of a given sensory state does not provide the organism with unique information as to the external stimulus giving rise to it. The organism is assumed to deal with this uncertainty by setting a criterion on any stimulus dimension such that sensory states whose values fall on one side of the criterion are interpreted as instances of a training stimulus and states whose values fall on the other side are attributed to a different stimulus. Observed behavior in tests of stimulus generalization must, therefore, depend both on the degree of overlap of the distributions of sensory states produced by different test stimuli and on the criterion adopted by the organism, which may in turn depend on motivational and reinforcement variables.

In much of the classical research on stimulus generalization and discrimination, it was possible to get by without appreciation of the role of the decision criterion since, in general, conditions of reinforcement and motivational variables were held constant. It is becoming clear, however, that the concept of the criterion needs to be taken into full account whenever one is concerned with interpreting behavior as a joint function of stimulus and motivational conditions.

Similarly, the background context in which experimentally manipulated conditioned or discriminative stimuli are administered is usually held constant and, thus, has often escaped explicit inclusion in models for generalization and discrimination. The arbitrariness of focusing one's attention on experimentally manipulated stimuli has gradually become apparent, however, and in the work of Spiker (1963) and Medin (1976), the idea is formally developed that performance and memory always depend jointly and, roughly speaking equally, on discriminative stimuli and the background contexts in which they occur. The one exception to this last generalization is perhaps the sphere of concept learning in which training is specifically arranged to develop independence of context. Investigators who have developed an appreciation of the way in which stimulus and context enter, usually inextricably but under special conditions separably, into conditioning and learning should perhaps be prepared for the otherwise apparently novel distinction between episodic and semantic memory that has rather suddenly become prominent in current interpretations of human memory, as will be brought out in the sequel.

10. Reward and Punishment, Feedback and Choice

One of the principal functions of learning in adaptation is to enable the organism to profit from experience with regard to the ways in which its actions lead to rewards and punishments. On the whole, instrumental behavior does serve this function, hence, the emergence of hedonistic principles early in the history of psychology and the long standing acceptance of the law of effect, at least as an empirical generalization.

Specific assumptions embodied in the law of effect as formulated by Thorndike (1931) are that rewarding outcomes lead to a direct and automatic strengthening of the association between the action and the situation in which it occurred; punishments lead to a corresponding weakening, but perhaps indirectly via the instigation of alternative behaviors that lead to more positive outcomes. Reinforcement theory as elaborated by Hull (1943) and Skinner (1938) continued to conform quite closely to this characterization.

In contrast, much current theorizing about reinforcement presumes a much looser coupling between rewarding or punishing outcomes and action tendencies (Atkinson & Wickens, 1971; Bolles, 1975; Buchwald, 1969; Estes, 1969a, 1969b, 1970; Miller, 1963). What I take to be the predominant contemporary view is that learning with regard to rewards and punishments is primarily a matter of the organism's storing information concerning relationships between situations, actions, and consequences so that, in effect, it has available at any time estimates of the conditional probability of various rewarding or punishing outcomes given the occurrence or nonoccurrence of particular actions in a given situation. In a situation calling for choice among possible actions, the organism, whether human or subhuman, is assumed in this view first to recall actions that it has employed on past occasions. Then, perhaps after initiating tentatively one or another response sequence, the organism generates expectations concerning the probable rewarding or punishing outcome and, finally, proceeds to carry out a given action or to inhibit it and engage in further "vicarious trial and error" as appropriate.

What view of reinforcement is more nearly "correct"? The answer, I suggest, depends on where one looks in the range of experimental situations that have been studied and in ontogenetic and phylogenetic sequences. On the one hand, I think there is little or no firm evidence against the narrower conception of the law of effect or operant conditioning principle in the case of trial-and-error behavior of the lower organisms and even of restricted subsystems (in particular, visceral responses) or behaviors in highly restricted situations in the case of higher organisms including man. In this last category would fall, for example, the effects of reinforcement observed in the case of mental defectives, psychotic individuals in institutions, even prisoners or others in highly limited and structured environments. In all of these cases, either because no elaborate memory system is available or because the environment severely restricts the actions that can be initiated, there is little occasion for choice among alternative behaviors. Rather, there is usually simply a choice between making or inhibiting some particular response, usually one dictated by the species-specific organization in the case of lower animals or by instructions and task environment in the case of human beings.

By contrast, in relation to much instrumental or operant behavior of higher animals and perhaps nearly all normal human behavior, reinforcement can only be effectively understood in terms of distinct processes of acquiring information regarding stimulus-outcome and response-outcome contingencies and employing this information in conjunction with overt or covert search or exploratory behaviors in order to allow choices among actions to be guided by information concerning probable consequences. In these latter cases, it is not generally necessary that the organism actually perform the correct (that is, potentially most highly rewarded) response in a given situation and observe its consequences, but only that information concerning contingencies be obtainable in some manner— as by the observation of models (Bandura, 1971) or even more indirect forms of communication (Estes, 1969a, 1972b).

11. Reinforcement Schedules

Over many decades a large part of the experimental literature on the control of behavior by reward has been concerned with various kinds of intermittency, most conspicuously the "partial reinforcement effect," or increased resistance to extinction of an instrumental or operant response following intermittent as compared to continuous reinforcement. Until recently interpretations of the phenomena associated with intermittent reinforcement and subsequent extinction were for the most part performance oriented and highly specific to particular experimental paradigms. The literature of operant conditioning, following the extensive analyses of Ferster and Skinner (1957), has focused largely on interval and ratio schedules, and on various complex schedules generated from these in combination. The descriptive system initiated by Skinner has been amplified and formalized by Schoenfeld, Cummings, and Hearst (1956), among others, but has rarely been augmented at a more theoretical level except for interpretations of specific phenomena in terms of contextual relationships. The central idea was that extinction of a previously rewarded response does not occur, or is mitigated, if at the beginning of extinction the context in which the organism finds itself (including traces of immediately preceding stimuli and responses) closely resembles a context in which it has previously been rewarded.

Still more performance oriented are the frustration hypothesis of Amsel (1967) and the cognitive-dissonance hypothesis of Lawrence and Festinger (1962). According to the former, extinction is a consequence of the frustrating effects of nonreward, and these effects are mitigated if the animal has experience with occasional nonrewards during the period of training preceding extinction. The idea of Lawrence and Festinger is essentially the converse of Amsel's, namely, that if an organism has continued experience with a response that is not always rewarded, the effect of the nonrewards is to increase the attractiveness of the state of affairs produced by the response and thus to maintain the behavior even during a period of extinction.

A new development during the present decade is the emergence of a body of theory dealing much more specifically with the nature of the information acquired by an organism under various routines or schedules of reinforcement that enable it to anticipate when outcomes of actions are likely to be rewarding or frustrating. In the context of experiments involving discrete trials (as with the runway or T-maze), these approaches embody the assumption, in effect if not explicitly, that the organism forms representations in memory of patterns of reward and nonreward that have been experienced over preceding trials of an experiment (even if these are widely spaced in time) and performs as though expecting these patterns to repeat themselves (for example, Capaldi, 1967). Thus, if the animal has repeatedly experienced a sequence of nonrewards followed by reward, then the occurrence of successive nonrewards at the beginning of an experimental extinction session would not in itself be expected to lead to any decrement in performance.

In the context of continuous trial experiments, the corresponding idea is that the organism forms representations in memory of time intervals terminating in reward or nonreward and at any given moment performs in accord with its estimate of the time likely to elapse before the next occurrence of reward (for example, Gibbon, 1977; Staddon, 1974). The central ideas of this latter approach, which as formalized by Gibbon seems to offer considerable explanatory power, are, in effect, that the organism stores in long-term memory representations of time intervals of various lengths in the situation together with the events (reward or nonreward) that terminate them and, further, at any moment has available in short-term memory a representation of the interval since the preceding reinforcing event in a form that can be matched against various representations in the long-term store in order to generate expectations.

C.   Concepts of Information Processing

Studies associated with the rubric of information processing typically deal with the extraction, storage, and manipulation of information without regard to immediate behavioral functions or purposes the information might be relevant to. These studies and the associated theory shade into learning at one boundary and into "higher" cognitive processes at the other. The body of research deals primarily with the processing of information that is explicitly categorical in character. It nearly always presupposes that the individual studied has permanently stored in memory an assemblage of informational units—for example, digits, letters, words. The tasks investigated deal with the recognition or identification of these units as they occur in stimulus inputs, with memory both for what units occurred and for their order, and with various kinds of judgments concerning relationships between units or sequences.

Basic concepts may be considered in four main categories, defined in reference to (a) structure of the processing system, (b) the units of information and their levels of organization or processing, (c) concepts having to do with processing stages, and (d) the sources of capacity limitation.

1. Memory Structure

A primary structural distinction recognized in some form in all theories of human information processing is that between a short-term buffer or working memory and long-term memory. The first of these is conceived to be an extremely limited capacity subsystem, capable of maintaining only a few items. These may come either from the very short-term modality-specific memory (icon, in the case of vision, or echoic memory, in the case of audition) generated by a sensory input or via associative routes from long-term memory. Although there is some controversy on this point, it is usually assumed that items decay from working memory unless maintained by some rehearsal process. Further it is generally assumed (see, for example, Baddeley, 1976) that cognitive operations such as comparative judgments, encoding operations, or linguistic transformations, can be performed only on the items currently held in working memory.

Long-term memory is conceived to be essentially unlimited in capacity and extremely diverse in content. For a reasonably full account of the principal concepts and related methods of investigation, one would need to consult at least the chapters by Smith in the present volume, Chase in Volume 5, Murdock and LaBerge in Volume 4, and Postman in Volume 3 of the *Handbook*. In attempting to bring order out of this array of phenomena and theory, I have found it most effective to begin with the distinction between *episodic* and *semantic* memory. As this distinction was proposed by Tulving (1968), episodic memory refers to representations of events an individual has experienced together with the contextual settings in which the events occurred. Thus, asking an individual whether the automobile involved in an accident he had witnessed was a Chevrolet or asking him to recognize the automobile from a photograph of the incident would be rather clear-cut instances of testing for episodic memory. Contrariwise, asking the same individual whether Chevrolets are expensive would not.

Most research on long-term memory conducted in the laboratory deals with episodic memory in that retention is usually traced by testing for recall or recognition of stimuli or materials presented on specific occasions. In general, tests for episodic memory involve the reinstatement of all or part of the context in which to-be-remembered events occurred. When the reinstatement is relatively full one usually speaks of recognition, when only some very restricted portion of the context is reinstated one generally speaks of recall, and in the latter case the element of context used to evoke recall is denoted a *retrieval cue* (Tulving, 1968).

The nonepisodic aspects of long-term memory, termed *semantic* in Tulving's classification, are not so easy to define constructively. The intention is certainly to include all information stored in memory concerning properties of entities or events and their interrelationships that obtain generally, without reference to particular times or places. Certainly, a person's knowledge of word meanings falls in this category, hence, the denotation *semantic*. However, it seems unreasonable to me to exclude from this class information that is not necessarily verbalizable—concerning, for example, melodies, visual forms, textures of objects—and consequently I prefer to use a broader term such as *categorical* rather than semantic.

Perhaps the reason why many investigators have been content with the term *semantic* to denote nonepisodic long-term memory is that so much current research in this area has involved tasks in which subjects are asked to verify sentences concerning class memberships of objects, thus revealing their knowledge of the meanings of the words denoting the classes and the exemplars. As has been thoroughly discussed by Smith in this volume (Chapter 1), theories of semantic memory growing out of this research have taken two at least superficially distinct forms, one revolving around the concept of an associative network and the other around the concept of semantic features. There is no need to review these theories again at this point, but I shall proceed to characterize each of the two types of theory briefly and indicate how I think they may fit together.

In the many influential models for semantic memory falling within the neoassociationistic approach (Figure 1), an individual's memory for words or concepts and their interrelationships is represented by a network of associations. Typically, in the models running from Feigenbaum (1963) through Collins and Quillian (1972) and Anderson and Bower (1973) to Collins and Loftus (1975), the entities associated in the model are simply nodes that have the function of representing in some abstract sense the corresponding words or concepts and of providing something to be associated by connecting pathways.

In nearly all of the current models falling within this approach, it is assumed further that the associative networks are hierarchical in form, with upper levels corresponding to higher level categories and lower levels to subcategories or exemplars, as illustrated in the fragment of a hypothetical network shown in Figure 2. In terms of the diagram, it would be assumed that the node for the highest category, *animal,* is connected by pathways to the subordinate categories, *mammal* and *bird,* then the subcategory *bird* to exemplars such as *canary, ostrich,* and so on. Activation of any one node in the network by a stimulus input (for example, by the individual's hearing an appropriate word) is assumed to lead to activation of others by way of the connecting pathways. But the conduction takes time and hence longer pathways are expected to take more processing time. Thus, on this type of model it is expected that hearing the word

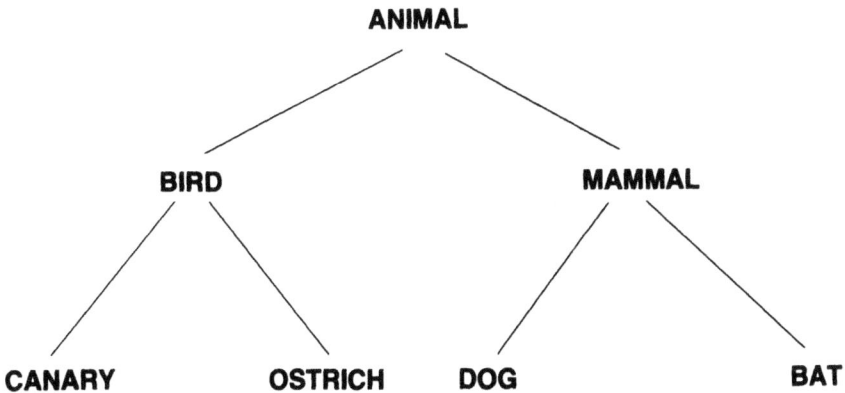

FIGURE 2.   A fragment of a hypothetical semantic-memory network, with associative pathways connecting superordinate categories to subordinate categories and exemplars.

canary would evoke memory of the word *bird* faster than it would evoke memory of the word *animal*.

In this particular instance, the implication has been borne out experimentally, but in other similar ones the evidence is not so clear. For example, the word *dog* evokes memory of *animal* with shorter reaction time than memory for *mammal*, which is not in accord with the model. It is possible for the word *dog* to evoke memory of the word *canary*, but only very indirectly, since there are no direct connections between items at the exemplar level, and thus an associative path would have to be traced upward from *dog* to the highest category and then down to *canary*. Activation of a category node, such as *bird,* is expected to generate excitation along all of the paths branching out from it downward and thus to activate at least partially all of the associated exemplars. Consequently, if, in the reaction-time experiments, the subject were presented first with the word *bird* and subsequently with one of the associated exemplars, say *canary,* he would be expected to respond to the latter more promptly than if *bird* had not been previously presented, a phenomenon termed *priming* in the current literature, and one nicely handled by the model.

In the other main family of semantic memory models (again fully reviewed by Smith in Chapter 1 of this volume), words or concepts are assumed to be represented in memory, not by nodes with connecting pathways but rather by hypothetical lists or vectors of semantic features. In Table 2 we give an illustration of the way in which the items that appeared in the fragmentary network in Figure 2 might be represented in a feature model. In the left-hand column is a listing of some of the attributes (for example, *respiration, reproduction*) that would enter into memory for meaning of the terms in question, and in the next three columns are possible values of these attributes (semantic features). The remaining columns show the features that would characterize memory for the

TABLE 2
Illustration of Semantic Feature Representations

Attribute	Value (feature)			Category	Subcategory		Exemplar		
	0	1	2	Animal	Bird	Mammal	Canary	Ostrich	Dog
Respiration	none	air breath	other	1	1	1	1	1	1
Reproduction	none	asexual	sexual	2	2	2	2	2	2
Growth	none	accretion	assimilation	2	2	2	2	2	2
Temperature	cold	warm			1	1	1	1	1
Coat	scales	feathers	fur		1	2	1	1	2
Locomotion	none	flies	runs				1	2	2

various category, subcategory, and exemplar terms. For example, the concept *animal* would be represented in terms of the features denoting that it breathes oxygen, undergoes sexual reproduction, and grows by assimilation. The concept *bird* would be characterized by these plus a feature denoting warm temperature and one denoting a feathered coat. Within the subcategory *bird,* a canary would be differentiated from an ostrich only by the feature referring to locomotion.

In this model, seeing or hearing a word denoting one of the categories or subcategories would evoke memory for the associated features, and this in turn would yield access to other concepts sharing the same features. For example, presentation of the word *animal* to an experimental subject would evoke memory for its features and thus in turn would weakly excite memory for all the sub-categories and exemplars sharing the same features, obviously providing a basis for the same priming phenomenon accounted for in a different way in the net-work model. If an individual were asked to verify a sentence such as, "A dog is an animal," it is presumed he would do so by remembering the features as-sociated with *dog,* then the features associated with *animal,* and making a term by term comparison on the list of attributes. If the features recalled for *animal* all matched some subset of those recalled for *dog,* then the response would be affirmative. If a mismatch were encountered on any attribute, then the response would be negative. Further, although this aspect does not seem to have been explicitly discussed by the authors of the principal semantic feature models, one would assume that encountering an object having a certain combination of fea-tures would evoke memory for the corresponding word (Estes, in press).

There have been numerous attempts to decide experimentally between network and feature models. The history has been that for particular realizations of each type of model, it has often been possible to obtain evidence favoring one or the other, but then it has always been possible to make local adjustments to the less favored of the two so that both account for the previously differentiating finding. Thus, the idea has come forward (Hollan, 1975; Smith, Chapter 1, this volume) that it is always possible to formulate a feature model that is homologous to any given network model, and vice versa. It is easy to see how either type of model can be mapped onto the other. Thus, the paths connecting *animal* with *bird* and *mammal* in Figure 2 can be taken simply as a visual characterization of the fact that the feature list for *animal,* shown in Table 2, has the same subset of elements in common with the list for *bird* and the list for *mammal* and so on for the other branches. Conversely, the tree diagram of the network models can be taken as a convenient way of sketching relationships between feature lists for words or concepts falling at different levels in the semantic-memory system. Given this equivalence, it would seem that the decisions between the two types of models can only be made for specific realizations that include both structural and processing assumptions in each case.

2. *Informational Units*

The items held in long-term memory are not conceived to be qualitatively all of a piece, but rather to comprise a number of units with systematic interrelationships at different levels of complexity. At the lowest level, it is conceived that an individual recognizes simple units such as individual letters or syllables that are heard or seen, not as holistic patterns, but rather as combinations of values on a few basic dimensions or attributes. These attributes, termed *critical features,* are relatively few in number. In the case of speech, there is considerable agreement on the basic ''vocabulary'' of features (Pisoni, Chapter 5, this volume). In the case of printed letters, no similar consensus exists, but a number of proposed systems are under investigation. In any event, it is assumed that all letters an syllables that can be identified in spoken discourse or printed text can be regarded as constructable from combinations of small numbers of these basic features. Words and still higher order linguistic units are then formed by combinations of letters or syllables. When an individual has encountered a spoken or printed display of linguistic material, the representation in memory takes the form of a listing of features, or a listing of words, or of higher order informational units depending on the degree of information processing that has been accomplished under the given task conditions. Generally, it is assumed that processing to levels of higher order units leads to more durable memory (Craik & Lockhart, 1972).

The early volumes of this *Handbook* were devoted primarily to the learning processes that give rise to these various information processing units, with this emphasis decreasing and giving way in the later volumes to a concentration on the nature of the units and the modes of interaction between perception and memory in tasks of differing levels of complexity. By way of an ''index,'' we can abstract from those more extensive treatments a summary of the processing units as shown in Table 3.

The concepts of features and feature detectors received their first major impetus in the neurophysiological studies of Hubel and Wiesel (1962) and of

TABLE 3
Informational Units Associated with Different Levels of Cognitive Processing

Process or mechanism	Units
Neurophysiological feature detection	Simple sensory attributes
Discrimination learning	Dimensionally encoded stimuli
Speech perception	Distinctive auditory features or phonological units
Reading	Critical features of letters
Short-term memory	Chunks, tags
Long-term memory	Semantic syntactic markers or features

Lettvin, Maturana, McCulloch, and Pitts (1959), showing selective responses of single cortical cells of animals to moving spots or contours with specific orientations in the visual field and, hence, suggesting that the cells serve as "detectors" for simple properties of the visual environment. More recently, the question has emerged whether the basic visual processing units, at least in the mammalian visual system, are better conceived in terms of detector channels attuned to limited ranges of spatial frequencies rather than detectors of contours or the like (Graham, in press). In any event, shortly thereafter, drawing primarily on behavioral rather than neurophysiological data, Mackintosh (1965) and Sutherland (1964) introduced the first of a new generation of discrimination-learning theories, based on concepts of selective attention, replacing the models of Hull (1950) and Spence (1937), in which stimulus analyzing had been treated as a matter of passive registration of environmental inputs. The approach of Mackintosh and Sutherland was built around the concept of *analyzers,* presumably innate mechanisms whereby the animal selectively attends to and processes sensory attributes or dimensions.

These developments at the levels of neurophysiology and animal learning primed, so to speak, investigators of human cognitive processes to seek similar feature analyzing mechanisms at still higher levels, but the form these were to take proved to be dictated not directly by the results of research on human perception and memory, but rather by inputs from linguistics. The entering wedge was the theoretical work of Jakobson, Fant, and Halle (1952), which suggested that the recognition of speech sounds can be accounted for on the basis of reactivity of the hearer to a small number of binary-valued *critical features,* as for example, tense versus lax consonant or grave versus acute vowel phonemes. This idea was taken up by experimental psychologists, for example, Wickelgren (1965), who showed that indeed confusion matrices obtained in experiments on speech perception and short-term memory can be well accounted for on the basis of a simple system of distinctive features. These successes in turn led Gibson (1969) and others to attempt similar analyses of the recognition of letters in reading in terms of distinctive features, an enterprise that continues to receive much attention in the literature, although so far with only limited success.

Current research on memory can fairly be said to be dominated by further extensions and elaborations of the feature concept. Thus, the conception of short-term memory as simply an image, in some sense, of the immediately preceding sensory experience has given way almost entirely to one of an encoding in terms of attributes or features. These attributes may refer to rather elementary visual or auditory features, as in the approach of Conrad (1967) or to abstract attributes such as repetition tags (Lee, 1976), chunks (Miller, 1956), or codes for groups of items (Johnson, Chapter 3, this volume). Similar ideas are making inroads even in the complex and hitherto almost unanalyzed area of human semantic memory with the concepts of semantic markers or features (fully discussed by Smith, Chapter 1, this volume).

3. *Factors Operative at Specific Processing Stages*

A principal characteristic of nearly all approaches to human information processing is the idea that the extraction and manipulation of information from stimulus inputs proceeds by way of a sequence of discrete stages of processing. At the first stage, patterns of stimulus information are registered on the receptor surfaces, and these patterns of activity are maintained for a short time, up to a second or two at most, in very short-term sensory memory systems: the visual persistence or "iconic memory" in the case of visual inputs and "echoic memory" in the case of auditory inputs. While the sensory pattern persists, values of the stimulus on various basic dimensions are evaluated by perceptual mechanisms, for example, feature detectors, and at the next processing stage outputs of simultaneously activated combinations of these detectors are compared with memory representations of alphanumeric characters or similar units. At either of these stages, depending on task requirements, a decision may be made as to whether properties of the input match representations in memory of features or feature combinations and an appropriate response can be generated. If responses are not called for at these stages, the process of comparison of the outputs of a preceding stage with representations in memory proceeds through higher levels of units (Estes, 1975; LaBerge, 1976).

The assumption that the successive stages of registration, encoding, matching, decision, and so on are nonoverlapping may not prove to be wholly satisfied in all instances. Nonetheless, the idea of serial processing through a succession of discrete stages has been extremely important for methodological purposes. On the supposition that each stage requires a measurable amount of processing time, which is in turn reflected in the individual's reaction time, estimates of the processing times of individual stages can be obtained by a subtractive procedure (Chase, 1978; Sternberg, 1975). Further, on the same assumption one can hope to determine whether the effects of various independent variables affect the same or different stages by ascertaining whether their effects on reaction time are additive (Sternberg, 1975). Pursuit of this method has yielded evidence, for example, that operations of stimulus degradation and variations in stimulus probability primarily influence encoding stages, whereas total memory load or processing load primarily affects stages of comparison or matching, and similarity or confusability between stimuli influences the stage of decision making.

The bodies of research reviewed in Volumes 4 through 6 of the *Handbook* yield a number of generalizations concerning the concepts and principles entering into the interpretation of tasks designed primarily to tap single stages of information processing. In the following summary we group factors associated with the three principal stages of search for signal or target stimuli, recognition or identification, and categorical decision.

a. Search.   In many if not most situations involving cognitive tasks, an individual must search overtly or covertly through an array or succession of noise stimuli or distractors in order to locate the signal stimulus carrying the sought for information. In the most systematic treatment of search processes to date (Schneider & Shiffrin, 1977; Shiffrin & Schneider, 1977), three factors have been implicated as primary determinants of the speed and accuracy with which individuals search through simultaneous or successive arrays of symbols such as alphanumeric characters. Perhaps most critical is constancy versus variability of the mapping of stimuli onto target versus noise categories. If in an individual's repeated experiences with a situation some subset of stimuli occur only as target or signal stimuli, and the remainder only as distractors or noise, a gradual shift occurs from what Schneider and Shiffrin term a *controlled* to an *automatic* search mode. In the controlled mode, the individual searches through an array of stimuli examining each in turn, with the search continuing until information accumulated permits a decision as to whether a sought for target is present and, if so, which of the stimuli encountered is the target. In this controlled mode, the search process is serial in character and relatively slow, proceeding, for example, at a rate on the order of 25 to 50 msecs per character through either visually presented arrays of letters or digits or collections of representations of letters or digits held in working memory.

Whether the search is exhaustive or self-terminating is determined to an important extent by the total memory load imposed by the task. When the load is relatively light, typically the search is exhaustive, that is, continuing through all members of the array with the decision being made after all possible targets have been examined. With heavier loads the search tends to be self-terminating, that is, proceeding only until a stimulus is encountered that meets the individual's criterion for a target.

If the mapping of stimuli into target versus noise categories varies from time to time, evidently this controlled mode of search is the only one available. But with sufficient experience under a constant mapping, individuals are found to shift to what Schneider and Shiffrin (1977) term *automatic processing,* a parallel process in which all distractor stimuli present are simultaneously and quickly rejected leaving only the target stimuli to receive any additional processing appropriate for the task. A conspicuous difference in data obtained under controlled versus automatic search conditions is that in the controlled mode, speed of locating a target is directly and strongly related to the size of the array in which the target is included, whereas in the automatic mode, speed of locating a target is virtually independent of the size of the array. Since automatic processing evidently develops only with experience in a specific type of situation, amount of practice must be considered in order to permit predictions of search efficiency together with constancy of mapping and total memory load.

b. Identification.   Whether signal stimuli are presented in backgrounds of noise or alone, one component of most cognitive tasks is a determination of the categories to which signal stimuli belong. One of the most important determiners of the efficiency of identification is the level of encoding of the stimulus, the levels that have been most studied being those corresponding to what Posner (1969, 1978) terms *physical* versus *name* matches. If, for example, the stimulus presented is an alphanumeric character visually displayed, the first stage of encoding involves simply the extraction of the combination of features making up the visual pattern. If a second stimulus is presented and a decision concerning similarity or difference required before encoding has progressed past this stage, the comparison must be made on the basis only of feature information. Comparisons at this level generally yield the shortest reaction times obtainable in comparison tasks. If an interval longer than about a second elapses between display of a character and the presentation of a comparison stimulus, the visually encoded representation of the first stimulus will have decayed before the second appears. In that case the task can be accomplished only if, while the visually coded representation of the first stimulus was available, processing continued to the point of assigning a label, typically a character name, to the stimulus. This name is then maintainable by rehearsal indefinitely and provides a basis for comparison with a stimulus presented later, once the latter also has been processed to the level of name assignment. Comparisons made at the name level may be as accurate as those at the feature level (although not always so, since there is some fallibility in the generation of names), and the reaction time for decisions at the name level is characteristically longer.

A second major determiner of efficiency of identification is commonly termed *priming*. By priming one refers to the observation that identification of any stimulus is more likely to be accurate if the same or a similar stimulus has recently been processed. If identifications or comparisons are being made at the feature level, they are facilitated only to the degree that a prior stimulus shares features with the one undergoing processing. If identification or comparison has to do with higher level, for example, semantic categories, then processing of a given stimulus, as, for example, a word, is primed if a preceding stimulus belongs to the same semantic category (see Chase, 1978; Posner, 1978).

c. Decision and response selection. One of the persisting and all but ubiquitous problems of cognitive psychology is that of separating cognitive processes (that is, those having to do with perceptual or memorial aspects of information processing) from decision processes. In the earlier literature having to do with the "new look" in perception, this problem appeared in the form of a confounding between frequency and other attributes of words. It was found, for example, that words with emotional associations tended to have different recognition thresholds than more neutral words (McGinnies, 1949), but on further examination it was found that the words of the two types often differed in frequency of usage in the language, and the frequency itself was a determiner of thresholds (Solomon & Howes, 1951). Somewhat similarly, in studies related to reading, it was found that the facilitating effects of meaningful verbal contexts were often confounded with transitional probabilities between successive words, and it was easy to show that people are sensitive to these probabilistic relationships (Miller, Bruner, & Postman, 1954).

A body of theory termed *sophisticated guessing theory*, took form to interpret and correct for an individual's tendency to use probablistic or frequency information in situations where perceptual information is incomplete or ambiguous (Broadbent, 1967; Catlin, 1969). The overall idea is that, in any perceptual task, an individual first uses perceptual information to the extent possible to narrow down possible response alternatives, then uses frequency or probablistic information to narrow further the subset of admissible possibilities before making a choice. This type of theory has been most thoroughly formalized and effectively applied to situations involving letter or word recognition by Treisman (in press).

In lines of research closer to psychophysics, the analogous problem arises, and one solution has been the development of a body of theory associated with choice models (Luce, 1959, 1963), in which a framework is provided for separately estimating parameters reflecting response bias and parameters reflecting use of stimulus information in discrimination or recognition experiments. As brought out most clearly in the recent work of Noreen (1977), choice models are closely related and in many instances strictly homologous to signal-detection models in which decision and stimulus factors are distinguished in terms of the observer's criterion on the one hand and the signal-to-noise ratio of the target stimulus relative to possible distractors on the other.

In the entire field of visual processing (as, for example tachistoscopic studies of letter recognition), one of the long standing problems is that of interpreting the fact that the perceptibility of a target letter appears to be strongly affected by the number and spacing of other letters in the display that includes the target. To some extent these effects of other letters must be attributable to some form of lateral interference or masking, but at the same time to the extent that target and distractors letters are confusable, there is a decision problem. Gardner (1973) and Shiffrin and Geisler (1973) have, in fact, developed models accounting in considerable detail for some of the effects of display size in terms of the assumption that different letters activate parallel, independent, perceptual channels and that the effects of increasing display size are solely a consequence of the increasing probability of confusion errors. Proceeding from this base, further research seems to have shown that this decision component is indeed important, but that, within the framework of a suitable model, it can be separated from genuine masking effects (Estes, 1974).

In recognition memory the problem of an observer's criterion arises in a form closely parallel to that familiar in psychophysics. When a person is presented with a stimulus and asked to make a judgment as to whether it has appeared before during the experimental session, the observer is characteristically faced with a situation in which the distributions of internal states aroused by new and old stimuli overlap, and some criterion must be set, categorizing these into the states that will lead to "yes" and "no" responses (Atkinson, Holmgren, & Juola, 1969; Murdock, 1976). The theoretical problem is more difficult than in signal detection, however, in that in the recognition problem the discrimination required is between internal memory representations rather than between external stimuli and distractors. Consequently, in the recognition problem there is no independent way of determining signal-to-noise ratio, and, consequently, reasoning within the framework of a model analogous to those of signal-detection theory is necessarily more indirect (Healy & Jones, 1973, 1975). Nonetheless, the approach has proved useful, and evidence from a variety of sources suggests that in many recognition situations individuals do indeed adjust their criteria in accord with changing tasks. These variations in the criteria must be taken into account in any attempt to trace the course of recognition memory. These problems have been examined in depth by Ratcliff (1978).

Even in studies of semantic memory, one encounters parallel problems. When a subject is asked to verify a sentence such as "A canary is a bird," evidence suggests a two-phase process in which a "yes" response may be generated with very short reaction time at the first stage if the overlap in terms of semantic features between the category and exemplar terms (bird and canary, respectively, in the example) exceeds the individual's criterion. The response is withheld until a more thorough memory search can be completed if the overlap falls short of the criterion, thus producing a longer reaction time (Smith, Shoben, & Rips, 1974).

At this point it seems safe to say that explicit attention to response biases and criteria is essential in every type of research arising in cognitive psychology. Always, some behavior on the part of the subject is used as an indicator of some not directly observable perceptual or memorial process under examination. And characteristically the behavioral indicator is subject to the effects of motivational and performance variables as well as those specifically at issue in a given study. Further, it has become exceedingly clear that progress toward separating cognitive from performance variables generally can be accomplished only within the framework of a theory or model, and this insight is proving one of the strongest sources of motivation toward increasing rigor and precision of theory in this area.

4. The Central Role of Capacity Limitations

Perhaps the most important single motif running through research on human information processing is the idea of capacity limitation. In part, the central role of this concept is no doubt due to the obvious empirical fact that people often can not accomplish all they might wish with respect to almost any intellectual task; and one of the principal tasks of cognitive psychology is to explain these limitations. But the notion of capacity limitation is also inherent in the information-processing analogy. One of the earliest substantial accomplishments of mathematical theories of information and communication was the development of a mathematical characterization of the concept of information that has proved central to the interpretation of the communication process. Thus, it naturally was hoped that the capacity of the human being in information-processing tasks could similarly be captured in models that would simply incorporate man as a component in information-processing systems. Some of the resulting lines of research and the many concepts arising therefrom can be organized into two principal categories, one having to do with structural and the other with process limitations.

a. *Structural limitations.*   Perhaps the earliest applications of information theory in psychology revolved around the notion of channel capacity and the hope that the human being's ability to perceive and transmit information from any stimulus display could be characterized in terms of the transmission of bits of information from stimulus to response by way of a channel having a fixed capacity. In the context of psychophysical scaling, some interesting results were obtained expressing an individual's ability to discriminate steps along a sensory continuum in informational units (see, for example, Attneave, 1959; Garner, 1962). And in the study of memory span, the notion of a fixed capacity in terms of the number of appropriately defined units (the magical numbers ranging from the 7 of Miller [1956] down to the 3 of Broadbent [1975]) achieved considerable visibility. Review of the more recent research literature (as, for example, Shiffrin, 1976) makes it clear, however, that the search for measures of fixed capacity has not proved fruitful and that the trend has instead been to seek the sources of capacity limitation in the parameters of cognitive processes themselves.

One major factor in the fall from popularity of fixed-capacity schemes was the emergence of signal-detection theory as the principal framework for much research on discrimination and recognition. In this framework it is recognized that in nearly all instances of information processing the individual must start from the initial problem of discriminating inputs that constitute signals from distractors that should be regarded as noise and that the signal-to-noise ratio is always a principal parameter. But also, in the signal-detection approach, it is recognized that the individual does not have direct access to stimulus inputs, but only to central representations generated by signals or distractors, and, consequently, that an individual's response to any input must depend on the criterion he has adopted as to which representations will be taken to represent signals and which to represent noise.

Further, a major aspect of research on early stages of both visual and auditory information processing bears on the fact that perceptual processes initiated by stimuli interact in important ways during the course of processing to the cognitive level where decisions can be made. These interactions are described in terms of various concepts of masking—lateral, backward, or forward depending on spatial and temporal relationships (Massaro, 1976; Shiffrin, 1976; Turvey, 1978). Thus, for example, a letter in a visual display must be separated by at least a critical distance from neighboring letters in order to be perceived at a given level of efficiency, and its appearance must similarly be separated by critical intervals from preceding and following patterned stimuli.

The limited resolving power of the perceptual systems in the temporal domain has given rise to much research concerned with establishing minimal durations for various processes. One of the earliest instances of this kind of research was that of Broadbent (1958) on switching time in auditory perception, followed somewhat later by a cluster bearing on the concept of encoding time in visual processing (reviewed by Ganz, 1975). Extensions of the same methods used in the case of sensory processing have made progress, further, in establishing minimal durations for more central cognitive operations, as, for example, comparison time per item in short-term memory scanning (dating from Sternberg, 1966) and minimal retrieval times from semantic memory networks (Anderson & Bower, 1973). These approaches and results are more fully reviewed by Chase (1978).

b. Capacity (resource) allocation.   Roughly speaking, structural factors account for only half the story with regard to capacity limitations on information processing. The many new and increasingly incisive methods for the study of attention that have appeared during the two decades from Broadbent (1958) to Shiffrin and Schneider (1977) have made it clear that, despite the limited resolving power of the sensory mechanisms and the many sources of masking, generally more stimuli pass the barriers of the peripheral sensory systems than can be dealt with at higher levels of cognitive processing. This fact is reflected in the distinction between structural and control processes in Atkinson and Shiffrin's (1968) approach to short-term memory and more recently in Norman and Bobrow's (1975) distinction between data limitations and resource limitations on processing capacity. In both of these instances the first component refers primarily to processes and factors that I have included in the previous section under structural limitations, and the second component refers to those remaining to be summarized under the heading of allocation.

The problem of allocating limited intellectual resources to accomplish simultaneous tasks or to meet multiple objectives concurrently takes several forms. One that is beginning to be reasonably well understood has to do with the fact that in almost any situation in which an individual must process information in order to obtain a basis for decision, the accrual of information over time generally follows a diminishing-returns function, and there is latitude with regard to the point at which the processing of information gives way to the initiation of a decision.

As a consequence, it is found in tasks ranging from simple choice reaction time through sentence verification and the comprehension of text that to some extent an individual can trade speed for accuracy. Hence, differences in times required to accomplish different tasks, or the same task under different conditions, cannot be taken to be direct measures of differences in central-processing time unless there is some way to ascertain that the same criterion has been adopted in each case with regard to the amount of information processed before a decision is initiated. Useful discussions of many aspects of this problem and some of the means of coping with it have been given by Pachella (1974) and Ratcliff (1978).

The concept of speed–accuracy tradeoff applies mainly to situations in which the information required for a decision can be obtained within a single brief interval or episode. But a somewhat analogous problem arises in situations requiring such large amounts of information to be processed that some must be held in memory while processing of new perceptual inputs continues. Another aspect of capacity limitation enters in that information can only be maintained in active working memory by a process of rehearsal, and the need for rehearsal brings in two additional bottlenecks. The first has to do with the fact that information that may have been processed perceptually in parallel can only be converted into a sequence of rehearsable items serially, a process that can evidently only be accomplished at a rate of about 200 msec per item (Shiffrin, 1976; Sperling, 1963). And even once the recoding is accomplished, an individual's rehearsal system can only maintain a limited number, perhaps up to about eight, items at a time. If the original input is processed in terms of simple units such as alphanumeric characters, the limitation on capacity of the rehearsal system may be increased somewhat by further recoding combinations of characters into higher order rehearsable units (syllables, words, "chunks"), but this activity requires time and evidently cannot be carried out in parallel with rehearsal of already coded items without interference.

The most efficient accomplishment of any intellectual task thus requires the individual to find an optimal allocation of time between perceptual processing, recoding, and rehearsal. There is scant reason to think that the optimum is ordinarily realized, but little can be said with assurance one way or the other, since methods for obtaining theoretically useful descriptions of resource allocation are just beginning to appear. In very current work of Norman and Bobrow

(1975) and Sperling and Melchner (in press), one sees applications of a concept of performance-operating characteristic that is somewhat analogous to the receiver-operating characteristic of signal-detection theory and that may conceivably play a similar role in enabling useful quantitative descriptions of resource allocation.

D.   Homologies between Concepts of Learning Theory and Information Processing

Because of the disjointness of the research settings, the kinds of subjects customarily studied, and the descriptive vocabularies employed in research on conditioning and learning on the one hand and cognitive psychology and information processing on the other, one may well get a distorted impression of the degree of novelty of the concepts and principles that have become current in the latter areas. Emphasizing differences rather than correspondences doubtless serves a protective function, helping investigators in either tradition by classifying as irrelevant much literature outside a given investigator's specialty that would otherwise be difficult to keep up with. There is a possible cost of indulging in this protective mechanism, of course, in the form of a lack of perspective that may encourage superficiality and shut off potentially stimulating or catalyzing inputs to the investigator's theoretical efforts.

On the premise that both the simpler or more primitive forms of conditioning and learning and the more complex forms of information processing and cognitive activity have evolved under the pressure of similar problems of adaptation arising in the course of interactions of organisms with their environment, one might expect to find significant analogies or even homologies in form and properties between concepts arising at these different levels or stages of psychological theorizing. In any event, in the course of studying closely the diverse contents and approaches represented in the six volumes of the present *Handbook,* I have been struck by the close parallelism discernible between the concepts of the two traditions, despite the differences in specific terms and their more superficial connotations. To document this impression in a compact way, I have brought together in Table 4 a sampling of parallel or homologous concepts from learning theory and information-processing theory, arranged roughly in the order of stages of processing from stimulus input through memory storage and retrieval to response decision or output. Examination of some of these entries will show, I think, that the correspondences are, at least in many instances, more than superficial analogies.

Consider conceptions of selective attention. One of the mainstreams of ideas associated with present-day research on human information processing emanated from Broadbent's studies of selective listening and his formulation of a perceptual filter model (Broadbent, 1958). In terms of one of the most familiar examples, a person's ability to follow a single conversation in a room in which many

TABLE 4
Parallel Concepts in Learning and Information-Processing Theory

	Concept	
Stage or factor	Learning theory	Information processing
1. Selective attention	Stimulus salience, distinctiveness	Priority level, perceptual filter
2. Initial encoding	Stimulus analyzers	Extraction of features or attributes
3. Higher encoding	Patterning	Unitization
4. Transient memory	Stimulus trace, reverberatory loop	Primary memory, working memory
5. Long-term memory	Association	Storage
	Context-dependent (state dependent) vs. independent	Episodic vs. semantic
	All-or-none vs. strength	Propositional vs. analog
6. Interference with storage or retrieval	Proactive and retroactive inhibition	Forward and backward masking
7. Facilitation of retrieval	Sensitization, reinstatement	Priming, rehearsal
8. Source of random error in retrieval	Stimulus fluctuation	Encoding variability
9. Memory search	Vicarious trial and error	Memory scanning
10. Decision	Threshold	Criterion

voices are speaking simultaneously was interpreted in terms of a selective attentional process, the perceptual filter, that effectively screens out voices other than the one to which the individual is momentarily attending. But nonetheless, a stimulus of high priority value, for example, the sound of the person's own name or a call for help, would pass the filter and capture attention. These notions have been further refined in the recent work of Schneider and Shiffrin (1977) on automatic versus controlled attentional processes. However, over the same period, theories of both animal and human discrimination learning have been almost fully transformed from the earlier conception of a passive process of selective strengthening and weakening of associations by reinforcement and nonreinforcement (for example, Spence, 1937) to theories organized around the central concept of selective attention (Lovejoy, 1968; Trabasso & Bower, 1968). But the parallel goes even deeper. In discrimination theories, as in information-processing theories, we find the same two aspects—a selective filtering process on the part of the organism, as in the concept of observing stimulus dimensions first formally developed by Zeaman and House (1963), and the concept of stimulus priority, in the case of discrimination models couched in terms of distinctiveness (Lawrence, 1963) or stimulus salience (Medin, 1976).

The close parallel continues through at least the early stages of stimulus encoding. All information-processing models include an early stage in which features or attributes of inputs are detected or abstracted, followed by a stage in which combinations of these form higher units, the elementary constituents of long-term memory. In conditioning and learning theory, from the first stage of stimulus input, processing is accomplished by stimulus analyzers (Sutherland & Mackintosh, 1971), or their counterparts in other theories, the outputs of the analyzers then entering into stimulus compounding (Hull, 1943), or patterning (Estes, 1959; Rescorla, 1973). At this point in the interpretation of encoding processes, the two approaches diverge somewhat in that in learning theory the compounds or patterns simply enter into associations with actions, whereas in cognitive theory they enter into higher order organizations in memory.

In the minds of cognitive psychologists, the concept of short-term, primary, or working memory belongs wholly to their own area, stemming from the work of such individuals as Peterson and Peterson (1959), Atkinson and Shiffrin (1968), and Waugh and Norman (1965). Nonetheless, other investigators have noted the close correspondence between the properties of Hull's (1943) conception of stimulus trace and those of the more modern concept of primary memory. In fact, in the hands of Ellis (1970), the concept of stimulus trace shades with no perceptible transition into interpretations of short-term memory. Also, in the extensive systematic treatment of conditioning theory by Konorski (1967), one finds a conception of short-term, transient memory maintained by a neural reverberatory process very similar in its properties to the seemingly more cognitive concept of primary memory.

In the case of long-term memory, treatments in terms of learning theory and cognitive psychology necessarily diverge more greatly as a consequence of the fact that research in the cognitive tradition has concentrated strongly on semantic properties and variables, which have no direct counterparts in learning theory. Nonetheless, and in spite of the fact that the term memory itself was not used much by learning theorists until recently, there are obvious parallels in the principal categorizations of concepts. Thus, the important distinction between propositional and analog representations in memory, a central issue for many current investigators of human information processing, is in some respects parallel to the distinction in learning theory between all-or-none associations and associative strength models.

Again, the distinction between episodic and semantic memory might seem wholly peculiar to cognitive psychology. However, one notes that a principal basis for this categorization is that episodic memory is presumed to include memory for the background context, both spatial and temporal, in which events occurred, whereas semantic memories are context independent. This same distinction between context dependent or state dependent associations, the rule in most forms of conditioning, and context independent associations, achievable by discriminative training in conceptual paradigms, is similarly important in learning theory.

Retrieval or recall from long-term memory is conceived to be facilitated, in information-processing models, if the to-be-recalled items have been rehearsed during a retention interval and if they are primed by the presence of appropriate related material just prior to attempted retrieval. Correspondingly, conditioned responses are most readily evoked after a long period if they have been refreshed by a manipulation termed *reinstatement* (Spear, 1976) and if sensitization has been provided by administration of an appropriate stimulus just prior to a test. Within information-processing models, the ability of an individual to encode successfully items of information so that they can be maintained in memory depends critically on the temporal relationship between the given item and others that might produce forward or backward masking during input (see, for example, Turvey, 1978). Correspondingly, in learning theory and classical interpretations of memory, retention of associations depends critically on the occurrence of other stimulus–response events shortly before or shortly after the input of the to-be-remembered items, the effects being interpreted in terms of proactive and retroactive inhibition.

Whether an item of information once encoded can be successfully retrieved after an interval filled with potentially interfering activities is assumed in information-processing theories to depend importantly on encoding variability. By this term one refers to the possibility that the same stimulus input may be encoded differently on a test than it had been during an earlier experience, in which case the encoding generated on the test would not make contact with the representation of the item in memory. It has been observed (Martin, 1971) that this concept of encoding variability almost exactly parallels in its dynamics, and sometimes even in the specific associated mathematical models, the conception of stimulus fluctuation earlier developed in the context of conditioning and learning theory (Estes, 1955a).

In the process of memory retrieval itself, the central interpretive concept in information-processing models is one of memory search or scanning. One would not expect to find these distinctively cognitive terms in conditioning and learning theory, but nonetheless consider the similarity between memory search and the concept of vicarious trial and error (VTE) developed many decades ago by Tolman (1938) and others. At first the notion of VTE was closely tied to the observable behavior of a rat at a choice point, the animal typically being observed to look from one side to another several times before actually entering a pathway, as though this overt examination of the stimulus alternatives were of help in arousing appropriate memories of past experiences. The identification of this perhaps rudimentary memory-search process with overt behaviors was quickly lost, however, in the continuing development of the VTE model in the hands of Bower (1959) and myself (Estes, 1959).

At the final stage of decision or response production, if we consider only the responses usually observed as the basis for reaction time and frequency measures in experimental research, the gap between information processing and learning-theoretic approaches virtually vanishes in that some variant of the criterion concept of signal-detection theory is coming to be the preferred model in both cases. There would seem to remain only the productive aspects of language as a so far almost unchallenged province of human cognitive psychology. Whether even this gap may be closed by study of the intensively tutored chimpanzees of Gardner and Gardner (1971), Premack (1971), and others remain to be seen.

E. Linguistic Functions

Although psycholinguistics is a readily identifiable research area, owing to the characteristic types of materials and the linguistic backgrounds of investigators, it is not easy to decide how language and the cognitive processes implicated in its comprehension and production should be categorized in a portrayal of the concepts and theories of cognitive psychology and information processing. One source of the difficulty is that language and verbal behavior pervade virtually all human cognitive activity, yet also may be treated as distinct objects of study in themselves. Verbal behavior is a well-defined form of performance, and language a relatively well-defined body of symbols and rules. But the theoretical question of central concern is the extent to which the cognitive processes, mechanisms, and structures that are used to interpret the results of psycholinguistic research are unique to linguistic functioning and to what extent they may be regarded as particular applications of general purpose processes and mechanisms. What one finds among psychologists is a conflict of strong beliefs on both sides.

The conception of linguistic functioning as simply a special form of performance (that is, verbal behavior) seems on the basis of actual evidence to deserve a mixed appraisal. Certainly, speech is among other things a form of performance and within limits (perhaps very strict ones) can certainly be modified by the same procedures of reinforcement as can other forms of behavior. The idea that research and theory cast in this mold would be sufficient for the understanding of linguistic functioning in all of its aspects (adopted enthusiastically by some students of operant behavior following the appearance of Skinner's 1957 book) has not, however, proved influential in the field at large.

At the other extreme, what evidence does one find for the view that there are major theoretical concepts of a psychological character that are wholly peculiar to linguistic function? Perhaps the clearest case of such a concept would be that of *linguistic universals*, basic to Chomsky's (1965) efforts to extend theories of linguistics to the status of explanatory theories that might interpret the acquisition and use of language. In Chomsky's approach the term *universal* expressed the supposition that a child must have some, presumably innate, general knowledge of the character of the language in order to be prepared to acquire its specific system of symbols and rules. The concept has certainly been influential in the thinking of psycholinguists, as indicated by its frequency of occurrence in the literature, but it is not clear to me that the concept has either accrued much specific support or undergone much refinement or elaboration as a consequence of a dozen years of psycholinguistic research.

Such concepts as *surface structure* and *deep structure*, introduced to refer to syntactic aspects of sentences at the level of observed tokens on the one hand and the inferred deeper level of understanding or comprehension on the other, are certainly peculiar to psycholinguistics within cognitive psychology. But, again, the notion of deep structure seems not to have matured theoretically as the result of research. Rather, substantial efforts to interpret comprehension of and memory for sentences have relied largely on the same types of concepts as concurrent efforts to deal with memory for other kinds of inputs. A good example would be semantic features, which do indeed refer specifically to attributes of linguistic units or expressions, but which nonetheless in most current work are assumed to be stored in memory, accessed, and subjected to cognitive operations such as comparison and matching according to essentially the same principles and rules as other kinds of features (Smith, Chapter 1, this volume).

Perhaps a sensible point of view is that it is premature to expend much energy on the question of whether there are cognitive processes unique to linguistic tasks or functions. Just as in the much older problem of the relation between psychology and physiology, there is likely to be little reward for being overimpressed either by superficial similarities or by superficial differences between concepts that enter into the interpretation of linguistic versus nonlinguistic information processing. Rather, one should expect important homologies and other significant relationships to develop at a relatively abstract level of theory. Consequently, the urgent need is for more constructive theory development on both fronts.

F. Comment on Generality of Laws and Principles

There is scarcely a more persistent theme in science than the continuing efforts in every empirical domain to progress toward laws and concepts of increasing generality. The idealized outcome, significantly realized in physics but a still unattained goal motivating biological and behavioral scientists, is the distillation of a small number of relatively fundamental concepts and laws from which predictions may be derived with regard to countless experimental or environmental conditions. In the heyday of the "systems" of psychology and the grandly projected learning theories of Tolman (1932) and Hull (1943), the inevitability of progress toward general laws was almost taken for granted. Perhaps the high point of optimism was associated with Hull's vision of a deductive system that would enable the derivation of the empirical laws of behavior in all its variations as theorems (Hull, 1937, 1943, 1950).

More recently, however, the pendulum of opinion has swung far in the other direction, and one sees numerous expressions of skepticism concerning the possibility of general laws or principles in psychology, at least in cognitive psychology. These have been perhaps best articulated by individuals strongly influenced by developments in ethology bearing on species-specific constraints on learning (for example, Seligman, 1970) but at least as vigorously by rediscoverers of individual differences and some adherents of computer-simulation approaches.

What has happened to shift the Zeitgist on a matter of strategy that should presumably have a deep rational basis? Perhaps part of the answer is simply that progress toward general theories was not fast enough to satisfy psychologists, who often seem to look for the same order of theoretical accomplishment in a decade that has taken a century in other sciences. Another factor is certainly the occurrence of some notable and well-publicized disappointments, especially on the part of investigators in the operant tradition, on finding that what had been taken to be laws of conditioning broke down upon seemingly small variations in empirical boundary conditions (for example, Breland & Breland, 1966). Perhaps most important is the emergence of behavior genetics as an independent discipline, together with the accumulating impact of ethology in generating increasing appreciation for the fact that laws of learning and cognition must operate within the framework of an intricate organization of behavioral dispositions shaped by genetic factors and species-specific genetic–environmental interactions. Finally, outside the sphere of academic science itself, public awareness and concern with ecological problems has tended to force everyone, scientists and nonscientists alike, toward increasing emphasis on the importance of individual differences with respect both to genetic backgrounds and to environmental situations.

Thus, one is led to wonder whether the current pessimism with regard to the possibility of truly general laws and theories in cognitive psychology will prove to be better justified than was the earlier optimism. As might be anticipated on the basis of my review of several aspects of cognitive theory in the preceding sections of this chapter, I think probably not. Rather, I anticipate that the strongest current of opinion will swing back toward the main line of continuing sustained effort toward general theory, but perhaps with better perspective as to the ways in which this goal may be realized in psychology as compared to other sciences. One ground for this view is the impression growing out of the extensive reviews of research and theory in the six volumes of the *Handbook* that there is in fact more generality in cognitive theory than we ordinarily appreciate, commonality of ideas often being obscured by variations in labels. What may often seem in retrospect to be unnecessary variations in terminology should not, however, be regarded as capricious. Rather, they are the natural outcome of a process in which general laws or principles operating in very different empirical circumstances generate phenotypically diverse descriptive principles and models, which are of course initially expressed in the vocabulary of particular empirical domains.

Another factor in my prognosis about the climate of opinion regarding generality is to be found in some signs of increasing sophistication in the treatment of individual differences. It is not always realized, but I think it should be, that general laws of learning or cognition need not be formulated in terms of average organisms and that individual differences may be subject to general laws and principles just as may uniformities. Thus, in very current research on individual differences in information processing, we find evidence that wide individual differences in particular forms of intellectual performance may signify not that general models are unattainable in principle but rather that, up to a point, different models may apply to different individuals (Hunt, 1978). There is little reason to expect quick or easy answers to the next question of what general principles might be responsible for these variations. Continuing progress toward generality seems only to be more difficult than one might have hoped for, not impossible, and to require as vigorous investigation of individual differences as of commonalities, together perhaps with some reshaping of our ideas as to what general laws and concepts of cognitive psychology should look like when we find them.

REFERENCES

Amsel, A. Partial reinforcement effects on vigor and persistence. In K. W. Spence & J. T. Spence (Eds.), *The psychology of learning and motivation.* Vol. 1. New York: Academic Press, 1967, Pp. 1–65.

Anderson, J. A. A theory for the recognition of items from short memorized lists. *Psychological Review,* 1973, **80,** 417–438.

Anderson, J. R., & Bower, G. H. *Human associative memory.* Washington, D.C.: V.,H. Winston, 1973.

Atkinson, R. C., & Estes, W. K. Stimulus sampling theory. In R. D. Luce, R. R. Bush, & E. Galanter (Eds.), *Handbook of mathematical psychology.* Vol II. New York: John Wiley & Sons, 1963. Pp. 121–268.

Atkinson, R. C., Holmgren, J. E., & Juola, J. F. Processing time as influenced by the number of elements in a visual display. *Perception & Psychophysics,* 1969, **6,** 321–326.

Atkinson, R. C., & Shiffrin, R. M. Human memory: A proposed system and its control processes. In K. W. Spence & J. T. Spence (Eds.), *The psychology of learning and motivation: Advances in research and theory.* Vol. 2. New York: Academic Press, 1968. Pp. 89–195.

Atkinson, R. C., & Wickens, T. D. Human memory and the concept of reinforcement. In R. Glaser (Ed.), *The nature of reinforcement.* New York: Academic Press, 1971. Pp. 66–120.

Attneave, F. *Applications of information theory to psychology: A summary of basic concepts, methods, and results.* New York: Henry Holt & Co., 1959.

Baddeley, A. D. *The psychology of memory.* New York: Basic Books, 1976.

Bandura, A. (Ed.). *Psychological modeling: Conflicting theories.* Chicago: Aldine-Atherton, 1971.

Bandura, A. Self-efficacy: Toward a unifying theory of behavioral change. *Psychological Review,* 1977, **84,** 191–215.

Bloomfield, L. *Language*. New York: Holt & Co., 1933.

Bolles, R. C. Learning, motivation, and cognition. In W. K. Estes (Ed.), *Handbook of learning and cognitive processes*. Vol. 1. Hillsdale, New Jersey: Lawrence Erlbaum Associates, 1975. Pp. 249-280.

Bower, G. H. Choice point behavior. In R. R. Bush & W. K. Estes (Eds.), *Studies in mathematical learning theory*. Stanford: Stanford University Press, 1959. Pp. 109-124.

Bower, G. H. A multicomponent theory of the memory trace. In K. W. Spence & J. T. Spence (Eds.), *The psychology of learning and motivation*. Vol. 1. New York: Academic Press, 1967. Pp. 229-325.

Breland, K., & Breland, M. *Animal Behavior*. New York: MacMillan, 1966.

Broadbent, D. E. *Perception and communication*. New York: Pergamon Press, 1958.

Broadbent, D. E. Word-frequency effect and response bias. *Psychological Review*, 1967, **74**, 1-15.

Broadbent, D. E. The magic number seven after fifteen years. In A. Kennedy & A. Wilkes (Eds.), *Studies in long-term memory*. London: John Wiley & Sons, 1975. Pp. 3-18.

Brown, J. L. *The evolution of behavior*. New York: Norton, 1975.

Buchwald, A. Effects of "right" and "wrong" on subsequent behavior: A new interpretation. *Psychological Review*, 1969, **76**, 132-143.

Bush, R. R., & Mosteller, F. A model for stimulus generalization and discrimination. *Psychological Review*, 1951, **58**, 413-423.

Capaldi, E. J. A sequential hypothesis of instrumental learning. In K. W. Spence & J. T. Spence (Eds.), *The psychology of learning and motivation*. Vol. 2. New York: Academic Press, 1967. Pp. 67-156.

Catlin, J. On the word-frequency effect. *Psychological Review*, 1969, **76**, 504-506.

Chase, W. G. Elementary information processes. In W. K. Estes (Ed.), *Handbook of learning and cognitive processes*. Vol. 5. Hillsdale, New Jersey: Lawrence Erlbaum Associates, 1978. Pp. 19-90.

Chomsky, N. *Aspects of the theory of syntax*. Cambridge, Massachusetts: M.I.T. Press, 1965.

Collins, A. M., & Loftus, E. F. A spreading-activation theory of semantic processing. *Psychological Review*, 1975, **82**, 407-428.

Collins, A. M., & Quillian, M. R. How to make a language user. In E. Tulving & W. Donaldson (Eds.), *Organization of memory*. New York: Academic Press, 1972. Pp. 309-351.

Conrad, R. Interference or decay over short retention intervals? *Journal of Verbal Learning and Verbal Behavior*, 1967, **6**, 49-54.

Craik, F. I. M., & Lockhart, R. S. Levels of processing: A framework for memory research. *Journal of Verbal Learning and Verbal Behavior*, 1972, **11**, 671-684.

Ellis, N. R. Memory processes in retardates and normals. In N. R. Ellis (Ed.), *International review of research in mental retardation*. Vol. 4. New York: Academic Press, 1970. Pp. 1-32.

Estes, W. K. Toward a statistical theory of learning. *Psychological Review*, 1950, **57**, 94-107.

Estes, W. K. Statistical theory of spontaneous recovery and regression. *Psychological Review*, 1955, **62**, 145-154. (a)

Estes, W. K. Statistical theory of distributional phenomena in learning. *Psychological Review*, 1955, **62**, 369-377. (b)

Estes, W. K. A random-walk model for choice behavior. In K. J. Arrow, S. Karlin, & P. Suppes (Eds.), *Mathematical methods in the social sciences*. Stanford: Stanford University Press, 1959. Pp. 265-276.

Estes, W. K. Theoretical treatments of differential reward in multiple-choice learning and two-person interactions. In J. H. Criswell, H. Solomon, & P. Suppes (Eds.), *Mathematical methods in small group processes*. Stanford: Stanford University Press, 1962. Pp. 133-149.

Estes, W. K. All-or-none processes in learning and retention. *American Psychologist*, 1964, **19**, 16-25.

Estes, W. K. Reinforcement in human learning. In J. Tapp (Ed.), *Reinforcement and behavior*. New York: Academic Press, 1969. Pp. 63-94. (a)

Estes, W. K. New perspectives on some old issues in association theory. In N. J. Mackintosh & W. K. Honig (Eds.), *Fundamental issues in associative learning*. Halifax: Dalhousie University Press, 1969. Pp. 162–189. (b)

Estes, W. K. *Learning theory and mental development*. New York: Academic Press, 1970.

Estes, W. K. Reward in human learning: Theoretical issues and strategic choice points. In R. Glaser (Ed.), *The nature of reinforcement*. New York: Academic Press, 1971. Pp. 16–36.

Estes, W. K. An associative basis for coding and organization in memory. In A. W. Melton & E. Martin (Eds.), *Coding processes in human memory*. New York: V. H. Winston & Sons, 1972. Pp. 161–190. (a)

Estes, W. K. Reinforcement in human behavior. *American Scientist*, 1972, **60**, 723–729. (b)

Estes, W. K. Memory and conditioning. In F. J. McGuigan & D. B. Lumsden (Eds.), *Contemporary approaches to conditioning and learning*. Washington, D.C.: V. H. Winston, 1973. Pp. 265–286.

Estes, W. K. Redundancy of noise elements and signals in visual detection of letters. *Perception and Psychophysics*, 1974, **16**, 53–60.

Estes, W. K. Memory, perception, and decision in letter identification. In R. L. Solso (Ed.), *Information processing and cognition: The Loyola symposium*. Hillsdale, New Jersey: Lawrence Erlbaum Associates, 1975. Pp. 3–30.

Estes, W. K. Structural aspects of associative models for memory. In C. N. Cofer (Ed.), *The structure of human memory*. San Francisco: Freeman, 1976. Pp. 31–53.

Estes, W. K. On the descriptive and explanatory functions of theories of memory. In L-G. Nilsson (Ed.), *Perspectives in memory research*. Hillsdale, New Jersey: Lawrence Erlbaum Associates, in press.

Estes, W. K., & Skinner, B. F. Some quantitative properties of anxiety. *Journal of Experimental Psychology*, 1941, **29**, 390–400.

Feigenbaum, E. A. Simulation of verbal learning behavior. In E. A. Feigenbaum & J. Feldman (Eds.), *Computers and thought*. New York: McGraw-Hill, 1963. Pp. 297–309.

Ferster, C. B., & Skinner, B. F. *Schedules of reinforcement*. New York: Appleton-Century-Crofts, 1957.

Fillmore, C. J. Types of lexical information. In D. D. Steinberg & L. A. Jakobovits (Eds.), *Semantics*, Cambridge: University Press, 1969. Pp. 370–392.

Flavell, J. H. *The developmental psychology of Jean Piaget*. New York: D. Van Nostrand Co., 1963.

Gagne, R. M. Contributions of learning to human development. *Psychological Review*, 1968, **75**, 177–191.

Ganz, L. Temporal factors in visual perception. In E. C. Carterette & M. P. Friedman (Eds.), *Handbook of perception*. Vol. 5. New York: Academic Press, 1975. Pp. 169–231.

Garcia, J., & Koelling, R. A. Relation of cue to consequence in avoidance learning. *Psychonomic Science*, 1966, **4**, 123–124.

Gardner, G. T. Evidence for independent parallel channels in tachistoscopic perception. *Cognitive Psychology*, 1973, **4**, 130–155.

Gardner, B. T., & Gardner, R. A. Two-way communication with an infant chimpanzee. In A. M. Schrier & F. Stollnitz (Eds.), *Behavior of nonhuman primates*. Vol. 4. New York: Academic Press, 1971. Pp. 117–184.

Garner, W. R. *Uncertainty and structure as psychological concepts*. New York: John Wiley & Sons, 1962.

Gelber, B. Investigations of the behavior of paramecium aurelia: I. Modification of behavior after training with reinforcement. *Journal of Comparative and Physiological Psychology*, 1952, **45**, 58–65.

Gibbon, J. Scalar expectancy theory and Weber's law in animal timing. *Psychological Review*, 1977, **84**, 279–325.

Gibson, E. J. *Principles of perceptual learning and development*. New York: Appleton-Century-Crofts, 1969.

Gormezano, I., & Kehoe, E. J. Classical conditioning: Some methodological–conceptual issues. In W. K. Estes (Ed.), *Handbook of learning and cognitive processes*. Vol. 2. Hillsdale, New Jersey: Lawrence Erlbaum Associates, 1975. Pp. 143–179.

Graham, F. K. Habituation and dishabituation of responses innervated by the autonomic nervous system. In H. V. S. Peeke & M. J. Herz (Eds.), *Habituation*. Vol. 1. New York: Academic Press, 1973. Pp. 163–218.

Graham N. Spatial frequency channels in human vision: Detecting edges without edge detectors. In C. S. Harris (Ed.), *Visual coding and adaptability*. Hillsdale, New Jersey: Lawrence Erlbaum Associates, in press.

Grant, D. A. A preliminary model for processing information conveyed by verbal conditioned stimuli in classical conditioning. In A. H. Black & W. F. Prokasy (Eds.), *Classical conditioning II: Current research and theory*. New York: Appleton-Century-Crofts, 1972. Pp. 28–63.

Groves, P. M., & Thompson, R. F. A dual-process theory of habituation: Neural mechanisms. In H. V. S. Peeke & M. J. Herz (Eds.), *Habituation*. Vol. 2. New York: Academic Press, 1973. Pp. 175–205.

Guthrie, E. R. Association as a function of time interval. *Psychological Review*, 1933, **40**, 355–368.

Harris, J. D. Forward conditioning, backward conditioning, and pseudoconditioning, and adaptation to the conditioned stimulus. *Journal of Experimental Psychology*, 1941, **28**, 491–502.

Harris, J. D. Habituatory response decrement in the intact organism. *Psychological Bulletin*, 1943, **40**, 385–422.

Healy, A. F., & Jones, C. Criterion shifts in recall. *Psychological Bulletin*, 1973, **79**, 335–340.

Healy, A. F., & Jones, C. Can subjects maintain a constant criterion in a memory task? *Memory & Cognition*, 1975, **3**, 233–238.

Hebb, D. O. *The organization of behavior: A neuropsychological theory*. New York: John Wiley & Sons, 1949.

Heinemann, E. G., & Chase, S. Stimulus generalization. In W. K. Estes (Ed.), *Handbook of learning and cognitive processes*. Vol. 2. Hillsdale, New Jersey: Lawrence Erlbaum Associates, 1975. Pp. 305–349.

Hilgard, E. R. An algebraic analysis of conditioned discrimination in man. *Psychological Review*, 1938, **45**, 472–496.

Hilgard, E. R. *Theories of learning*. New York: Appleton-Century-Crofts, 1948.

Hinde, R. A. Constraints on learning: An introduction to the problems. In R. A. Hinde & J. Hinde (Eds.), *Constraints on learning*. New York: Academic Press, 1973. Pp. 1–19.

Hollan, J. D. Features and semantic memory: Set-theoretic or network model? *Psychological Review*, 1975, **82**, 154–155.

Hubel, D. H., & Wiesel, T. N. Receptive fields, binocular interaction and functional architecture in the cat's visual cortex. *Journal of Physiology (London)*, 1962, **160**, 106–154.

Hull, C. L. Knowledge and purpose as habit mechanisms. *Psychological Review*, 1930, **37**, 511–525.

Hull, C. L. Goal attraction and directing ideas conceived as habit phenomena. *Psychological Review*, 1931, **38**, 487–506.

Hull, C. L. Mind, mechanism, and adaptive behavior. *Psychological Review*, 1937, **44**, 1–32.

Hull, C. L. *Principles of behavior*, New York: Appleton-Century-Crofts, 1943.

Hull, C. L. Simple qualitative discrimination learning. *Psychological Review*, 1950, **57**, 303–313.

Humphrey, G. *The nature of learning*. New York: Harcourt, 1933.

Hunt, E. Mechanics of verbal ability. *Psychological Review*, 1978, **85**, 109–130.

Irwin, F. W. *Intentional behavior and motivation: A cognitive theory*. New York: J. B. Lippincott Co., 1971.

Jakobson, R., Fant, C. G. M., & Halle, M. *Preliminaries to speech analysis*. Cambridge, Massachusetts: M.I.T. Press, 1952.

Johnson, N. F. Coding processes in memory. In W. K. Estes (Ed.), *Handbook of learning and cognitive processes.* Vol. 6. Hillsdale, New Jersey: Lawrence Erlbaum Associates, 1978. Pp. 87–129.

Kamin, L. J. Selective association and conditioning. In N. J. Mackintosh & W. K. Honig (Eds.), *Fundamental issues in associative learning.* Halifax: Dalhousie University Press, 1969. Pp. 42–64.

Kendler, H. H., & Kendler, T. S. From discrimination learning to cognitive development: A neobehavioristic odyssey. In W. K. Estes (Ed.), *Handbook of learning and cognitive processes.* Vol. 1. Hillsdale, New Jersey: Lawrence Erlbaum Associates, 1975. Pp. 191–247.

Kimble, G. A. *Hilgard and Marquis' conditioning and learning.* New York: Appleton-Century-Crofts, 1961.

Kimmel, H. D., & Yaremko, R. M. Effect of partial reinforcement on acquisition and extinction of classical conditioning in the planarian. *Journal of Comparative and Physiological Psychology,* 1966, **61,** 299–301.

Kintsch, W. *The representation of meaning in memory.* New York: John Wiley & Sons, 1974.

Klahr, D., & Wallace, J. G. *Cognitive development.* Hillsdale, N. J.: Lawrence Erlbaum Associates, 1976.

Konorski, J. *Conditioned reflexes and neuron organization.* New York: Cambridge University Press, 1948.

Konorski, J. The role of central factors in differentiation. In R. W. Gerard & J. W. Duyff (Eds.), *Information processing in the nervous system.* Amsterdam: Excerpta Medica Foundation, 1962. Pp. 318–329.

Konorski, J. *Integrative activity of the brain.* Chicago: University of Chicago Press, 1967.

LaBerge, D. Perceptual learning and attention. In W. K. Estes (Ed.), *Handbook of learning and cognitive processes.* Vol. 4. Hillsdale, New Jersey: Lawrence Erlbaum Associates, 1976. Pp. 237–273.

Lawrence, D. H. Acquired distinctiveness of cues: I. Transfer between discriminations on the basis of familiarity with the stimulus. *Journal of Experimental Psychology,* 1949, **39,** 770–784.

Lawrence, D. H. The nature of a stimulus: Some relations between learning and perception. In S. Koch (Ed.), *Psychology: A study of science.* Vol. V. New York: McGraw-Hill, 1963. Pp. 179–212.

Lawrence, D. H., & Festinger, L. *Deterrents and reinforcement.* Stanford: Stanford University Press, 1962.

Lee, C. L. Repetition and acoustic contrast in short-term memory for letter sequences. *Journal of Experimental Psychology: Human Learning and Memory,* 1976, **2,** 695–704.

Lettvin, J. Y., Maturana, H. R., McCulloch, W. S., & Pitts, W. H. What the frog's eye tells the frog's brain. *Proceedings of the Institute of Radio Engineering,* 1959, **47,** 1940–1951.

Levine, M. *A cognitive theory of learning: Research on hypothesis testing.* Hillsdale, New Jersey: Lawrence Erlbaum Associates, 1975.

Lovejoy, E. *Attention in discrimination learning.* San Francisco: Holden-Day, 1968.

Lubow, R. E. Latent inhibition. *Psychological Bulletin,* 1973, **79,** 398–407.

Luce, R. D. *Individual choice behavior.* New York: John Wiley & Sons, 1959.

Luce, R. D. Detection and recognition. In R. D. Luce, R. R. Bush, & E. Galanter (Eds.), *Handbook of mathematical psychology.* Vol. 1. New York: John Wiley & Sons, 1963. Pp. 103–189.

Mackintosh, N. J. Selective attention in animal discrimination learning. *Psychological Bulletin,* 1965, **64,** 124–150.

Mackintosh, N. J. From classical conditioning to discrimination learning. In W. K. Estes (Ed.), *Handbook of learning and cognitive processes.* Vol. 1. Hillsdale, New Jersey: Lawrence Erlbaum Associates, 1975. Pp. 151–189.

Martin, E. Verbal learning theory and independent retrieval phenomena, *Psychological Review,* 1971, **78,** 314–332.

Massaro, D. W. Auditory information processing. In W. K. Estes (Ed.), *Handbook of learning and cognitive processes.* Vol. 4. Hillsdale, New Jersey: Lawrence Erlbaum Associates, 1976. Pp. 275-320.

McGeoch, J. A., & Irion, A. L. *The psychology of human learning.* New York: Longmans, Green, 1952.

McGinnies, E. Emotionality and perceptual defense. *Psychological Review,* 1949, **56**, 244-251.

Medin, D. L. A theory of context in discrimination learning. In G. H. Bower (Ed.), *The Psychology of Learning and Motivation: Advances in Research and Theory.* New York: Academic Press, 1975, Pp. 263-314.

Medin, D. L. Theories of discrimination learning and learning set. In W. K. Estes (Ed.), *Handbook of learning and cognitive processes.* Vol. 3. Hillsdale, New Jersey: Lawrence Erlbaum Associates, 1976. Pp. 131-169.

Medin, D. L., & Cole, M. Comparative psychology and human cognition. In W. K. Estes (Ed.), *Handbook of learning and cognitive processes.* Vol. 1. Hillsdale, New Jersey: Lawrence Erlbaum Associates, 1975. Pp. 111-149.

Miller, G. A. *Language and communication.* New York: McGraw-Hill, 1951.

Miller, G. A. The magical number seven, plus or minus 2: Some limits on our capacity for processing information. *Psychological Review,* 1956, **63**, 81-97.

Miller, G. A., Bruner, J. S., & Postman, L. Familiarity of letter sequences and tachistoscopic identification. *Journal of General Psychology,* 1954, **50**, 129-139.

Miller, N. E. Some reflections on the law of effect produce a new alternative to drive reduction. In M. R. Jones (Ed.), *Nebraska symposium on motivation.* Lincoln: Nebraska University Press, 1963. Pp. 65-112.

Murdock, B. B., Jr. Methodology in the study of human memory. In W. K. Estes (Ed.), *Handbook of learning and cognitive processes.* Vol. 4. Hillsdale, New Jersey: Lawrence Erlbaum Associates, 1976. Pp. 91-131.

Murdock, B. B., Jr. *Human memory: Theory and data.* Hillsdale, New Jersey: Lawrence Erlbaum Associates, 1974.

Neimark, E. D. Model for a thinking machine: An information processing framework for the study of cognitive development. *Merrill-Palmer Quarterly,* 1970, **16**, 345-368.

Nelson, T. O. Savings and forgetting from long-term memory. *Journal of Verbal Learning and Verbal Behavior,* 1971, **10**, 568-576.

Newell, A., & Simon, H. A. *Human problem solving.* Englewood Cliffs, New Jersey: Prentice-Hall, 1972.

Noreen, D. L. Relations among some models of choice. *Mathematical Psychology Meetings (10th annual),* Los Angeles, 1977.

Norman, D. A., & Bobrow, D. G. On data-limited and resource-limited processes. *Cognitive Psychology,* 1975, **7**, 44-64.

Norman, D. A., & Rumelhart, D. E. A system for perception and memory. In D. A. Norman (Ed.), *Models of human memory.* New York: Academic Press, 1970. Pp. 19-64.

Nuttin, J., & Greenwald, A. G. *Reward and punishment in human learning.* New York: Academic Press, 1968.

Pachella, R. G. The interpretation of reaction time in information processing research. In B. Kantowitz (Ed.), *Human information processing: Tutorials in performance and cognition.* Hillsdale, New Jersey: Lawrence Erlbaum Associates, 1974. Pp. 41-82.

Pavlov, I. P. *Conditioned reflexes.* London: Oxford University Press, 1927.

Peeke, H. V. S., & Herz, M. J. (Eds.). *Habituation.* Vol. 1. New York: Academic Press, 1973.

Peterson, L. R., & Peterson, M. J. Short-term retention of individual verbal items. *Journal of Experimental Psychology,* 1959, **58**, 193-198.

Pisoni, D. B. Speech perception. In W. K. Estes (Ed.), *Handbook of learning and cognitive processes.* Vol. 6. Hillsdale, New Jersey: Lawrence Erlbaum Associates, 1978. Pp. 167-233.

Posner, M. I. Abstraction and the process of recognition. In G. H. Bower & J. T. Spence (Eds.), *The psychology of learning and motivation: Advances in research and theory.* Vol. 3. New York: Academic Press, 1969. Pp. 43–100.

Posner, M. I. Chronometric analysis of abstraction and recognition. In W. K. Estes (Ed.), *Handbook of learning and cognitive processes.* Vol. 5. Hillsdale, New Jersey: Lawrence Erlbaum Associates, 1978. Pp. 143–188.

Postman, L. Methodology of human learning. In W. K. Estes (Ed.), *Handbook of learning and cognitive processes.* Vol. 3. Hillsdale, New Jersey: Lawrence Erlbaum Associates, 1976. Pp. 11–69.

Premack, D. On the assessment of language competence in the chimpanzee. In A. M. Schrier & F. Stollnitz (Eds.), *Behavior of nonhuman primates.* Vol. 4. New York: Academic Press, 1971. Pp. 185–228.

Prytulak, L. S. Natural language mediation. *Cognitive Psychology,* 1971, **2,** 1–56.

Ratcliff, R. A. A theory of memory retrieval. *Psychological Review,* 1978, **85,** 59–108.

Rescorla, R. A. Pavlovian conditioning and its proper control procedures. *Psychological Review,* 1967, **74,** 71–80.

Rescorla, R. A. Probability of shock in the presence and absence of CS in fear conditioning. *Journal of Comparative and Physiological Psychology,* 1968, **66,** 1–5.

Rescorla, R. A. Informational variables in Pavlovian conditioning. In G. Bower (Ed.), *The psychology of learning and motivation.* Vol. 6. New York: Academic Press, 1972. Pp. 1–46.

Rescorla, R. A. Second-order conditioning: Implications for theories of learning. In F. J. McGuigan & D. B. Lumsden (Eds.), *Contemporary approaches to conditioning and learning.* Washington, D.C.: Winston, 1973. Pp. 127–150.

Rescorla, R. A. Pavlovian excitatory and inhibitory conditioning. In W. K. Estes (Ed.), *Handbook of learning and cognitive processes.* Vol. 2. Hillsdale, New Jersey: Lawrence Erlbaum Associates, 1975. Pp. 7–35.

Rescorla, R. A., & Wagner, A. R. A theory of Pavlovian conditioning: Variations in the effectiveness of reinforcement and nonreinforcement. In A. H. Black & W. A. Prokasy (Eds.), *Classical conditioning II: Current theory and research.* New York: Appleton-Century-Crofts, 1972. Pp. 64–99.

Restle, F. *Psychology of judgment and choice: A theoretical essay.* New York: John Wiley & Sons, 1961.

Ross, L. E., & Ross, S. M. Cognitive factors in classical conditioning. In W. K. Estes (Ed.), *Handbook of learning and cognitive processes.* Vol. 3. Hillsdale, New Jersey: Lawrence Erlbaum Associates, 1976. Pp. 103–129.

Rudy, J. W. Stimulus selection in animal conditioning and paired-associate learning: Variations in the associative process. *Journal of Verbal Learning and Verbal Behavior,* 1974, **13,** 282–296.

Rudy, J. W., & Wagner, A. R. Stimulus selection in associative learning. In W. K. Estes (Ed.), *Handbook of learning and cognitive processes.* Vol. 2. Hillsdale, New Jersey: Lawrence Erlbaum Associates, 1975. Pp. 269–303.

Schneider, W., & Shiffrin, R. M. Controlled and automatic human information processing: I. Detection, search, and attention. *Psychological Review,* 1977, **84,** 1–66.

Schoenfeld, W. N., Cumming, W. W., & Hearst, E. On the classification of reinforcement schedules. *Proceedings of the National Academy of Science,* 1956, **42,** 563–570.

Seligman, M. E. P. On the generality of the laws of learning. *Psychological Review,* 1970, **77,** 406–418.

Shettleworth, S. J. Constraints on learning. *Advances in the study of behavior,* 1972, **4,** 1–68.

Shiffrin, R. M. Capacity limitations in information processing, attention, and memory. In W. K. Estes (Ed.), *Handbook of learning and cognitive processes.* Vol. 4. Hillsdale, New Jersey: Lawrence Erlbaum Associates, 1976. Pp. 177–236.

Shiffrin, R. M., & Geisler, W. A. Visual recognition in a theory of information processing. In R. L. Solso (Ed.), *Contemporary issues in cognitive psychology: The Loyola symposium.* Washington, D.C.: Winston, 1973. Pp. 53–101.

Shiffrin, R. M., & Schneider, W. Controlled and automatic human information processing: II. Perceptual learning, automatic attending, and a general theory. *Psychological Review*, 1977, **84**, 127–190.

Skinner, B. F. *The behavior of organisms: An experimental analysis.* New York: Appleton-Century-Crofts, 1938.

Skinner, B. F. *Verbal behavior.* New York: Appleton-Century-Crofts, 1957.

Smith, E. E. Theories of semantic memory. In W. K. Estes (Ed.), *Handbook of learning and cognitive processes.* Vol. 6. Hillsdale, New Jersey: Lawrence Erlbaum Associates, 1978. Pp. 1–56.

Smith, E. E., Shoben, E. J., & Rips, L. J. Structure and process in semantic memory: A featural model for semantic decisions. *Psychological Review*, 1974, **81**, 214–241.

Sokolov, Ye. N. *Perception and the conditioned reflex.* Oxford: Pergamon Press, 1963.

Solomon, R. L., & Howes, D. H. Word frequency, personal values, and visual duration threshholds. *Psychological Review*, 1951, **58**, 256–270.

Spear, N. Retrieval of memories: A psychobiological approach. In W. K. Estes (Ed.), *Handbook of learning and cognitive processes.* Vol. 4. Hillsdale, New Jersey: Lawrence Erlbaum Associates, 1976. Pp. 17–90.

Spence, K. W. The differential response in animals to stimuli varying within a single dimension. *Psychological Review*, 1937, **44**, 430–444.

Sperling, G. A model for visual memory tasks. *Human Factors*, 1963, **5**, 19–31.

Sperling, G., & Melchner, M. Visual search, visual attention and the attention operating characteristic. In *Attention and Performance VII*. Hillsdale, New Jersey: Lawrence Erlbaum Associates, in press.

Spiker, C. C. The hypothesis of stimulus interaction and an explanation of stimulus compounding. In L. P. Lipsitt & C. C. Spiker (Eds.), *Advances in child development and behavior.* Vol. 1. New York: Academic Press, 1963, Pp. 233–264.

Staddon, J. E. R. Temporal control, attention, and memory. *Psychological Review*, 1974, **81**, 375–391.

Staddon, J. E. R. Learning as adaptation. In W. K. Estes (Ed.), *Handbook of learning and cognitive processes.* Vol. 2. Hillsdale, New Jersey: Lawrence Erlbaum Associates, 1975. Pp. 37–98.

Sternberg, S. High-speed scanning in human memory. *Science*, 1966, **153**, 652–654.

Sternberg, S. Memory scanning: New findings and current controversies. *Quarterly Journal of Experimental Psychology*, 1975, **27**, 1–32.

Stevenson, H. W. *Children's learning.* New York: Appleton-Century-Crofts, 1972.

Stevenson-Hinde, J. Constraints on reinforcement. In R. A. Hinde & J. Hinde (Eds.), *Constraints on learning.* New York: Academic Press, 1973. Pp. 285–296.

Sutherland, N. S. The learning of discriminations by animals. *Endeavour*, 1964, **23**, 148–152.

Sutherland, N. S., & Mackintosh, N. J. *Mechanisms of animal discrimination learning.* New York: Academic Press, 1971.

Syz, H. C. Psycho-galvanic studies on sixty four medical students. *British Journal of Psychology*, 1926, **17**, 54–69.

Thorndike, E. L. *The psychology of learning (educational psychology II).* New York: Teachers College, 1913.

Thorndike, E. L. *Human learning.* New York: Century Co., 1931.

Thurstone, L. L. The learning function. *Journal of General Psychology*, 1930, **3**, 469–493.

Tolman, E. C. *Purposive behavior in animals and men.* New York: Appleton-Century, 1932.

Tolman, E. C. The determiners of behavior at a choice point. *Psychological Review*, 1938, **45**, 1–41.

Trabasso, T., & Bower, G. H. *Attention in learning: Theory and research.* New York: John Wiley & Sons, 1968.

Treisman, M. A theory of the identification of complex stimuli with an application toward recognition. *Psychological Review*, in press.

Tulving, E. Theoretical issues in free recall. In T. R. Dixon & D. L. Horton (Eds.), *Verbal behavior and general behavior theory*. Englewood Cliffs, New Jersey: Prentice-Hall, 1968. Pp. 2-36.

Tulving, E., & Donaldson, W. *Organization of memory*. New York: Academic Press, 1972.

Turvey, M. T. Visual processing and short-term memory. In W. K. Estes (Ed.), *Handbook of learning and cognitive processes*. Vol. 5. Hillsdale, New Jersey: Lawrence Erlbaum Associates, 1978. Pp. 91-142.

Underwood, B. J. Attributes of memory. *Psychological Review*, 1969, **76**, 559-573.

Waugh, N. C., & Norman, D. A. Primary memory. *Psychological Review*, 1965, **72**, 89-104.

White, S. H. Evidence for a hierarchical arrangement of learning processes. In L. P. Lipsitt & C. C. Spiker (Eds.), *Advances in child development and behavior*, 1965, **2**, 187-220.

Whitlow, J. W., Jr. The dynamics of episodic processing in Pavlovian conditioning. In D. L. Medin, W. A. Roberts, & R. T. Davis (Eds.), *Processes of animal memory*, Hillsdale, New Jersey: Lawrence Erlbaum Associates, 1976. Pp. 203-227.

Wickelgren, W. A. Short-term memory for phonemically similar lists. *American Journal of Psychology*, 1965, **78**, 567-574.

Wickelgren, W. A., & Norman, D. A. Strength models and serial position in short-term recognition memory. *Journal of Mathematical Psychology*, 1966, **3**, 316-347.

Wickens, D. D., & Wickens, C. D. A study of conditioning in the neonate. *Journal of Experimental Psychology*, 1940, **25**, 94-102.

Zeaman, D., & House, B. J. The role of attention in retardate discrimination learning. In N. R. Ellis (Ed.), *Handbook of mental deficiency*. New York: McGraw-Hill, 1963. Pp. 159-223.

Author Index

Numbers in *italics* refer to pages on which the complete references are listed.

Subject Index

For Product Safety Concerns and Information please contact our EU
representative GPSR@taylorandfrancis.com
Taylor & Francis Verlag GmbH, Kaufingerstraße 24, 80331 München, Germany

9 781848 723993